LEGAL RIGHTS AND THE INSTITUTIONAL IMAGINATION

This book presents a contemporary perspective on legal rights centred on the longstanding will theory–interest theory debate. Starting with classical rights literature, central aspects of the debate in its modern idiom are contextualised within a social theory setting developed from the writings of Max Weber.

The book explores the idea that the institutional and coercive character of legal enforcement necessitates viewing legal rights as a locus of social power residing within the 'institutional imagination': that is, in the decision-making of key institutional actors such as judges, prosecutors, police, governmental authorities – and ultimately supreme court judges – who routinely mobilise coercive mechanisms towards the enforcement of legal rights and powers. This marks a departure from the trend of rights literature to view legal rights largely from the standpoint of the right-holder.

The book also touches on whether the emerging perspective points towards a 'third way' beyond the traditional two theoretical approaches.

A major task of the study is the construction of an archetypal supreme court judge – personifying the 'institutional imagination' – fashioned, via Weberian sociology, from a critique of Ronald Dworkin's 'Herculean' judge and measured against doctrinal exegesis that draws on sources which include UK higher appellate court judgments.

Legal Rights and the Institutional Imagination

Hamish Ross

• HART •
OXFORD • LONDON • NEW YORK • NEW DELHI • SYDNEY

HART PUBLISHING

Bloomsbury Publishing Plc

Kemp House, Chawley Park, Cumnor Hill, Oxford, OX2 9PH, UK

1385 Broadway, New York, NY 10018, USA

Bloomsbury Publishing Ireland Limited, 29 Earlsfort Terrace, Dublin 2, D02 AY28, Ireland

First published in Great Britain 2026

A catalogue record for this book is available from the British Library.

A catalogue record for this book is available from the Library of Congress.

ISBN: HB: 978-1-50997-900-4
ePDF: 978-1-50997-898-4
ePub: 978-1-50997-899-1

Typeset by Compuscript Ltd, Shannon

For Sam, Nicky and Kip

PREFACE

This book contextualises a longstanding debate – between will and interest theorists of rights – within a classical social theory (Weberian) setting, building on aspects of the author's 2001 book, *Law as a Social Institution* (Hart Publishing), at the same time as drawing on the writings of a range of legal philosophers from the mid-twentieth century to the early twenty-first century: for instance, HLA Hart, Neil MacCormick, Joseph Raz, Matthew Kramer and Nigel Simmonds. The book promotes the idea that legal rights can be viewed as a locus of social power ultimately centred upon the decision-making of key institutional actors: hence the focus of the book on the 'institutional imagination'. Institutional decision-makers – who ultimately mobilise legal enforcement mechanisms – are epitomised in a constructed archetypal supreme court judge ('*Iudex*') fashioned, via writings of Max Weber, from a critique of Ronald Dworkin's 'Herculean' archetype.

In Chapter 1, important aspects of the two leading theories of rights are identified in the context of an outline of theoretical developments since the early 1960s. An exploration of the antinomy, and the potential scope for theoretical interpenetration, of the rival theories points among other things to a recurring theme of the book, the principle of protective empowerment: *that which protects also empowers*. This reflects the possibility that the idea (from interest theory) that rights are protective of interests and the idea (from will theory) that rights are empowering (and *also* empowering because *protective*) are mutually complementary, rather than irreconcilable, theoretical positions. At the same time, the conventional image of the legal right as something to be viewed from the standpoint of the right-holder – as in *right-holder* empowerment, and protection of *right-holder* interests – is challenged. It is argued that the institutional and coercive character of legal enforcement necessitates viewing legal rights as a repository of social power that resides in some measure in the decision-making of institutional actors such as judges, and ultimately supreme court judges of a legal system's highest appeal court: given their involvement, in the final analysis, in mobilising coercive agencies towards enforcing legal rights. This prefigures the central theme of the book which is an examination of legal rights viewed from a significant institutional perspective – that of the so-called '*Iudex*' (a constructed archetypal ultimate supreme court judge).

Chapter 2 examines more closely the rights theories advanced respectively by HLA Hart (will theory) and Neil MacCormick (interest theory), considering the extent to which the two theorists attempted to integrate the distinctive versions of their theories with their more general theories of law. A key aim of the discussion is to reach a preliminary view on whether an improved understanding of the nature of legal rights is better promoted by one or other theoretical approach. While the approach outlined overall in the book is an elaboration of Hartian will theory, drawing upon social theory and incorporating important aspects of classical interest theory, the view is taken that MacCormick – unlike Hart – advances a more holistic conception of a legal right, his theoretical positions – both general and particular – being mutually reinforcing. MacCormick's thesis is that a legal right is an institution of law and, by reason of that, an institutional fact, or cluster of institutional facts. That position lends itself to the development of an ontological exploration of legal rights which not only complements the overarching institutional theme of the book but paves the way for the development of a modified position on MacCormick's thesis in Chapter 9. Essentially Chapter 2 lays the groundwork for developing an ontology of legal rights out of MacCormick's idea of law as institutional fact, but with a sociological orientation that MacCormick's philosophical approach all but neglects.

The central thesis of the book is framed in Chapter 3, where it is argued that versions of will theory and interest theory offer problematic accounts of the nature and existence conditions of a legal right. The focus of the chapter, drawing on key positions outlined in Chapters 1 and 2, is to consider whether the legal right – or, to be accurate, its content, scope and effect – might be viewed as being constructed in the 'institutional imagination' (specifically, the 'judicial consciousness'), marking a departure from the tendency of the leading theories of rights to adopt a perspective that places the consciousness (ie awareness, understanding, etc) of the *right-holder* or *duty-bearer* at the centre of the explanatory process. In approaching an understanding of the content (and scope and effect etc) of legal rights, a '*Iudexian*' perspective is argued to be a necessary corrective to the perspectives of the individual right-holder or duty-bearer. Unlike the latter perspectives, a '*Iudexian*' perspective, with its concomitant hypothesis of the ultimate judgment, encompasses a fully informed knowledge of the content (etc) of given legal rights, and applicable legal rules, principles and standards. Institutional decision-makers are epitomised in a constructed archetypal supreme court judge ('*Iudex*') – personifying the 'institutional imagination' – fashioned, via Weberian sociology, from a critique of Ronald Dworkin's 'Herculean' judge (see Chapter 7) and measured against doctrinal exegesis that draws on sources including UK higher appellate court decisions (see Chapter 8). Decisions at the *Iudexian* level are also authoritative and final in a way that decision-making of the right-holder or duty-bearer are not. The *Iudexian* perspective is empirically significant because, arguably, the social power inhering in legal rights *in the final analysis* resides in the decision-making of institutional actors, such as *Iudex*, who are in a position to mobilise coercive agencies (possessing significant social power) towards enforcing legal rights.

The *Iudexian* perspective and the related hypothesis of the ultimate judgment, outlined in the preceding chapters, are further developed in Chapter 4. This chapter draws upon insights from Hans Kelsen's *Pure Theory of Law* as reinterpreted in the light of a theoretical position that views Kelsenian theory (unusually) as drawn by the gravitational pull of Weberian social theory. Aspects of both Kelsen's and Weber's writings have common roots in nineteenth-century German idealist and Neo-Kantian philosophy which, arguably, make it problematic for Kelsen to break free entirely from influences that compromise the 'purity' of his pure theory. Chapter 4, among other things, seeks to show how Kelsen's concept of the Reconstructed Legal Norm or *Rechtssatz* (as formulated in the *Pure Theory of Law*) and the Kelsenian concept of legal meaning or *rechtliche Bedeutung* gravitate in striking ways towards Weberian interpretive sociology or, minimally, towards its philosophical roots. The analysis invites the possibility of a sociological repositioning of the Reconstructed Legal Norm not only in replicating the hypothesis of the ultimate judgment (handed down, in theory, by *Iudex*) but serving in its own right as an 'artefact' of interpretive sociology. In this way, Kelsen's Reconstructed Legal Norm provides a basis for a discussion of where the final, most authoritative, acts of legal interpretation in a given legal system factually reside, redoubling the idea that the theoretical construct, *Iudex*, is such an ultimate repository of legal meaning. The themes developed in Chapter 4 are revisited in Chapter 9, where the ontological implications of Kelsen's concept of the Reconstructed Legal Norm and the idea of legal meaning are further contextualised within the overarching themes of the book.

Mirroring Chapter 4 but with the focus on HLA Hart, Chapter 5 examines aspects of the gravitational pull exerted by (Weberian) social theory on elements of *The Concept of Law* considering, among other things, how this might impact Hart's analysis of legal 'rights correlative to obligations' in chapter VII of Hart's major work, *Essays on Bentham*. The possibility, touched upon in Chapter 1, that the (Hartian) legal 'right correlative to obligation' may be viewed as an instrument of social power is further explored in this chapter. A core tenet of Hartian will theory characterises a legal right as a power of control (residing in a right-holder) over a correlative obligation (residing in a duty-bearer). It is argued that it is possible to identify echoes of the same social power dynamic in Weber's concept of *Herrschaft*, which Weber scholars have characterised as a structure of superordination and subordination, and as a relational concept centred upon the impact of one person upon another where the behaviour of one (that of the duty-bearer) is seen to be determined by another (the right-holder). The idea of the legal right as a locus of social power complements the more general approach established in the book which treats legal rights as an *instrument* of social power – viewed from an institutional ('*Iudexian*') perspective – reinforced by the presence of ultimately coercive institutional structures that serve to empower, and to afford various types of protection to the interests of, right-holders.

The focus on Hartian will theory in Chapter 6 continues the exploration of one of the major tasks of the book to harness the insights of that theory towards constructing an image of the legal right as an instrument of social power. Chapter 6 contributes to this aim by re-examining Neil MacCormick's influential critique of Hartian will theory which, among other things, maintains that will theory is unable to provide a satisfactory explanation of children's rights, or even to accommodate the possibility of such rights as a tenable proposition. Possible defences of Hart's theoretical position are outlined in Chapter 6, taking in lines of analysis pursued in earlier chapters. The aim is to examine persistently recurring criticisms of Hartian will theory that have, over decades, achieved almost the status of 'articles of faith' of dominant (interest theory-based) perceptions of will theory that have tended to undermine Hart's theoretical outlook on rights. The ensuing revised approach to Hartian will theory serves to reinforce the overarching thesis, touched upon in Chapter 1 and elsewhere, that the (will theory) idea that rights are empowering and (interest theory) idea that rights are protective of interests are actually mutually complementary theoretical positions.

In Chapter 7 an expository and critical assessment of elements of Ronald Dworkin's Herculean archetype is undertaken as a basis for the development, in Chapter 8, of an outline of the *Iudexian* perspective. Although in many respects Dworkin's Herculean archetype is found to be overly idealised and utopian – for instance, envisaging a judge of superhuman talent with endless time at his disposal – the fact that the archetype generally fails to capture the decision-making activities of 'real judges' does not imply that *none* of its elements resonates with the experience of judges of the common law tradition. Dworkin's Herculean archetype appears to be designed for a practical, yet 'reflective', purpose: namely, to represent best judicial practice for 'real world' judges. Now while that position arguably represents an overreach of the practical utility of the Herculean archetype the view is ultimately taken in Chapter 8 that it is possible to appropriate some elements of Dworkin's Herculean archetype in the construction of a *Iudexian* archetype. Be that as it may, in the final analysis, the *Iudexian* archetype is designed to be anchored more in the activities of 'real world' judges than those of an imaginary, idealised and essentially utopian judge such as Hercules.

Chapter 8 explores, among other things, the possibility of drawing upon Dworkin's Herculean archetype for inspiration in outlining the elements of an archetypal judge, *Iudex*, representing a paradigmatic institutional perspective from which legal rights – viewed as a significant repository of social power – may be imagined. One issue considered early in the chapter, and arising out of Dworkin's characterisation of the Herculean archetype, is whether the most rigorous possible 'fit' of a judicial decision with past judicial decisions, and the moral authority of the decision, might be relevant considerations in making a judicial decision – especially one that approximates to a 'Herculean' one – proof against review by a higher court, such as in a situation where Hercules is a lower-court (appellate) judge. (Dworkin's archetype is not framed explicitly as an ultimate, or supreme court, judge.)

An important line of enquiry pursued in the chapter turns on identifying possible instances where 'real judges' appear to replicate some of the more realistic 'Herculean' avenues of approach to decision-making. This may be in the quest for a doctrinally 'unassailable' decision. If that is what a judge is aiming for, it may be more a matter of the judge's adopting a rigorous approach to judicial method than any conscious attempt to imitate the attributes of an imaginary judge such as Dworkin's Hercules. In further developing the *Iudexian* archetype, a case study – based upon decision-making at the level of higher appellate courts in the UK – is employed, enabling possible characteristics to be assigned to the hypothetical *Iudexian* archetype. The chapter ends with an exploration of further possible characteristics of the *Iudexian* perspective. First, there is consideration of whether ultimate judicial decision-making is in any sense distinctive and set apart from non-ultimate decision-making. Secondly, the idea that (collective) ultimate judicial decision-making might be, essentially, a *social activity* is contrasted with the idea that such decision-making may also be viewed as a creative (even solitary) process. In the resulting modified Herculean position outlined in Chapter 8, primacy is given to the idea of *Iudex*, including higher appellate-level judges, striving to achieve doctrinal 'unassailability' in their decision-making.

A number of lines of enquiry pursued in earlier chapters reach their point of convergence in Chapter 9. The main focus is on ontological questions, with a discussion, later in the chapter, of whether the overarching argument of the book could form the basis of a 'third way' approach to understanding legal rights beyond Hartian will theory and interest theory as expounded by Raz and MacCormick, among others. To this end there is discussion of Gopal Sreenivasan's position as a representative of contemporary, so-called 'third way', literature. Consideration is again given to Hart's claim that *The Concept of Law* can be regarded as an 'essay in descriptive sociology': in particular to the idea that Hart's book – to the extent that it had any kind of claim to a sociological viewpoint – arguably exploits not only the particularising (idiographic) possibilities characteristic of such a science, but the generalising (nomothetic) possibilities as well. Hart's generalising approach is exemplified in (among other things) the generic concept of the social rule; the idea of the internal aspect of rules; and the critical reflective attitude to rules.

Issues of perspective also arise for discussion in Chapter 9. There is further development of the idea of legal rights as a repository of social power residing to a significant degree in judicial decision-making, presupposing a standpoint integral to the 'institutional imagination', captured in the constructed 'consciousness' of the ultimate institutional (judicial) actor, *Iudex*. This part of the discussion gives way to further analysis of Weber's concept of a legal right which not only synthesises central tenets of will theory and interest theory but strikes out in an explicitly sociological direction. To that end, Weber's viewpoint serves to reinforce the social power dimension of legal rights using the frame of reference of the core concept, *Herrschaft*. This reflects the possibility of right-holders imposing their will upon the behaviour of others with the support of, and protection afforded by, relevant institutional structures. Later in the chapter, the discussion of Gopal Sreenivasan's 'third way' approach points, among other things, to a credible attempt on Sreenivasan's part to outline an area of theoretical interpenetration of will theory and interest theory. The idea of interpenetration (initially taken up in Chapter 1) dovetails with the overall approach outlined in this book as largely an elaboration of Hartian will theory, drawing upon social theory, but incorporating aspects of classical interest theory that reinforce that approach.

ACKNOWLEDGEMENTS

I wish to acknowledge the friendly critical advice given to me by scholars previously attached to the (former) Department of Jurisprudence at the University of Glasgow: in particular, Elspeth Attwooll, David Goldberg and the late Esin Örücü. Over a number of years Elspeth, David and Esin acted as a sounding board for some of the more outlandish ideas that, in a more restrained incarnation, have come to be incorporated in this book. A special word of thanks is due to Elspeth for reading and commenting on an earlier version of Chapter 2. Back in the 1990s Elspeth was a constant source of encouragement to me when I was lecturing and tutoring in jurisprudence at Glasgow.

My association with London School of Economics as a tutor in jurisprudence in the early 2000s led to a number of fruitful exchanges of ideas with David Schiff and Nicola Lacey regarding the impact of social theory on Hartian analytical jurisprudence and its continuously evolving secondary literature.

The writings of the late Neil MacCormick have exerted a profound and continuing influence on the development of a range of positions outlined in this book. Neil's influence also played out on a more personal level when he was asked by the University of Glasgow to become my doctoral supervisor in the late 1980s. Numerous conversations with Neil at that time helped to shape lines of approach to law as an institutional social phenomenon which now inform a number of themes underlying this book.

I also owe debts of gratitude to Timothy Endicott for reading and commenting on an earlier version of Chapter 3; and to Iain Stewart for reading and commenting on an earlier version of Chapter 4. I am especially grateful to Lord Hope of Craighead who as a former 'ultimate judge' at the highest level of the UK's judicial system(s) – in other words, a '*Iudex*' in the sense of key lines of analysis pursued in this book – read and commented insightfully on a near-final version of Chapter 8. I also benefited from conversations with Lord Eassie and David Christie that fed into the case study in Chapter 8.

My writing-up of this book has benefited immensely from the enthusiastic and friendly editorial team at Hart Publishing, extending to anonymous peer reviewers and freelance editors. I acknowledge, with special thanks, the input of Kate Whetter, Sasha Jawed, Andrew Devine and Linda Goss.

Finally, thanks are due to my wife and son, Sam and Nicky, for putting up with my interminable absences when writing and re-writing the manuscript into something approaching an intelligible narrative.

CONTENTS

TABLE OF CASES

1

Legal Rights and Contemporary Scholarship – The Antinomy of Interest Theory and Will Theory

1.1. Introduction

There are occasions, when reflecting upon the two leading theories of rights – the interest (or benefit) theory and the will (or choice or power) theory[1] – that one may be left wondering whether, for instance, it is possible for there to be a right that is not predicated upon the existence of some kind of interest that the right is said to protect; or (alternatively) whether it is possible for there to be a right that does not entail, or necessarily imply, the need for an exertion of the right-holder's will towards the exercise of a legally recognised or conferred choice to control the behaviour of another. Thus, we may find that it is perfectly possible for there to be a legal right that the right-holder regards as more burdensome than advantageous, thereby casting doubt on the idea that the right is, in any accepted sense, *and at least for that particular right-holder*, protecting any perceived interest of the right-holder. Rights are, in other words, 'foisted upon' unwilling and reluctant subjects, supposedly protecting 'interests' that they may regard as not worth having, still less protecting.[2] Likewise, some may argue that an infant who is the claimed holder

[1] For convenience, reference is made respectively to the interest theory [of rights] and the will theory [of rights]. Adherents to the will theory of rights have included Friedrich Carl von Savigny and HLA Hart. See FC von Savigny, *System of the Modern Roman Law* (W Holloway (tr), Higginbotham 1867) vol I, 2nd book, ch I, 6: 'If we regard the position of Right as in practical life it surrounds and penetrates us on all sides it appears to us as the power justly appertaining to the individual person: a territory in which his will rules and rules with our consent. This power we call a right of this person synonymous with privilege; some call it right in a subjective sense.' Ihering and Bentham are commonly looked upon as adherents to the interest theory. Hart discusses Bentham's distinctive 'benefit theory of rights' at length. See HLA Hart, *Essays on Bentham: Jurisprudence and Political Theory* (Clarendon Press 1982) (hereafter, in this chapter, '*Essays on Bentham*') ch VII, especially 174–188.

[2] As Neil MacCormick points out: 'Perhaps there are some people who have been more harmed than benefited by an inheritance. Perhaps in some cases property inherited – eg slum properties subject to statutory tenancies at controlled rents – are literally more trouble than they are worth, and, besides, something of an embarrassment to their proprietor.' See DN MacCormick, 'Rights in Legislation' in PMS Hacker and J Raz (eds), *Law, Morality, and Society: Essays in Honour of HLA Hart* (Clarendon Press 1977) (hereafter, in this chapter, 'Rights in Legislation') 202. Raz makes essentially the same point. See J Raz, 'On the Nature of Rights' (1984) 93 *Mind* 194 (hereafter, in this chapter, 'On the Nature of Rights') 208.

of a right, but is personally incapable of recognising, to say nothing of exercising, any choice to control or determine the behaviour of others, cannot in the result be possessed of a right in any conventional sense.[3] Ultimately, those of us grappling with these difficulties may have little alternative but to question the very existence of the right if the thing claimed to be essential to its existence – such as the presence of an interest in need of protection, or of a choice or capacity or ability to control others' actions – is absent.

One possible approach to resolving the difficulties in question is to examine closely the two main theories of rights on the (for the time being untested) supposition that what may be creating unnecessary obstacles to understanding are the two competing theories themselves rather than the phenomena they seek to illuminate.[4] Both theories offer insights into (among other things) the conditions of existence of rights, suggesting more than a passing interest in the ontological foundation of rights. This seems a suitably fertile area for enquiry because as soon as we embark upon an exploration of the existence conditions of something it is necessary to examine the closely related matter of *what it is the existence of which is being asserted*. In other words, for a theory to suggest that the existence conditions of X are A, B and C, even the most rudimentary idea of what X is is called for. Thus, a theory of rights should offer an explanation – which, in an ideal situation, would approach a complete explanation – of what a right *is*: what its nature and fundamental characteristics are.

This book offers a perspective on legal rights centred around the longstanding debate between adherents to the will theory of rights and the rival interest theory of rights. Critical consideration is given to writings of will (or 'choice') theorist HLA Hart and of interest theorists Joseph Raz and Neil MacCormick. Critical attention is also given to more recent writing, such as of Matthew Kramer, Nigel Simmonds and Gopal Sreenivasan. Expanding upon themes originating in the author's 2001 book,[5] important aspects of the debate, in its modern idiom (ie from and after Hart), are contextualised within a classical social theory setting developed out of the writings of Max Weber.

One key argument underlying the discussion is that the idea that rights are protective of interests (traceable to interest theory) and the idea that rights are empowering, or literally *are* powers of a kind, (mainly traceable to the Hartian variant of will theory) are mutually complementary, rather than irreconcilable,

[3] See generally DN MacCormick, 'Children's Rights: A Test Case for Theories of Right' (1976) 62 *Archiv für Rechts- und Sozialphilosophie* 305. (This article is also reprinted with modifications as chapter 8 of DN MacCormick, *Legal Right and Social Democracy: Essays in Legal and Political Philosophy* (Clarendon Press 1982).)

[4] For the idea that there may, or may not, be 'life' beyond the two main theories, see generally, R Cruft, 'Rights: Beyond Interest Theory and Will Theory?' (2004) 23 *Law and Philosophy* 347; and MH Kramer and H Steiner, 'Theories of Rights: Is There a Third Way?' (2007) 27 *Oxford Journal of Legal Studies* 281. See also G Sreenivasan, 'A Hybrid Theory of Claim-Rights' (2005) 25 *Oxford Journal of Legal Studies* 257.

[5] H Ross, *Law as a Social Institution* (Hart Publishing 2001).

theoretical positions. It is argued that this points to the need for an exploration of what gives *legal* rights – the primary focus of this book – their protective *and* empowering force, encompassing important tenets of both interest theory and will theory. This in turn precipitates a reassessment of the conventional image of the legal right – reflected in writings of both will theory and interest theory – as something to be viewed primarily from the standpoint of the right-holder: where legal rights are invariably seen as giving *the right-holder* control over the actions of others or as protecting interests (primarily) *of the right-holder*. (See generally the discussion in section 3.2.3 (Chapter 3, below).) It is maintained that a shift in perspective is called for which is necessitated by the essentially institutional and coercive character of legal enforcement mechanisms. A major task of the book, therefore, is to explore the less conventional image of the legal right viewed from an *institutional perspective* on the basis that legal rights are a significant repository of social power *reinforced by the presence of institutional structures*, some of which are directly involved in enforcing legal rights and affording various types of protection to right-holders. (This is reflected in the title of this book.) Of course, this is not to diminish, or deny the importance of, the perspective of the right-holder; or that of a duty-bearer. But a shift of perspective, it is argued, is critical to a proper understanding of the protective and social power dynamics that animate and underpin legal rights.

The institutional perspective in question takes the form of a (Weber-inspired) ideal type which hypothesises the decision-making role of a hypothetical common law judge, called *Iudex*, whose output, in terms of judicial decision-making could be described as: (A) the synthesised judgment of a collectivity of judges sitting in the highest appeal court in a hypothetical judicial system which (B) represents a final, unappealable, decision of that court. The judicial decision-making of *Iudex* could be said to represent a legally conclusive position on the rights of the parties in a hypothetical case.[6] The hypothesis of the ultimate judgment (ascribable to *Iudex*), which has resonances of Hans Kelsen's concept of the Reconstructed Legal Norm or *Rechtssatz*, as developed in the *Pure Theory of Law*,[7] is taken to represent a final determination of the content, scope, import and effect of any given legal right for the (essentially practical) purpose of the mobilisation of the coercive apparatuses of the legal system in question towards enforcement of the judicially declared rights. The empirical significance of this perspective turns not only on

[6] As Neil MacCormick has put it (in the context of a critique of the so-called '*Iudexian*' perspective): 'There are also courts and judges, and clusters of surrounding officers of court and other officials. For many approaches to legal theory these are the quintessentially legal institutions, though not all have been as articulate about the reasons for taking what Hamish Ross has called a "Iudexian" approach as he has been. His argument is that the standpoint of a judge in a highest-level state court is the one that can enable us to discern most clearly the most prominent features of the legal landscape.' N MacCormick, *Institutions of Law: An Essay in Legal Theory* (Oxford University Press 2007) at 55. See also H Ross, *Law as a Social Institution* (Hart Publishing 2001) ch 5. For more detailed discussion, see section 3.3 (Chapter 3, below); and sections 4.4, 4.5 and 4.6 (Chapter 4, below).

[7] See in particular section 3.2.3 (Chapter 3, below); and sections 4.4 and 4.5 (Chapter 4, below).

the fact that enforcement mechanisms – extending to the possible use of force (and including awards of damages, fines, incarceration and other punishments and orders made by the court) – tend to be activated or mobilised in response to the decision of a court of law or tribunals; but on the accepted reality that countless individuals – including professionals such as solicitors, barristers, court officials, clerks, (non-ultimate) judges, government bodies, civil servants, banks, regulatory agencies and commercial organisations – in attempting to imagine the legal consequences of their action and that of others 'out of court' often consciously or otherwise adopt a perspective that replicates that of an 'ultimate judge' such as the hypothetical *Iudex*. (In effect the question they ask is what would the legal result be if, following the occurrence of certain events, a dispute were to arise or criminal proceedings were to be brought, and this dispute or those proceedings were to be litigated or tried to a point in the system where a final and authoritative determination was made?)

The book significantly develops the *Iudex* ideal type by adapting aspects of Ronald Dworkin's so-called 'Herculean' judge as a point of departure. Arising from a critique of Dworkin's imaginary judge, a range of characteristics – to be assigned to a more developed '*Iudexian*' perspective – are developed from, and tested and evaluated against, empirical criteria drawn from sources including UK appellate court decisions and academic and other literature that provide insights into the modes of reasoning, and decision-making processes, adopted by supreme court (or 'ultimate') judges in common law jurisdictions.

Ultimately, the view is taken that legal rights are inseparable, and ought not (at the risk of distortion) to be viewed in isolation, from the institutional setting in which authoritative legal meaning is conferred upon them – a process that is explicitly determinative of the content, scope, import and effect of any actual legal right for the purpose of mobilising the coercive apparatuses of the legal system towards enforcement of the judicially declared rights. To a greater extent than can be accommodated within the constraining influence of either the will theory of rights or the interest theory of rights, the legal right is argued to be, in important ways, a 'creature' of the institutional (judicial) imagination or judicial consciousness.

The remainder of this chapter serves as a brief introduction to a few of the core themes to be developed later in the book, the emphasis being on contemporary writings on the subject of moral and legal rights. The particular point of departure for the discussion to follow is the antinomy of interest theory and will theory: exploring significant ways in which interest theory and will theory stand opposed to one another.

1.2. The Antinomy of Interest Theory and Will Theory

When reviewing some of the more influential recent writings in the area of interest theory and will theory it becomes apparent that important themes and lines of analysis developed in the early 1960s, such as by Hart,[8] and in the 1970s and 1980s by (respectively) MacCormick and Raz,[9] were still playing out by the late 1990s (eg Kramer, Simmonds and Steiner)[10] and into the first and second decades of the new millennium (eg Kramer and Wenar, both writing in 2013).[11] Clearly, any contemporary writing must engage with those aspects of the debate that have been reverberating for well over half a century.

What emerges in particular from *A Debate Over Rights* – which is given some attention in this chapter – is that the territory of what might be described as *classical modern* versions of, on one hand, interest theory (MacCormick and Raz) and, on the other, will theory (Hart) remains very much in the frame in terms of continuing to afford compelling lines of analysis for critical evaluation, as a step towards progressing, and (if need be) rehabilitating, the debate for a new era. It is immediately striking that the *core* theoretical positions reformulated, restated and discussed in contemporary writings are not radically different from the classic (core) positions developed by theorists such as Hart, MacCormick and Raz between the 1960s and 1980s, emphasising the continuing relevance of those earlier theoretical writings. Nigel Simmonds, for instance, despite being an adherent to will theory, emphasises his rejection of important aspects of the Hartian version of the theory, such as where he calls attention to Hart's 'confusion' in framing his concept of a 'right correlative to obligation' in terms of the various 'powers' that (according to Hart) characterise such rights. In Simmonds's view, by introducing 'powers' into the analysis (eg power of waiver; power of enforcement – which Hart also frames as right-holder 'choices') Hart confuses different levels in the Hohfeldian analysis, where his analysis of the claim-right–duty jural relation (corresponding to the Hartian 'right correlative to obligation') appears to factor in elements of Hohfeld's power–liability jural relation.[12] This, according to Simmonds, results in Hart's theory seemingly confusing 'the importantly distinct categories of primary and secondary legal relations'.[13]

[8] See, in particular, HLA Hart, *Essays on Bentham* (this chapter, n 1) ch VII. This essay builds upon earlier work dating (apparently) from 1962: HLA Hart, 'Bentham: Lecture on a Master Mind' (1962) 48 *Proceedings of the British Academy* 297.

[9] See generally, for instance, DN MacCormick, 'Rights in Legislation' (this chapter, n 2); and J Raz 'On the Nature of Rights' (also this chapter, n 2).

[10] See MH Kramer, NE Simmonds and H Steiner, *A Debate Over Rights: Philosophical Enquiries* (Oxford University Press 1998) (hereafter, in this chapter, '*A Debate Over Rights*').

[11] See MH Kramer, 'Some Doubts about Alternatives to the Interest Theory of Rights' (2013) 123 *Ethics* 245; and L Wenar, 'The Nature of Claim-Rights' (2013) 123 *Ethics* 202.

[12] NE Simmonds in *A Debate Over Rights* (this chapter, n 10) 220–221. (Simmonds's chapter contribution to the book has the title: 'Rights at the Cutting Edge'.)

[13] ibid 221. According to a more accommodating interpretation of Hart's position, which does not diminish Simmonds's argument, an ostensibly narrow claim-right can be viewed as part of a wider regime of legal empowerment extending beyond the core. Hart makes the point that the powers attending a claim-right are 'legal powers'. For instance, he comments: 'These legal powers (*for such they are*) over a correlative obligation [eg power to waive or extinguish the obligation] are of great importance to lawyers … They are therefore a natural focus of legal attention, and there are I think many signs of the centrality of those powers to the conception of a legal right'. See HLA Hart, *Essays on Bentham* (this chapter, n 1) 184 (emphasis added).

Yet, at the same time as taking issue with Hart, Simmonds welcomes two particular aspects of the Hartian version of will theory that he describes as virtues. One is the idea that a right is something that is 'exercised' by right-holders; with the manner of exercise being the subject of choices made by the right-holder. Rights, therefore, give us choices; and this seemingly accords with our intuitions about how rights behave.[14] The other (virtue) is Hartian will theory's promotion of the idea that a legal right is a reason *in itself* for the action that the right-holder demands of another. As Simmonds puts it, rights ground *peremptory demands* that we may make against others.[15] Interest theory (eg in the variant advanced by Raz) effectively stifles this idea by emphasising how rights are to be looked upon merely as 'grounds' of duties – in other words, interest-based reasons, which are not exhaustive of *possible* reasons, for others to act in accordance with the relevant duty.[16] So, under will theory, a legal right immediately 'crystallises' in a duty whose performance can be insisted upon by the right-holder. But under interest theory, the right (such as it is) is merely one factor among others when considering the scope or operation of any purported duty.

Simmonds's reiteration of familiar points of analysis, traceable to Hart's *Essays on Bentham* and in writings of MacCormick and Raz, is echoed in Kramer's lengthy essay, 'Rights Without Trimmings',[17] though Kramer's approach is in many respects more narrowly focused on points of analytical detail than Simmonds's.[18] Kramer's reassessment of the core positions recognises that each of the rival theories rests upon what appear on the face of it to be relatively straightforward points of departure. The broad focus of interest theory is upon how [legal] rights protect interests; while will theory emphasises the right-holder's will, 'the exercise of which is definitive for the existence of' a right.[19] In its Hartian variant, the will of the right-holder is expressed in the making of relevant choices, such as to enforce the right, waive it or leave

[14] Interestingly, as we have seen, Simmonds regards Hart's idea of framing choices in terms of 'powers' (eg to enforce, or to waive, a right) as confusion in Hart's thinking; but sees the more general *principle* of the idea of choice as a virtue. There is no contradiction in holding an analytical strength to (nonetheless) have weaknesses (if that is what they are).

[15] See NE Simmonds in *A Debate Over Rights* (this chapter, n 10) at (for instance) 216, 225, 226 at n 138. At p 176 Simmonds also comments: '[T]he initial connection between rights and coercion reflects our sense that rights are in some sense peremptory: that if I have a *right* that you should perform a certain act, your performance of that act is not a matter for calculation or debate, but may be demanded "as of right". In the currently fashionable Interest Theory of rights, however, the "peremptory" character of rights is lost'.

[16] See the more extensive discussion of Raz's position in section 3.2.2 (Chapter 3, below). Otherwise, see J Raz, 'Legal Rights' (1984) 4 *Oxford Journal of Legal Studies* 1, at 5, 14.

[17] See MH Kramer in *A Debate Over Rights* (this chapter, n 10) 7–111.

[18] Simmonds is engaged in an entirely different type of project. As Kramer comments in the Introduction to *A Debate Over Rights*: 'Unlike Kramer, Simmonds believes that one's conception of the formal aspects of rights should hinge centrally on one's moral/political values; he perceives Kramer's austerely analytical approach as arid'. See MH Kramer in *A Debate Over Rights* (this chapter, n 10) at 3.

[19] See TD Campbell, 'The Rights of the Minor: as Person, as Child, as Juvenile, as Future Adult' (1992) 6 *International Journal of Law and the Family* 1, 4.

it unenforced. Simmonds, as we have seen, embraces this as a virtue of Hart's theory. Yet the relative simplicity of the rival theories' core positions belies the disparities in theoretical perspective that underpin the antinomy, particularly at the level of theoretical elaborations *beyond* the core points of departure. Kramer usefully identifies the core theoretical tenets or principles that characterise the two theories at the same time as taking stock of what it is that necessarily divides the theories. In the remainder of this section it is instructive to examine briefly the points of difference and similarity that Kramer highlights for discussion.[20]

Essentially Kramer – in his overview of the debate in 'Rights Without Trimmings' – frames the most fundamental tenets of will theory and interest theory, centring around the existence conditions of rights, in terms of propositions of *necessity* and of *sufficiency*.

Kramer's synopsis adopts a modified perspective on Hartian will theory that, additionally and simultaneously, rejects core tenets of interest theory.[21] According to the synopsis, it is *necessary and sufficient* for the holding or actual possession of a right that the right-holder is competent and authorised to demand or waive enforcement of the right; while (towards opposing interest theory) the protection or preservation of an interest[22] is *not necessary and not sufficient* for such holding or possession. Classic Hartian will theory would frame the core tenet more straightforwardly in terms of *control* and *choice* in that a measure of control of enforcement or waiver of a correlative obligation is not only necessary, but is also sufficient, for the holding or actual possession of a right (being a 'right correlative to obligation' in Hart's analysis), putting the right-holder in a position to make choices such as between waiving a right or enforcing it.[23]

Similarly, Kramer frames the core tenets of interest theory in terms of positions developed in various writings of Raz and MacCormick which, additionally and simultaneously, reject core tenets of will theory. According to Kramer's synopsis, the protection or preservation of an interest is *necessary* for the holding or actual possession of a right; while it is *not necessary and not sufficient* that the right-holder

[20] The theoretical points of departure of (respectively) will theory and interest theory that Kramer identifies – initially in 1998 and later in 2013 – and the ways in which he frames them, are more or less identical. The earlier of these, as we have seen, is Kramer's essay 'Rights Without Trimmings': see MH Kramer in *A Debate Over Rights* (this chapter, n 10) 7–111. The later essay, an article, is MH Kramer, 'Some Doubts about Alternatives to the Interest Theory of Rights' (2013) 123 *Ethics* 245.

[21] See MH Kramer in *A Debate Over Rights* (this chapter, n 10) 61–63; and MH Kramer, 'Some Doubts about Alternatives to the Interest Theory of Rights' (2013) 123 *Ethics* 245, 245–249.

[22] When framing core tenets of interest theory, Kramer speaks of a right that 'preserves' interests in 'Rights Without Trimmings'; though on the same page, when framing two core tenets of will theory (that contrast with interest theory), he mentions 'protect' and 'protection' of interests. See MH Kramer in *A Debate Over Rights* (this chapter, n 10) 62. In his later article, in framing the core tenets of interest theory, he settles for 'protects'. See MH Kramer, 'Some Doubts about Alternatives to the Interest Theory of Rights' (2013) 123 *Ethics* 245, 246. The idea that rights are *protective* of interests is, without doubt, the classic position.

[23] See HLA Hart, *Essays on Bentham* (this chapter, n 1), for instance at 183–184; and for the idea of a legal right as a legally respected individual choice see (for example) at 189, 193.

is competent and authorised to demand or waive enforcement of the right (the latter position being an *interpretation* of classic Hartian will theory, rather than a precise replication of one of its core tenets).[24]

According to Kramer, both will theory and interest theory go at least a step further, and indeed concur, in maintaining that protection or preservation of an interest – while it may be necessary under interest theory though *not* will theory – is *not sufficient* for the holding or actual possession of a right. This is an important point at which will theory and interest theory appear to coincide, but it serves perhaps to emphasise a certain ontological impoverishment in interest theory which (in contrast to will theory) apparently succeeds only in identifying necessary conditions (among possible others) for the holding or possession of a right: not necessary and sufficient conditions.[25]

Ultimately Kramer's synopsis raises the question whether the core theoretical positions are simply 'opposed' because they incorporate what might be described as 'reciprocal negations'; or are genuinely, irreconcilably, opposed at the level of substantive, theoretical principle. They resemble contrasting 'belief systems'. So, if theory A holds to principle X *but explicitly not* principle Y, and theory B holds to principle Y *but explicitly not* principle X, it does not necessarily, though it *might*, follow, that principles X and Y are irreconcilable. That would certainly be the case if the value of X, say, is 100 degrees Celsius (boiling point of water) and that of Y is 0 degrees (freezing point of water). These are simple irreconcilables.

What is clear from Kramer's synopsis is that the 'reciprocal negations' of the core theoretical positions – where core will theory rejects core interest theory and the converse – revolve more around the emphasis or focus of the respective theories than points of principle that are irreconcilably divergent. Interest theory asserts that it rejects the core tenets of will theory, instead giving primacy to right-holders' interests in its elucidation of rights. Will theory asserts that it rejects the core tenets of interest theory, instead placing the emphasis on right-holders' ability to demand or waive enforcement of the right (which Hart explicitly frames

[24] Hart synoptically frames the contrast between the positions he adopts in relation to (respectively) interest theory and will theory in the following terms: 'The analysis of a right correlative to obligation which is suggested by the foregoing criticisms of the benefit [interest] theory is that for such a right to exist it is neither sufficient nor necessary for the person who had the right to be the beneficiary of the obligation [which Hart would maintain is a core tenet of interest theory]; what is sufficient and necessary is that he should have at least some measure of the control, described above, over the correlative obligation'. See HLA Hart, *Essays on Bentham* (this chapter, n 1) 187–188.

[25] That said, Kramer acknowledges that interest theory must admit of a further desideratum to account for the existence of a (legal) right. What is needed is some *law:* a statute, a judicial ruling, a constitutional provision, an administrative regulation, an incorporated moral principle, a contract, or some other authoritative legal norm that confers the right upon the right-holder. (See MH Kramer, 'Some Doubts about Alternatives to the Interest Theory of Rights' (2013) 123 *Ethics* 245, 247.) It is unclear why the need for a law would be a requirement of interest theory (only) and not of interest theory *and* will theory. Hart does, however, create difficulties for will theory when his necessary and sufficient conditions for the existence of a legal right do not explicitly include a law (or authoritative legal norm), but centre around powers and choices that are simply 'there', or simply 'materialise'; there being little in the way of investigation (by Hart) of any rule-based origins of legal rights.

in terms of right-holders' control over a correlative obligation and right-holders' resultant choices).

However, at the level of the detail of critical analyses of the respective theories, adherents to one or other theory may find numerous points of disagreement that may or may not be so intractable that they are literally irreconcilable. For instance, Neil MacCormick (in the interest theory camp) points to the existence of rights that are legally incapable of waiver in order to refute a key theoretical position that he attributes to Hart.[26] Essentially, MacCormick maintains that Hartian will theory holds to the (in his opinion, mistaken) view that for a right to exist it is necessary that the right-holder in every case has (among other abilities) the ability to waive the right.[27] Ultimately, this allows him to maintain the paradox that the more inalienable (in effect, *incapable of waiver*) a right is, the less can it be a right.[28] There is, on the face of it, no straightforward way of reconciling that aspect of will theory with any corresponding (but *opposed*) position in interest theory given that the latter theory (in its core tenets) makes no significant claim in relation to rights that are incapable of waiver. In a similar way, MacCormick's noteworthy position in relation to the untenability of accommodating children's rights within Hartian will theory has no direct counterpart in any key position upheld by interest theory.[29] It is fully possible to argue that Hartian will theory is beset by the theoretical difficulties identified by MacCormick without the need to take up a contrary position in interest theory. (Indeed, critics of Hartian will theory – who could actually be located within the 'will theory camp' – would have no need to share MacCormick's commitment to interest theory in order to align themselves (more narrowly) with MacCormick's critique.)

It seems clear – at least on the basis of Kramer's synopsis – that there is nothing in a core tenet of one theory that so conflicts with a corresponding aspect of the rival theory that we are forced to conclude that in the relevant respect the two *theories* are irreconcilable. Instead, what we find is that theorists from one or other camp set out to refute a key tenet of the rival theory. The refutation, if tenable, may support a claim of 'irreconcilability'. So, taking MacCormick's 'inalienable rights' argument, if a will theorist is (correctly) held to the claim that for a right to exist it is necessary that the right-holder, without exception, has the ability to waive the right, while an interest theorist claims that that is *not* necessary,

[26] See DN MacCormick, 'Rights in Legislation' (this chapter, n 2) 195–199.

[27] ibid at 196: 'If there be no power to waive or assert the immunity, the claim, or whatever, upon some matter, upon that matter there is, *by definition*, no right either'.

[28] ibid 198–199.

[29] For example, Kramer's synopsis highlights the protection or preservation of an interest as a substantive tenet of interest theory, and only mentions the (mental) competence and authorisation of a given right-holder *as an aspect of a subsidiary tenet* of interest theory – ie in the context of a tenet of interest theory that refutes or negates what Kramer identifies as a core tenet of will theory. So, in other words, there is nothing in interest theory that obviously and directly engages – in the same way as will theory – the issues and controversies surrounding the cognitive or volitional capacity of a given right-holder (eg a child).

then the claims of the theorists in the rival camps are plainly at variance and may be irreconcilable.[30] One camp claims X is necessary; the other camp claims X is not necessary. These positions negate each other and cannot straightforwardly be reconciled. So, a *theorist* may hold to a position that is irreconcilable with that held by another theorist, even if core aspects of the theories themselves are not necessarily, irreconcilably, and directly in conflict. This points to the desirability of considering areas of overlap or convergence between will theory and interest theory on the basis that this might serve not only to delimit the boundaries of one theory from the other, but to assist the development of a more encompassing frame of reference within which to explore the nature, characteristics and conditions of existence of legal rights.

1.3. Towards Theoretical Interpenetration

As we have seen, Kramer identifies at least one point of convergence between will theory and interest theory, which is that protection or preservation of an interest – while it may be necessary under interest theory though not will theory – is not, under *both* theories, *sufficient* for the holding or actual possession of a right. Essentially, then, under interest theory the presence of an interest is necessary but not sufficient for the holding or possession of a right; while under will theory the presence of an interest is neither necessary nor sufficient for the holding or possession of a right. This somewhat restricted question of [lack of] sufficiency, then, appears to be common to the two theories. Now, if that were the only point at which the two theories coincide then, needless to say, they would have little in common.

But perhaps this is also in some way accountable to a corresponding lack of commonality in the philosophical roots of the theories: interest theory having a broadly utilitarian or welfarist origin and will theory having a broadly Kantian origin. Thus Hart, when commenting on Bentham's leanings towards an interest theory of rights – where, for Hart, the key emphasis is more in the direction of *benefits conferred* by rights, rather than, strictly, interests protected by them – notes that 'at some important points … [Bentham's] utilitarianism gets in the way of his analytical vision'.[31] The core idea is that interest theory – focusing on benefits conferred, or interests secured, through the performance of a correlative obligation – views rights through the lens of a philosophical tradition that gives primacy to the notion of maximising human happiness. In this there lies the beginnings of an approach to understanding rights based on a system of normative ethics that is fundamentally consequentialist. The same approach can also accommodate the most diverse range of interests. At the same time, Kramer and Simmonds both

[30] DN MacCormick, 'Rights in Legislation' (this chapter, n 2) 198–199.
[31] See HLA Hart, *Essays on Bentham* (this chapter, n 1) 162.

point to the *welfarist* philosophical origins of interest theory, which has obvious resonances with utilitarianism.[32]

Now while the philosophical roots of interest theory may be traceable to the consequentialism of (utilitarian) welfarism, the arguably Kantian origins of will theory would seek to emphasise the *intrinsic* rightness or wrongness of actions. So, essentially, while one philosophical tradition (Kantianism) would claim (plausibly or otherwise) to disregard the consequences of actions, another claims to place consequences at the centre of its thinking (utilitarianism). Kantianism would also seek to delimit areas of freedom within which the individual acts.[33] The Kantianism of will theory may furthermore engage Kant's categorical imperative which, according to a conventional formulation, urges us to *act only on that maxim which we can at the same time will as a universal law*.[34] Applied to legal rights – and to the determination of their scope – ideally an area of freedom assigned to one right-holder by rights should not encroach materially upon the freedom enjoyed by other right-holders. So, if by universalising the right in a given case a right-holder's own freedom would be materially curtailed or harmed by the (resultant encroaching) rights of others, this would not be a right that given right-holders would either wish to have for themselves, or for others to possess. Expressed another way, Kant's imperative urges the pursuit of individual freedom only so far as compatible with the like pursuit of the freedom of others.[35] This in turn envisages the demarcation of a sphere of mutually coexistent, and compatible, freedoms with which rights are said to invest a given right-holder. In Hartian will theory this idea could be manifested in (appropriately constrained) freedoms – in other words, not only the narrow freedom of *choice* (or discretion) associated with each and every legal right to exercise a measure of control over the correlative obligation that corresponds to the right, but at the level of the substantive content of rights.[36]

[32] See MH Kramer in *A Debate Over Rights* (this chapter, n 10) 62; and NE Simmonds (ibid) 205–211.

[33] See generally NE Simmonds in *A Debate Over Rights* (this chapter, n 10) 123.

[34] See R Scruton, *Kant* (Oxford University Press 1982) 69–70.

[35] See NE Simmonds in *A Debate Over Rights* (this chapter, n 10) 135, quoting I Kant, *The Metaphysics of Morals* (M Gregor (tr), Cambridge University Press 1991) 51: 'Kant believed that it was possible to delineate principles which would flesh out this notion of equal freedom: "Right is therefore the sum of the conditions under which the choice of one can be united with the choice of another in accordance with a universal law of freedom".'

[36] One way of imagining the idea of 'freedom' in the context of what might be said to be the 'Hohfeldian straitjacket' of Hartian 'rights correlative to obligations' – which is apparently Hart's adopted frame of reference for the development of his will theory of rights – is to consider the position of someone who has a right to a piece of land. AM Honoré would argue that the right carries with it: (i) a subsidiary right of exclusion (placing countless others under a correlative obligation not to (civilly) trespass on the land); and (ii) an immunity with which the right-holder is invested that constrains others from dispossessing the right-holder of the land (or indeed divesting the right-holder of a *title* to the land). (See generally HLA Hart, *Essays on Bentham* (this chapter, n 1) ch VII. See also AM Honoré, 'Rights of Exclusion and Immunities Against Divesting' (1959–1960) 34 *Tulane Law Review* 453.) Armed with the right to the land (ie a title and a plethora of subsidiary rights, powers, immunities and so on) the right-holder has the freedom to enjoy the land, to stroll around it undisturbed, to build on it, to plant and uproot trees and shrubbery at will, to pick and eat apples and pears 'with abandon', and to do

By opting for an explanation of legal rights based on interest theory, society is viewed as being on a quest, through the operation of legal rights, to alleviate or resolve conflicts of interest before they arise or are anticipated to arise. By opting for an explanation of legal rights based on will theory, society is seen to be on a quest to ensure that all coexistent freedoms, expressed through the medium of legal rights, are mutually compatible. Although the route may differ, both end states will often come to the same thing, ultimately. And even the process of arriving at a particular end state might, in practical terms, involve the same or similar trade-offs or concessions.

Yet, against a background of theoretical divergence that recognises contrasting philosophical origins for will theory and interest theory, it is possible to discern a further point of convergence beyond the minor one identified at the beginning of this section. On one hand, the idea that rights are protective of interests (traceable to interest theory) and, on the other, the idea that rights are empowering, or literally *are* powers (mainly traceable to the Hartian variant of will theory),[37] emerge as mutually complementary, rather than irreconcilable, theoretical positions. And their complementarity is seen to turn on something very practical: that is, the *institutionality* of legal rights. Differing aspects of this perspective are developed in some detail later in this book. But examining the fundamental idea in more concrete terms if, in order to secure my castle against an invading enemy, I heighten and strengthen the walls, deepen the moat, and enlist new recruits into my private army, the steps I have taken to protect my interests – namely, the interest in safeguarding my castle against attack and preserving my property from pillage – surely *empower* me. I am now more secure than if I had taken no steps to reinforce the castle and its defences. When 'translated' into institutionally secured legal rights, the critical area of overlap between the domain of protection and that of empowerment can be expressed in a straightforward idea: namely, *that which protects also empowers*. Simple as it may be, this pivotal principle – that of protective empowerment – underlies important aspects of the analysis to follow.

For the moment, suffice it to say that when legal rights are observed operating in the context of (ultimately coercive) institutional processes the protection of interests that they afford to right-holders, allied to right-holder empowerment, appear to reinforce the core tenets of (respectively) interest theory and will theory identified earlier in this chapter.[38] For an interest to be seen to be protected, and

a multitude of things denied to others who have various obligations of non-interference that, at one and the same time, serve (at least in part): (a) to delimit *their* actions (and their freedom) when interacting with the land, and (b) to define the freedom of the right-holder (the land-owner) when interacting and transacting with the land.

[37] See discussion in section 5.3.4 (Chapter 5, below) and generally Chapter 9 below.

[38] As Kramer comments: 'For the Interest Theorists, the essence of a legal right consists in its tendency to safeguard some aspect of the well-being of its holder; for the Will Theorists, contrariwise, the essence of a legal right consists in its provision of opportunities for its holder to make significant choices. In the eyes of the Interest Theorists, the chief desideratum accruing to the holder of a legal right is *security*. In the eyes of the Will Theorists, the chief desideratum is *control*'. See MH Kramer, 'Some Doubts about Alternatives to the Interest Theory of Rights' (2013) 123 *Ethics* 245, 248 (emphasis added). At this

for a right-holder to be considered to be empowered, the focus inevitably turns to the practical – extending to physically coercive – ways in which institutional coercive apparatuses (or the threat of them) may be engaged directly or indirectly to induce particular behaviours. Protection is, however, not limited to physically coercive (institutional) means of enforcement; it encompasses *normative* protection, turning on the idea that those in possession of a legal right may have a justified expectation of performance of the subject matter of the right, whilst duty-bearers (for a variety of reasons beyond the mere existence per se of the right) may consider that they *ought to* render performance to the right-holder. Thus, there are physical (coercive) *and* cogitative (normative) manifestations of protection; and they complement one another.

Hartian will theory, in particular, adopting the position of the right-holder, places the emphasis on a regime of control with 'three distinguishable elements' (each of which affords relevant choices to right-holders), maintaining that – in the context of 'rights correlative to obligations' (or 'duties', taking into account shifts in Hart's terminology) – right-holders are invested with the following powers:

> (i) the right holder may waive or extinguish the duty or leave it in existence; (ii) after breach or threatened breach of a duty he may leave it 'unenforced' or may 'enforce' it by suing for compensation or, in certain cases, for an injunction or mandatory order to restrain the continued or further breach of duty; and (iii) he may waive or extinguish the obligation to pay compensation to which the breach gives rise.[39]

These elements of right-holder empowerment occupy a temporal continuum extending from the point in time prior to judicial enforcement; through the enforcement process; and ultimately to its aftermath. Looking briefly at each of Hart's three elements in turn, in the case of (i) above,[40] the institutional processes (eg involving the possibility of escalating to enforcement action such as court proceedings) can be disengaged where a right-holder takes action to waive or extinguish the (substantive) right. Alternatively, simply leaving the right in existence (as Hart suggests) neither explicitly engages nor disengages any institutional process; so a 'neutral' state of affairs obtains unless and until the right-holder asserts the right: such as by explicitly demanding performance from the duty-bearer

level of analysis, not only is there theoretical complementarity; there is also a step towards theoretical interpenetration which the coupling of security and control implies. Security flows from the protection of the right-holder's interests which the right affords; while control flows from the empowerment that the right provides to the right-holder. Commenting on the latter, Simmonds notes: '… the Will Theory treats control by the will as being the very essence of a right'. See NE Simmonds in *A Debate Over Rights* (this chapter, n 10) 229.

[39] See HLA Hart, *Essays on Bentham* (this chapter, n 1) 183–184. This is also discussed in sections 3.2.1 and 3.2.3 (Chapter 3, below) at respectively nn 11 and 33. Note that Hillel Steiner extends the scope of – and the scope of the discussion of – the powers enumerated by Hart in *Essays on Bentham*. In so doing, he instructively explores interrelationships, and the interplay, between and among the various Hartian powers (as extended). See H Steiner in *A Debate Over Rights* (this chapter, n 10) 240–247.

[40] '[T]he right holder may waive or extinguish the duty or leave it in existence.'

(and that may, of course, stop short of institutional engagement). In the case of (ii) above,[41] an institutional process is explicitly engaged when a right is enforced through (for example) civil proceedings. But, again, simply leaving the right unenforced is a 'neutral' state of affairs unless and until, as in (i), the right-holder in some way asserts the right. In the case of (iii) above,[42] judicial proceedings that have run their course may result in a court-imposed obligation to pay compensation, in the form of an order of the court. But an *unenforced* obligation – such as a breach of contract that has not been, and is not intended to be, the subject of judicial redress – probably also falls within Hart's third category.

Yet while Hart refers to the three elements of right-holder empowerment as investing a right-holder with the 'fullest measure of control', in truth the judicial elements of the process – involving court proceedings – invariably lie beyond a right-holder's immediate control or power, diminishing the choices that (Hart would claim) are entailed in the possession of a right. In short, as soon as it becomes necessary for a right to be enforced by way of a judicial process, the right-holder experiences some measure of loss of control as institutional (court) apparatuses take over and rules of evidence and procedure are engaged. All of this, to a not insignificant extent, erodes the personal autonomy and agency that a right-holder might imagine would be entailed in the possession and exercise of a legal right.[43] Clearly this raises questions concerning the asymmetry between rights enforcement outcomes based around, on one hand, right-holder autonomy or self-help – ie what a right-holder asserting a right can directly achieve when not engaging institutional processes (eg sending a letter to the duty-bearer formally requesting performance) – and outcomes involving institutional enforcement (for instance, judicial intervention or less formalised dispute-resolution processes).

These questions are further explored at a number of points in the analysis to follow. In the next section, more specifically, a few elements of the relationship between the protection of interests by rights and right-holder empowerment are discussed to lay the groundwork for later analysis.

1.4. Resonances of Protection and Empowerment in Social Theory

As we have seen, the principle of protective empowerment touched upon in the preceding section – *that which protects also empowers* – represents a point of complementarity between a core position upheld in mainstream interest theory

[41] '[A]fter breach or threatened breach of a duty [the right holder] … may leave it "unenforced" or may "enforce" it by suing for compensation.'

[42] '[The right holder] … may waive or extinguish the obligation to pay compensation to which the breach gives rise.'

[43] See the discussion of loss of (right-holder) control in section 5.3.4 (Chapter 5, below).

and a similarly pivotal stance maintained in Hartian will theory. Thus Neil MacCormick argues that one of interest theory's key contentions is that the legal (or moral) protection or promotion of one person's interests as against some other person or the world at large is 'essential to the constitution of a right'.[44] According to MacCormick, protection and promotion (of relevant interests) are secured by the imposition of duties, disabilities, or liabilities which the right-holder is in a position to demand of the duty-bearer.[45] At the same time, as we have seen, a key contention of Hartian will theory is that the right-holder is invested with some measure of control of enforcement or waiver of a correlative obligation to which a duty-bearer is subject.[46] The right-holder is therefore empowered to enforce or waive a right; while that right, in turn, operates to protect or promote some interest that the right-holder might claim to have.

The idea that protection of interests (following interest theory) and right-holder empowerment (following will theory) are complementary theoretical positions resonates with classical social theory. For instance Max Weber, unconstrained by the need that would later evolve in Anglo-American jurisprudence to visualise a legal right as falling only within one explanatory pigeonhole or the other, moves between conceptions of legal rights that are characteristic of both interest theory and will theory – in fact, Weber appears to *combine* the protectionist rationale of interest theory and the empowerment rationale of will theory.[47] For instance, in emphasising the role of a legal right in promoting interests, Weber observes that – viewed in sociological terms – the possession of a legal right gives the right-holder, pursuant to the 'consensually accepted interpretation of a legal norm' (which is a function of the judicial system), the ability to invoke in favour of 'his ideal or material interests' the aid of a 'coercive apparatus' which stands in readiness to give effect to, and to enforce, the right. Weber argues that, typically, the 'aid' in question consists in the readiness of certain persons to support the right-holder 'in the event that they are approached in the proper way' (assuming this support is guaranteed by a legal norm).[48] Weber's oblique reference to institutional mechanisms of enforcement – such as courts and (eg) civil enforcement agencies – clearly operates at the level of both interest protection and right-holder empowerment, though the latter is more explicitly articulated in the context of Weber's generic concept of social power, where a legal right is to be seen as a manifestation of *Herrschaft*.

[44] See DN MacCormick, 'Rights in Legislation' (this chapter, n 2) 192.

[45] ibid.

[46] See HLA Hart, *Essays on Bentham* (this chapter, n 1) 183–184.

[47] While the two 'camps' of interest theory and will theory already existed in some shape or form at the time Weber was writing, they were not perhaps as 'polarised' as they became (especially in Anglo-American jurisprudence), later in the twentieth century.

[48] See M Weber, *Economy and Society: An Outline of Interpretive Sociology* [*Wirtschaft und Gesellschaft: Grundriss der Verstehenden Soziologie*] (G Roth, C Wittich and others (trs and eds), Bedminster Press Inc 1968) (hereafter, in this chapter, '*Economy and Society*') 315.

Thus Guenther Roth characterises *Herrschaft* relationally and correlatively as a 'structure of superordination and subordination, of leaders and led, rulers and ruled'.[49] In the legal context, Weber's concept of *Herrschaft* equates to a 'power to command', but in the sense of a 'meaningful interrelationship'.[50] As an exertion of will, Weber sees *Herrschaft* in terms of social power, reflecting 'the possibility of *imposing one's ... will upon the behavior of other persons*'.[51] Power in that sense is to be seen percolating down to the case where, according to Weber, a customer places an order with a shoemaker for a pair of shoes, or employees assert their claim to wages from their employer. Being contractual rights, the powers in question also occupy the territory of legal rights. Weber in fact views private law as the decentralisation of *Herrschaft* (or 'domination') in the hands of those upon whom legal rights have been conferred.[52] 'From this angle, the worker would have the *power to command*, ie, 'domination' over the entrepreneur to the extent of his wage claim'.[53] For Weber, '[t]he concept of power is sociologically amorphous. All conceivable qualities of a person and all conceivable combinations of circumstances may put him in a position to *impose his will* in a given situation'.[54]

There is perhaps more than a resonance of Weber's viewpoint in Hart's characterisation of a right-holder's 'control' as 'exclusive control, more or less extensive, over another person's duty so that in the area of conduct covered by that duty the individual who has the right is a small-scale sovereign to whom the duty is owed'.[55] But setting Hart aside for the moment, the emerging picture is one in which classical social theory appears to accommodate the principle of protective empowerment (*that which protects also empowers*) that straddles interest theory and will theory. More specifically, Weber's writings support the idea that a legal right which is protective of a right-holder's interests at the same time operates to invest the right-holder with the power, by way of an exertion of will, to ensure that effect is given to the right. Not only are right-holders, through the exercise of their legal rights, personally in a position to impose their will in a given situation (as Weber suggests), but they are able to do this with the aid of a coercive apparatus – in other words, an institutional structure

[49] See M Weber, *Economy and Society* (this chapter, n 48) 61–62 n 31. (Translators have conventionally rendered *Herrschaft* as 'domination'.)

[50] ibid 942, 1378.

[51] ibid 942 (emphasis added).

[52] ibid. See also M Weber, *Max Weber on Law in Economy and Society* (M Rheinstein (ed), Harvard University Press 1954) 323–24, 328.

[53] M Weber, *Economy and Society* (this chapter, n 48) 942 (emphasis added). See further discussion in section 5.3.4 (Chapter 5, below). Weber also comments that '[i]t is essential to include the criterion of power of control and disposal (*Verfügungsgewalt*) in the sociological concept of economic action if for no other reason than that an exchange economy involves a complete network of contractual relationships, each of which originates in a deliberately planned process of acquisition of powers of control and disposal'. See M Weber, *The Theory of Social and Economic Organization* (AM Henderson and T Parsons (trs and eds), The Free Press 1947) 163.

[54] M Weber, *Economy and Society* (this chapter, n 48) 53 (emphasis added).

[55] See HLA Hart, *Essays on Bentham* (this chapter, n 1) 183. This metaphor is also examined in more detail in section 5.3.4 (Chapter 5, below).

whose functioning is integral to the empowerment factually afforded by the right.

Yet despite the apparent sociological dependence of the concept of a legal right on the ability of a right-holder to invoke the aid of a coercive apparatus, there is no suggestion in the (Weberian) sociological analysis of legal rights that the perspective of any part of the coercive apparatus itself, such as that of a judicial institutional structure, might be adopted to throw light on the idea of a legal right.[56] This is not only arguably a lacuna of (Weberian) sociology but of both mainstream interest theory of rights and Hartian will theory also.[57] It is a surprising omission given the dependence of the related ideas of protection and empowerment on institutional – and ultimately coercive – intervention. The presence of institutional enforcement structures is always a backdrop – often no more than an 'unstated assumption' – when the protective and empowering dimensions of legal rights are under discussion, even in cases where explicit institutional intervention is not in contemplation. Beyond the point of such intervention, when the process is initiated, most right-holders – for instance, in the case of civil law rights – largely surrender control of the process to professionals such as lawyers who are engaged by the right-holder for that purpose. This may, or may not, result in the right-holder's original conception of the right being upheld. So, to continue to view the standpoint of the right-holder – and right-holder autonomy – as pre-eminent, once institutional intervention has entered the frame, draws the discussion towards analytical distortion.

In any institutional reckoning of the content or scope of a legal right – such as where a civil law right (say) is disputed – what appears, on the face of it, to be a straightforward and relatively transparent claim, may come up against a number of hurdles, such as evidential, jurisdictional or procedural barriers to the pursuit of the claim. For instance, is there credible evidence of the existence of the right? In order to establish a claim, is one of the litigating parties actually in default in performing a legal duty (and is there credible evidence of that)? Does the particular court in which the claim is raised have jurisdiction? Is the claim time-barred? If an institutional process such as civil litigation is engaged to protect an interest claimed to be protected by a legal right – and if at the same time a claimant is empowered by the ability to resort to that institutional process – the practical hurdles in question would need to be cleared. In other words, the operational and practical efficacy of a *disputed* legal right may be contingent on the successful prosecution of a claim within an appropriate institutional process. And if a claimant falls foul of any significant hurdle, such as a time-bar, the claim may be defeated. Thus, *both* protection of relevant interests

[56] An appropriate institutional point of view – that of an idealised hypothetical common law judge, *Iudex* – is discussed in some detail in later chapters. Further discussion of the '*Iudexian*' perspective is held over until those later chapters in order not to pre-empt that later discussion. (See, for instance, section 3.2.3 (Chapter 3, below) and generally Chapter 8.)

[57] This is taken up again in Chapter 3, below. See section 3.2.3.

(maintained as a characteristic of interest theory) *and* right-holder empowerment (maintained as a characteristic of will theory) may be critically dependent on the successful conduct of a claim, such as litigation prosecuted in a court of law. And in other cases – such as a non-court setting, where no claim is contemplated – a realistic assessment of the content and scope of a given legal right (even if merely hypothetical) must take account of the institutional context in which the right will invariably and ultimately reside, extending to the projected institutional response to the right in question if the right is ever the subject of an institutional (eg judicial) process.

1.5. Concluding Reflections

Several of the themes touched upon in this chapter are revisited and developed later in the book. For instance, some aspects of the position – straddling both interest theory and will theory – that legal rights may be protective of interests *at the same time as* they empower right-holders (essentially through the protective tutelage of institutional structures) are explored further in Chapters 3 and 9 below.[58] The essential point to emerge from the foregoing discussion in this chapter is that social theory is thought to be an appropriate context in which to examine such a position, even if derivable from theoretical assumptions that are more immersed in a tradition of legal philosophy that has been evolving since the mid-twentieth century than in Weberian sociology. The possibility of viewing legal rights as an instrument of social power – contextualising the discussion within both a Hartian and classical (Weberian) social theory setting – is taken up in section 5.3.4 (Chapter 5, below) and in Chapter 9. It will be maintained, ultimately, that legal rights are to be seen as a repository of social power reinforced by the presence of institutional structures. The perspectival shift away from the image of the legal right as something to be viewed primarily from the standpoint of the right-holder urges the adoption of an alternative image of the legal right – viewing rights from a standpoint that resides within the 'institutional imagination' (or, more narrowly, 'judicial consciousness',[59] epitomised in a (Weber-inspired) ideal type which hypothesises a supreme court judge, *Iudex*, whose decision-making is recognised as legally conclusive for the jurisdiction in question. It is argued that, in the final analysis, it is 'a *Iudex*' who mobilises the (ultimately coercive) mechanisms of the legal system towards the enforcement of legal rights, whether this is

[58] Power, as Hart would put it, resides in the idea of the right-holder having 'exclusive control, more or less extensive, over another person's duty'. See HLA Hart, *Essays on Bentham* (this chapter, n 1) 183. Essentially, the idea (traceable to interest theory) that legal rights are protective of interests converges with the idea (traceable to will theory) that legal rights empower the right-holder. This convergence is expressed in the principle of protective empowerment, outlined earlier in this chapter, namely: *that which protects also empowers.*

[59] See section 3.1 (Chapter 3, below), n 3; and generally Chapters 7 and 8.

directly in court proceedings (such as by way of the decision of a supreme court); or indirectly, where relevant institutional actors, including lower court judges, imaginatively reconstruct the consciousness or mindset of 'a *Iudex*' in the context of their own decision-making.

The possibility of developing an institutional (ie judicial, or *Iudexian*) perspective on legal rights is further explored in Chapter 3. And in Chapter 8, using a critique of Ronald Dworkin's imaginary 'Herculean' judge (outlined in Chapter 7) as a point of departure, a developed version of the *Iudexian* ideal type construct is benchmarked against empirical criteria drawn from sources that include decision-making at the level of higher appellate judges in the UK.

2

Theories of Rights and Theories of Law*

2.1. Introduction

In this chapter, and Chapter 3, key aspects of the two main theories of rights – will (or choice or power) theory and interest (or benefit) theory – are examined. The focus of the discussion across the two chapters is on particular variants of those theories: namely, the version of will theory advanced by HLA Hart; and the versions of interest theory advanced respectively by Joseph Raz and Neil MacCormick. Whereas in Chapter 3 the focus is on three so-called 'constraining factors' which, it will be argued, subvert the two theories of rights in ways that have implications for enquiries pursued later in this book, the fundamental question for consideration in this chapter is the extent to which two leading representatives of the rival theories of rights attempted to integrate the distinctive versions of their rights theories with their more general theories of law. For the relatively narrow purpose of this chapter, it is proposed to consider whether – and, if so, the extent to which – Hart integrated his version of the will theory of rights, as principally developed in his *Essays on Bentham*, with the core of his general theory of law, as outlined in writings such as 'Definition and Theory in Jurisprudence' and in his major work, *The Concept of Law*.[1] Likewise, it is proposed to consider whether – and, if so, the extent to which – Neil MacCormick integrated his distinctive version of the interest theory of rights, outlined in writings such as his essay 'Rights in Legislation',[2] with his general institutional theory of law, presented in writings as diverse as his inaugural lecture, 'Law as Institutional Fact' and *Institutions of Law*, one of the tetralogy of books completed shortly before his death.[3]

* Elspeth Attwooll kindly commented on an earlier draft of this chapter.

[1] See generally HLA Hart, *Essays on Bentham: Jurisprudence and Political Theory* (Clarendon Press 1982) (hereafter, in this chapter, '*Essays on Bentham*'); HLA Hart, *The Concept of Law* (2nd edn, Clarendon Press 1994); and HLA Hart, 'Definition and Theory in Jurisprudence' (1954) 70 *Law Quarterly Review* 37 (hereafter, in this chapter, 'Definition and Theory'). Note that 'Definition and Theory' is also reprinted in HLA Hart, *Essays in Jurisprudence and Philosophy* (Clarendon Press 1983) ch 1 (Essay 1). In this chapter, references are to the reprinted (1983) essay. Hart acknowledges certain defects in 'Definition and Theory' in the Introduction to *Essays in Jurisprudence and Philosophy*, 4–6.

[2] DN MacCormick, 'Rights in Legislation' in PMS Hacker and J Raz (eds), *Law, Morality, and Society: Essays in Honour of HLA Hart* (Clarendon Press 1977) ch 11 (hereafter, in this chapter, 'Rights in Legislation').

[3] See generally DN MacCormick, 'Law as Institutional Fact' (1974) 90 *Law Quarterly Review* 102 (hereafter, in this chapter, 'Law as Institutional Fact'); and N MacCormick, *Institutions of Law: An Essay in Legal Theory* (Oxford University Press 2007) (hereafter, in this chapter, '*Institutions of Law*').

The working assumption underlying the discussion in this chapter is that if two influential legal philosophers could maintain, as they did, intelligible theoretical and philosophical positions in relation to the general idea of law, viewed as a distinctive type of social and institutional phenomenon, one might expect to discern some application, more or less explicit, of the same modes of explanation, and explanatory frames of reference, in such of their writings that focus more narrowly on the fundamental concept of the legal right. That assumption is in turn rooted in a broader assumption that, in terms of theoretical and philosophical enquiry, what holds for the *general* (ie law in the wider sense) holds for the *particular* (ie core concepts such as the legal right). At a more fundamental level of enquiry, any disjunction or incompatibility that might be found to exist between, respectively, Hart's and MacCormick's particular and general theoretical positions may have implications not only for the coherence of the approach adopted by each theorist in framing his general theoretical outlook, but for the integrity of his analysis of the basic concept of the legal right in terms of how that plays out in the distinctive versions of will theory and interest theory that they respectively promoted. Conversely, if it would appear that Hart or MacCormick (or both) were found to have successfully integrated their respective *particular* theoretical positions on legal rights with their general theoretical positions then the question will arise as to the extent to which the resultant analyses, viewed more holistically, might be used to advance our understanding of legal rights more effectively.

The end point of the enquiry pursued in this chapter – which will feed into lines of analysis and discussion taken up in later chapters – is consideration of whether there are lessons to be learnt not only about the nature of law and legal rights based on contrasting theoretical positions, but on the coherence, explanatory power and tenability of those theoretical positions themselves: in other words, the theoretical enquiries into the nature of law and legal rights pursued by Hart and MacCormick respectively.

Commencing the discussion with Hart, then, it is appropriate to examine the extent to which Hart's version of the will theory of rights was integrated with elements of his general theory of law in several of his more important writings. A parallel discussion will follow later in this chapter: considering the extent of integration of MacCormick's version of interest theory with elements of his more encompassing institutional theory of law.

2.2. HLA Hart's Ordinary Language Methodology and Will Theory of Rights

In 'Definition and Theory' – an important essay published in January 1954 and later reprinted with some acknowledgment of errors and defects – Hart set out a 'manifesto' for what has come to be regarded as his radically new philosophical and theoretical approach to the elucidation not only of generic ideas such as the concept of 'law' itself, but of more particular, if nonetheless fundamental, legal concepts such as 'right' and 'duty'.[4] Hart's approach derived from the ordinary language philosophy of JL Austin, itself influenced by writings of the philosopher Ludwig Wittgenstein.[5] The general approach announced by Hart in 'Definition and Theory' was later reinforced in his major work, *The Concept of Law*. In that book, in his approach to the subject matter of his enquiry – which, to use his own phraseology, includes 'municipal legal system' (or 'municipal law') and a variety of fundamental legal concepts[6] – Hart developed a broader range of methodological insights than were to be found in 'Definition and Theory'. One of these, for instance, is the idea (to use Hart's own words) of the 'internal aspect of rules seen from their internal point of view'.[7] It goes without saying that, in its totality, Hart's work has gained recognition for making a pioneering contribution to jurisprudence and legal philosophy, with no small part of that being accountable to the general approach and methodological insights that Hart first developed in 'Definition and Theory'.[8]

The core methodological principle that emerges from 'Definition and Theory' had originally been the subject of an injunction voiced by Bentham, cautioning that, in approaching the problematic task of elucidating core legal concepts such as 'right' or 'state' or 'corporation', we should not take these words in isolation 'but [must] consider whole sentences in which they play their characteristic role'.[9] As Hart puts it, it was futile to 'hammer away at single words'. Instead of focusing narrowly on the concept in hand or seeking a definition – which could lead the lawyer into (as Hart describes it) a 'forbidding jungle of philosophical argument' or an encounter with an 'incubus of theory'[10] – the adopted approach would involve consideration of the import of (typical) *whole sentences* in which a given concept

[4] See generally HLA Hart, 'Definition and Theory' (this chapter, n 1).

[5] See CA Auerbach, 'On Professor HLA Hart's Definition and Theory in Jurisprudence' (1956) 9 *Journal of Legal Education* 39. Auerbach cites Wittgenstein's *Philosophical Investigations*, which has been published in a number of editions. But for one of the earlier editions of the book, first published in the early 1950s, see L Wittgenstein, *Philosophical Investigations* (GEM Anscombe (tr) and GEM Anscombe and others (eds), Basil Blackwell Limited 1953).

[6] Hart's concept of '[modern] municipal legal system' (or 'municipal law [in a modern state]') is explored briefly in Chapter 5, below, in the context of a discussion of the possible use by Hart of social science typologies. Particular instances of the use of this related terminology are to be found in *The Concept of Law* (this chapter, n 1). See (eg) at 5, 17, 100 ('[modern] municipal legal system'); and at 79, 122, 199 ('municipal law [in a modern state]').

[7] See HLA Hart, *The Concept of Law* (this chapter, n 1) 90. The possibility that the internal aspect of rules (as Hart envisages this in *The Concept of Law*) resonates with the Weberian idea of the subjective meaning [of social action] – seen not merely as a characteristic of rules per se but as a methodological principle – is discussed in Chapter 5, below.

[8] Hart makes clear his intention to continue the approach established in 'Definition and Theory' when he states in the Preface to *The Concept of Law*: 'Many important distinctions, which are not immediately obvious, between types of social situation or relationships may best be brought to light by an examination of the standard uses of the relevant expressions and of the way in which these depend on a social context, itself often left unstated'. (See HLA Hart, *The Concept of Law* (this chapter, n 1) v.)

[9] See HLA Hart, 'Definition and Theory' (this chapter, n 1) 26. Hart's reference to Bentham at the start of section II of the essay perhaps comes as a surprise when one might have expected such a pivotal methodological principle to have originated, say, in the writings of JL Austin.

[10] See HLA Hart, 'Definition and Theory' (this chapter, n 1), respectively, at 21, 23.

played its characteristic role. Once the enquirer had discovered or formulated a suitably representative sentence, the concept could be explained by first specifying the conditions under which the *whole sentence* is true, and secondly by showing how the concept is used in drawing a conclusion of law from (legal) rules in a particular case.

The question arising for consideration at this point in the discussion is that of the extent to which Hart applied this general approach in later writings in which he outlined his will theory of rights. It is apparent, in considering this question, that there is significant overlap between aspects of his general analysis of the legal right in 'Definition and Theory' and his separate analysis in chapter VII ('Legal Rights') of *Essays on Bentham*.[11] In 'Definition and Theory', Hart explicitly applies a general method derived from linguistic philosophy but focused on the elucidation of legal concepts. In this way, or possibly by other means, he arrives at a number of tenets outlined at the end of section III of that essay. (These are considered in some detail below.)[12] The explicit application of this general method, however, is absent from his analysis in chapter VII of *Essays on Bentham*.[13] Given that the analysis in that chapter has, for some, come to define the core of his will theory of legal rights,[14] this omission at first sight seems surprising, particularly as one might have expected the same basic approach to be manifested in both the earlier and later writings. The point is that 'Definition and Theory' – importantly, unveiling his general linguistic philosophical method and using for this purpose the concept of the legal right among others as his 'test subject' – without doubt lays some of the groundwork for key aspects of the analysis that he later pursues in chapter VII of *Essays on Bentham*. Carrying forward selected aspects of the earlier analysis to the later analysis, albeit absent the fundamental methodological insights outlined in the earlier analysis,[15] is not the least productive line of approach that Hart could have adopted, given that a settled position is presented in some detail in the earlier analysis, with the result that the two discrete analyses are mutually

[11] See HLA Hart, *Essays on Bentham* (this chapter, n 1) ch VII, 162–193.

[12] See section 2.2.1 (this chapter, below).

[13] So, in other words when, in reference to the class of 'rights correlative to obligations', Hart outlines a version of the will theory of rights – whose exponents had included figures as prominent as Friedrich Carl von Savigny and Hans Kelsen – the idea of examining the expression 'right', contextualised in a sentence with some claim to typicality, is seemingly passed over. In chapter VII of *Essays on Bentham*, therefore, there are no instances of the expression 'right' or 'a [legal] right' being embedded in a typical sentence in which it plays a characteristic role, with the sentence in turn being subject to 'exegetical' scrutiny (that being the broad approach recommended in 'Definition and Theory'). Yet, in contrast, Hart's analysis in chapter VIII of *Essays on Bentham*, where the subject matter of the discussion is legal powers, actually *commences* with an attempt to make sense of the expression 'legal power' by considering how it is used in 'a range of situations, familiar in the ordinary working of a modern legal system'. (See HLA Hart, *Essays on Bentham* (this chapter, n 1) ch VIII, 194.)

[14] For example, see DN MacCormick, 'Rights in Legislation' (this chapter, n 2) especially at 192.

[15] It is perhaps also notable that Hart does not refer to 'Definition and Theory' when explicitly restating, in chapter VII of *Essays on Bentham*, parts of the analysis previously (and recognisably) formulated in 'Definition and Theory'.

reinforcing. (Could it be argued that, in the later analysis, Hart simply omits to 'show his workings'?)

Perhaps a more pressing question (than the preliminary question outlined above) is whether the relevant analyses *taken together* – where the methodological insights of 'Definition and Theory' are seen to be combined with the analytical insights of chapter VII of *Essays on Bentham* – exhibit coherence, persuasive force and (ultimately) explanatory power. To address that question, what is needed, it is suggested, is: first, a reassessment (in overview) of Hart's general linguistic philosophical method set out in 'Definition and Theory'; secondly, a brief examination of the points of overlap between: (A) Hart's elucidation of the concept of the legal right in 'Definition and Theory' and (B) relevant aspects of the analysis of the legal right in chapter VII of *Essays on Bentham*; and, thirdly, some drawing of appropriate conclusions from the emergent analysis.

2.2.1. Hart's Ordinary Language Philosophical Method

It is well recognised that Hart's general linguistic philosophical method for elucidating core and 'perplexing' legal concepts – otherwise, his ordinary language approach – has three main elements which are briefly restated here, namely:

(A) embodying a key legal concept – such as [legal] 'right' – in a 'typical' sentence in which the concept plays its characteristic role;
(B) specifying the conditions under which the resulting *whole sentence* is true; and
(C) specifying how the concept is used in drawing a conclusion of law from (legal) rules in a particular case.[16]

It is worth recalling Hart's claim, derived from Bentham, that it is pointless to focus on a philosophically problematic concept (such as 'right' or 'legal right') in isolation: in other words (as Hart puts it) to 'hammer away at single words'. Contextualising the concept in a typical sentence was Hart's suggested way forward: this would be a first step towards properly elucidating the concept. What is immediately striking about this approach is that in 'Definition and Theory' Hart proposes no criteria of 'typicality'. What counts as a 'typical' sentence? Or how is a sentence in which a key concept such as 'right' plays a characteristic role to be identified?[17] A theorist might be tempted to select, or to devise, a sentence that delivers the most favourable explanatory outcome at the same time as downplaying obvious hindrances

[16] HLA Hart, 'Definition and Theory' (this chapter, n 1) 34–35.

[17] Hart, for instance, speaks interchangeably of 'examples of typical contexts where these words [such as 'right' or 'duty'] are at work'; and of the embodying of words such as 'right' or 'duty' 'in a sentence … where it plays a characteristic role': see HLA Hart, 'Definition and Theory' (this chapter, n 1), respectively, at 27, 34. So, a sentence selected for scrutiny will be 'typical'; or a key [legal] concept (eg 'right') will play a 'characteristic role' in such a sentence.

to explanation. For instance, Hart's seemingly randomly chosen sentence – 'X has a right' – connects the concept of a right with: (i) an individual, X, who is (ii) in possession of a right. There is, in other words, an underlying, or pre-theoretical, assumption that a legal right is something that: (i) 'someone' can (ii) 'have'. That might not seem especially revelatory, but given that Hart was instituting a new theoretical approach to elucidating and explaining problematic legal concepts – where, ideally, his starting point should be a 'blank sheet of paper' – pre-theoretical assumptions of that kind (as discussed more fully below) would inevitably have a hand in predetermining or precipitating a given analytical outcome.

So, what constitutes a typical sentence in which the expression (legal) 'right' occurs? As already noted, Hart offers no criteria of 'typicality', yet nonetheless proposes 'X has a right' as an example of a typical sentence. Without direction as to what does and does not constitute a 'typical' sentence, the question arises as to whether any sentence – or sentence type – is ruled out in the quest for 'typicality'. Indeed, we might ask how 'ordinary' a sentence needs to be when ordinary language philosophical methods are employed. It so happens that legal rights-language use may be more prevalent in 'technical' legal settings than in 'ordinary' (non-legal or non-professional) settings so that, in terms of the given content, this can represent 'ordinary' use *of a kind*. A typical context for the use of rights-language is the judicial setting. Hart's quest for 'typicality' does not rule out instances of rights-language use to be found in that setting – and in similar (legal) professional contexts – where the use of rights-language is all-pervasive: for instance, law text-books. Thus, Hart urges reflection upon 'statements made on a particular occasion by a judge or an ordinary lawyer',[18] while saying little about the precise or anticipated content of such statements in these more 'technical' legal settings.

Yet, as soon as we observe what appears to be a 'typical' use of rights-language in a judicial setting and apply the ordinary language philosophical method of analysis to it, we find that the resulting analysis may lead the lawyer into at least as forbidding a jungle of *legal* analysis as the 'jungle of philosophical argument' that Hart had sought to avoid.[19] One result of this is that even the most ordinary use of rights-language in a judicial context throws us upon *technical legal* uses an understanding of which is indispensable to the proper elucidation of the concept *as used in that setting*. Take, as a random example, an observation of Lord Buckmaster in *Donoghue v Stevenson*:

> The principle contended for must be this: that the manufacturer, or indeed the repairer, of any article, apart entirely from contract, owes a duty to any person by whom the article is lawfully used to see that it has been carefully constructed. All rights in contract

[18] See HLA Hart, 'Definition and Theory' (this chapter, n 1) 27, and also 28–29. Hart also makes reference to pronouncements made by game umpires (at 29).

[19] Towards the end of section 2.2.2 (this chapter, below), the extent to which the judicial setting – where rights discourse inevitably becomes (legally) highly technical – may be used as an example of the genuinely 'ordinary' settings that appear to be necessitated by an ordinary language philosophical enquiry is questioned.

> must be excluded from consideration of this principle; such contractual rights as may exist in successive steps from the original manufacturer down to the ultimate purchaser are ex hypothesi immaterial.[20]

For someone properly versed in the technical legal use of rights-language this is straightforward enough, at least at first sight. But a moment's reflection on Lord Buckmaster's use of such language reveals at least three issues worthy of further exploration when considered against the background of applying Hart's ordinary language approach.

First, Lord Buckmaster explicitly uses rights-language to exclude contractual rights from the scope of a principle that turns on the presence of a 'duty': a duty of care. However, can 'rights' be excluded from a 'duty' (or a 'principle', for that matter)? On the face of it, excluding rights *from other rights* makes more sense. It is clear that the rights under discussion are, in fact, tort- or delict-based rights arising by operation of law, *but framed in terms of 'duty'*. So, Lord Buckmaster excludes contractual rights from a more encompassing and varied class of rights. This may be to clear 'space' for a discussion of precisely those non-contractual rights that are framed in terms of a duty of care.

Secondly, it is clear that in the context of a discussion of the scope and content of a unique category of non-contractual rights, Lord Buckmaster frames the central principle not in terms of a right but in terms of a duty. Person A owes a duty 'to any person [B] by whom … [an] article is lawfully used to see that it has been carefully constructed'. It would be clear to any lawyer that in this situation B has a right, *which is to be inferred from a duty of care* owed to B by A. Lord Buckmaster envisages that compliance with the relevant duty of care by A (a manufacturer or repairer of an article) is something that B as right-holder is in a position, in some sense, to insist upon.

Thirdly, as we have seen, a lawyer coming upon a legal duty framed in these terms would typically *infer* the presence of a legal right corresponding, and correlative, to the duty. It is an instance of the class of rights that Hart refers to as 'rights correlative to obligations',[21] which in turn is closely associated with the idea of 'jural correlativity' identified in Hohfeld's analysis, where (among other types of rights or powers) a legal claim-right in the 'strict' sense correlates with a legal duty or obligation.[22] But what is most notable about this part of Lord Buckmaster's speech is that the discussion of what is clearly a right correlative to a duty does not turn literally on use of the expression 'right'. The concept of a legal *duty* is used in Lord Buckmaster's formulation of the key principle in a situation where the concept of a right might have been used instead. What this suggests is something that a lawyer knows only too well: the obvious fact that a right can in many contexts be established by law, or can be *inferred*, in the absence of an explicit use

[20] *Donoghue v Stevenson* [1932] AC 562, 577.
[21] See HLA Hart, *Essays on Bentham* (this chapter, n 1) generally ch VII; but particularly 174–188.
[22] See generally WN Hohfeld, *Fundamental Legal Conceptions as Applied in Judicial Reasoning* (WW Cook (ed), Yale University Press 1919).

of the expression 'right'.[23] And, if that is so, some knowledge of rights and their 'behaviour' needs to be brought to bear in understanding the nature of a right that is not explicitly identified as such. And while this may not strengthen the case for applying Hart's ordinary language approach to understanding legal rights per se – in terms of contextualising the expression 'right' in a typical sentence in which it plays a characteristic role – a defender of Hart might object (not unreasonably) that the opportunity to apply that approach direct to Lord Buckmaster's opinion would see the concept of a legal 'duty' at the centre of that enquiry; not the concept of a legal 'right'. That said, the inconveniences attending the practical application of the ordinary language approach to an understanding of legal rights in circumstances where the expression 'right' is not literally used – despite the obvious presence to a lawyer of an 'inferred right' – does little to facilitate that approach or render it workable.

Fourthly, Lord Buckmaster is enunciating a principle that in substance he *rejects*. His speech is a dissenting one and he makes a point of clearly stating the principle to be upheld not by him but by the majority of the court in the same judgment – ie the duty of care owed by a manufacturer to an end-user of a product – in order to highlight its potential weaknesses (as he perceives them). Perhaps this emphasises the truism that it is possible to discuss and argue over real *or hypothetical* rights without being in any way 'invested' in the rights in question: eg accepting them, rejecting them, possessing them, calling for them (when they are not there) and welcoming them (when they are). But as Lord Buckmaster makes clear, the case provides a basis for the recognition of what in essence became – consequent upon the decision in *Donoghue v Stevenson* – a new, or certainly a newly recognised, principle of law where relevant rights were established under the English law of tort (and Scots law of delict), subsisting independently of any contractual arrangements already in place. In order to make sense of the relevant passage from Lord Buckmaster's speech it is necessary to recognise a 'lawyer's distinction' between contract-based rights and legal rights grounded in the general law of tort (English law) or delict (Scots law). At the same time, Lord Buckmaster's particular use of rights-language applies either to a right that did not yet exist; or to a nascent right that would only become established or recognised – essentially for the first time – when the judgment was handed down. This was, of course, an early incursion into the field of consumer rights. So, the point is that rights-language can apply to [legal] rights that are hypothetical or imaginary, nascent or prospective; they need not be fully established and be legally enforceable. This raises the question of what can be learnt from an interrogation of the truth conditions of

[23] Even a situation where a tortfeasor is considered to have a 'liability' to compensate a wronged party – without any necessary or explicit use of the expressions 'duty' or 'obligation' – gives rise to the inference that the wronged party has a 'right' to compensation, though in this context 'liability' is equivalent to 'duty' or 'obligation' (to compensate) under the law of tort. Given that the entire law of negligence turns on the idea of breach of duty, judicial discussion of a finding that there has, or has not been, negligence in a particular case is as likely to turn on consideration of whether there is a 'duty' or 'breach of a duty' or a 'liability' as it is to place the idea of a 'right' as the focal point of the discussion.

a sentence such as 'A has a right' (applying Hart's methodology) if we happen to know that the right in question is merely hypothesised or is a right not yet in existence. (In that circumstance, can A in truth be said to *have* 'a right'?) Moreover, for a fuller understanding of the rights in question, an important 'lawyer's distinction' needs to be recognised between rights grounded in contract and rights grounded in the general law.

The final point, overlapping significantly with the first, centres on the idea that Hart's ordinary language approach to explaining concepts such as a 'right' may become redundant or inutile in situations where the expression 'right' is not even discoverable in a typically occurring sentence, such as the instance seen in the passage reproduced from Lord Buckmaster's speech, where a key proposition, from which a lawyer would not hesitate to infer a right, is framed in terms of 'duty'.[24] As we have seen, Hart's approach involves exploring key characteristics of a typical sentence in which an expression, such as 'right', is embedded, by specifying the conditions under which the sentence is true, and by showing how the concept is used in drawing a conclusion of law from (legal) rules in a particular case. In the case of a (legal) right, it is apparent that when a typical sentence does not even contain the expression 'right', but instead uses a related concept from which the presence of a right is to be inferred, some prior understandings, or pre-theoretical assumptions, are necessarily brought to bear in reaching a proper understanding of the character of the (inferred) right in question.

Yet it also seems no less arguable that in the case of Hart's analysis of simple, and 'typical', sentences such as 'A has a right', a *similar* set of understandings, or pre-theoretical assumptions, must be engaged. If the ordinary language approach is neither facilitating nor constraining of understanding then the same analysis might be pursued, and the same conclusions might be reached, without resort to that approach. The question, then, is whether situating a 'perplexing' or problematic concept such as 'right' in a typical sentence is a redundant (extra) step in analysing the nature and characteristics of the concept in question. Everything, it seems, turns on the content of the resultant analysis and of any relevant prior understandings, or pre-theoretical assumptions, relied upon. Support for this position appears to come from a surprising quarter: literally from Hart himself. The apparent redundancy of Hart's general approach is apparent in his analysis

[24] In one of the key passages of the leading opinion of Lord Atkin, the notion of a right can still be *inferred* even though the right in question (giving rise, in turn, to a right of action) is several steps removed from the foundational duty (of care) under discussion. Lord Atkin argues that the central proposition of his opinion is that 'by Scots and English law alike a manufacturer of products … with the knowledge that the absence of reasonable care in the preparation or putting up of the products will result in an injury to the consumer's life or property, owes a duty to the consumer to take that reasonable care'. (See *Donoghue v Stevenson* [1932] AC 562, 599.) Here, the consumer is, or becomes, a right-holder whose right can be inferred from: (i) the existence of a duty of care on the part of a manufacturer, that (ii) is breached, (iii) causing injury to the consumer and giving rise to (iv) a liability on the part of the manufacturer to compensate the consumer in respect of the injury caused. The right in question is the reflex of the tortious or delictual *liability* (equivalent to a duty to compensate). And, needless to say, in the passage in question, Lord Atkin makes no explicit mention of any 'right'.

of the legal right in the context of his discussion of the will theory of rights in chapter VII of *Essays on Bentham* where he makes no mention of this approach but nevertheless restates key parts of the analysis (of a 'right') developed in 'Definition and Theory'. In other words, parallel, and similar, analyses are pursued in two separate (and chronologically distinct) settings; with only the earlier analysis appearing, on the face of it, to be dependent upon the general (ordinary language philosophical) approach outlined there.

It is useful to consider the implications of this position in more detail: examining the extent to which Hart's analysis of a right in 'Definition and Theory' coincides with his analysis in chapter VII of *Essays on Bentham*, at the same time considering the extent of reliance of the latter analysis on the general (ordinary language) approach outlined in the former.

2.2.2. Overlap between Hart's 'Definition and Theory' and Chapter VII of *Essays on Bentham*

In both 'Definition and Theory' and chapter VII of *Essays on Bentham*, Hart emphasises the same fundamental point, namely, that the notion of a legal right and other core legal concepts had in the past proved to be 'very elusive' and a source of perplexity or puzzlement.[25] And in the case of those same writings, despite their separation by the passage of nearly two decades,[26] works of Bentham, such as his *Of Laws in General*,[27] remained, for Hart, a source of inspiration and an enduring point of departure for the analysis of major legal concepts. Hart's writings have undoubtedly carried the explanatory process to a higher level. Perhaps the most significant overlap between the earlier and later analyses – marking something of a departure from any stance that could be attributed directly to Bentham – is a line of analysis centring on the notion of the right-holder's *will* upon which Hartian will theory turns. One might say that it is the idea that puts the 'will' into will theory; and is the key to differentiating Hartian will theory not only from the version of interest theory that Hart attributes to Bentham, but from interest theory in general. The genesis of this idea is to be found in a key passage in Hart's 'Definition and Theory'; and essentially the same position is taken up in chapter VII of *Essays on Bentham*. In the passage in question, Hart explicitly applies his ordinary language approach to a (typical) statement incorporating the expression 'right'. Hart urges exploration of the truth conditions of such statements. Thus

[25] See HLA Hart, *Essays on Bentham* (this chapter, n 1) 162; and HLA Hart, 'Definition and Theory' (this chapter, n 1) 21, 23, 31–33.

[26] Chapter VII of *Essays on Bentham* was originally published as 'Bentham on Legal Rights' in AWB Simpson (ed), *Oxford Essays in Jurisprudence: Second Series* (Clarendon Press 1973). But that essay sought to build, to an extent, on an earlier work from 1962: HLA Hart, 'Bentham: Lecture on a Master Mind' (1962) 48 *Proceedings of the British Academy* 297.

[27] See J Bentham, *Of Laws in General* (HLA Hart (ed), Athlone Press 1970).

the statement 'X has a right' is true if certain conditions, including the following (using Hart's numbering), are met:

(b) Under a rule or rules of the system some other person Y [ie a duty-bearer, being someone other than the right-holder, X] is, in the events which have happened, obliged to do or abstain from some action.
(c) This obligation is made by law dependent on the choice … of X … so that either Y is bound to do or abstain from some action only if X … so chooses or alternatively only until X … chooses otherwise.[28]

In a parallel analysis of the concept of a legal right in *Essays on Bentham*, not only is there no explicit mention of the ordinary language approach upon which the analysis in 'Definition and Theory' turns, Hart appears to pursue the very approach that he had disavowed in that essay: that is, he 'hammers away' at a single concept – the legal right.[29] Thus, in chapter VII of *Essays on Bentham*, Hart arrives at a position broadly equivalent to that outlined in 'Definition and Theory', not through identification of truth conditions of a typical sentence incorporating the expression 'right' but through identification of the *existence conditions* of a certain type of legal right: namely, the class of rights which he identifies as 'rights correlative to obligations'.[30] Taking Hart's condition (b) above, what serves as one of the truth conditions of the statement 'X has a right' in 'Definition and Theory' – ie the state of duty-bearer Y's being obligated to right-holder X – merely becomes part of the definition of the class of rights selected for analysis in chapter VII of *Essays on Bentham*. (The point is that any analysis of 'rights correlative to obligations' must minimally, *definitionally*, presuppose the presence of obligations to which the relevant rights correlate.)[31] More significant, however, is Hart's adoption of the position, in condition (c) above, that the truth condition of the sentence 'X has a right' which (in 'Definition and Theory') views the performance of Y's correlative obligation as being dependent on X's *choice* – an exertion of X's will – becomes (in *Essays on Bentham*) a *necessary and sufficient condition* of the *existence* of the right.[32] In short, one of the truth conditions of a typical sentence incorporating the expression 'right' in the earlier analysis (applying the ordinary language approach) is recast as an existence condition of a right in the later analysis. Inevitably, that raises the question: *whither the ordinary language approach*? It seems that truth conditions of a typical sentence incorporating the expression 'right' can readily be reframed as existence conditions of a 'right' without reference to the sentence. If the use of an interposing step – ie the use of a sentence with an indeterminate

[28] See HLA Hart, 'Definition and Theory' (this chapter, n 1) 35.
[29] ibid 26.
[30] See HLA Hart, *Essays on Bentham* (this chapter, n 1) (principally) 168–169, 174–188.
[31] ibid 168: 'All rights correlative to obligations are rights to services which consist in the performance of their correlative obligation and with two exceptions all legal obligations or duties have correlative rights'. (Hart goes on to describe the two exceptions as 'self-regarding duties' and 'obligations by which no one at all benefits'.)
[32] See section 3.2.1 (Chapter 3, below).

claim to typicality – seemingly adds nothing to the analysis is there a need for that step? If not, can the step be jettisoned? In a review of Hart's 'Definition and Theory', published in 1969, PMS Hacker asks a similar question in a different way:

> Hart's own truth-conditional definition of 'legal claim-right' involves the use of the following concepts: the existence of a legal system, rules, systems of rules, obligation, choice recognized by law, action and others. Yet these perplexing terms cry out for philosophical analysis no less than 'a right'. If one is permitted to use these in a truth-conditional definition, why is one forbidden to use them in an analytic definition?[33]

Hacker is referring here to the range of truth conditions of the statement 'X has a right' cited in Hart's 'Definition and Theory', including not only those mentioned above – at (b) and (c) – but Hart's condition (a) which necessitates the presence of (nothing less than) a functioning legal system as the environment within which legal rules (and legal rights) operate. Beyond the stated truth conditions, Hart, as we have seen, further maintains that a 'statement of the form 'X has a right' is used to draw a conclusion of law in a particular case which falls under such rules', suggesting the need to bring to bear a knowledge of syllogistic reasoning.[34] It is clear that in examining the statement 'X has a right', Hart is impelled to 'bring to the table' a range of pre-theoretical understandings of the concept of a legal right and a knowledge of appropriate reasoning processes. The need for institutional structures must also be factored in: legal system, courts, and so on. All of this necessitates some prior insight into the nature and characteristics of legal rights which no straightforward elaboration of a statement of the form 'X has a right' could possibly arrive at. Key parts of the analysis in Hart's 'Definition and Theory' presuppose a more or less fully worked-through concept of a legal right which is critically dependent on an understanding of related concepts or ideas that are as beset with conceptual difficulty as the concept of a legal right itself: for instance, the concept of a legal rule; the idea of a system [of rules] (indeed a legal system); the notion of [legal] obligation; the idea of choice; and so on. On that basis, it seems clear that in 'Definition and Theory' Hart has in mind a quite developed idea of legal right which he goes on to develop further in *Essays on Bentham*. But, it is suggested,

[33] PMS Hacker, 'Definition in Jurisprudence' (1969) 19 *Philosophical Quarterly* 343, 346. Amid other objections to Hart's approach, Hacker points out particular weaknesses in Hart's general position that the expression 'a right' has meaning only as a part of a sentence the function of which as a whole is to draw a conclusion of law from a specific kind of legal rule. As Hacker points out, '[u]nless it is the case that all words have meaning only in sentences, then there is no apparent reason to deny meaning to "a right" or "duty" outside a sentential context'.

[34] Simply put, if X has a right on the occurrence of circumstances N, the right will come into existence whenever circumstances N occur. For instance, a legal rule might be interpreted such that an individual (X) is deemed to have a right to (for example) the intestate estate of a deceased uncle (Y) if circumstances N obtain. So, if we assume that Y has died and all other conditions N are satisfied (such as, for example, that Y did not leave a will, and dies without being survived by a spouse, or children, or remoter descendants) then the conditions may be met for the assertion (which is a 'conclusion of law') 'X has a right to Y's intestate estate' to be considered to be true.

this does not, and cannot, 'with one bound', spring forth from an analysis of the simple statement 'X has a right'.[35]

Against that background, the need to embody the expression 'a right' in a typical sentence such as 'X has a right' in chapter VII of *Essays on Bentham* might have distracted from the more important task that Hart set himself in that chapter where, in effect, he lays much of the groundwork for his version of will theory. The fact that the ordinary language approach does not feature in that chapter is perhaps recognition of this. That is not to suggest that Hart's use of the ordinary language approach is redundant in every situation. In many places in *The Concept of Law*, and in other writings (including *Essays on Bentham*), Hart's use of this technique is illuminating. The foregoing discussion, then, perhaps highlights a few of its limitations. On the most fundamental questions such as 'what is a (legal) right?', it seems there is little which Hart's methodology – placing the expression 'right' in a statement and examining its truth conditions – adds to the analysis which would not emerge from an independent elucidation of that concept: in other words, 'hammering away' at the concept of a 'right'. This is what Hart does when he simply posits the existence conditions of a right in chapter VII of *Essays on Bentham*.

A possible further reason for any claimed lack of success of the ordinary language approach in progressing understanding of the legal right in Hart's 'Definition and Theory' is that, often enough, the characteristics of legal rights are demonstrated in more 'technical' settings, such as in the context of judicial opinions. The question, then, is whether those (more 'technical') settings can possibly serve as the 'ordinary' settings necessitated by ordinary language philosophical enquiry. At the same time, viewing legal rights as, at least in part, an 'institutional artefact', calls for recognition that the discernment of those rights is often in the hands of specialists – for instance, judges and other trained professionals. So when, at a level furthest removed from the so-called private citizen, legal rights are formulated or constructed, say, in the opinions of judges of a supreme court, the ordinary language approach – to the extent that that may have regard to the perceptions and understandings of 'ordinary' individuals – may have little to add to the institutional perception, whether of legal rights generally or of specific rights that are the subject of judicial proceedings. (This point is taken up again in Chapter 3.)

[35] Referring to a position held by Brian Tamanaha, Nicola Lacey argues that Hartian theory 'is torn between a thoroughgoing conventionalism that attempts to theorize any phenomenon treated as law within a social group, and a more essentialist position that assumes that law has some core and invariant structural features'. It is difficult to escape the notion that Hart's analysis of the legal right – in both 'Definition and Theory' and chapter VII of *Essays on Bentham* – tends towards an 'essentialism' manifested in the simple positing of a selection of structural characteristics of a legal right, but under the guise of narrating (certainly in the case of 'Definition and Theory') the truth conditions of a randomly selected and typical sentence containing the word 'right'. It seems untenable that the characteristics in question could somehow be arrived at through a kind of 'exegesis' applied to such a rudimentary sentence. On Hart's 'essentialism', see N Lacey 'Analytical Jurisprudence versus Descriptive Sociology Revisited' (2006) 84 *Texas Law Review* 944, 949–950, referring in turn to BZ Tamanaha, *A General Jurisprudence of Law and Society* (Oxford University Press 2001) 135.

The idea of viewing the legal right as an institutional artefact perhaps marks a convenient point in the discussion for turning to consider the general institutional theory of law advanced by Neil MacCormick, and its connection (if any) with MacCormick's interest theory of rights.

2.3. Neil MacCormick's Institutional Theory of Law and Interest Theory of Rights

We have briefly considered whether HLA Hart, in seeking to explain the fundamental concept of the legal right according to his version of the will theory of rights, applied the same explanatory frame of reference to the concept of the legal right as he applied in his more general approach to explaining the concept of law. Having considered the extent to which Hart's will theory of rights was integrated with elements of his general theory of law, it is instructive now, in similar fashion, to consider the extent to which Neil MacCormick integrated his distinctive interest theory of rights with his general institutional theory of law.

With its origins in his influential inaugural lecture, 'Law as Institutional Fact',[36] MacCormick developed a version of his theory that became increasingly sophisticated over four decades. In retrospect, the institutional theory, thus developed, formed a significant part of his life's work, culminating in *Institutions of Law*, published in 2007.[37] It is clear that at least an echo of MacCormick's earliest work in viewing law as an institutional phenomenon – in particular, his inaugural lecture – finds its expression in his (also quite early) outline of a version of the interest theory of rights.[38]

In his essay, 'Rights in Legislation', MacCormick argues in support of his version of interest theory. Given that the essay is a chapter of a *Festschrift* dedicated to Hart, MacCormick takes the opportunity to outline a critical position in relation

[36] DN MacCormick, 'Law as Institutional Fact' (this chapter, n 3).

[37] See N MacCormick, *Institutions of Law* (this chapter, n 3). As MacCormick explains in the Preface at p v: 'This book sets out my version of the institutional theory of law. This theory has been taking shape since my 1973 inaugural lecture, "Law as Institutional Fact". Many of the ideas in it have been put forward in more tentative or preliminary form in other papers and books, and in lectures over the past thirty-five years. The theory has evolved beyond the legal positivist tenets to which I subscribed in 1973'.

[38] See generally DN MacCormick, 'Rights in Legislation' (this chapter, n 2). See also DN MacCormick, 'Children's Rights: A Test Case for Theories of Right' (1976) 62 *Archiv für Rechts- und Sozialphilosophie* 305. This article is also reprinted with modifications as chapter 8 of DN MacCormick, *Legal Right and Social Democracy: Essays in Legal and Political Philosophy* (Clarendon Press 1982) (hereafter, in this chapter, 'Children's Rights: A Test Case'). (In this chapter, references are to the article reprinted as a book chapter in 1982.) It seems to make sense to identify, at this stage of the discussion, whether there was any cross-fertilisation or overlap between MacCormick's early, yet significant, account of law as an 'institutional' phenomenon (such as in 'Law as Institutional Fact') and his near-contemporary accounts of a version of the interest theory of rights (such as in 'Rights in Legislation' and 'Children's Rights: A Test Case') which have retained a certain significance in terms of outlining a position that explicitly opposed Hart's will theory of rights.

to Hart's version of the rival will theory. With much of the focus of his essay upon perceived inadequacies of Hartian will theory – while all the time reinforcing the case for viewing interest theory as a credible alternative – MacCormick makes only a passing reference to his previously published 'Law as Institutional Fact'.[39] Towards the end of 'Rights in Legislation', MacCormick notes that in order to reach what is only a *practical* understanding of rights it is necessary to 'envisage them as "institutional" concepts'.[40] He concludes by briefly recalling his familiar tripartite classification of the laws structuring institutions of law, namely, institutive (or investitive) laws, consequential laws and terminative (or divestitive) laws.[41] In 'Rights in Legislation', elements of institutional theory only superficially complement the version of interest theory advanced in that essay. But perhaps that was as it should be given that – in contrast to 'Rights in Legislation' – 'Law as Institutional Fact', published around three years earlier, was directed towards a more ambitious aim. Viewing the law and legal concepts as 'institutional facts', and attempting an explication of the *full range* of fundamental legal concepts, was doubtless part of a grander theoretical project where legal rights would have an important place, but they would not be exhaustive of the field.

Suffice it to say, at this point in the discussion, that by 2007, in *Institutions of Law*, MacCormick appeared to be pursuing a more holistic approach in his treatment of the relationship between interest theory and institutional theory in that elements of both theoretical postures (institutional theory and interest theory) could be viewed, in a discernible way, as interdependent. (This is considered in further detail below.) So, if by 2007, elements of interest theory and institutional theory are seen to have reached a point of convergence – not mere complementarity – was there an aspect of institutional theory, in particular, that might have made that a realistic possibility?

The beginnings of an answer, it is suggested, lie in the fact that, first and foremost, MacCormick's general theory, as first expounded in 'Law as Institutional Fact', is explicitly ontological in its outlook – focusing on the conditions of existence, and facticity, of law and of major legal concepts.[42] That perhaps makes it peculiarly suited to accommodating *any* and *potentially every* fundamental legal concept encompassed within its range. Legal rights, most obviously, are prime candidates for inclusion within the category of concepts to be viewed as

[39] See DN MacCormick, 'Rights in Legislation' (this chapter, n 2) 206–207.

[40] ibid.

[41] This is first outlined in 'Law as Institutional Fact' (this chapter, n 3) 106–107. MacCormick notes in 'Law as Institutional Fact', n 6, that Raz, following Bentham, had touched upon essentially the same classification using the terminology, 'investitive', 'constitutive' and 'divestitive' laws. See J Raz, *The Concept of a Legal System: An Introduction to the Theory of Legal System* (2nd edn, Clarendon Press 1980) 175–183.

[42] See for instance, 'Law as Institutional Fact' (this chapter, n 3) 106–107 where MacCormick comments on the existence conditions of an institution of law. '[T]he law lays down that on the occurrence of a certain (perhaps complex) act or event a specific instance of the institution in question comes into existence. It is thus possible to state in the form of a separate rule of law the conditions which are essential to the existence of an instance of any such institution.'

'institutional facts'. This serves to differentiate theoretical positions adopted by MacCormick in 'Rights in Legislation' from those adopted by Hart, and indeed Joseph Raz, because, as discussed in Chapter 3, key aspects of the respective theories of rights advanced by Hart and Raz – on one hand, a version of will theory; and on the other, a version of interest theory – are directed towards examining *conditions of existence* of legal rights. It may be that, for his part, MacCormick had no need to address in detail such conditions in writings where he specifically set out his interest theory of rights, such as 'Rights in Legislation', because he had already laid the groundwork for that in 'Law as Institutional Fact'. That is not to suggest that the idea of law as institutional fact may be taken as read when considering MacCormick's earlier writings on interest theory. On the contrary, it is necessary to give close critical attention to the theoretical position first outlined in 'Law as Institutional Fact' because – whether it complements interest theory (in earlier writings) or is more integrated with that theory (in later writings) – in the final analysis it is not possible to give an encompassing critical account of MacCormick's interest theory of rights without giving proper consideration to his institutional theory of law. This is because, for MacCormick a legal right is an 'institution of law'.[43]

To that end, then, it is useful to consider briefly a few of the key elements of MacCormick's institutional theory as originally set out in his inaugural lecture. 'Law as Institutional Fact' is at least chronologically proximate to writings such as 'Rights in Legislation', where MacCormick outlined his interest theory of rights.[44] In 'Law as Institutional Fact' MacCormick identifies two main senses in which law can be described as 'institutional': a philosophical sense and a sociological sense.[45] It is appropriate to consider each of these in turn.

2.3.1. MacCormick on the Philosophical Institutionality of Law

At one level, as we have seen, MacCormick is explicitly concerned with the ontology of law and legal concepts, extending to their factual existence, expressed in theoretically conceived conditions of existence. The material reality of law is not, as MacCormick puts it, on the level of 'brute creation': not, in other words, on the same plane as 'shoes and ships and sealing wax'. It is, rather, a matter of 'institutional fact'; and that depends on the occurrence of, *and application of rules to*, 'acts or events in the world'.[46] MacCormick attributes this key insight to the work of

[43] It makes sense to focus on existence conditions given that, for MacCormick, a legal right is an instance of an 'institution of law' whose existence conditions are outlined in 'Law as Institutional Fact'.

[44] MacCormick also outlines aspects of his interest theory of rights in 'Children's Rights: A Test Case' (this chapter, n 38).

[45] See 'Law as Institutional Fact' (this chapter, n 3) 110–111.

[46] ibid 105.

philosopher John Searle.[47] Turning to Searle for the moment, instances of 'human institutions', marriage, baseball, money and trials (ie in the sense of criminal or civil proceedings), are identified. As Searle observes:

> [A]t an even simpler level, it is only given the institution of money that I now have a five dollar bill in my hand. Take away the institution and all I have is a piece of paper with various gray and green markings … Every institutional fact is underlain by a (system of) rule(s).[48]

MacCormick similarly identifies marriage as an instance of an 'institution' but he extends the category to contracts, rights of ownership, wills, trusts and corporations.[49] Even legislation is to be viewed as a 'legal institution'.[50] Yet the origins of this fundamental idea – that of the application (and significant consequences of the application) of rules to 'acts or events in the world' – is traceable not only to the work of Searle, writing in the 1960s; it can also be traced to writings of the legal philosopher, Hans Kelsen, at least as early as the 1930s when the first edition of *Reine Rechtslehre*, his seminal *Pure Theory of Law*, emerged.[51] Arguably, not every instance of the application of legal rules to acts or events in the world will result in something describable as an 'institution' or an 'institution of law'. This can be illustrated in observations made by Kelsen where he outlines a position that is in significant respects not dissimilar to that advanced by MacCormick.

The distinction between 'brute fact' and 'institutional fact' promoted by MacCormick is probably reflected in Kelsen's attempted separation of the world of law from the world of fact, expressed in the *normativity thesis* (here, following Stanley Paulson's account).[52] But whereas Kelsen attempts to maintain a credibly strict separation of law and fact, MacCormick attempts a synthesis of law and fact, where a special realm of 'institutional fact' results from the 'confrontation' of 'brute creation', or 'acts or events in the world', with relevant, applicable laws – that being the point of departure of institutional theory.[53] Kelsen, while still maintaining the idea of law and fact as separate domains, postulates the idea of legal meaning (*rechtliche Bedeutung*), that serves to bridge the gap between law and fact. In essence, Kelsen views the 'confrontation' of fact with law in a quite distinctive way, which resonates with the notion of the 'institutional fact'.[54] For Kelsen, certain acts that

[47] JR Searle, *Speech Acts: An Essay in the Philosophy of Language* (Cambridge University Press 1969).

[48] ibid 51. See also GEM Anscombe, 'On Brute Facts' (1958) 18 *Analysis* 69. Anscombe develops a concept of 'institutional facts' to complement the concept of 'brute facts'. See also D Dwyer, 'Beyond Kelsen and Hart? MacCormick's *Institutions of Law*' (2008) 71 *Modern Law Review* 823, 824.

[49] See 'Law as Institutional Fact' (this chapter, n 3) 106, 116, 119.

[50] ibid 119.

[51] See generally H Kelsen, *Pure Theory of Law* (published as Hans Kelsen, *Introduction to the Problems of Legal Theory* [*Reine Rechtslehre. Einleitung in die rechtswissenschaftliche Problematik*]) (BL Paulson and SL Paulson (trs and eds), Clarendon Press 1992) (hereafter, in this chapter, '*Pure Theory of Law*').

[52] ibid xix to xxix.

[53] For 'brute creation', see 'Law as Institutional Fact' (this chapter, n 3) 103.

[54] The idea, expressed here, of 'confronting' facts with laws originates in the Paulsons' translation of *Pure Theory of Law* at p 10 (see passage cited, this chapter, at n 56). For his part, as we have seen, MacCormick uses the expression 'apply' and its derivatives – so, he envisages the 'application' of laws

are 'perceptible to the senses, taking place in time and space'[55] may be endowed with special legal significance. Describing how murder is to be distinguished from the act of executing the death penalty, Kelsen observes:

> That a material fact is not murder but the carrying-out of a death penalty is a quality, imperceptible to the senses, that first emerges by way of an act of intellect, namely, confrontation with the criminal code and with criminal procedure.[56]

But where would murder – as opposed to the act of carrying out the death penalty – sit within MacCormick's and Kelsen's respective theories? As a practical matter, in Kelsen's pure theory, relevant acts – for example, a fatal stabbing (premeditated, say, and on the face of it, amounting to murder) – would be 'confronted' with relevant criminal laws. This would coincide broadly with Kelsen's treatment of an entirely separate type of act, the act of voting – where, again, relevant events are 'confronted' with relevant laws:

> People assemble in a hall, they give speeches, some rise, others remain seated – this is the external event. Its meaning: that a statute is enacted.[57]

MacCormick would doubtless go along with this (Kelsenian) interpretation of the act of voting. His institutional theory can accommodate the idea of voting as not only an institutional fact but as an *institution of law*.[58] So, a general election – involving voting on a large scale – could be regarded as such an institution. So also could any isolated act of voting at the level of the individual voter. According to Kelsen's stance, the act of voting is something that engages the idea of legal meaning in that, in practical terms, an act of intellect – involving the 'confrontation' of relevant acts or events with relevant laws – confers legal meaning upon those acts or events. It is clear that for *both* theorists 'acts or events in the world'

to facts. Obviously, this usage is common in a legal setting. See 'Law as Institutional Fact' (this chapter, n 3) 105, citing Searle: '[A] proposition whose truth depends not merely upon the occurrence of acts or events in the world, but also upon the *application* of rules to such acts or events, is a proposition of institutional fact'. (Emphasis added.)

[55] See *Pure Theory of Law* (this chapter, n 51) 8: 'There is an act perceptible to the senses, taking place in time and space, an external event, usually an instance of human behaviour. And there is a specific meaning, a sense that is, so to speak, immanent in or attached to the act or event … A merchant writes a certain letter to another merchant, who writes back in reply. This means they have entered into a contract'. In places there are striking parallels observable between MacCormick's (and others') concept of the institutional fact and Kelsen's notion of acts or events possessed of immanent legal meaning. In 'Law as Institutional Fact' (this chapter, n 3) 104, MacCormick refers to the act of boarding a bus and paying the fare: '[T]he act in question belongs to a class of acts whose performance the law treats as operative to make a contract. And what makes that matter is that the law ascribes certain rights and duties to individuals conditionally upon the existence of contracts'.

[56] *Pure Theory of Law* (this chapter, n 51) 10.

[57] ibid 8.

[58] MacCormick defines 'institution of law' thus: 'The term "institution of law", as I shall use it, is therefore to be understood as signifying those legal concepts which are regulated by sets of institutive, consequential and terminative rules, with the effect that instances of them are properly said to exist over a period of time, from the occurrence of an institutive act or event until the occurrence of a terminative act or event'. See 'Law as Institutional Fact' (this chapter, n 3) 108.

are in effect 'confronted' by relevant laws. For Kelsen, an act of conferring legal meaning is involved; while for MacCormick, a process resulting in the establishment of *institutional facts* is involved. But while the idea that institutional theory must take matters a step further by declaring certain acts or events so 'confronted' institutions of law, is relatively unproblematic in the case of voting and general elections, the place and status of murder in MacCormick's theory seem less straightforward.

In Kelsen's pure theory, the legal meaning of this or that assemblage of facts, when 'confronted' with the criminal code, is murder. But while that may broadly be the position in the perspective of institutional theory, and while it might be appropriate, using MacCormick's frame of reference, to view murder as an 'institutional fact', is it tenable to view it as an 'institution of law'? Can we speak of the 'institution' of murder? Given that, for MacCormick, the establishment of institutional facts, and the creation of institutions of law, are dependent on the occurrence of, and application of rules to, 'acts or events in the world',[59] it is not unreasonable to ask whether for MacCormick, murder – being a relevant act or acts 'confronted' with relevant laws – is an 'institution'. (It cannot be denied that 'murder' is a *legal* concept; whilst noting that MacCormick argues that 'institutions of law' are to be defined as 'legal concepts'.)[60]

Institutions such as a contract, or a general election, in the sense of institutional theory are usually 'instituted' (established) for a purpose – which may be, for instance, economic or social or political or cultural – and which may be perceived by some as beneficial or advantageous; playing out over time and delivering on their presumed benefits or advantages. Ordinary usage has permitted slavery to be described as an 'institution', at least historically if not in the modern age,[61] doubtless because it has always had a commercial and economic rationale that murder, or indeed other criminal acts such as arson, rape, incest, or assault, do not have. (Yet it would be difficult to deny that criminal activities such as drug-dealing and money laundering have an economic rationale.) If we adopt, unqualified, the position outlined by MacCormick in 'Law as Institutional Fact' can we properly speak of the 'institution' of rape; the 'institution' of money laundering? When criminalised, is prostitution an institution of law? Do *any* criminal activities qualify as institutions of law? In civil law, is the commission of a negligent act or other civil wrong, or the condition of having a tax liability, an institution of law? Indeed, in both the criminal *and* civil law, is the privilege of diplomatic immunity an institution of law? When does a given set of institutional facts – acts or events in the world 'confronted' by relevant laws – qualify as

[59] 'Law as Institutional Fact' (this chapter, n 3) 105.

[60] See MacCormick's definition, this chapter at n 58.

[61] Slavery is referred to as an 'institution' in writings such as KM Stampp, *The Peculiar Institution: Slavery in the Ante-Bellum South* (Alfred A Knopf 1956). Doubtless slavery is in a different position having been not simply an activity historically protected by law but was at the relevant time, among other things, an integral part of the economies of countries involved in trading slaves or exploiting their labour. Modern slavery is for the most part outlawed.

an institution of law in MacCormick's theoretical world view? What identifying criteria are to be applied?

MacCormick does allude in passing to Buckland's standard work on the main institutions of Roman private law, initially suggesting that what is conventionally referred to as an institution of law may be restricted to a category which – being tied to the discipline of law – is quite narrow.[62] But in institutional theory, the 'confrontation' (in the abstract) of facts with laws results in the creation of institutional facts that may, for MacCormick, be 'institutions of law' that are as generic as the universe of legal rights and obligations (including, as we have seen, legislation – with the result that every statute is to be seen as an institution of law);[63] or as specific as rights of intestate succession and obligations of reparation.[64] Ultimately, conventional usage may have more of a hand in determining when and whether a phenomenon can properly be regarded, or be referred to, as an institution of law in a given case. It may be that the expression 'institution' (such as in 'institution of law') is reserved only for practices around which a particular usage happens to have grown up – even once extending to the historically lawful, if abhorrent, practice of slavery. Nonetheless, MacCormick appears to suggest that *any* 'confrontation' of relevant facts with relevant laws – or, at any rate, any 'application' of rules (of law) to 'acts or events in the world', to use his phraseology – will yield institutional facts. And in some circumstances, it seems, the same collection of institutional facts will also comprise institutions of law. Apart from the definition provided,[65] and his citation of specific instances, MacCormick perhaps offers too little in the way of criteria for identifying such institutions. The result of that is that it is unclear whether certain legal states of affairs (or indeed what may pass as 'institutional facts') are included in, or excluded from, the general class of institutions of law. As we have seen, criminal offences and civil wrongs appear to lie within a particular grey area in institutional theory.

This seeming lack of clarity over the task of differentiating clusters of institutional facts classifiable as institutions of law from other (on the face of it) institutional facts that may not be so classifiable, is a theoretical lacuna. Yet it may come down to a mere matter of usage or semantics which the theory leaves unexplored. And while that may be problematic for institutional theory in its early manifestation in 'Law as Institutional Fact' a perhaps more intractable difficulty arises from the implications of the theory's ontological leanings where there is

[62] See 'Law as Institutional Fact' (this chapter, n 3) 105, citing WW Buckland, *The Main Institutions of Roman Private Law* (Cambridge University Press 1931). There was also a tradition for Scotland's so-called institutional writers to write authoritative legal treatises that were entitled 'institutions' or 'institutes'. See, for example, Sir James Dalrymple of Stair, *The Institutions of the Law of Scotland* (1681); and J Erskine, *An Institute of the Law of Scotland* (1773). See also JW Cairns, 'Institutional Writings in Scotland Reconsidered' (1983) 4 *Journal of Legal History* 76.

[63] 'Law as Institutional Fact' (this chapter, n 3) 119.

[64] ibid at 105. MacCormick's diverse inventory of institutions of law explicitly includes ownership, trust, testation, rights of intestate succession, incorporation, personality, obligations of reparation, real security, marriage and adjudication.

[65] ibid 108.

a focus on the conditions of existence of law and major legal concepts – their facticity. As we have seen, MacCormick brings that discussion under the first main sense in which, he claims, law can be described as 'institutional' – the philosophical sense. This places much of the emphasis of the ontological insights of the theory on its philosophical aspect, arguably at the expense of the other main sense in which, according to MacCormick, law can be described as 'institutional' – its *sociological* sense. Inevitably, this raises the question as to what extent a sociological understanding of law and legal concepts as institutional facts or as institutions of law might contribute to an ontological awareness of law and legal concepts. Essentially, the question is whether the sociological sense in which law is describable as 'institutional' has any role to play in setting conditions of existence of law and major legal concepts or even whether, according to institutional theory, the sociological aspect of the theory plays as prominent a role in that as its philosophical aspect. It is therefore appropriate now to give some attention to that question.

2.3.2. MacCormick on the Sociological Institutionality of Law

We have seen that in 'Law as Institutional Fact' MacCormick identifies, as one of the two main senses in which law can be described as 'institutional', a *sociological* sense. Sociology concerns itself, among other things, with explaining and attaining an understanding of social action, social relationships and types of structured behaviour – for example, where activities are organised towards a particular end or purpose or are structured around political or legal institutions.[66] Types of structured behaviours that can be characterised as 'institutions', as MacCormick notes, include universities, libraries and civil service departments.[67] But there are organised institutional structures that carry out specifically legal, or law-related, tasks, such as interpreting, applying and enforcing the law. MacCormick mentions the courts, the police and the legal profession.[68] There is no doubt that institutionality in that sense is an important attribute of law of a certain kind – for

[66] For instance, Max Weber outlines (behavioural) typologies that have an obvious institutional underpinning, such as the ideal type of *legal authority with a bureaucratic administrative staff*. See M Weber, *Economy and Society: An Outline of Interpretive Sociology* [*Wirtschaft und Gesellschaft: Grundriss der Verstehenden Soziologie*] (G Roth, C Wittich and others (trs and eds), Bedminster Press Inc 1968) (hereafter, in this chapter, '*Economy and Society*') 217–226. Related to this is the concept of a 'legitimate order' (ibid 31–36). See also the brief discussion of Weberian ideal types in section 5.3.5 (Chapter 5, below). Weber attempts definitions of sociology and of social action in M Weber, *The Theory of Social and Economic Organization* (AM Henderson and T Parsons (trs and eds), The Free Press 1947) 88. See section 4.4 (Chapter 4, below) at n 38.

[67] See 'Law as Institutional Fact' (this chapter, n 3) 110.

[68] As MacCormick observes: 'Such I shall call "social institutions". To this class it is obvious that courts, parliaments, police forces, civil service departments, the Faculty of Advocates, and the Law Society, all belong'. See 'Law as Institutional Fact' (this chapter, n 3) 110.

instance, the paradigm of the law of a Western state with centralised organs of government.[69]

Given the evident importance, to MacCormick, of the sociological sense of law as an institution, one might have expected to see some elaboration of the implications of this position in 'Law as Institutional Fact': for instance, mirroring the ontological insights afforded by his discussion of the philosophical sense of law's institutionality. Instead, MacCormick appears to take as a given the existence, role and functions of relevant legal institutions (for instance, the courts) without engaging in any kind of explicit sociological analysis designed to contextualise law and relevant legal institutions, even in a rudimentary way, within a conventional sociological frame of reference, such as might be provided in the writings of Weber; or indeed in a related setting, such as legal anthropology.[70] MacCormick merely touches upon the sociological aspect of the institutional dimension of law, having nonetheless emphasised its importance. In the result, the possibility of fruitful sociological enquiry is passed over, and sociology in the main is left unexplored.[71]

But the neglect of the work of leading sociologists is not where the most obvious of MacCormick's theoretical lacunae could be said to lie. In terms of understanding the factual existence – the conditions of existence – of laws and legal concepts, MacCormick's discussion of the philosophical sense of law's institutionality is insightful. It turns on the idea of key concepts, such as a legal right, comprising institutions of law in a specially defined sense. Yet, crucially, MacCormick fails to identify or explain the ways in which there might be a significant point of intersection between his philosophical, and sociological, characterisations of law's institutionality. For instance, does the existence of a legal right – predicated on the application of relevant laws to 'acts or events in the world' – rest on just *anyone's* 'say-so'? It surely matters, in a practical sense, *who* determines or declares the existence of (for example) a given right, or a duty, or an immunity, or a liability.

[69] See this chapter at n 6; and see also section 5.2 (Chapter 5, below) at n 10.

[70] Paul Bohannan, citing Malinowski, defines 'social institution' as 'a group of people who are united (and hence organized) for some purpose; who have the material and technical means of achieving that purpose or at least of making rational attempts at it; who support a value system, ethics, and beliefs validating that purpose; and who repeat more or less predictable activities and events in the carrying out of the purpose'. Bohannan distinguishes legal from non-legal institutions (his idea of a 'legal institution' being perhaps overly focused on dispute-resolution): 'A legal institution is one by means of which the people of a society settle disputes that arise between one another and counteract any gross and flagrant abuses of the rules of the other institutions of society'. See P Bohannan, 'Law and Legal Institutions' in WM Evan (ed), *The Sociology of Law* (Free Press 1980) ch 1, 5. (See also, generally, B Malinowski, *The Dynamics of Culture Change: An Inquiry into Race Relations in Africa* (Yale University Press 1945).) Two distinctive patterns of behaviour identified by Weber are reflected in Bohannan's definition of 'social institution': *zweckrational* and *wertrational* behaviour: respectively, instrumentally rational action (taking into account consequences and means of achieving set goals), and value-oriented action (being action oriented to, for example, religious, ethical or philosophical beliefs). See M Weber, *Economy and Society* (this chapter, n 66) 24–26.

[71] MacCormick never fully embraces sociology even in later writings, though he makes informative observations on the possible classical social theory grounding of Hart's internal and external points of view. See N MacCormick, *HLA Hart* (Edward Arnold (Publishers) Ltd 1981) 36–40.

There is a need for MacCormick's philosophical outlook on institutionality – which partly centres on his analysis of the existence and status of institutional facts and institutions of law (such as a particular legal right or legal duty) – to be complemented by his sociological outlook on institutionality. This would call for some discussion of the role of legal institutions (in MacCormick's sociological sense) – particularly the role of the courts – at the point where that role is determinative of institutional facts that go to make up institutions of law in specific cases. For instance, say a court of law makes an authoritative determination that a particular contract, with its attendant rights, duties and contractual provisions, exists. In that situation there might have been some doubt as to whether the (purported) contract which is the subject of the proceedings was in fact valid and enforceable (or indeed the very opposite – whether it was a legal nullity). The court's role may therefore be critical in determining the existence of what MacCormick would argue is a cluster of institutions of law that go to make up the contractual relationship obtaining between the contracting parties. In other words, the judgment of the court (assuming a judgment of validity as opposed to nullity) will serve to determine authoritatively that the whole gamut of legal states including claim-rights, duties, powers, liabilities, discretions, immunities, and so on, exists. Of course, it will always be arguable that evidence of the existence of the (disputed) contract – pre-dating the court's determination – subsisted in some shape or form, and that that determination added nothing to the pre-existing state of affairs. However, that would misleadingly represent the role of the court in rendering a decision that is more than merely declaratory of a given state of affairs. The court's decision may also be regarded as being *foundational* in that it serves to reinforce or re-establish what was (arguably) already there. The court's decision does this formally and authoritatively, and may indeed innovate upon what was (disputably) in place prior to the raising of the proceedings.

It could be said that a process of 'secondary institutionalisation' is at work where (predominantly) courts of law as legal institutions – in MacCormick's sociological sense – are recognised for theoretical purposes as making authoritative determinations as to the existence, content, scope, incidence or effect of relevant institutions of law; with the result that these institutions are seen to have a role in 'institutionalising' or 're-institutionalising' relevant institutional facts (such as institutions of law – eg a right or a duty). The status of these determinations (being in some sense authoritative) is, of course, different from the status of a determination made by a 'random' private individual.[72] But, undeniably, the court's role has

[72] Raz views the tension between the position of the courts and that of the private individual in terms of the authority invested in the courts to make binding determinations. 'Courts and tribunals have power to determine the rights and duties of individuals. But cannot any person do the same? … The difference between a court and a private individual is not merely that courts are provided with better facilities to determine the facts of the case and the law applying to them. Courts have power to make an *authoritative* determination of people's legal situation. Private individuals may express their opinion on the subject but their views are not binding.' See J Raz, *The Authority of Law: Essays on Law and Morality* (Clarendon Press 1979) 108.

ontological significance. In particular, in a case coming before a court, a given (disputed) right, say, may have no practically reliable existence until the court makes its determination. The most complete assessment of the factual conditions of existence of laws and legal 'objects' such as rights (essentially institutions of law as characterised by MacCormick) may reside in an ontological enquiry that includes some consideration of the nature of relevant institutional roles and functions, seen as a *sociological* fact. Sociological analysis, in other words, may have something significant to contribute to an ontological enquiry centring on the conditions of existence of laws and legal concepts. MacCormick's outlook on the philosophical institutionality of law may thus to an extent be analytically dependent on his outlook on the sociological institutionality of law. It is questionable, ultimately, whether MacCormick makes sufficient allowance for this in his characterisation of the philosophical *and the sociological* sense of law's institutionality in 'Law as Institutional Fact'.

We return to this line of analysis – adopting the hypothetical perspective of a theoretically conceived supreme court judge, *Iudex* – in Chapter 3.

2.3.3. MacCormick's General (Institutional) Theory of Law and Interest Theory of Rights

It is appropriate to take stock of the extent to which MacCormick (arguably) integrated his distinctive interest theory of rights with his general institutional theory of law.

MacCormick first attempts what one might describe as a synthesis of his general institutional theory and his interest theory of rights in his chapter in the Hart *Festschrift*, *Law, Morality, and Society: Essays in Honour of HLA Hart*, published around three years after the appearance of 'Law as Institutional Fact' in the *Law Quarterly Review*.[73] In the *Festschrift* chapter MacCormick advances a classic position on interest theory, viewing the concept of a (legal) right as an advantage or benefit conferred by rules designed to protect or promote 'one person's interests as against some other person or the world at large, by the imposition on the latter of duties, disabilities, or liabilities in respect of the party favoured'.[74] We have seen that towards the end of 'Rights in Legislation' the idea of a legal right, thus outlined, is associated with familiar elements of institutional theory as these had been presented in 'Law as Institutional Fact'.[75] Institutional facts and institutions of law, therefore, are to be seen as occupying a position in time and space in that they are created on the occurrence of institutive facts (governed by institutive laws or provisions – such as contractual

[73] See DN MacCormick, 'Rights in Legislation' (this chapter, n 2).
[74] ibid 192. See also 202.
[75] ibid 206–207.

provisions); they subsist for a time during which legally determined incidents and consequences of their existence play out (governed by consequential laws or provisions); and they cease to exist on the occurrence of terminative facts (governed by terminative laws or provisions). There is a compelling parallel to be made with biological life forms which are born or are generated, live for however long (more or less actively); and, after the passage of time, perish or die.

So it is that in the span of two seminal writings, spaced approximately three years apart, MacCormick had integrated aspects of his interest theory of rights with key aspects of his institutional theory. And as if to underline that position, in his late writings, his characterisations of institutional theory and interest theory essentially become part of one overarching narrative. In *Institutions of Law*, MacCormick maintains that 'rights are legal positions of a normally advantageous kind, hedged around with remedial rights and powers to obtain enforcement of them'.[76] Elsewhere he reiterates themes from his earlier writings on institutional theory consistently developed over four decades, by (among other things) reinforcing his core ontological position on the existence and continuity through time of rights seen as institutions of law whose presence turns on institutive, consequential and terminative laws or provisions, and relevant acts or events interpreted by reference to the same laws or provisions.[77]

Be that as it may, MacCormick develops his thinking at least one significant step further in *Institutions of Law*. The step is perhaps the culmination of institutional theory's preoccupation with the facticity of law and of institutions of law. In the context of an analysis of legal obligations viewed as institutions of law, MacCormick maintains that these are 'capable of being *reified*, that is, considered as a species of incorporeal thing'.[78] There is a question whether, by extension or inclusion, legal rights (as institutions of law) might be regarded as having a more obvious claim to being viewed in reifying terms than obligations. On the other hand, if law is institutional *fact*; then perhaps all the artefacts of law – law's 'commodities': rights, powers, obligations, immunities, liberties (even legal rules), and all the others – are to be viewed in the same way: namely, as intangible and incorporeal 'things'.[79] We may not touch or see them in any physical sense, but they are maintained in existence no less palpably than shoes and ships and sealing wax. As soon as a legal right is, in terms of MacCormick's version of interest theory, to be viewed as something – some *thing*: an 'institutional artefact' – that is normally advantageous and which promotes one person's interests as against some other person or the world at large, it is transformed into a kind of possession or

[76] *Institutions of Law* (this chapter, n 3) 123.

[77] ibid 36, 139, 146.

[78] ibid 118 (emphasis added).

[79] Richard Wasserstrom, commenting on the status of *human rights*, maintains that such rights are 'commodities' of a special kind: 'If there are any such things as human rights, they have certain important characteristics and functions just because rights themselves are valuable and distinctive moral "commodities"'. See R Wasserstrom, 'Rights, Human Rights and Racial Discrimination' (1964) 61 *The Journal of Philosophy* 628, 629.

commodity that, for its bearer, for the most part has intrinsic value and practical utility.[80]

2.4. Concluding Reflections

The central question posed at the outset of this chapter is whether two leading philosophers of law, HLA Hart and Neil MacCormick, in seeking to explain the fundamental concept of the legal right in terms of (in the case of Hart) the will theory of rights, and (in the case of MacCormick) the interest theory of rights, applied the same modes of explanation and explanatory frames of reference to that narrower concept as they applied in their more general approaches to explaining the concept of law. The key assumption here was that, in terms of theoretical and philosophical enquiry, what holds for the general (ie law in the wider sense) should hold for the particular (ie the core concept of the legal right). It was noted that any disjunction or incompatibility that might be found to exist between, respectively, Hart's and MacCormick's particular and general theoretical positions might have implications not only for the coherence of the approach adopted

[80] This line of argument also complements the position that MacCormick adopts in 'Rights in Legislation' (this chapter, n 2) (at 206) when insisting on the indispensability of the use of 'rights' terminology as a means of achieving complex legal protections by means of short and simple words. In a given case, the expression 'right', used in a legal context, will have the potential to convey a myriad of Hohfeldian atomic relationships (including, for instance, sets of correlative duties) which no reductive act – ie reducing the right without residue to all of its constituent components – could hope to reproduce with the same economy of expression. The right – the expression 'right' – becomes a facilitating device for all the legal incidents that can be inferred from its possession. To use a simplistic mathematical analogy, it will always be more convenient to speak of 'x' in shorthand when $x = a + b + c + d + e$ than to enumerate at length everything comprised in x on each occasion that the subject of x arises for discussion or (where x is a right) in formal juristic contexts such as in a statute. So, a legal right, with all of its attendant legal 'baggage', becomes a 'vessel' – a 'thing' – which in some sense exceeds the sum of its component parts. (It is not clear from MacCormick's analysis, however, why this 'shorthand function' of 'rights' terminology should be regarded as a peculiar characteristic of the interest theory of rights, rather than of *both* interest theory and will theory; though the overriding point of MacCormick's line of analysis is narrowly to meet Hart's 'charge of redundancy' levelled at interest theory. See section 3.2.1 (Chapter 3, below).) Interestingly, Richard Tuck attributes to Hart (as a will theorist) a position that in the final analysis is not dissimilar to that of MacCormick (as an interest theorist) when he comments: 'If any right can be completely expressed as a more or less complex set of duties on other people towards the possessor of the right, and those duties can in turn be explained in terms of some higher-order moral principle, then the point of a separate language of rights seems to have been lost, and with it the explanatory or justificatory force possessed by references to rights'. Tuck takes the view that Hart may have been troubled by this possibility and that it led him to give recognition to the attribution of rights to people that would give them 'some kind of 'sovereignty' over their moral world'. (Tuck views 'sovereignty' as close to the idea of 'dominium'.) Tuck cites HLA Hart, 'Are There Any Natural Rights?' (1955) 64 *Philosophical Review* 175, especially 184. See R Tuck, *Natural Rights Theories: Their Origin and Development* (Cambridge University Press 1979) at 6 and n 4. Tuck, in the same chapter (ch I), goes on to discuss scholarship centring on the compelling notion that Roman law had no concept of a 'subjective right' (ibid 7–13). See further, in particular, the discussion of the Hartian idea of right-holders as 'small-scale sovereigns' in section 1.4 (Chapter 1, above) and section 5.3.4 (Chapter 5, below).

by each theorist in framing his general theoretical outlook, but for the integrity of each theorist's analysis of the particular concept of the legal right in terms of the distinctive version of the theory of rights promoted by him. The point of the enquiry, ultimately, would be to reach a preliminary view on whether an improved understanding of the nature of law and legal rights was better promoted by one or other theoretical approach.

In his analysis of legal rights in chapter VII of *Essays on Bentham*, Hart appears to (at least temporarily) abandon his general approach to elucidating problematic or 'perplexing' legal concepts such as those itemised in 'Definition and Theory'. In the case of a legal right, for instance, this would entail placing the expression 'a right' in a statement with some claim to typicality, and examining the truth conditions of the resulting statement. Instead of pursuing that approach, however, as we have seen, Hart directly outlines and discusses a set of existence conditions of legal rights, essentially omitting the intervening step involving the use of a typical statement. What that implies for the particular line of enquiry pursued here is that Hart's analysis of key characteristics of rights in his will theory of rights does not appear to be well integrated with his more general epistemological outlook, even if the latter makes claims about its explicit focus on legal concepts such as 'right' (and other fundamental concepts such as, for example, 'duty' and 'corporation'). On the face of it, therefore, there is a failure to follow through with the general approach outlined in key writings when examining the concept of the legal right in the context of his outlook on will theory: specifically, the class of 'rights correlative to obligations'. It may be that this merely serves to highlight the limitations, and the redundancy in certain contexts, of Hart's general approach. Hart's analysis of 'rights correlative to obligations' in his version of the will theory of rights is arguably unimpaired – in other words, it has no less explanatory power – in consequence of the apparent caesura that is claimed (in this chapter) to exist between Hart's particular and general theoretical positions. But the question of overall explanatory power probably comes back to haunt Hart when we reflect upon what is (found to be) a more integrated theoretical approach adopted by MacCormick.

For his part, in contrast, MacCormick advances a more holistic conception of a legal right. In his later writings in particular, his version of the interest theory of rights is closely integrated with his institutional theory of law. The result is that the two theoretical positions are mutually reinforcing. For MacCormick, a legal right is an institution of law and, by reason of that, an institutional fact, or cluster of institutional facts. At the same time, a right, along with other institutions of law, such as legal obligations, may be seen as capable of reification. They are to be viewed as incorporeal *things*, designed to promote interests. For MacCormick, it originates in the world of institutional fact in two ways. First, aspects of factual reality come to be 'confronted' with and, from a practical standpoint, they are interpreted by reference to, applicable legal rules – legal rules themselves (such as where these are in the form of statutes) being institutions of law. And secondly, from a sociological perspective, institutions – in the sense of structures of organised behaviour, such as courts – are tasked with administering and enforcing the law and, crucially, interpreting, applying it, and also developing it, such as in a common law setting.[81] MacCormick's conception of a legal right, viewed through the prism of interest theory, is inseparable from his general position where law and fundamental legal concepts are to be viewed as institutional artefacts: institutional 'things'. MacCormick therefore delivers a perspective on law and legal concepts that perhaps has greater coherence and internal consistency than Hart's. But that is not to deny or diminish the power of Hart's theoretical positions, or indeed the fact that Hart throws light on aspects of legal rights that MacCormick does not – though clearly that works both ways. Both theories illuminate legal rights in different ways while neither theory offers the complete picture. And indeed, both theories leave room for the work of other theorists – Raz being an obvious candidate, as is seen in Chapter 3.

[81] Sociological institutionality, as we have seen, is significantly less developed in MacCormick's writings.

3

The Legal Right Constructed in the Judicial Consciousness*

3.1. Introduction

In this chapter it is argued that one of the difficulties with the approaches adopted by versions of will theory and interest theory is that each theory offers only a selective, and in key respects incomplete or problematic, account not only of claimed existence conditions of a legal right but of what a legal right actually is.[1] That is not to say that the theories do not shed light on very significant aspects of legal rights. Moreover, the two main theories of rights are neither inherently, nor are they irreconcilably, 'opposed'. This position is maintained in Chapter 1, where areas of complementarity – such as the protective and empowering functions of rights corresponding to core tenets of interest theory and will theory respectively – are identified. In a given case we may opt for one theory in preference to the other on the basis that each theory offers an arguably better explanation of some facet of a right than the other: in short, *this* theory explains *these* things well, and *that* theory explains *those* things well.[2] The focus may then fall upon what the two theories of rights leave unaddressed or what the theories fail to explain adequately or, for that matter, misdescribe. This chapter explores those questions, but with a focus, ultimately, upon consideration of the extent to which the legal right – or its *content* (extending to related matters such as scope and effect) – might be viewed

* Timothy Endicott kindly commented on an earlier draft of this chapter.

[1] According to Nigel Simmonds, classical interest and will theories of rights were first and foremost theories of the grounds of legitimacy of rights rather than 'austerely analytical clarifications of a concept'. See NE Simmonds, 'Rights at the Cutting Edge' in MH Kramer, NE Simmonds and H Steiner, *A Debate Over Rights* (Oxford University Press 1998) 113. It is towards that more 'austere' task that this chapter inclines: that is, more towards discovery of the form than the content (and legitimacy) of legal rights. But that is not to question Simmonds's fundamental point – if not to distort the point that he makes more elegantly – that complex separations and dependencies exist between form and content that blur the boundaries between conceptual analyses and substantive moral and political theories. Inevitably, a failure properly to identify those separations and dependencies may result in analytical and theoretical distortion or aridity. That is indeed a challenge for the task – primarily of conceptual analysis – that is tackled in this chapter and elsewhere in this book.

[2] The main theories can also, in some way, be 'defined' by what they 'do badly', thereby impelling a flight from one theory to the other. Thus, Matthew Kramer sets out 'to bolster the Interest Theory by impugning the chief alternatives to it'. See MH Kramer, 'Some Doubts about Alternatives to the Interest Theory of Rights' (2013) 123 *Ethics* 245, 259.

as a construct of the judicial consciousness, marking (to the relevant extent) a departure from the tendency of the leading theories of rights to adopt a perspective that places the *right-holder* – or both right-holder and duty-bearer – at the centre of the explanatory process.[3]

3.2. Theories of Rights – Three Constraining Factors

It is proposed to argue that the two seminal theories of rights – represented in the writings of legal philosophers such as HLA Hart, Joseph Raz and Neil MacCormick – are attended by theoretical constraints when (specifically) *legal* rights are set within their relevant frames of reference.[4] The emergent theoretical positions, it will be argued, are narrowly conceived and are, in the result, incomplete in certain important respects. The point of departure is to assert the existence of 'constraining factors' attending the scope of the two main theories of rights. These are limitations that contribute to the theories being lacunate in certain respects and point to an inability of the theories to provide not only an ontologically adequate account

[3] The idea of 'consciousness' has a role to play in the discussion to follow (given the chapter title). No necessarily fixed idea of consciousness is intended by the use of this expression here; nor is the idea to be seen to be rooted in any particular philosophical or scientific tradition, though John Locke refers to 'consciousness' in the most general terms as 'the perception of what passes in a man's own mind'. (See J Locke, *An Essay Concerning Human Understanding* (26th edn, printed for T Tegg, R Griffin & Co and J Cumming 1828) 59.) A reference in this and later chapters to the 'consciousness' of a right-holder, or to 'judicial consciousness' or 'institutional imagination', minimally implies the presence of some mental content, attitude or mental disposition. In the context of legal rights, the idea of some level of awareness or understanding of such rights is intended – for instance, recognition of their existence, content, scope, effect, and so on. Rights consciousness (in reference to legal rights) may vary in intensity from the most general and abstract awareness of particular rights to the most specific and informed awareness. In a given case, however, there may be an *absence* of such awareness. (See the discussion of rights of children in Chapter 6.) Awareness of rights may be coloured by more general attitudes and beliefs (including *systems* of belief), religious precepts, ethical principles, moral sentiments, political leanings, professional practices, and so on – all coming within the scope of the general idea of 'consciousness'. The idea of 'judicial consciousness' or 'institutional imagination', viewed through the prism of (for example) professional methodologies and practices, will ordinarily be something quite different in content from the consciousness of a private individual such as a given right-holder. In the specifically legal context, for instance – as we have seen in section 2.3.1 (Chapter 2, above) – Hans Kelsen (in the Paulson translation) refers to judicial acts 'of intellect' where relevant acts or events are 'confronted' with relevant laws, with the aim of conferring 'legal meaning' (*rechtliche Bedeutung*) upon those acts or events. (See H Kelsen, *Pure Theory of Law* (published as Hans Kelsen, *Introduction to the Problems of Legal Theory* [*Reine Rechtslehre. Einleitung in die rechtswissenschaftliche Problematik*]) (BL Paulson and SL Paulson (trs and eds), Clarendon Press 1992) 8–10.) In the analysis to follow, significant perspectival differences are explored in parallel with the development of an outline of the idea of 'consciousness' or 'institutional imagination' generally, and 'judicial consciousness' in particular. This largely corresponds to the perspective of the hypothetical ultimate judge, *Iudex*. (See especially, Chapters 7 and 8 below.)

[4] One reason for the focus in this chapter on relatively modern, yet nonetheless 'historical', literature is that the writers in question effectively set terms of reference for discussion and debate that continued to resonate for decades. (This is touched upon in Chapter 1.) That may be a measure of the quality of the writing. But for every matter that may have been challenged and laid to rest there are, and were, other issues of which the writings in question stimulated discussion, yet which were never fully or satisfactorily addressed or resolved in the intervening years.

of the conditions of existence of legal rights, but fully convincing explanations of the related matter of the nature and key characteristics of legal rights.

The three constraining factors – considered in more detail below – are as follows:

I. that the primary emphasis of will theory (or at least its Hartian variant) is on what rights 'do': in other words, the idea that (according to Hart) rights give a right-holder control over the behaviour of a duty-bearer – empowering the right-holder; this being facilitated by the conferment of relevant choices upon the right-holder;
II. that the primary emphasis of interest theory (exemplified in writings of MacCormick and Raz) is on what rights are 'for': in other words, the idea that rights exist, or are created, to protect interests;[5]
III. that both theories, in their core or definitional formulations, fail to give adequate attention to outlining an appropriate institutional perspective when theorising about legal rights; exemplified in the idea that interest theory and will theory primarily adopt the perspective of the right-holder when analysing and explaining legal rights, thereby (sometimes problematically) placing the right-holder's consciousness at the centre of the explanatory process. (This has already been touched upon in section 2.3.2 (Chapter 2, above); and is more fully developed in this, and later, chapters.)

Under constraining factors I and II, explanations of legal rights (eg their nature, key characteristics, existence conditions and so on) are regarded as constrained

[5] Superficially *both* theories can be framed in terms of (A) what rights 'do' (they: (i) give control and (ii) protect interests) and (B) what rights 'are for' (they exist in order to: (i) give control and (ii) protect interests). However, the primary emphasis of will theory (in its Hartian variant as discussed in this chapter, below) may best be seen as the discovery of an *active* or facilitative dimension to rights, where a given right-holder is recognised as having an ability or choice to require performance of a course of behaviour from a given duty-bearer. (Here the focus is more upon what rights 'do' than what they are 'for'.) The primary emphasis of interest theory, on the other hand, may best be seen as something *passive*, serving as it does as an *explanation of why* the right exists in the first place – ie to protect interests. (Here the focus is more upon what rights 'are for' than what they 'do'. As Simmonds points out, '[f]or all varieties of the Interest Theory, the right-holder is essentially a bearer of interests rather than a locus of choice or will. Classical versions of the Interest Theory find it necessary to identify legal rights by means of an inquiry into the *purpose* of the relevant duty-imposing rules.' See NE Simmonds, 'Rights at the Cutting Edge' in MH Kramer, NE Simmonds and H Steiner, *A Debate Over Rights* (Oxford University Press 1998) 224–225.) Essentially this approach – identifying will theory with what rights 'do'; and interest theory with what rights 'are for' – underlies the position developed in the analysis to follow. It is worth noting at this point in the discussion that there is no necessary incompatibility between a theory that examines what rights 'do' and one that examines what right 'are for'. Indeed, in at least one key respect, previously discussed, the theories are complementary. (See section 1.3 (Chapter 1, above).) They just 'do different things'. And as we have also seen in Chapter 1, Matthew Kramer highlights the safeguarding of some aspect of the well-being of a right-holder – captured in the idea of *security* – as the essence of a legal right, seen from the point of view of interest theory. So, in a sense this is slightly more about what a right is 'for' than about what it 'does'. At the same time (for Kramer), the essence of a legal right viewed in terms of will theory consists in its provision of opportunities for its holder to make significant choices. This is captured in the idea of *control*. Again, this is perhaps significantly more about what a legal right 'does' for someone possessed of it than about what it is 'for'. See MH Kramer, 'Some Doubts about Alternatives to the Interest Theory of Rights' (2013) 123 *Ethics* 245, 248.

to the extent that they rest upon contrasting notions of functionality.[6] In the case of Hartian will theory, for instance, by placing the emphasis on what legal rights 'do' (and 'do' for right-holders in particular), there is arguably insufficient emphasis on what legal rights *are*. Of course, some degree of focus on functionality must be conceded to any properly ontological enquiry centring upon the nature of rights. The difficulty, as will be suggested, is in the scope of that enquiry. Knowing what something 'does' or what it is 'for' might tell us something about what it is. But ultimately this may explain too little, or may set a false agenda for the relevant enquiry.

Constraining factor III focuses on how legal rights might be viewed from an empirically significant perspective which is not that of the right-holder. Conventionally, versions of will theory and interest theory are framed in terms of perspectives that emphasise the central position of the right-holder: focusing respectively on right-holder's will, right-holder's interests. Arguably there is too little emphasis on the detached perspective of those who occupy empirically significant institutional roles such as a judge making a determination about the existence and content of a right in the setting of a court of law.[7] This constraining factor highlights a perspectival issue which, it will be maintained, is critical in the context of examining the institutional nature of the legal right. The point of the enquiry is to consider the extent to which important elements of the legal right can be viewed as capable of being constructed within the judicial consciousness. Here the focus is on how explanations of legal rights, and explanatory frames of reference, have shortcomings when constructed exclusively or primarily around the consciousness and understandings of the holder of a legal right. Adopting the standpoint of the right-holder can advance the explanation of legal rights only so far, it is suggested. Legal rights are intensively bound up with institutional practices and processes which arguably must be given a more prominent place in theories of legal rights than such theories conventionally allow.

3.2.1. Constraining Factor I – Will Theory: HLA Hart

Turning to what is arguably his core formulation of will theory in *Essays on Bentham*, Hart identifies characteristics of rights that are to be viewed as in some sense definitive or defining: their presence being *necessary and sufficient* conditions of the existence of a right within a specific, albeit extensive, category of rights,

[6] That the will and interest theories of rights might be regarded as theories of rights *functionality* is recognised by (for example) Wenar. See L Wenar, 'Rights', *The Stanford Encyclopedia of Philosophy* (Fall edn, 2015) para [2.2] https://plato.stanford.edu/entries/rights/#2.2 (accessed 28 July 2025). See also, for (among other things) generalised discussion of functions of rights, L Wenar, 'The Nature of Rights' (2005) 33 *Philosophy and Public Affairs* 223.

[7] In this context, empirical significance turns on the fact that enforcement mechanisms – extending to the possible use of force (and including incarceration, fines and other punishments) – tend to be activated or mobilised in response to the decision of a court of law or certain tribunals.

namely, 'rights correlative to obligations'.[8] Hart maintains that what is necessary and sufficient for this type of right to exist is that the right-holder should have some measure of control over a correlative obligation the performance of which falls upon a corresponding obligation-bearer.[9] Control in this context, and being possessed of control, are actually *constitutive* of the right. The state of being invested with such control, and thus being invested with a right, give the right-holder power and the *choice*, by way of an exertion of will, to enforce the right, waive it, or leave it unenforced.[10] In other words, the presence of control in this special sense, for Hart, calls a right 'into existence'. This follows from Hart's claim that 'control' (in the relevant sense) is not only a necessary, but a *sufficient*, condition of the existence of a right.[11] (Something that is (merely) necessary needs to be there; but something that is necessary *and sufficient* is *all* that needs to be there.) Thus, Hart's defining theoretical position on rights has an ontological basis.

In response to Hart's position, Neil MacCormick argues that the control, and related choice, elements of a right – the ability to enforce it, waive it, or leave it unenforced – are simply incidents of a right – something that happens to go hand-in-hand with its possession. It is neither to be identified with a right nor is it an essential or defining characteristic.[12] It should be noted that Hart (on the face of

[8] See HLA Hart, *Essays on Bentham: Jurisprudence and Political Theory* (Clarendon Press 1982) (hereafter, in this chapter, '*Essays on Bentham*') ch VII, especially 174–188. A key focus of Hart's analysis of legal rights in that chapter is upon 'rights correlative to obligations'. In both his exposition and his critique of Bentham's position, Hart maintains that such rights are to be found in both the criminal law and the civil law even if 'rights correlative to obligations as these appear in the civil law' are to be regarded as the 'paradigm' (see Hart's observation at 186), where, according to Hart, rights are *directly enforceable by a right-holder* in contrast to the position under the criminal law where the enforcement of 'rights', such as they are, is largely in the hands of prosecuting officials. In that situation, a person protected only by the criminal law has 'no unique power to determine whether the duties of the criminal law should be enforced or not'. (See 184.)

[9] ibid 183–184, 185, 188. At 188 Hart maintains that '[t]he case of a right correlative to obligation then emerges as only a special case of legal power in which the right-holder is at liberty to waive or extinguish or to enforce or leave unenforced another's obligation'.

[10] ibid 184.

[11] ibid 188: '[W]hat is sufficient and necessary [for a right to exist] is that [the right-holder] … should have at least some measure of the control, described above, over the correlative obligation'. Elsewhere, Hart refers to such control as 'a *defining feature* of legal rights correlative to obligations' (at 186, emphasis added). At 183–184, Hart comments: 'The fullest measure of control comprises three distinguishable elements: (i) the right holder may waive or extinguish the duty or leave it in existence; (ii) after breach or threatened breach of a duty he may leave it "unenforced" or may "enforce" it by suing for compensation or, in certain cases, for an injunction or mandatory order to restrain the continued or further breach of duty; and (iii) he may waive or extinguish the obligation to pay compensation to which the breach gives rise'.

[12] See generally DN MacCormick, 'Children's Rights: A Test Case for Theories of Right' (1976) 62 *Archiv für Rechts- und Sozialphilosophie* 305. This article is also reprinted with modifications as chapter 8 of DN MacCormick, *Legal Right and Social Democracy: Essays in Legal and Political Philosophy* (Clarendon Press 1982) (hereafter, in this chapter, 'Children's Rights: A Test Case'). (In this chapter, references are to the article reprinted as a book chapter in 1982.) Although MacCormick does not put it this way, Hart appears to commit a logical fallacy. From the proposition: *if a right exists, the individual in possession of the right has control (or power) and certain choices*, Hart appears to derive its converse: *if an individual has control (or power) and certain choices, then a right [necessarily] exists*. The latter is untenable. Control, power and choices can come from having a right, just as well as they can

it, narrowly) delineates for discussion a category of rights – namely, *rights correlative to obligations* – that has, as an integral feature, the presence of a correlative obligation which is the reflex of the right. So, it would seem that the control that the right-holder asserts over the correlative obligation, with its attendant choices, cannot be anything other than a defining characteristic. In other words, a 'right correlative to an obligation' cannot be explained without reference to the obligation that correlates with it. And by extension, the position of the right-holder is unintelligible unless reference is made not only to the obligation of which the right-holder may demand performance, but to the presence of an obligation-bearer from whom performance may be demanded.[13]

At first sight it may seem that Hart selects what appears to be a narrow category of rights when outlining a version of will theory that happens to have become, for some (certainly, for MacCormick), a classic exposition of the fundamentals of the will theory of *rights in general*. However, the class of rights correlative to obligations identified by Hart probably best corresponds to the category that WN Hohfeld (and Hohfeldians) refer to as claim-rights or rights *stricto sensu* (having duties as their correlative) and is arguably the most extensive and wide-ranging single category of legal rights in the universe of (legal) rights.[14] Moreover, a few of the core features of rights that Hart identifies as characteristic of 'rights correlative to obligations' – such as control and attendant choices – could be regarded as features of other types of (legal) rights; for instance, extending beyond legal rights *stricto sensu* into the legal power family of legal rights.

But perhaps where Hart's analysis, and MacCormick's interpretation of Hart's analysis, are at least in one important respect aligned is in relation to the idea that Hart adds something essentially new, through his elaboration of the idea of *control*. Control invests the right-holder with an ability – through an exertion of will and associated choices – to enforce a correlative obligation, or to waive it, or to leave it unenforced. For Hart, this characteristic of the particular type of right under scrutiny – which is one of Hart's necessary and sufficient conditions of existence

come from sitting in a cabin operating a crane – which of course does not imply the necessary presence of a right. MacCormick appears to concede the tenable (Hartian) position that having a right invests one with control (or power) and certain choices that are incidental to possession of the right when he describes powers of waiver or enforcement as 'essentially ancillary to, not constitutive of, rights'. See DN MacCormick, 'Children's Rights: A Test Case' at 164.

[13] The point is that Hart could not have failed to capture the essential and defining characteristics of the category of right selected for discussion when the definiendum ('right correlative to obligation') has more or less the same content as the definiens (a right that gives a measure of control over a correlative obligation). That said, as discussed in this chapter, below, it is the element of *control* that, according to Hart, gives Hartian will theory something of an explanatory edge over versions of interest theory.

[14] See generally WN Hohfeld, *Fundamental Legal Conceptions as Applied in Judicial Reasoning* (WW Cook (ed), Yale University Press 1919). The enduring centrality of Hohfeld's analysis in contemporary literature focusing on theories of rights can be seen, for example, in MH Kramer, 'Rights Without Trimmings' in MH Kramer, NE Simmonds and H Steiner, *A Debate Over Rights* (Oxford University Press 1998) 7–111. Earlier influential secondary writings on Hohfeld's analysis have included M Radin, 'A Restatement of Hohfeld' (1938) 51 *Harvard Law Review* 1141y.

of such a right – makes his version of will theory among other things immune to the 'charge of redundancy' which (Hart argues) had beset interest theory, where rights (of one) could be considered exhaustively reducible to duties (of another), with the result that:

> all that can be said in a terminology of such rights can be and indeed is best said in the indispensable terminology of duty. So the … [interest] theory appears to make nothing more of rights than an alternative formulation of duties …[15]

Hart's idea of control with its attendant choices – marking a decisive break with the idea of a right-holder as merely the passive beneficiary of a correlative obligation performable by another – makes it difficult for critics of Hartian will theory to dismiss the theory as offering, at best, *nothing beyond*, and at worst *less than*, interest theory. On the other hand, MacCormick's critique is striking for a number of reasons. For example, he points out that the lack of an ability to waive certain rights – viewed as one of the Hartian necessary and sufficient existence conditions of a right being, as it is, an integral part of the control (and associated choices) with which a right-holder is said to be invested – could lead to the absurdity that the more unwaivable, and correspondingly entrenched, a right happens to be the less can it be regarded as a right.[16]

Furthermore, and more importantly, MacCormick argues that the inability of Hartian will theory to accommodate or properly account for children's rights impels abandonment of the theory.[17] Thus, a child who does not have the cognitive or volitional capacity to take action (for example) to enforce a correlative obligation, or to waive it, cannot (according to MacCormick's reading of Hartian will theory) be the possessor of a right. One might say that the relative absence of cognitive or volitional capacity on the part of a child (for example, an infant) – a capacity that varies in degree according to where a child happens to be on the journey from infancy to adulthood – renders the whole notion of children's rights in Hart's version of will theory problematic, if not (for some) untenable.[18] (This is discussed more fully in Chapter 6.)

[15] HLA Hart, *Essays on Bentham* (this chapter, n 8) 181–182.

[16] MacCormick gives as examples of unwaivable rights the right not to be subjected to a serious assault nor to a surgical operation carried out by an unqualified person. See DN MacCormick, 'Rights in Legislation' in PMS Hacker and J Raz (eds), *Law, Morality, and Society: Essays in Honour of HLA Hart* (Clarendon Press 1977) (hereafter, in this chapter, 'Rights in Legislation') 197. See, further, the more extensive discussion in Chapter 6, below.

[17] DN MacCormick, 'Children's Rights: A Test Case' (this chapter, n 12) 158. That message is reinforced in DN MacCormick, 'Rights in Legislation' (this chapter, n 16) 198.

[18] This is one of the more 'notorious' corollaries of Hart's theoretical focus on the will of the right-holder and has led Tom Campbell to comment: '[I]f rights are defined (as they are on the "will theory" of rights) as normative powers to determine the obligations of others by the exercise of the will of the right holder, and if it is assumed, as it must be, that children do not have the relevant volitional capacities to claim rights, then children cannot properly be said to have any rights whatsoever. In this case, the distinctive thing about children's rights is that there are none'. See TD Campbell, 'The Rights of the Minor: as Person, as Child, as Juvenile, as Future Adult' (1992) 6 *International Journal of Law and the Family* 1, 2.

If we take a step back from those details of Hart's analysis that MacCormick singles out for critical attention, there are questions concerning the Hartian version of will theory that relate more fundamentally to the analysis pursued here. For instance, the aspect of will theory that leaves Hart vulnerable to the charge that he imposes theoretical constraints when framing his version of the theory is the idea that the most obvious of the most fundamental questions that Hartian theory can ask appears not to be 'what *are* [legal] rights?' but 'what do [legal] rights '*do*'? And the answer which the theory offers, in its core formulation, is this: what they 'do' is give a right-holder a measure of control over a correlative obligation the performance of which falls upon someone other than the right-holder; and this control gives the right-holder power and the choice, by way of an exertion of will, to enforce a right, waive it, or leave it unenforced. Looked at this way, Hartian will theory is reduced to a theory of rights functionality which does not venture far into the more problematic territory of what a legal right is.[19] Hartian will theory, in its core, definitional, formulation, thus instructs us that rights operate to give right-holders a range of competencies of not insignificant practical utility.

But there is without doubt more to Hart's position than suggested. The focus of Hartian will theory is certainly upon what rights 'do', how they work, and what they give to right-holders. So, any critic of the theory can be forgiven for highlighting this as a limitation in that it urges our understanding more in the direction of functional insight (*how does a right function – what does it 'do'?*) than towards discernment of the nature of a right (what actually *is* a right?) A theory or conception of a legal right that maintains, as Hartian will theory does, that the right *is to be identified with* an ability to control a correlative obligation of another goes some way towards identifying a right as some kind of power (a power of control); and that in turn suggests that the idea of a legal right, in an elaboration of Hartian will theory, can be accommodated within a variety of frames of reference that are not exclusively juridical – for example, paradigms of philosophy or social theory (such as those of Max Weber, say) – where rights can be viewed as a type of power (social power).[20] To that extent Hart's analysis without question contributes to our understanding of the *nature* of legal rights. Indeed, on this view, legal rights *are* powers, and this insight serves to reinforce the impression that the core of Hartian theory points to the possibility of a more encompassing ontological awareness of legal rights.[21] This position is further developed at various points in the analysis to follow.

[19] See texts cited in this chapter at n 6.

[20] This is examined in more detail in section 1.4 (Chapter 1, above) and in Chapter 5, below. It appears that, to the extent that Hart views certain rights as powers, these are to be seen in the stricter sense of *legal* powers. We have seen that Hart regards the concept of a right correlative to obligation as a special case of legal power where the right-holder may waive, extinguish, enforce or leave unenforced the obligation of another. (See HLA Hart, *Essays on Bentham* (this chapter, n 8) 188.)

[21] In other words, the Hartian position could be said to edge beyond an examination of the conditions of existence of rights towards an enquiry focusing on the essential nature of rights: what legal rights *are*.

3.2.2. Constraining Factor II – Interest Theory: MacCormick and Raz

In his critique of Hartian will theory, Neil MacCormick highlights a 'clash of theories' entailed in the contrast (as he puts it) between will theory and interest theory.[22] This implies what is probably well-recognised: namely, that there is a choice for legal theorists between one or other of the two theories, with the curious result that theorists not attracted or convinced by one theory tend to be 'thrown upon' the rival theory. For those seeking an enquiry offering an ontological insight into legal rights – including a more encompassing insight into the nature of legal rights generally, such as their key characteristics or conditions of existence – the choice has without doubt tended to be limited to the two rival theories.

In a modest way mirroring Hartian will theory, with its apparent leaning towards discovery of what rights 'do' – exemplified in the idea of a right investing a right-holder with a power of control over the behaviour of a duty-bearer – the version of interest theory promoted by Neil MacCormick is also quite focused on rights functionality but with a significantly different emphasis to that of Hartian will theory. Essentially, MacCormick addresses the question of what rights are 'for'. Hence, rights exist, or are constituted, or function, *to protect or promote interests*.[23]

Like MacCormick, Joseph Raz asserts a relationship between rights and interests in which he maintains a focus on the protection and promotion of interests as a function of rights. To that extent, there is significant overlap between Raz's and MacCormick's respective versions of interest theory. Raz, however, asserts both a basic position (which aligns with MacCormick's) and a generally more sophisticated position which expands upon, but ultimately represents a step-change beyond, the basic position. Thus, Raz's basic position asserts not only that 'rights are protected interests' but that 'legal rights are legally-protected interests'.[24] He also maintains – again, in relation to legal rights specifically, and affirming a position adopted by Bentham – that the 'law creates rights … by imposing duties with the intention to protect someone's interest thus endowing him with a legal right'.[25]

For MacCormick, rights directly protect or promote interests; whereas for Raz – in his more developed version of interest theory – rights *serve* interests, albeit *indirectly* through the interposing mechanism of duties. In other words, performance of a duty – which is the reflex of a right – serves interests associated with the right.

[22] See DN MacCormick, 'Rights in Legislation' (this chapter, n 16) 192.

[23] As MacCormick observes: 'The "interest theory" … contends that what is essential to the constitution of a right is the legal (or moral) protection or promotion of one person's interests as against some other person or the world at large, by the imposition on the latter of duties, disabilities, or liabilities in respect of the party favoured'. See DN MacCormick, 'Rights in Legislation' (this chapter, n 16) 192.

[24] J Raz, 'Legal Rights' (1984) 4 *Oxford Journal of Legal Studies* 1 (hereafter, in this chapter, 'Legal Rights') 12.

[25] ibid 14.

We can trace the origin of this and other aspects of Raz's version of interest theory to statements of his core position in his seminal essay on legal rights. The following probably captures the essence of Raz's position:

> To say that a person has a right is to say that an interest of his is sufficient ground for holding another to be subject to a duty, ie a duty to take some action which will serve that interest, or a duty the very existence of which serves such interest. One justifies a statement that a person has a right by pointing to an interest of his and to reasons why it is to be taken seriously. One uses the statement that a right exists to derive (often with the aid of other premises) conclusions about the duties of other people towards the right-holder.[26]

Taking stock of their complementary if contrasting positions, MacCormick and Raz both view rights as functioning to protect interests, while Raz, in his more developed position, views rights as the reflex of duties *the performance of which (duties) functions to serve interests.* In both versions of interest theory, functionality is an obviously significant factor: a right either directly protects interests (MacCormick and Raz); or it indirectly serves interests through the performance of duties (Raz). Like Hartian will theory, both versions of interest theory are predicated on a nexus that is recognisably 'Hohfeldian',[27] where a claim-right or right *stricto sensu* has a duty as its correlative.[28] Yet, for Raz, not

[26] ibid 5.

[27] Examples (beyond the claim-right–duty nexus) include the Hohfeldian (so-called) power–liability nexus; and, yet another, is the immunity–disability nexus. In this chapter the expression 'Hohfeldian nexus' (and also, in places, related expressions such as Raz's expression 'correlativity thesis') are used conveniently to denote the figure of a relationship between right-holder and duty-bearer where right and duty are each to be seen as the reflex of the other: as 'correlatives', in other words; each implying the other. Hohfeld captures this relationship by the use of the expression 'jural relation'. See generally WN Hohfeld, *Fundamental Legal Conceptions as Applied in Judicial Reasoning* (WW Cook (ed), Yale University Press 1919). The use of the expression 'Hohfeldian nexus' (and similar expressions) – for example in reference to writings of Hart, Raz or MacCormick – is thus not intended to suggest any more extensive a commitment to aspects of Hohfeld's analysis than those theorists themselves explicitly professed. It should be noted that Hillel Steiner examines aspects of the 'Hohfeldianism' of Hartian will theory, maintaining that the various controls that a legal right-holder is in a position to exercise over the correlative obligation to which the duty-bearer is subject are, essentially, 'Hohfeldian powers'. See H Steiner, 'Working Rights' in MH Kramer, NE Simmonds and H Steiner, *A Debate Over Rights* (Oxford University Press 1998) 239–247, especially 239–240. See also the related discussion, this chapter, at n 28.

[28] Hart takes the view that in analysing the notion of a legal right Bentham had proved to be 'a more thought-provoking guide than Hohfeld'. See HLA Hart, *Essays on Bentham* (this chapter, n 8) 162. Raz explores the implications – and also the limitations – of the 'correlativity thesis', which doubtless has a resonance of Hohfeld's analysis. See J Raz, 'On the Nature of Rights' (1984) 93 *Mind* 194 (hereafter, in this chapter, 'On the Nature of Rights') 199–200. In different ways, Hart (and Hartian will theory), and both Raz and MacCormick (and their respective versions of interest theory) may possibly be dependent upon – even if they tend to underplay the centrality of – the conceptual apparatus of the Hohfeldian nexus (principally the claim-right–duty nexus), and Hohfeld's analysis generally, when defining their core theoretical positions. It should be noted, however, that Hohfeld's analysis (and the correlativity thesis) are prefigured in the analytical writings of both Bentham and John Austin. Austin defines a legal right thus: 'My definition briefly is this:– A party has a right, when another or others are bound or obliged by the law, to do or to forbear, *towards* or *in regard of* him'. See J Austin, *Lectures on Jurisprudence: The Philosophy of Positive Law* (abridged edn, R Campbell (ed), Henry Holt and

only do rights indirectly serve interests, interests are seen as *justifying* rights: serving to explain why a particular right is in existence at all. In Raz's version of interest theory, interests thus feature in two important ways: they are (indirectly) served by rights and at the same time they justify or explain why (the same) rights exist. This dimension of interests as justifications reinforces Raz's version of interest theory as a theory that emphasises rights functionality. So, whereas for MacCormick the (functional) question of what rights are for, induces as a response: *rights protect or promote interests*; for Raz, the same question induces a more sophisticated response: *rights indirectly – through the mechanism of associated (correlative) duties – serve the interests that justify them*. (In the less developed version of his theory, of course, rights (echoing MacCormick) *protect* interests.)

In his version of interest theory Raz's focus upon what rights are for – what their function is: namely, serving or protecting interests – necessitates his making an analytical connection between rights and interests. Both rights and their conditions of existence, on one hand; and interests, on the other; are seen to stand in an intimate relation to the overarching functional question: *what are rights for?* We have seen that for Raz rights indirectly, via the mechanism of associated (correlative) duties, serve the interests that justify them; which begins to address the question of what rights are for. Raz develops his theoretical stance on rights functionality towards formation of a relatively narrow ontological position on rights that might have paved the way for his variant of interest theory to address the wider question of what rights (*legal rights*, in particular) actually *are*. That wider question is, however, left relatively underdeveloped; and this, arguably, has a constraining effect upon the explanatory power of his theoretical position overall. Even Raz's narrower ontological position, being more developed than the wider question, is constrained in certain ways. Thus, his ontological outlook, discernible in his core account and finding its expression in a tightly framed set of existence conditions of rights that connect rights and interests in a unique way, is beset by difficulties centring upon Raz's characterisation of *interests*.

Against that background it is appropriate to examine Raz's basic ontological position and the difficulties and limitations which appear to beset it. The primary emphasis, in the discussion to follow, is upon *legal* rights.

The existence conditions of rights, deriving from Raz's core account, can be restated such that for Raz, a given right-holder, A, can be said to have a right:

(i) if A has an identifiable interest, capable of being 'taken seriously';
(ii) if there is a duty-bearer, B, who has a duty to A associated with A's interest – this is predicated upon a Hohfeldian nexus (see discussion above, and (v) below);

Co 1875) 193 (Austin's emphasis). Manifestations of the Hohfeldian nexus (and indeed, the correlativity thesis) in Austin's conception of a right, and in his conceptions of varying *types* of rights, are to be found at many places throughout that work.

(iii) if A's interest constitutes a 'sufficient ground' or justification for B to have the relevant duty to A;
(iv) if the performance by B of B's duty, or the very existence of B's duty, serves A's interest.

Over and above his general position, Raz maintains (so far as *legal* rights in particular are concerned):

(v) that '[a]n individual has … a legal right if it is recognized by law, that is if the law holds his interest to be sufficient ground to hold another to be subject to a duty. *This is the core of the account here proposed*.'[29]

On closer scrutiny, Raz's conditions of existence of legal rights are not entirely unproblematic, three of the above conditions being particularly noteworthy for comment. First, for a right to exist, A's interest must be capable of being taken seriously. (See (i) above and passage cited this chapter at n 26.) In other words, it needs to be in some sense a 'weighty' interest; worthy of having the protection of law. Secondly, A's interest must constitute a *sufficient* ground or justification for B to have the relevant duty to A (which is the reflex of A's right). (See (iii) above and same passage cited at n 26.) And thirdly, according to Raz, for rights to be legal rights, they require to be recognised by law. (See (v) above.)

There are at least three inter-related practical difficulties here, corresponding to three of the highlighted existence conditions. First, a condition of existence that entails taking an interest 'seriously' appears to require an interposing judgment for its realisation. Does the existence or non-existence of a right literally turn on the presence of such a judgment, made by an unidentified person? Let us assume that the legislature deems an interest to be sufficiently weighty for the introduction of a law conferring a right on the party whose interest is, in the result, legally protected. The enactment of the new law will constitute the act of creation, for legal purposes, of the legal right; and this will supersede any antecedent interest that impelled the introduction of the new law. So, following enactment, the interest protected by the law will become (more or less) redundant for purposes of any assessment of whether the right exists or not.[30] The interest may continue to be relevant to, for example, judicial opinions, as part of the historical circumstances that, at some

[29] See J Raz, 'Legal Rights' (this chapter, n 24). Points (i) to (iv) are mainly derived from Raz's analysis on p 5; while point (v) derives from his analysis on p 14 (with emphasis added). Further, at p 12, Raz comments: 'If rights are protected interests in that a person has a right if and only if an interest of his is a sufficient ground for holding another to be subject to a duty then legal rights are legally-protected interests.'

[30] It is worth recalling Raz's point that 'law creates rights … by imposing duties.' See J Raz, 'Legal Rights' (this chapter, n 24) 14. See also J Raz, *The Concept of a Legal System: An Introduction to the Theory of Legal Systems* (2nd edn, Clarendon Press 1980) 21. Likewise Hart, in the course of endorsing a position maintained by Bentham, comments that '[r]ights resulting from obligation are conferred by (or as Bentham puts it, "have as their base") coercive laws; rights resulting from the absence of obligation have as their base discoercive or permissive laws.' See HLA Hart, *Essays on Bentham* (this chapter, n 8) 165. For his part, MacCormick discusses at length the possibility of rights being created by legislation which owe their existence *directly to law* rather than to either the presence of interests or any exertion of will on the part of a right-holder. 'The first point to be made about legal rights must seem, when made, to be of breath-taking banality. The point is that legal rights are conferred by legal rules,

time in the past, precipitated the introduction of the rights now enshrined in the (new) law. But to maintain that the existence of the right is dependent in perpetuity upon the existence of the interest that inspired its creation (by a legislative act) is to concede too much to the idea that interests condition the existence of rights.

The second difficulty turns on the idea that a condition of existence that necessitates treating an interest as a *sufficient ground* for constitution of a duty correlating with a right not only requires the making of a judgment for its realisation (thereby marking the re-emergence of the first difficulty discussed above), but, more critically, as a purely practical proposition places the existence of rights in the arena of a *question of degree*. At what point does an interest become a 'sufficient ground', and what is the status of the nascent right meantime? At what point, in other words, does a given right, such as it is, pass from a state of non-existence to a state of 'fully-fledged' existence? Is there a point at which 'critical mass' is reached? If so, how is this point defined? Upon whose judgment does this depend?[31]

The third difficulty under discussion centres on the idea of legal recognition. A condition that makes the existence of a legal right dependent upon recognition suggests the need to identify either a figure whose task is to confer legal recognition upon a legal right (or upon a 'candidate right' for recognition as a legal right), or a set of appropriate recognition criteria, applicable within a given legal system.[32] Again, as a purely practical proposition, by whom, and from whose standpoint, is a right to be adjudged a legally recognised right? Neither Raz nor MacCormick, in their respective versions of interest theory – nor Hart in his version of will theory – seeks to outline such a theoretical perspective. As this question is taken up and addressed in some detail under the third constraining factor, it is to that topic of discussion that we now turn.

3.2.3. Constraining Factor III – Theoretical Perspectives

The will theory of rights is, inescapably, a theory that places the will of the right-holder at the centre of the explanatory process. Hart's distinctive version of will theory reflects and reinforces that basic preoccupation.[33] But such is the centrality

or (if you will) by laws. What could be more obvious?' See DN MacCormick, 'Rights in Legislation' (this chapter, n 16) 189.

[31] Considerations such as the presence of significant interests, and the treatment of such interests as a sufficient ground for the constitution of a duty (being the reflex of the corresponding right), might feature in decisions (eg by a legislature or by a contracting party) whether or not to *introduce* a particular right – eg one that comes to be enshrined in a statute or in a contract. The idea that the presence of a relevant interest might be regarded in its own right as an *existence condition* of a duty (or of a corresponding right), when weighed against processes of enactment of statutes, or processes attending the formation of contracts, does not seem credible.

[32] A Hartian rule of recognition might be used to amplify Raz's analysis.

[33] As we have seen, this fundamental position is consistently traceable to writings as historically and geographically removed from the Hartian genre of theorising as those of Savigny. Based on a reading of Hartian will theory, the *will of the right-holder* equates to an imaginative determination on the part of

of – and the *definitional* dependence of the concept of a right upon – the right-holder's will in Hartian will theory that MacCormick, for one, asserts that if someone (such as an infant) by reason of incapacity, lacks the power personally to waive or assert an immunity, or a 'claim, or whatever, upon some matter, upon that matter there is, *by definition*, no right' under Hartian will theory.[34] Even without the (added) difficulty of definitional dependence, the consciousness or mental disposition of the right-holder – and its role in Hartian will theory – is no mere incident: to have a right, according to Hart, is to have a measure of control over the acts of another and, at least so far as Hartian *theory* is concerned, this explicitly engages the will of the right-holder towards the exercise of choices to take, or not to take, enforcement action, or towards consciously giving up (or waiving) the right altogether. Thus, will theory in its Hartian variant necessarily views rights through the eyes of the right-holder. It is not credible to have a notion of will theory that is not in some sense founded upon the consciousness of, at the same time as implying the need for exertions of will on the part of, the right-holder.[35]

Versions of interest theory also place the consciousness of the right-holder at the centre of the explanatory process though, unlike the Hartian version of will theory, the right-holder's consciousness (or will) is not *definitionally integral* to the concept of a right. For instance, Raz's conception (or 'definition' or 'account')[36] of a right is self-evidently dependent upon the presence of interests of the right-holder; and this marks an obvious point of differentiation between will theory and interest theory. As we have seen, Raz maintains that '[t]o say that a person has a right is to say that an interest *of his* is sufficient ground for holding another to be subject to a duty'.[37] It is clear from this that Raz, towards

the right-holder – being an element of the right-holder's consciousness (see this chapter, above, at n 3) – to bring about a particular outcome, expressed as a duty imposed upon a duty-bearer, that has its origin in, or is derivable from, the presence and availability of a legal right. In Hartian will theory, this determination is generally confined to the choice to act in one of three ways: (i) enforce the right, (ii) waive or extinguish the right, or (iii) leave the right unenforced. Here, such a determination is considered to reside generally within a right-holder's consciousness (this chapter, n 3), coexisting with elements that could include (for instance) a Hartian critical reflective attitude in relation to the laws that underpin (and are creative of) the right. See further, section 5.3.2 (Chapter 5, below). Hart also outlines a broader position, discussed at section 1.3 (Chapter 1, above), where an exercise of the given choices relate, by extension, to breach or threatened breach of a duty and the obligation to pay compensation. See HLA Hart, *Essays on Bentham* (this chapter, n 8) 183–184.

[34] DN MacCormick, 'Rights in Legislation' (this chapter, n 16) 196 (MacCormick's emphasis). This is discussed further in Chapter 6 below.

[35] As previously indicated, Hart is referring to what is arguably one of the most extensive categories of rights – 'rights correlative to obligations' (which is a manifestation of the Hohfeldian claim-right–duty nexus). (See this chapter at n 3 and n 33 for discussion of the idea of viewing the will of the right-holder as an integral part of a right-holder's 'consciousness'.)

[36] In the more 'generic' of his two seminal articles on rights, Raz maintains that his efforts are directed towards the development of a 'definition' of rights. See J Raz, 'On the Nature of Rights' (this chapter, n 28) 194–196, 199–200, 204, 207 (and at other places in the article). In the more 'focused' of his two articles (ie on *legal* rights), Raz maintains that he is offering (variously) an 'account', or an 'explanation', of [the nature of] legal rights. See J Raz, 'Legal Rights' (this chapter, n 24): for 'account' see, for example, 5–6, 12, 14; and for 'explanation' see, for example, 12, 14.

[37] J Raz, 'Legal Rights' (this chapter, n 24) 5 (emphasis added). Doubtless the interests in question in some cases will lie within the consciousness of the right-holder (see this chapter, n 3), though Raz

reinforcing the centrality of the consciousness of the holder of a (legal) right, situates both right-holder and duty-bearer within what is recognisably a binary Hohfeldian nexus – a jural relation.[38] Thus, for Raz, the scope of any given legal right, and conceptions of a legal right, are seen to be (theoretically) tied to the immediate participants in a jural relation – that is, the relationship implied by the possession of a Hohfeldian claim-right (having a duty as its reflex). This can also perhaps be seen as a *juris vinculum* or legal bond,[39] where participants in the relationship who are properly apprised of their legal situation view their respective positions in terms of what the right-holder (legally) can demand from the duty-bearer and what the duty-bearer needs to do in order reasonably to satisfy the right-holder's legitimate demand. In Raz's account, given the obvious presence of a Hohfeldian nexus (which Raz does not explicitly acknowledge to be such), both the right and interest of the right-holder are to be seen from the respective viewpoints of the participants in the relationship. But they may also be seen from the exclusive viewpoint of the right-holder (or indeed, more narrowly still, the viewpoint implied by relevant *interests* of the right-holder): in other words, *my* interest secured by *my* right.[40]

In significant respects, then, both will theory (in its Hartian variant) and interest theory (in the version formulated by Raz) view a legal right from the perspective of those most immediately involved in its possession and exercise, or (by extension) in the performance of the duty or obligation associated with it. This theoretical stance is reinforced to the extent that key aspects of each version of the relevant theory are predicated upon a recognisably Hohfeldian nexus, placing a renewed emphasis on the viewpoint of each of the parties to the relationship. So, on one hand, an explanation of legal rights turns directly on the content of the will or consciousness of the right-holder; while, on the other hand, the explanation proceeds from taking stock of relevant interests that will often lie within the perception of the right-holder. Yet, in both cases, the microcosm of the Hohfeldian

allows for the possibility of extraneous interests playing a role in the origination of rights, provided the interest of the right-holder subsists alongside the relevant extraneous interests (such as the public interest, for instance). See J Raz, 'On the Nature of Rights' (this chapter, n 28) 207.

[38] Interestingly, the Hohfeldian element of Raz's version of interest theory overlaps with the corresponding element of Hart's version of will theory: both theoretical outlooks, in other words, are 'Hohfeldian' in significant respects. (See this chapter at n 27 and n 28.) For use of the expression 'Hohfeldian nexus' in reference to the work of Raz, Hart and MacCormick, see this chapter at n 27.

[39] See A Kocourek, *Jural Relations* (2nd edn, The Bobbs-Merrill Company 1928) 41–42.

[40] There may be a question as to whether interests, and the pursuit or enjoyment of interests protected by legal rights, are the sole preserve of right-holders. Raz, in the main, emphasises right-holders' interests. However, duty-bearers may also be seen to be in possession of relevant interests. Take a commercial organisation that willingly takes on the burdens of a lucrative contract (acting, to that extent, primarily as 'duty-bearer') in order to win further lucrative contracts. Here, the organisation has an interest in performing its contractual obligations to the best of its ability to ensure a productive ongoing relationship with a significant client. An alternative way of looking at the same situation, which reinforces Raz's account, is that (ordinarily) the organisation in question will be paid for its provision of relevant goods or services to the client, and to that extent will simultaneously occupy the position of duty-bearer and right-holder – which, in the case of the latter, will involve possession of a right, ultimately, to demand payment from the client.

nexus – lying within the consciousness of the parties to the relationship – has a central place.

It is not immediately clear, then, when adopting the viewpoint of narrowly conceived participants' perspectives, how the distinctive *institutional* dimension of legal rights is to be accommodated within these theoretical positions. In Chapter 1 the discussion of legal rights that are protective of interests at the same time as they empower right-holders – representing core and complementary tenets of interest theory and will theory respectively – implies that protection and empowerment would be ineffectual if they went no further than the resources individually available to a right-holder: for instance, force of personality, status, personal charisma, and so on. Essentially, institutional reinforcement and backing are needed to secure the necessary protection and empowerment; and in some cases it may be needed to assist in convincing a (reluctant) duty-bearer to perform a legal obligation. Although Raz, in relevant writings, comments briefly on a narrow concept of 'institutional rights',[41] his core position on the concept of a right – which he also describes as a 'definition'[42] – does not explicitly accommodate institutionality as an integral element. It is, however, important to recognise that Raz's aim is to state a position, or to arrive at a definition, that encompasses both legal rights *and moral rights*.[43] A position or definition centring only upon the specifics of legal rights (including their distinctive institutional dimension) would tend either to frustrate, or to fail to advance, that aim. Also, we saw in section 2.3.2 (Chapter 2, above) that while MacCormick's philosophical outlook on institutionality – which focuses in part on his analysis of the existence and status of so-called 'institutional facts' and 'institutions of law' (such as a particular legal right or legal duty) – was insightful, there was a need to offer a more developed sociological outlook on institutionality. It was argued that this could include discussion of the role of legal institutions (in MacCormick's 'sociological' sense) – particularly the role of the courts – at the point where that role is literally *determinative* of the content and other features of institutional facts that go to make up relevant institutions of law (in MacCormick's sense) such as legal rights, in specific cases.

Similarly, Hart, with his focus upon core theoretical elements of the extensive category of 'rights correlative to obligations', advances a theoretical position on legal rights that is perhaps too narrowly tied to the figure of a Hohfeldian jural relation (and the correspondingly narrow perspective of participants in the relation – right-holder, duty-bearer) for the institutional dimension of legal rights to

[41] J Raz, 'Legal Rights' (this chapter, n 24) 2–3. Raz describes as 'institutional rights' those rights which are 'conferred by the rules of associations such as political parties, trade unions, educational institutions and sports associations'.

[42] See this chapter at n 36.

[43] Raz's claim that his general stance in relation to rights can be applied both to moral and legal rights is to be found in 'Legal Rights' (this chapter, n 24) 1, referring to the more 'general account of rights' expounded in J Raz, 'On the Nature of Rights' (this chapter, n 28). This point is reinforced at p 12, where Raz notes that his account gives 'rights' the same sense in both legal and non-legal contexts.

be properly accommodated.[44] These theoretical constraints – the third 'constraining factor' under discussion here – have implications that it is appropriate to consider now at greater length.

The departure point is an examination of the limitations of a perspective on legal rights that places the right-holder at the centre of the explanatory process and at the same time within the frame of reference of a Hohfeldian jural relation. The key question to arise is whether the standpoint of the right-holder (or indeed that of both right-holder and duty-bearer) is necessarily the most appropriate for capturing the existential condition of being in possession of a legal right. We have already seen, from reflecting briefly upon MacCormick's critique of Hartian will theory, the difficulties which an emphasis on the consciousness of the right-holder creates for the very possibility of children's rights.[45] Yet, surely what holds for children holds for *anyone* (including adults) whose cognitive or volitional capacities are impaired or deficient. And if that is correct, the deficiencies of will theory highlighted by MacCormick apply in principle to a more extensive range of cases; thereby potentially rendering aspects of Hartian will theory more problematic than MacCormick acknowledges.

In defence of Hartian will theory, it is argued in Chapter 6 below, that the more drastic implications of MacCormick's critique – which point to the possibility that children are to be regarded (at least in the 'eyes' of legal theory) as incapable of the possession and enjoyment of rights – may be questionable. Among other things, Hart explicitly accommodates children's rights when outlining his version of will theory in *Essays on Bentham*, a matter which MacCormick appears to overlook.[46] Indeed, Hart makes clear the necessity for representative legal mechanisms to be provided to compensate for cognitive and volitional incapacities of children.[47] Vulnerable adults are also attended by such incapacities, so without

[44] It will be recalled from section 2.2.2 (Chapter 2, above) that one of the truth conditions of the statement 'X has a right' cited by Hart includes the not insignificant presupposition of the presence of a functioning legal system as the environment in which legal rules (and legal rights) operate. An analysis in which presuppositions of that kind multiply (without further elaboration) would surely leave many critical areas unexplored.

[45] This is also discussed at length in Chapter 6, below.

[46] Nothing is said about Hart's stated position (see this chapter at n 47) either in DN MacCormick, 'Children's Rights: A Test Case' (this chapter, n 12) or in DN MacCormick, 'Rights in Legislation' (this chapter, n 16).

[47] Hart's broad position on (specifically) the rights of the child is to be found in a footnote: 'Where infants or other persons not *sui juris* have rights, such powers and the correlative obligations are exercised on their behalf by appointed representatives and their exercise may be subject to approval by a court … [T]he powers are regarded as belonging throughout [minority] to them and not to their representatives, though they are only exercisable by the latter during the period of disability'. See Hart, *Essays on Bentham* (this chapter, n 8) 184 n 86. See also 185 n 88. MacCormick's view as to Hart's position on children's rights might have been coloured by a less accommodating position that Hart had previously announced and to which MacCormick refers (and implicitly objects). See DN MacCormick, 'Children's Rights: A Test Case' (this chapter, n 12) 164 n 2. Hart had argued that to ascribe rights to babies or animals is to make 'an idle use of the expression "a right"'. See HLA Hart, 'Are There Any Natural Rights?' (1955) 64 *The Philosophical Review* 175, 181. It appears that Hart's position may have changed between the 1950s and 1980s.

such mechanisms, many of the ends of the law would regularly be defeated. For a variety of reasons an attempt to reach an understanding of the nature of a legal right that is, in significant ways, informed by the consciousness of the right-holder – extending, for example, to interests encompassed within the perception of the right-holder – may be quite instructive. However, what if the consciousness of the right-holder is infected with error, or incomprehension, or incomplete knowledge? The standpoint of the right-holder, or of others closely associated with the possession of a right, may not serve to generate hypotheses that best illustrate the most important characteristics of a legal right.[48] The difficulty with any theoretical position that makes the conditions of existence of a right in some way dependent upon a right-holder's consciousness (ie awareness, understanding; and recognition of its existence, content, scope, effect, and so on) – such as that adopted by Hart in the context of his version of will theory[49] – is that any deficiency in rights-literacy will count in some way against the *existence* of a right in the case of any given right and right-holder.

It is clear, when reflecting upon the unique characteristics of *legal* rights, that the perspective and consciousness of the right-holder – which (Hartian) will theory and the versions of interest theory advanced by Raz and MacCormick appear, in their core (or definitional) formulations, to adopt or reflect or reinforce – are best seen as a usually necessary, albeit non-exhaustive, part of a wider explanatory frame of reference. Viewing the world through the eyes of the acting individual or of persons most closely connected with unfolding events – and adopting that viewpoint in explaining those acts or events – has its place, of course.[50] But, just as any attempt to pass over or downplay an important perspective, such as that of right-holders when explaining the nature of their rights, could result in distortion, particularly given the centrality accorded to such a perspective in theories of rights, so, to disregard or downplay other important perspectives likewise has the potential for (explanatory) distortion. So far as *legal* rights are concerned, it is necessary to adopt or replicate a perspective that extends beyond explanations based narrowly on the point of view of the right-holder.

It is suggested that, as a practical and theoretical proposition, and for reasons to be clarified in this and later chapters, relevant perspectives *must* include the judicial perspective, whether at the level of lower courts or that of appellate or supreme courts. This is an imperative of *legal culture*: which is of particular importance

[48] See the related discussion in section 6.2.3 (Chapter 6, below), discussing the awareness of legal rights that a typical right-holder may, or may not, have.

[49] This is on the assumption that MacCormick's critique of Hartian will theory, and its full implications, actually have force. MacCormick's critique is extensively discussed in Chapter 6, below.

[50] This approach is rooted in the philosophy of the human sciences generally and, more particularly, the philosophy of social science. Inevitably such a viewpoint tends to be a 'first resort' in undertaking relevant explanatory and theoretical tasks. See generally P Winch, *The Idea of a Social Science and its Relation to Philosophy* (2nd edn, Routledge 1990). See also generally (such as in reference to the work of Max Weber) LA Coser, *Masters of Sociological Thought: Ideas in Historical and Social Context* (Harcourt Brace Jovanovich 1971).

where common law jurisdictions are concerned. It is a corollary of the presence of norms of legal professional practice, where an emphasis is placed on the use of *precedent* in judicial decision-making. For instance, in common law jurisdictions, where the principle of *stare decisis* has primacy,[51] *anyone* (such as right-holders, duty-bearers, legal professionals, teachers of law, journalists, private individuals; indeed *judges*) with an interest in discerning the most legally sound and authoritative expression of the content, scope, effect (etc) of a given right is necessarily 'thrown upon' judicial precedent, such that, unless their discernment is consistent and compatible with relevant judicial precedent (if any), it may prove unsafe and open to question. The adoption, or formulation of some kind of theoretical replication, of a judicial perspective is critical when theorising about legal rights posited in systems that are both hierarchical and located within the legal culture of the common law tradition. In particular, in hierarchical judicial systems, rulings on relevant rights – their existence, content, and import – when considered at the highest judicial level, such as a final court of appeal (a supreme court), are treated *for the system in question* not only as authoritative, but as final and conclusive and (therefore) legally beyond challenge.

Elsewhere an outline of just such a perspective has been attempted – the so-called *Iudexian* perspective[52] – which hypothesises the decision-making role of a (hypothetical) common law judge, *Iudex*, whose output (in terms of judicial decision-making) could be described as:

(i) the synthesised judgment of a collectivity of judges sitting in the highest appeal court in a hypothetical judicial system, delivering a judgment in the instant case before them, which takes account of fact-finding and other judicial outcomes at all lower levels of the judicial hierarchy; and
(ii) representative of a final, unappealable, decision (in effect, the 'last word') as regards the decision rendered in that case.[53]

In *Institutions of Law*, one of the last writings published before his untimely death, MacCormick critiques the *Iudexian* perspective – ie the perspective (as MacCormick puts it) of 'a judge in a highest-level state court'. MacCormick points out that this standpoint might be thought of as 'one that can enable us to discern most clearly the most prominent features of the legal landscape' or one 'from which to obtain a particularly rich vision and understanding of law'.[54]

[51] See R Cross and JW Harris, *Precedent in English Law* (4th edn, Clarendon Press 1991) ch III (*stare decisis*) and ch IV (exceptions to *stare decisis*).

[52] See H Ross, *Law as a Social Institution* (Hart Publishing 2001) ch 5. See also sections 4.5 and 4.6 (Chapter 4, below) and generally Chapter 8, below.

[53] The judicial decision-making of *Iudex* could be said to represent a conclusive position on the rights of the parties in a hypothetical case. The hypothesis of the ultimate judgment is taken to represent a final determination of the content and scope of the relevant rights for the (essentially practical) purpose of mobilising the (ultimately) coercive apparatuses of the legal system in question towards enforcement of the judicially declared rights. See H Ross, *Law as a Social Institution* (Hart Publishing 2001) 112–114.

[54] N MacCormick, *Institutions of Law: An Essay in Legal Theory* (Oxford University Press 2007) (hereafter, in this chapter, '*Institutions of Law*') 6, 55.

MacCormick expresses a preference for the adoption of an alternative point of view – that of an 'observer-from-within', corresponding to a 'professorial' standpoint.[55] He strongly hints – though does not explicitly state – that his adopted standpoint would be immune from any presumed narrowness of vision that might be thought to beset a *Iudexian* perspective: 'It is perhaps a particular feature of legal theorizing in common law countries to be so strongly judge-centred'.[56] In commenting on the *Iudexian* perspective, MacCormick appears to take the view that such a perspective necessarily excludes other possible, and equally insightful, perspectives.[57] Yet, the idea that our understanding of legal rights might be advanced by a point of view as promisingly eclectic as MacCormick's professorial standpoint doubtless reinforces the point that, in an effort to reach such an understanding, it is possible to adopt a range of different viewpoints where one adopted viewpoint might have more explanatory power in certain contexts and for certain purposes, than other viewpoints. The point is that no credible perspective need be ruled out as a candidate for affording insight into the nature or existence conditions of legal rights.[58]

Arguably, one of the merits of a *Iudexian* perspective is that legal rights that are constructed within, and imagined to emerge from, that (hypothetical) perspective are informed by a level of institutional insight that in most cases will be absent from a viewpoint constructed narrowly around the consciousness of the right-holder. The *Iudexian* perspective, hypothesising an ultimate judgment,[59] necessarily transcends any individual right-holder's rights awareness, establishing an institutional position untainted by such matters as (right-holder) error,

[55] 'By contrast with such, the present work unapologetically adopts a professorial standpoint. There is no reason to doubt that the systematization of law, to the extent that it has come to pass, has been primarily an achievement of legal science rather than of legal practice. This is not to deny that persons occupying the position of Ross's "*Iudex*", or others in other forms of legal practice, have been extremely prominent in developing a rational and "scientific" study of law. Nor should one deny that judicial expositions and interpretations of legal doctrine have a particularly authoritative role in developing legal doctrine in contemporary polities living under law.' See N MacCormick, *Institutions of Law* (this chapter, n 54) 6.

[56] ibid 55 n 40. Of course, a distinction must be drawn between the 'panoramic' (or indeed 'pantheistic') perspective adopted by a theorist (on one hand) and (on the other) a narrower perspective analytically constructed by the theorist, so as to form an integral *part* of the theory, which is designed purely as a heuristic device. A *Iudexian* perspective is the latter; whilst MacCormick's professorial standpoint is the former. MacCormick does not apparently recognise this key distinction.

[57] As pointed out in *Law as a Social Institution*: 'The *Iudexian* viewpoint is to be seen merely as a counterpoint to *other* viewpoints … There is nothing to prevent a conception of the world as it happens to be to, for instance, a marginalised indigenous community being expressed through that community's world view and given the scrutiny afforded by an appropriate methodology.' See H Ross, *Law as a Social Institution* (Hart Publishing 2001) 114.

[58] So, for instance, in one context, a detached observer's perspective or a (non-judicial) institutional insider's perspective, may have greater explanatory power, and be more informative, than (say) a 'bad man's' or a 'puzzled man's' perspective. See HLA Hart, *The Concept of Law* (2nd edn, Clarendon Press 1994) 40. In the same context, Hart reminds us that the principal function of law as a means of social control is not to be seen in how its consequences play out in courts of law. Rather, '[i]t is to be seen in the diverse ways in which the law is used to control, to guide, and to plan life out of court'.

[59] See this chapter at n 53.

incomprehension, incomplete knowledge (such as of the applicable law or relevant facts), or any cognitive or volitional incapacity affecting the right-holder. Such a perspective need not supplant – and indeed may actually incorporate – elements of right-holders' perceptions so far as bearing on their rights, or insights derived from their knowledge or understanding of their rights (which may be informed by legal advice). These perceptions or insights – for example, a factually established intention to enter into a legally binding contract – may come to play an important role in a court's decision-making. In the case of a court deciding whether a contract exists, the presence (or absence) of the requisite degree of contractual intent on the part of a claimant – a matter of evidence – may come to be at least partly determinative of the question. A *Iudexian* perspective may also serve to address lacunae left unaddressed by right-holders' often limited perceptions of the existence, content, and import of their rights – for instance, legal and other 'technical' matters not ordinarily falling within the knowledge of a typical right-holder. A *Iudexian* hypothesis may encompass a fully informed knowledge of the content of relevant legal rights – and of applicable legal rules, norms, standards, principles, doctrines, precedents, and so on – and knowledge of the prevailing legal culture, including insights into the workings of a system's judicial processes.[60]

A theoretical approach to understanding the nature and origin of legal rights that gives a central place to a *Iudexian* viewpoint is not incompatible with an approach grounded in elements of the consciousness (awareness, understanding etc) of the right-holder. In the case of interest theory (as advanced by Raz and MacCormick), attention focuses on the presence of interests possessed by, and ordinarily lying within the awareness and understanding of, a right-holder. In the case of will theory (as advanced by Hart), the focus is on exertions of will by a right-holder towards the exercise of control over the behaviour of others. An approach employing a *Iudexian* perspective would make no necessary claim as to the nature or existence of legal rights turning on the key issues identified by interest theory or will theory; but as we have seen, both of those theories *in their core (or definitional) formulations* in the writings of Hart, Raz and MacCormick,[61] at least tacitly adopt viewpoints, centred around the consciousness of the right-holder, that are too narrow properly to account for the institutional dimension of legal rights. Moreover, as we have seen, Raz acknowledges, in a position that he describes as 'the core of the account here proposed', that a right cannot be a legal right in the absence of legal recognition,

[60] An imaginary judge possessing a few of the qualities of a Dworkinian 'Hercules' comes to mind. See R Dworkin, 'Hard Cases' (1975) 88 *Harvard Law Review* 1057, 1083–1109. See generally K Greenawalt, 'Policy, Rights, and Judicial Decision' in M Cohen (ed), *Ronald Dworkin and Contemporary Jurisprudence* (Gerald Duckworth & Co Ltd 1984) ch 5. An extensive discussion of Dworkin's Herculean archetype follows in Chapter 7, below.

[61] See, for instance, passages reproduced and cited in this chapter at n 11 (Hart), n 23 (MacCormick) and nn 26 and 29 (Raz).

asserting that '[a]n individual has … a legal right if it is recognized by law'.[62] Raz, *within that core position*, leaves unaddressed the question of the form that legal recognition might take; but a typical mechanism, albeit perhaps more a creature of theory than of institutional reality, might equate to a (Hartian) rule of recognition.

The emergent theoretical position calls attention to the idea that critical insights into important elements of a legal right – the content, scope, effect, and indeed the very existence, of the right – may be gained by viewing those elements as being in some sense constructed within the judicial imagination or consciousness. In other words, key elements of a legal right – essentially viewed in their totality as a construct of the judicial consciousness – may be seen to reside within the hypothesised point of view of an ideal supreme-court-level judge, *Iudex*. The *Iudexian* perspective on legal rights reflects those criteria of recognition, and processes of legal argumentation, analysis and rationalisation, that are appropriate for the given judicial system and legal culture. Viewed in more practical terms, if the highest appellate court of a given jurisdiction – applying all relevant criteria of recognition for the system in question – would decline to recognise a purported or 'candidate' right as a right of the system, then this will simply fail to qualify as such.[63] Conversely, if such a court declares a purported or 'candidate' right to be a right of the system, with this or that content, scope, effect, and so on, then the declared right will be (at least for the time being, pending a later, inconsistent, decision of the same court) legally conclusive and unassailable. The ontological question whether a right exists as a *legal* right – in other words, as a right of a given legal system – and the content of the individual right, would turn on what is contained within the hypothesis of an ultimate judgment emerging from the *Iudexian* perspective. Such a judgment, although theoretical and hypothetical, may be taken to represent an authoritative determination and characterisation of the right in question.

Urging the adoption of a *Iudexian* perspective towards purely theoretical ends – in the face of MacCormick's critique of that perspective – is not to suggest that judges somehow have a 'monopoly' on legal rights or that legal rights are in some sense the 'personal property' or 'playthings' of judges. Rather, in the context of a relatively narrow discussion of core (or definitional) tenets of the two main

[62] See J Raz, 'Legal Rights' (this chapter, n 24) 14.

[63] The criteria of recognition in question might include an elaboration of Hart's rule of recognition along the lines suggested (for example) by MacCormick. See N MacCormick, *HLA Hart* (2nd edn, Stanford University Press 2008) ch 10. The wider question, explored in section 4.5 (Chapter 4, below), focuses on how a *Iudexian* perspective might shape the mindset of those concerned to know the law or the content, scope and effect of particular (or hypothetical) legal rights. For instance, an academic lawyer writing a textbook will usually seek to identify the best and highest authority on a given question; and, in the absence of a direct authority, may apply processes of reasoning that seek to replicate, as closely as possible, the outlook and approach of an ultimate supreme court judge for the practical purpose of anticipating how institutional exercises of power might play out, first, in determining the content of a [hypothetical] right and, secondly, in activating relevant coercive enforcement mechanisms. Others may do likewise: eg law students, prosecutors, legal advisers, tax accountants, court officials, compliance officers, and so on.

theories of rights, will theory and interest theory, a *Iudexian* perspective might be seen as a necessary corrective or addition to any explanatory frame of reference that would seek to place the consciousness of the right-holder – or others similarly closely connected with the possession and exercise of legal rights – exclusively at the centre of the explanatory process. As we have seen here and elsewhere (but particularly in MacCormick's critique of Hartian will theory where the 'will' of the right-holder takes centre stage), such an approach is enduringly problematic; not least because explanations of the nature and existence conditions of legal rights are precarious where right-holders are seen to be beset by, among other things, an absence of cognitive or volitional capacity. Yet it seems entirely understandable and credible, when considering the existence, scope and content of A's legal right to X for theoretical discussion to be centred around what precisely it is that A can be said to 'have' when possessed of a legal right and for the focus therefore to fall upon (among other things) A's consciousness, awareness, understanding, and so on. But the very possibility of a *Iudexian* perspective on A's legal right or claimed legal right – involving the adoption of the perspective of an imaginary supreme court judge – raises potentially wider issues around whether (and if so, the extent to which) key elements of the institutional artefact that is the legal right can be viewed as a construct of – or, at any rate, capable of being constructed within – the judicial consciousness.

3.3. Ontological Implications of the Three Constraining Factors

The analysis of aspects of will theory and interest theory presented in this chapter identifies a number of limitations in the explanatory power of those theories, centring upon the scope and analytical reach of their core or definitional tenets.

Will theory: In apparently promoting an explanation of legal rights – or a class of legal rights, namely, 'rights correlative to obligations'[64] – based upon what rights 'do', Hartian will theory asserts that legal rights give a right-holder a power to control the behaviour of others, at the same time affording the right-holder the choice, by way of exertions of will, to enforce the right, waive it, or leave it unenforced. Ontologically, Hartian will theory is constrained by the need to demonstrate an analytical connection between the existence of a legal right and the will of the right-holder, where an exertion of will entails an exercise by a right-holder of the power of control (and associated choices) with which the right-holder is said to be invested. When, as MacCormick points out, the existence of a right is, for Hart, definitionally dependent on the will, or aspects of the mental disposition, of right-holders – arguably implying the need for a right-holder to have the volitional and

[64] See observations in this chapter at n 8.

cognitive capacity to exercise a right before the right can even exist – Hart's conditions of existence of rights, and his definition of right, become problematic.

Interest theory: In apparently promoting an explanation of rights based upon what rights are 'for', the versions of interest theory advanced by Raz and MacCormick assert that rights protect or promote interests; though Raz takes this a step further: rights indirectly – through the mechanism of associated (correlative) duties – serve the interests that justify them; whilst legal rights, in particular, are rights that have been afforded recognition by law.[65] Ontologically, the version of interest theory advanced in particular by Raz is constrained by the need to demonstrate an analytical connection between the existence of a right and the presence of interests. When Raz's characterisation of interests is beset by difficulties – namely, the three inter-related practical difficulties outlined in section 3.2.2 (this chapter, above) – his conditions of existence of rights (which also serve in some way to define the concept of a right) become problematic.

Beyond positing (arguably) problematic existence conditions and, where relevant, definitions, of the concept of a [legal] right, neither theory, in its core or central or definitional propositions, ventures significantly into the wider question of what a legal right actually is in terms of any broader frame of reference. That said, Hartian will theory, as previously noted, contends that legal rights can be viewed as a kind of power;[66] while Raz inclines to the view that rights (reflecting the role that they play in practical reasoning) 'indicate intermediate conclusions between statements of the right-holder's interests and another's duty'.[67] But, in asserting elsewhere that rights actually *are* interests,[68] Raz appears to promote the view that rights do not merely *protect* interests or, via correlative duties, *serve* the interests that justify them, but literally *are* interests.[69] Both theorists' positions nonetheless offer promising points of departure for a more thorough exploration of the nature and key characteristics of legal rights.

Less promising is the notion that in the case of Hartian will theory, and both Raz's and MacCormick's versions of interest theory, the right-holder's consciousness is apparently placed at the centre of the explanatory enterprise.[70] This, as has

[65] See observations in this chapter at, or around, n 29.

[66] This, as noted above – see in particular section 1.4 (Chapter 1, above) – raises the possibility of aspects of Hartian will theory being accommodated within relevant social theory frames of reference.

[67] J Raz, 'Legal Rights' (this chapter, n 24) 5.

[68] ibid 12 for example, where Raz states: 'If *rights are protected interests* in that a person has a right if and only if an interest of his is a sufficient ground for holding another to be subject to a duty then *legal rights are legally protected interests*'. (Emphasis added.)

[69] The analysis is impaired by circularity. The difficulty is how can a right function to protect an interest at the same time as it literally *is* (identical to) the interest that the right purportedly protects?

[70] Hart, Raz and MacCormick are by no means the only jurists who give a central place to the viewpoint of the parties subject to a Hohfeldian jural relation. Thus, George Goble characterises Hohfeld's power–liability relationship as follows: '[Power] … describes a relationship of two persons from the viewpoint of the dominant or controlling party. The same relationship is described from the viewpoint of the servient or controlled party by the term *liability*'. See GW Goble, 'A Redefinition of Basic Legal Terms' (1935) 35 *Columbia Law Review* 535, at 535. And as Kelsen comments: 'The reflex right is only

been maintained at various places above, is a constraining factor: a *perspectival* constraint; and it lies at the heart of the question, to be taken up in this part of the discussion, of the extent to which key elements of the institutional artefact that is the legal right can be viewed as a construct of – or, at any rate, as capable of being constructed within – the judicial consciousness.

Essentially, the central or definitional accounts or explanations of legal rights (such as those to be found in some of the key writings of Hart, Raz and MacCormick) turning on the consciousness or self-perception of right-holders, or those most closely connected with the possession and enjoyment of rights, fall short of capturing what is characteristically 'legal' about legal rights: namely, their institutional character.[71] The view promoted here is that in order properly to capture something of the characteristic institutionality of legal rights it is appropriate to adopt, or to adopt a suitably modified version of, a *Iudexian* perspective – being the standpoint of a hypothetical supreme court judge (*Iudex*)[72] – on a basis that recognises its conceptual and theoretical limitations. It would be going too far to suggest that the existence or content or characteristics of a given legal right might be *exhaustively* accounted for through the adoption of such a perspective. We have already touched upon a few general limitations attending the *Iudexian* perspective, such as that legal rights are not the exclusive 'preserve' of judges. At the same time, an explanation of legal rights that did not in some way take account of the perspective of the right-holder would surely be incoherent. For instance, it could leave unstated and unexplored much of what Hart has identified as coming within the consciousness of individuals possessing legal rights: for example, attitudes of right-holders to the power of control that rights give them over the behaviour of others, such as choices around the exercise (or not) of the rights in question. It is undeniable that the perspective of individual right-holders is empirically significant.

the legal obligation, seen from the viewpoint of the individual toward whom the obligation has to be fulfilled'. See H Kelsen, *Pure Theory of Law* (2nd edn, University of California Press 1967) 166.

[71] In the present context, the related concepts of 'institutional' and 'institutionality' reflect the idea that, in purely empirical terms, the institution of positive (or *posited*) law is the enterprise of placing human behaviour under the governance of rules, principles and other explicitly articulated standards (laws). This entails installing structures of organised human behaviour comprising: (i) legislative institutions to enact the relevant laws; (ii) judicial institutions to administer and apply the laws so enacted; and (iii) coercive agencies to guarantee the performance and enforcement of the relevant laws. Weber's concept of 'guaranteed law' (being a manifestation of state law) is instructive, referring as it does to a system where there exists a 'coercive apparatus' comprising 'one or more persons whose special task it is to hold themselves ready to apply specially provided means of coercion (legal coercion) for the purpose of norm enforcement'. See M Weber, *Economy and Society: An Outline of Interpretive Sociology* [*Wirtschaft und Gesellschaft: Grundriss der Verstehenden Soziologie*] (G Roth, C Wittich and others (trs and eds), Bedminster Press Inc 1968) 313. See also Weber's concept of 'legal order' at 317. In common law jurisdictions, of course, judicial institutions that carry out adjudicatory functions may actually have a hand in creating new law in the process. See generally R Cross and JW Harris, *Precedent in English Law* (4th edn, Clarendon Press 1991).

[72] See section 3.2.3 (this chapter, above); and see, in particular, H Ross, *Law as a Social Institution* (Hart Publishing 2001). See further, sections 4.5 and 4.6 (Chapter 4, below).

In what limited respects, then, might key elements of the institutional artefact of the legal right be thought to be constructed within the judicial consciousness in the context of a core or definitional account or explanation of the conditions of existence – or content or characteristics – of a legal right? An alternative – if narrower – way of framing the same question is to ask what could be assumed to reside within a hypothetical *Iudexian* perspective on legal rights that would not ordinarily reside within an imaginary (typical) right-holder's perspective? We have already touched upon a few aspects of that question. For instance, typical right-holders are unlikely to have a fully informed – and more importantly, *entirely accurate* – knowledge of the content and implications of their legal rights, even with the benefit of (the best available) legal advice. It is, however, theoretically possible for such a fully informed, detailed, encompassing and accurate knowledge to be assigned to 'a *Iudex*' on the hypothesis that an authoritative and final determination has been made in relation to, among other things, rights that are the subject of relevant, if, again, hypothetical, criminal, civil or other (eg declaratory) proceedings.[73]

There is an ontological dimension to this (as we have seen) if it is assumed that a judgment emerging from the highest appellate court of a legal system – which takes account of all applicable recognition criteria including tests of legal validity – incorporates, or by necessary implication encompasses, a finding that the rights that are the subject of the hypothetical judgment *exist as valid and enforceable rights of the legal system in question*. The finality of such a judgment ensures that the rights so declared – at any rate, pending any subsequent change in the law – subsist at least for the time being.[74] But whereas the securing of a *Iudexian*-type judgment corresponding to literally every right ever to have existed now or in the past in a particular jurisdiction would be a practical impossibility; it is tenable as a *theoretical* proposition.

It has been suggested (above) that a *Iudexian* perspective – if need be, suitably modified – might be seen as a necessary corrective to an explanatory frame of reference that would place the consciousness (awareness, understanding etc) of the right-holder at the centre of the theoretical enterprise. The day-to-day beliefs and imaginings of right-holders concerning the content and import of their rights

[73] It may seem that there might be no limits upon what could be assigned to the consciousness of 'a *Iudex*' on the basis that, being hypothetical, anything is possible, and only a failure of imagination could exert any constraining influence. In other words, why not, like Dworkin, use a 'Herculean' judge as a point of departure? (See this chapter at n 60.) A reason for *not* adopting a fully Dworkinian approach is, in a word, *verisimilitude*. Arguably, 'a *Iudex*' should, so far as possible, be modelled on a supreme court judge of 'ordinary competence', to borrow an idea from English case law. (See *Bolam v Friern Hospital Management Committee* [1957] 1 WLR 582, 586 (McNair J).) A paradigm with no counterpart in the real world would, it is suggested, lack practical utility and credibility. See Chapters 7 and 8, below.

[74] This is not to suggest that for any legal right to exist there is literally a need for a declaratory judgment of a supreme court. Clearly, the *Iudexian* perspective is a theoretical device – an idealisation – which reflects what happens in the real (legal) world in a tiny number of instances when the full appellate processes of a legal system are engaged. It is furthermore designed to assist understanding of legal rights from an empirically significant perspective that is not that of the right-holder.

(or rights that they believe they have) will rarely be informed or displaced by some perception in the right-holder's mind of a 'legally supreme' take on those (real or imagined) rights. So-called private citizens do not ordinarily spend all day poring over a casebook or a statute book. Day-to-day life carries on regardless. The mismatch between the consciousness of the right-holder, on one hand, and the judicial consciousness on the other (represented, in its highest form of expression, by a judgment of a supreme court) reflects, in the theoretical context, a dilemma. What if the viewpoint of typical right-holders yields an interpretation of the content of their right that is, legally, hopelessly misconceived and inaccurate?[75] What if the interpretation is so awry that the claimed 'right' does not represent even the beginnings of a valid right of the given legal system? Should not the risk of distortion which that threatens be reflected in a theoretical position that properly addresses that risk?

On the other hand, we might ask whether a *Iudexian* perspective is too esoteric, and too divorced from day-to-day reality, to account for legal rights in their ordinary setting. And this may in turn invite consideration of competing perspectives such as MacCormick's professorial perspective. The particular reason for giving primacy, in a theoretical setting, to a *Iudexian* perspective – and not that of a randomly-selected individual right-holder – is that such a perspective has legal cultural significance, especially in the context of common law jurisdictions. Such a perspective is also empirically significant for a number of reasons. One of these is that numerous agencies and bodies which may be invested with significant social power – such as government departments, tax authorities, local (government) authorities, police, prisons, the legal profession, lower courts and tribunals, and commercial and regulatory bodies – explicitly align their behaviour and activities with decisions and rulings emerging from courts and tribunals: particularly those in the higher echelons of the system. Many private individuals also so align their behaviour. Conventionally, common law legal method and legal culture adopt the practice of looking to the highest available authority in a given jurisdiction. That may be a decision of a supreme court, or of an appellate court or, in the absence of such decisions, a

[75] To use imagery that perhaps makes light of the situation, a right-holder may entertain the belief, and enter legal proceedings assuming, that the content of a (claimed or purported) right is a 'zebra', only to find, when the proceedings have run their course, that the right has been reconstituted by the court (and indeed, where relevant, by the highest court in the judicial system) as a 'giraffe'. In other words, what went in a 'zebra' (in the mind of the right-holder) came out a 'giraffe' (in the mind of the court). This is because (professionalised) judicial method and culture – at any rate, within the common law world – demand an approach that, in stating or restating, framing or reframing, legal rights and their content and import, ordinarily takes account of all relevant and applicable laws, legal rules, principles, doctrines and other standards, whether drawn from statute, case law or other authoritative sources. That interpretive process, particularly at the highest judicial level, plays out in a rarefied environment far removed from the circumstances of everyday life. Critically, the output of the highest court represents, for all legal purposes – that is, for purposes of the activation of apparatuses of enforcement and wider (eg doctrinal) purposes – *the* legally correct and unassailable statement of the content of any legal rights under consideration or in dispute.

ruling of a lower court or tribunal. As we have seen, Raz maintains as a core tenet of his version of interest theory that an individual has a legal right 'if it is recognized by law, that is if the law holds his interest to be sufficient ground to hold another to be subject to a duty'.[76] As a matter of institutional practice, the courts are the primary repository of rights recognised as legal rights. The ideas and beliefs of an individual right-holder are not. So, the ontological questions that Raz poses (tacitly, if not in actuality) – namely, *by what mechanism is recognition of a right as a legal right established?* – is arguably not satisfactorily addressed by a cluster of core tenets that, in setting the conditions of existence of a legal right, place only the holder of a legal right at the centre of theoretical enquiry, leaving no place for key institutional actors (the courts, the judiciary). If this critique holds for Raz's version of interest theory then it holds *a fortiori* for Hartian will theory which (certainly in the view of Neil MacCormick) seeks to *define* an important class of legal rights ('rights correlative to obligations') by reference to exertions of will, or the mental content, or the mental disposition, of individual right-holders.[77]

Undoubtedly all three theorists give recognition to the institutional character of legal rights in their wider writings.[78] What is called for, it seems, is a modest theoretical corrective that reflects the fact that the existence, content, scope, import and effect of legal rights are authoritatively declared by courts and tribunals, and, ultimately by the highest (supreme) courts of a given jurisdiction. In a purely theoretical context, this corrective might equate to the need to recast ontologically significant *core and definitional tenets* of both Hartian will theory, and the versions of interest theory advanced by Raz and MacCormick – in other words, the stated conditions of existence of legal rights – in the light of shifts of emphasis which an approach embodying a *Iudexian* perspective would necessitate.

3.4. Concluding Reflections

In following through the call for the development of a theoretical corrective, more can be said towards building upon and further developing, a *Iudexian* perspective. By adopting such an approach, albeit in the light of the limitations and qualifications already discussed, it may be possible to arrive at a more developed position regarding the extent to which key elements of the institutional artefact that is the

[76] J Raz, 'Legal Rights' (this chapter, n 24) 14.

[77] DN MacCormick, 'Rights in Legislation' (this chapter, n 16) 196.

[78] Few have explored this more extensively than MacCormick. See, for example, DN MacCormick, 'Law as Institutional Fact' (1974) 90 *Law Quarterly Review* 102; and N MacCormick, *Institutions of Law* (this chapter, n 54). For his part, Raz has left few stones unturned in his influential writings on the authority of law. See generally, for example, J Raz, *The Authority of Law: Essays on Law and Morality* (2nd edn, Clarendon Press 2009).

legal right might be thought of as a construct of – or, at any rate, as capable of being *constructed within* – the judicial consciousness at a supreme or ultimate court level. In pursuing that objective, some further groundwork is laid in the following two chapters, exploring the possibility of formulating a classical social theory context for discussion centred around particular perspectives on the work of Hans Kelsen and HLA Hart derived from an examination of the gravitational pull of classical (mainly Weberian) social theory on significant writings of those influential twentieth century legal theorists.

4

Hans Kelsen and the Gravitational Pull of Social Theory*

4.1. Introduction

This chapter considers aspects of the relationship between academic disciplines that have rarely been thought to be mutually compatible – on one hand the academic study of law (specifically, the theoretical part of jurisprudence, exemplified by Hans Kelsen's *Pure Theory of Law*) and on the other hand the academic study of human behaviour and society (specifically, interpretive sociology, exemplified by the writings of Max Weber). A passage from Nicola Lacey's biography of HLA Hart, *A Life of HLA Hart: The Nightmare and the Noble Dream*, sets the scene whilst prefacing lines of discussion to be pursued further here. The passage concerns the occasionally disputed question of whether Hart read, and was influenced by, the work of Max Weber.

> [T]here is an interesting question here about the influence of sociological thought on Herbert's [Hart's] work. On one occasion, John Finnis consulted one of Herbert's volumes of Max Weber and found it heavily annotated (as was the case with most of the books which Herbert read closely). Finnis later asked him on two separate occasions about Weber's influence on his account of the 'internal aspect of rules'. Herbert denied that any such influence existed, ascribing the origins of the idea instead to Peter Winch's *The Idea of a Social Science*. Finnis felt unable to respond to his denial by saying that he had seen the counter-evidence in his copy … Weber's discussion of the variety of ways in which conduct may be orientated towards certain maxims within an order is marked [on Hart's copy of *Max Weber on Law in Economy and Society*] 'Good, like it, likely to be useful'.[1]

Lacey suggests that Hart's seeming reluctance to acknowledge any intellectual debt to Weber may have originated in the fact that in the predominantly philosophical world that Hart inhabited, any indebtedness to Weber would have been unlikely to win Hart much praise. Hart may thus have been disinclined to be seen to have

* This chapter was previously published as H Ross, 'The *Pure Theory of Law* and Interpretive Sociology – a Basis for Interdisciplinarity?' in M Freeman (ed), *Law and Sociology* (Current Legal Issues 2005, vol 8) (Oxford University Press 2006) ch 5. (Some minor updating changes and corrections are made here.) Iain Stewart kindly commented on an earlier version of this chapter.

[1] N Lacey, *A Life of HLA Hart: The Nightmare and the Noble Dream* (Oxford University Press 2004) 230.

grounded key aspects of *The Concept of Law* – for instance, the 'internal aspect of rules' – on the work of a 'mere' sociologist, even if the sociologist in question, Max Weber, happened to be a towering figure in the development of sociology as an academic discipline as well as a renowned jurist in his own right. Indeed, Hart once commented with little sympathy on the – as he perceived it – apparent lack of intellectual and analytical rigour attending 'average' books on sociology:

> I think that no candid student of sociology could deny that, valuable as the insights have been which it has provided, the average book written in the sociological vein ... is full of unanalyzed concepts and ambiguities ... Both psychology and sociology are relatively young sciences with an unstable framework of concepts and a correspondingly uncertain and fluctuating terminology.[2]

The question whether Hart may have been influenced by Weber when writing *The Concept of Law* is touched upon in Chapter 5 in the context of a wider discussion of possible resonances between the writings of Hart and Weber.[3] The primary aim of this chapter is instead to examine a number of issues that arise from possible resonances between the writings of *Kelsen* and Weber. But the attitude of seeming mutual antipathy between leading analytical jurists and sociologists during the twentieth century – weighing, more often than not, against sociology – is an instructive point of departure for an assessment of a few aspects of the autonomous domain that Kelsen claimed to have created for his *Pure Theory of Law*. Kelsen's theory aspired to the possibility of severing legal theory from the influence of 'foreign' disciplines such as sociology, biology or ethics. Any attempt to 'mix' disciplines was 'syncretism' – without doubt, for Kelsen, a malign and futile undertaking.[4]

Yet the enduring question of whether the *Pure Theory of Law* – ostensibly purged of any 'syncretic' tendency – achieved the theoretical independence that Kelsen claimed for it assumed a paradoxical turn with Richard Tur's observation that Kelsen's theory is in fact a model for 'a collectivist *verstehende* sociology'.[5] Could such a paradigm of theoretical purity – on the face of it, perhaps, as far removed as it is possible to be from the spectre of interdisciplinarity or 'syncretism', to use Kelsen's more pejorative expression – possibly serve as a blueprint for an approach to theoretical jurisprudence embedded in interpretive sociology? That is a question the beginnings of which will be taken up in this chapter: without, however, engaging in extensive critical engagement with Kelsen's pure theory as

[2] HLA Hart, 'Analytical Jurisprudence in Mid-Twentieth Century: A Reply to Professor Bodenheimer' (1957) 105 *University of Pennsylvania Law Review* 953, 974.

[3] This is also examined in H Ross, *Law as a Social Institution* (Hart Publishing 2001).

[4] See H Kelsen, *Pure Theory of Law* (published as Hans Kelsen, *Introduction to the Problems of Legal Theory* [*Reine Rechtslehre. Einleitung in die rechtswissenschaftliche Problematik*]) (BL Paulson and SL Paulson (trs and eds), Clarendon Press 1992) (hereafter, in this chapter, '*Pure Theory of Law*') xxi and n 14. For usage of the expression 'syncretism', see M Eliade (ed), *The Encyclopedia of Religion* vol 14 (Macmillan Publishing Company, 1987) 218–227.

[5] R Tur, 'The Kelsenian Enterprise' in R Tur and W Twining (eds), *Essays on Kelsen* (Clarendon Press 1986) 149. See also 178, 182, n 4.

such. Tur's challenging observation will frame a discussion that seeks to develop that question from aspects of Kelsen's theory that are merely *suggestive* of areas for sociological theoretical development. So while the discussion will not pretend to 'dispose' of the question, some remarks will be made as to what might be learnt from the exercise of viewing some aspects of Kelsen's pure theory, albeit 'sociologically repositioned', as a model for 'a collectivist *verstehende* sociology'.

4.2. Kelsen's Reconstructed Legal Norm (*Rechtssatz*)

For reasons to be clarified, it is proposed to consider Tur's observation in the context of Kelsen's concept of the Reconstructed Legal Norm (*Rechtssatz*).[6] In the *Pure Theory of Law* the Reconstructed Legal Norm is a 'legal category' that is 'cognitively and theoretically transcendental in terms of the Kantian philosophy'. Kelsen uses this device in part to assist in the task of separating the 'legal world' from the 'moral world' and the 'natural world'.[7] Yet, more significantly for the present discussion, its status in the pure theory as 'hypothetical judgment' – and (thus, as will be argued) as the hypothesised outcome of the judicial interpretive process of conferring legal meaning on legally relevant facts and events – raises the question of whether, and how far, it can be regarded as capable of rendition as an 'artefact' of interpretive or *verstehende* sociology.

For Kelsen, the Reconstructed Legal Norm – the 'quasi-technical' *Rechtssatz* of the pure theory – represents a hypothetical judgment expressing the linking of a conditioning material fact with a conditioned legal consequence. This feature serves to distinguish legal norms from moral norms – facilitating Kelsen's project of carving out an autonomous domain for legal theory. Kelsen suggests that the notion that both legal and moral norms assume an imperative form – for instance, 'thou shalt not …' – had led 'traditional theory' into the error of assimilating one with the other.[8] As these were imperatives the question could be asked whether it was tenable to regard them as the 'same thing'. Kelsen's Reconstructed Legal Norm

[6] As the Paulsons observe, the expression 'Reconstructed Legal Norm' ('*Rechtssatz*') is Eugenio Bulygin's terminology for Kelsen's hypothetically formulated legal norm: see H Kelsen, *Pure Theory of Law* (this chapter, n 4) 23, n 20. See also *Pure Theory of Law*, 132–134. The Paulsons comment that the Reconstructed Legal Norm has a 'quasi-technical use' in the pure theory: *Pure Theory of Law*, Supplementary Notes, at 133. In other words, in Kelsen's usage in the specific context of the pure theory it is not (as is seemingly the case with other jurists and indeed with Kelsen in the context of other writings) a synonym for '*Rechtsnorm*' or 'legal norm'. It would appear to represent a theoretically conceived or 'ideal form' of the legal norm posited by legal science, as opposed to any instance of an actual legal norm existing in some enacted form or capable of extrapolation as a principle or doctrine from an authoritative source such as a judicial precedent. Bulygin had rendered the *Rechtssatz* as one type of 'reconstruction of a norm'. (See *Pure Theory of Law*, 133.)

[7] See generally H Kelsen, *Pure Theory of Law* (this chapter, n 4) 22–25.

[8] ibid 23 and, generally, Supplementary Notes at 133 where the Paulsons observe: 'Kelsen enquires into the 'ideal form' of the legal norm as part of his effort to distinguish legal norms from norms of morality. Earlier theorists had argued that both legal and moral norms have the same imperative form, a view Kelsen believes to be mistaken and a source of confusion generally about the law and morality'.

rendered that assimilation impossible because unlike the moral world a legal consequence – for instance a criminal penalty imposed by a court – is linked to a legal condition, for example, the commission of a crime. In the pure theory the legal norm is understood 'as a hypothetical judgment that expresses the specific linking of a conditioning material fact with a conditioned consequence':[9] 'If A commits an unlawful act, A ought to be punished'.[10] Such a linkage could not realistically be made in the moral world because – whatever the 'consequence' of a course of behaviour adjudged 'immoral' might be (manifested, for example, in outrage, criticism, censure, and so on) – that response is nowhere specifically predetermined as an outcome in the same sense that legal consequences would be in the legal world.

For Kelsen the conceptual act of linking a perceived act with the consequence that in law ought to follow it is an act of 'imputation'. In the pure theory this further differentiates the legal from the natural world: separating the 'is' from the 'ought'. According to this view, in the natural world *causality* is the linking principle between one natural event and another. Thus, according to Kelsen, laws of nature take the form: 'if *A* is, then *B* [causally] must be'. Laws of the legal world take the form: 'if *A* is, then *B* [normatively] ought to be'. Kelsen's doctrine of the Reconstructed Legal Norm allows him to connect 'legal condition and legal consequence' through the medium of the 'ought' as a (Kantian) 'category of the law' without reliance upon the linking principle of causality.[11]

Kelsen additionally places the legal norm – theoretically refashioned in the Reconstructed Legal Norm – in an institutional context. In that setting the legal norm has the additional property of being *coercive* in nature. It is a norm 'providing for coercion'.[12] The consequence attaching to a certain condition is 'the coercive act of the state – comprising punishment and the civil or administrative use of coercion'.[13] The behaviour constituting (say) a delict is set in the Reconstructed Legal Norm as the condition of a specified consequence. The positive legal system, as Kelsen observes, responds to this behaviour with a coercive act. The role of coercion in the law is to induce human beings to behave in a legally prescribed manner by means of the technique of visiting an 'evil' upon anyone who fails so to behave. Human beings thus treat this coercive act as an evil to be avoided. The 'efficacy' of the legal system lies in its potential to *motivate* behaviour towards the avoidance of relevant sanctions.[14]

[9] ibid 23.

[10] As Kelsen notes: 'Positive laws say: "if *A* is, then *B* ought to be"'. See H Kelsen, *Pure Theory of Law* (this chapter, n 4) 24.

[11] ibid 24–25.

[12] ibid 26.

[13] ibid.

[14] Kelsen, however, concedes a degree of uncertainty as to the motivational force of legal coercion and sanctions: 'It is difficult to decide whether human behaviour that conforms to the legal system is actually an effect of the notion engendered by the threat of a coercive act … The motive is by no means always fear of sanction or of the coercive act being carried out; there are religious and moral reasons for doing this or that, there is regard for social custom, concern about social ostracism, and very often there is simply no stimulus to behave contrary to law …' (See H Kelsen, *Pure Theory of Law*

Two strands of analysis in Kelsen's pure theory, each gravitating around the concept of the Reconstructed Legal Norm, are suggestive of the possibility of a sociological repositioning of that concept towards the *interdisciplinary* approach to theoretical jurisprudence alluded to in section 4.1 (this chapter, above).[15]

First, the Reconstructed Legal Norm as the 'hypothetical judgment' of a court of law can be taken to represent the hypothesised outcome of the judicial interpretive process of conferring legal meaning on legally relevant facts and events. Put another way, for a judge to conclude – from a determination of the fact that 'A is' – that 'B [legally] ought to be' is an interpretive act, ie an act of interpretation of the legal signification of fact A, or the legal consequences that should flow from a situation involving fact A. In other words, it is an act of conferring legal meaning or sense upon fact A. Just as importantly, it is 'social action' in Weber's sense, and for Weber, social action is the key concept, and the very object, of interpretive sociology.[16] (The connection with Kelsen's concept of 'legal meaning' (*rechtliche Bedeutung*) is briefly outlined in section 4.4 (this chapter, below).)

Secondly, Kelsen's acceptance of the *motivational* dimension of the legal norm prevents the legal norm from being viewed as some kind of 'causative force' – ie a 'cause' that *impels* an 'effect' such as in the case of (eg) a transfer of energy in the natural world. Instead – to the extent that the legal norm functions to motivate human behaviour – the norm comes to be incorporated into the meaningful (mental) processes of the actor so motivated. It does not, in other words, directly 'enact' behaviour in the sense (say) that a red billiard ball striking a green billiard ball causes the latter to move towards a side pocket.

Both of these strands of analysis run in parallel with comparable analyses in mainstream sociological writings. In particular, Kelsen appears to acknowledge subjective meaning (*Sinn*) – in the sense that Weber conceives this – as a

(this chapter, n 4) 31.) Weber similarly concedes uncertainty. A legal norm may be seen as merely *one* determinant of human behaviour in a given instance. There may be a range of degrees of consciousness of the influence exerted on action by determinants such as legal norms. See M Weber, 'The Concept of "Following a Rule"' in WG Runciman (ed), *Max Weber, Selections in Translation* (Cambridge University Press 1978) ch 5, especially 105.

[15] Such an approach – doubtless amounting to Kelsenian 'syncretism' – would surely be anathema to Kelsen. It is not, of course, suggested that the 'sociological repositioning' to be proposed here is anything other than an 'inventive step' or extrapolation from a Kelsenian point of departure towards a decisively *non-Kelsenian* theoretical end. Kelsen's pure theory by no means endorses, nor indeed does it necessarily imply, that proposed end. The expression 'interdisciplinary' suggests, on one hand, theoretical jurisprudence in the specific sense of Kelsen's *Pure Theory of Law*, and on the other hand, interpretive sociology in the sense of the sociological writings of Weber. For the latter, see generally, M Weber, *The Theory of Social and Economic Organization* (AM Henderson and T Parsons (trs and eds), The Free Press 1947); M Weber, *Economy and Society: An Outline of Interpretive Sociology* [*Wirtschaft und Gesellschaft: Grundriss der Verstehenden Soziologie*] (G Roth, C Wittich and others (trs and eds), Bedminster Press Inc 1968); and M Weber, '"Objectivity" in Social Science and Social Policy' ['*Die 'Objektivität' sozialwissenschaftlicher und sozialpolitischer Erkenntnis*'] in M Weber, *Max Weber On The Methodology of the Social Sciences* (EA Shils and HA Finch (trs and eds), The Free Press 1949) ch II.

[16] See this chapter at nn 31 and 38.

component, and the meaningful content, of human behaviour (or *legally directed* human behaviour, to be more specific): 'only the human being, endowed with reason and will, can be motivated by the notion of a norm, motivated to behave in conformity with that norm'.[17] Where law is viewed causally, lawmaking acts are looked upon as causes of certain effects, manifested in the regularity of patterns of human behaviour. But Kelsen holds that that ignores the normative nature of law. It deprives law of its normative *meaning*.

4.3. Subjective Meaning – *Sinn*

The possibility has been alluded to that subjective meaning – as the ideative component of human behaviour in the sense developed by Weber (ie *Sinn*) – resonates with aspects of Kelsen's pure theory. In particular, the concept of the Reconstructed Legal Norm or *Rechtssatz* – which along with other concepts such as the *Grundnorm*, lies at the centre of the Kelsenian enterprise of attaining a 'pure' legal science – when viewed as a 'hypothetical judgment' of a court of law, incorporates an interpretive element. Its function is as a kind of theoretical reconstitution of the acts of interpretation brought to bear by a judge on facts presented to a court in the context of a legal process. That interpretive element can be positioned within the wider frame of reference of Weberian interpretive sociology as a step towards the sociological repositioning of the Reconstructed Legal Norm attempted later in this chapter. As Julien Freund observes:

> Weber introduced the interpretive method. Some historians of sociology even refer to it as his 'interpretive sociology'. [Weber] was not the inventor of the interpretive method, nor even of the distinction between explaining (*erklären*) and understanding (*verstehen*). Droysen before him had tried to apply it to history, and Dilthey had made of it the cornerstone of the general methodology of the human sciences (*Geisteswissenschaften*). Weber's merit is to have elaborated this method conceptually with more rigor, applying it to sociology.[18]

Human beings act 'meaningfully' in reflecting upon and interpreting their *own* behaviour, for instance pursuing goals, acting evaluatively or conscientiously, participating in rule-following behaviour, engaging in political activity, and so on. Furthermore, they reflect upon and interpret the behaviour of *others*, often as a basis for their own behaviour.[19] Knowledge of these meaningful

[17] See H Kelsen, *Pure Theory of Law* (this chapter, n 4) 29. See also I Stewart, 'The Critical Legal Science of Hans Kelsen' (1990) 17(3) *Journal of Law and Society* 273, 283 (and articles cited at n 76). The 'paralleling' of analyses referred to here is considered in H Ross, 'Hans Kelsen and the Utopia of Theoretical Purism' (2001) 12 *King's College Law Journal* 174, 180–184.

[18] J Freund, 'German Sociology in the Time of Max Weber' in T Bottomore and R Nisbet (eds), *A History of Sociological Analysis* (Heinemann Educational Books Ltd 1978) ch 5, 167.

[19] As Freund further comments (ibid at 167): 'Unlike the naturalist, the sociologist does not work on inert matter, analyzing instead social relations and an activity (*Handeln*), that is to say forms of social

processes – the science of the mental component of human behaviour or 'human sciences' (*Geisteswissenschaften*) – was achievable through experience and understanding, using techniques that included re-experiencing, re-living and empathy. The empathic technique, in particular, involved the investigator in an introspective process, drawing on the investigator's own reservoir of experience, and bridging the gap between that and the subjective states of the actor under investigation by a kind of 'projection' into the 'expressions' of the actor. The greater the correspondence between the investigator's experiences and those of the actor under investigation, the more exhaustive and enlightened would be the investigator's understanding.[20]

Critically for Dilthey, *as for Weber*, knowledge of human behaviour – *scientific* knowledge, to be sure – proceeded from the attainment of a grasp of mental processes. It was legitimate to make mental processes, or 'objects' of the mind, possible candidates for theoretical discussion and ultimately *scientifically* valid knowledge. Thus the 'acquired structure of mental life' as Dilthey called it – which included valuations and purposes affecting behaviour, influencing ideas, organising impressions and controlling emotional states – could be abstracted from the pattern of experience and subjected to scientific scrutiny.[21]

Unlike Dilthey – indeed, *contrary* to Dilthey – Weber held that 'positivistic' methods – ie those appropriate to the natural sciences or *Naturwissenschaften* – still had to be brought to bear in the study of human behaviour as a critical *verifying* procedure so that the knowledge thus acquired could attain the 'dignity' of 'scientific' knowledge.[22] For his part, indeed, Kelsen exalted the value of 'purity' as a scientific aspiration. The detachment and objectivity implied by the notion of scientific 'purity' not only seemingly endowed Kelsen's theory with the 'prestige' of a 'natural science' such as theoretical physics, pure mathematics, and such like, but proclaimed legal science as a discipline *no less* detached, objective and prestigious

behavior which are always evolving with the constant development of circumstances. Since man's activity never ceases, he is not a passive object. Now, human activities, which produce social relations, are affected by a quality absent in natural phenomena *meaning*. To act socially is, on the one hand, to take part in a conventional context of institutions, customs, rules and laws, created by men with certain ends in mind; second, to give oneself a goal or an end which justifies the activity, and finally, to appeal to certain values, aspirations, or ideals as motives for activity. Meaning plays a role on all three of these levels'.

[20] See generally HP Rickman (tr and ed), *W Dilthey Selected Writings* (Cambridge University Press 1976) 172. For Dilthey, an 'expression' was any manifestation of mental content, foremost among these being basic modes of human communication such as language, gestures, facial expressions, and so on. So far as understanding (*verstehen*) is concerned, Dilthey comments as follows (ibid 170–171): 'The approach of higher understanding to its object is determined by its task of discovering a vital connection in what is given. This is only possible if the context which exists in one's own experience and has been encountered in innumerable cases is always – and with all the potentialities contained in it – present and ready. This state of mind involved in the task of understanding we call empathy, be it with a man or a work … If, therefore, understanding requires the presence of one's own mental experience this can be described as a projection of the self into some given expression'.

[21] ibid 170–171.

[22] See LA Coser, *Masters of Sociological Thought: Ideas in Historical and Social Context* (2nd edn, Harcourt Brace Jovanovich Inc 1977) 220–221.

than the sciences of the natural world. In the *Pure Theory of Law* Kelsen, if merely by implication and omission, appeared to exaggerate the dependence of sociology on 'positivistic' methods thereby de-emphasising the hermeneutic or *verstehende* dimension of (specifically) Weberian interpretive sociology.[23] (We might legitimately ask this: Is the Kelsenian argument in support of 'purity' and against 'syncretism' – eg in the sense of the 'uncritical mixing' of (say) sociology with the legal conceptual analysis characteristic of jurisprudence – somehow reinforced or fortified if a Comteian 'positivistic' sociology is presented as being characteristic of *sociology in general*?)[24]

In Weberian sociology the observation of regular relations – such as of 'cause' and 'effect' – between external events necessarily *complemented* the essentially hermeneutic task of discerning and interpretively understanding the subjective meanings underlying the behaviour of actors under investigation. For Weber: 'Immediate intuitions of meaning can be transformed into valid knowledge only if they can be incorporated into theoretical structures that aim at causal explanation.'[25]

4.4. Legal Meaning (*Rechtliche Bedeutung*) and *Rechtssatz*

Remarkably – for a jurist espousing an approach to the scientific analysis of the legal world that sought to eschew anything 'sociological' in character – one of Kelsen's key insights into the workings of the legal world resonates quite consonantly with

[23] See H Ross, 'Hans Kelsen and the Utopia of Theoretical Purism' (2001) 12 *King's College Law Journal* 174, 177–178. And see especially H Kelsen, *Pure Theory of Law* (this chapter, n 4) 13–14: '[C]ognition in legal sociology is not concerned with the legal norm *qua* specific meaning; rather, it is directed to certain events quite apart from their connection to norms that are recognized or presupposed as valid. Legal sociology does not relate the material facts in question to valid norms; rather, it relates these material facts to still other material facts as causes and effects.' The fact that this characterisation of legal sociology does not hold for *Weber's* sociology of law is probably recognised by Kelsen in his *General Theory of Law and State*. (See this chapter, n 24.)

[24] Elsewhere Kelsen presents a more balanced perspective on (Weberian) social theory. Kelsen argues in effect that to be fully intelligible 'sociological jurisprudence' is dependent upon and must, of necessity, incorporate the conceptual apparatus of 'normative jurisprudence'. But this concession requires some acknowledgment of the *ideative* dimension of sociology – doubtless, however, the sociology more characteristic of a Weber than of a Comte. See H Kelsen, *General Theory of Law and State* (A Wedberg (tr), Harvard University Press 1945). See particularly at 177 where Kelsen observes: 'Sociology of law, as defined by Max Weber, is possible only by referring the human behavior which is its object to the law as it exists in the minds of men as contents of their ideas. In men's minds, law exists, as a matter of fact, as a body of valid norms, as a normative system. Only by referring the human behavior to law as a system of valid norms, to law as defined by normative jurisprudence, is sociological jurisprudence able to delimit its specific object from that of general sociology.' For discussion of the historical context of sociological positivism in the sense of Auguste Comte see A Giddens, 'Positivism and its Critics' in T Bottomore and R Nisbet (eds), *A History of Sociological Analysis* (Heinemann Educational Books Ltd 1978) ch 7.

[25] LA Coser, *Masters of Sociological Thought: Ideas in Historical and Social Context* (2nd edn, Harcourt Brace Jovanovich Inc 1977) 220–221.

one of the key aims of Weberian interpretive sociology – attaining an understanding (and explanation) of the meaningful subjective states underlying human behaviour. For Kelsen a critical factor differentiating the domain of law from that of objects in the 'natural world' was that of *legal meaning* (*rechtliche Bedeutung*). In the legal world, as elsewhere, there are acts and events capable of being perceived by the senses and existing in time and space. But those same acts and events may also possess the quality of being endowed with immanent 'legal sense' or significance. Kelsen gives the example of the enactment of a statute:

> People assemble in a hall, they give speeches, some rise, others remain seated – this is the external event. Its meaning: that a statute is enacted.[26]

For Kelsen, meanings could be either subjective or objective and those meanings could – though need not necessarily – coincide. Legal meaning had 'objective', as opposed to 'subjective', status. Kelsen gives the example of a secret society acting outside the law but in accordance with its own norms. If the society condemns to death and then executes a traitor, the 'subjective' meaning of this act *to the society members* (interpreted by reference to the society's norms) is 'lawful' execution. But the same act also carries an 'objective' meaning – its *legal* meaning – which is that it constitutes *murder*, not the carrying out of a death penalty in the conventional legal sense. Legal meaning thus derives from a legal norm whose content, according to Kelsen, refers to a relevant act or event and 'confers' legal meaning upon it. According to this view acts are to be perceived as either 'legal' or 'illegal' to the extent that they correspond (or fail to correspond) to the relevant content of a valid legal norm. In the judicial setting when, in Kelsen's view, a judge establishes a material fact or concrete event as (for example) a *delict* his cognition is firstly directed towards the fact as an event in the 'natural' world. But the cognition becomes 'legal' through the application of a legal norm to the established material fact when the fact is interpreted *as* a delict: for example, as theft or fraud:

> The specifically legal sense of the event in question, its own peculiarly legal meaning, comes by way of a norm whose content refers to the event and confers legal meaning on it; the act can be interpreted, then, according to this norm. The norm functions as a scheme of interpretation.[27]

In his analysis of legal meaning in the *Pure Theory of Law* Kelsen uses strikingly similar imagery to that used by Weber. For instance Weber argues that we cannot 'understand' the behaviour of cells in the same way that we might 'understand' meaningful human behaviour. All we can hope for is to observe the relevant functional relationships and generalise on the basis of these observations.[28] Similarly, in differentiating the legal realm from the natural realm Kelsen notes that human

[26] See H Kelsen, *Pure Theory of Law* (this chapter, n 4) 8.
[27] ibid 10.
[28] M Weber, *The Theory of Social and Economic Organization* (AM Henderson and T Parsons (trs and eds), The Free Press 1947) 94.

behaviour can declare its own sense if expressed verbally, this being 'a special characteristic of the material dealt with in social and in particular in juristic knowledge'. However:

> A plant can convey nothing about itself to the research worker who is trying to define it. It makes no attempt to explain itself scientifically. But a social act can very well carry with it an indication of its own meaning.[29]

Kelsen's notion of legal meaning is more than anything the key to what might be loosely described as his '*Geisteswissenschaft* tendency' or, more specifically, his tendency to be drawn by the 'gravitational pull' of elements of Weberian interpretive sociology.[30] The act of bringing a vehicle to a halt at red traffic lights may have 'meaning' on many different levels: for instance, *safety* (as perceived by the driver and other road users), *utility* (as perceived by traffic-flow planners), *convenience* (as perceived by pedestrians who cross the road when traffic is halted). The specifically legal meaning of the act as perceived by (say) an *institutional* actor – for example, traffic police, judges, prosecutors – may be in terms of legal *necessity*: what is prescribed by the criminal law and is thereby rendered non-optional. The act is perceived as a legal duty or obligation. If it is a requirement of the law that drivers comply with a relevant legal norm then, in the view of law enforcement officials, they have no option but to comply. The legal meaning of the act of *stopping* at red lights is an act in compliance with the law. The legal meaning of the act of driving through the red lights *without stopping* is an act in violation of the law, an offence; a crime.

Whilst the Kelsenian idea of legal meaning or *rechtliche Bedeutung* appears to resonate with (eg) the 'Diltheian' assumptions underlying human sciences or *Geisteswissenschaften* and the Weberian idea of subjective meaning or *Sinn*, it generally lacks the explicit behavioural context of *Sinn*. For Weber *Sinn* is the ideative component of socially directed human behaviour (social action). It is the mental component of social action and includes anything that motivates the individual or makes a particular course of action meaningful.[31] Kelsen does not

[29] See H Kelsen, 'The Pure Theory of Law' (1934) 50 *Law Quarterly Review* 478, 480–481. See also H Kelsen, *Pure Theory of Law* (M Knight (tr), 2nd edn, University of California Press 1967) 2–3.

[30] Note that Kelsen, in *Pure Theory of Law* (this chapter, n 4) at 15, explicitly maintains that legal science is a human science in the sense of *Geisteswissenschaft*: 'In marking off the law from nature, the Pure Theory of Law seeks the boundary between the natural and the ideal. Legal science belongs not to the natural sciences, but to the human sciences'. ('*Indem die Reine Rechtslehre das Recht gegen die Natur abgrenzt, sucht sie die Schranke, die die Natur vom Geist trennt. Rechtswissenschaft ist Geistes-, nicht Naturwissenschaft.*') On the other hand, as the Paulsons observe (ibid 131): 'Kelsen himself … had never been content with the notion of *Geisteswissenschaft* either, and he in fact rarely appeals to it … He prefers a distinction between *normative sciences* and *natural sciences*'. The Paulsons also point out that Kelsen's appeal to *Geisteswissenschaft* in *Pure Theory of Law* at p 15 is 'one such rarity'. In H Ross, 'Hans Kelsen and the Utopia of Theoretical Purism', (2001) 12 *King's College Law Journal* 174, there is fuller discussion of *other* ways (ie beyond resonances of *Geisteswissenschaften*) in which Kelsen's *Pure Theory of Law* appears to run analytically parallel to the sociological writings of, and the scientific approach adopted by, Max Weber.

[31] According to Weber: 'Action [in the general sense of human behaviour] is social in so far as, by virtue of the subjective meaning attached to it by the acting individual (or individuals), it takes account of the behaviour of others and is thereby oriented in its course'. See M Weber, *The Theory of Social and Economic Organization* (AM Henderson and T Parsons (trs and eds), The Free Press 1947) 88.

explicitly identify legal meaning as the exclusive preserve of *any specific actor* though, of course, he does refer to what is cognised by a *judge* when an event is interpreted in legal terms:

> His [a judge's] cognition becomes legal at the point at which he brings together the material fact he has established and the statute he is to apply; that is to say, his cognition becomes legal when he interprets the material fact as 'theft' or 'fraud'.[32]

Arguably lying behind legal meaning is a set of 'behavioural' assumptions which, if not made, would render the notion unintelligible. Yet paradoxically for Kelsen legal meaning is seemingly taken to be 'conferred' upon a human act or other event '*by*' a legal norm, the norm being thereby severed from human agency:

> The specifically … legal meaning [of an event], comes by way of a norm whose content refers to the event and confers legal meaning on it.[33]

Taking this as a mere curiosity of expression arguably *could* allow it to be lightly disregarded because no one really believes that legal norms as such actually 'do' things: literally 'confer', truly 'interpret', and so on. But if the point is pressed further it becomes possible to discern a genuine substantive objection to Kelsen's approach: an objection that, ultimately, finds its expression in the idea that the pure theory engages in a kind of 'reductionism' of human behaviour *to* legal norms. On that basis legal norms virtually take on the role of 'protagonist', to use Donald Galloway's expression.[34] This manipulation arguably retards the pure theory's slide wholesale towards (say) a sociology of judicial action. But it creates a distortion that is scarcely compensated for in terms of the 'payoff' that comes from the idea that the pure theory defines an autonomous realm for legal science, entirely independent of 'foreign', non-law disciplines. Seen

[32] *Pure Theory of Law* (this chapter, n 4) 11. This cognitive dimension of the judicial role has greater significance in the context of the line of argument to be pursued later in this chapter. From the point of view of Kelsen's pure theory, however, the act of a judge's cognising material facts legally – for example, interpreting a factual scenario as 'theft' or 'murder', and so on – is seemingly offered by Kelsen as merely one, albeit a particularly characteristic, instance of legal cognition. Arguably Kelsen could have maintained that a lawyer (*any* lawyer) arguing their case before a court of law, or giving legal advice to their client, engages in no less characteristic an act of legal cognition. Indeed *anyone* 'applying' a law to a factual situation engages in such legal cognitive acts. The main point of departure of the argument pursued in section 4.5 (this chapter, below), however, is that certain judicial cognitive acts – specifically those of judges sitting in the hierarchically supreme court of a given jurisdiction – have a special status as authoritative and final acts of legal cognition: in other words, authoritative and final acts of conferring legal meaning upon relevant facts established in evidence. More significantly, the hierarchically supreme judicial actor personified in the conceptual device referred to as *Iudex* becomes a special repository of final, authoritative legal meaning for the legal system in question. See further, sections 3.2.3 and 3.3 (Chapter 3, above), sections 4.5 and 4.6 (this chapter, below), generally Chapter 8 below; and sections 9.2 and 9.4 (Chapter 9, below).

[33] *Pure Theory of Law* (this chapter, n 4) 10. And see the entire passage from *Pure Theory of Law* cited, this chapter, at n 27.

[34] See D Galloway, 'The Axiology of Analytical Jurisprudence: A Study of the Underlying Sociological Assumptions and Ideological Predilections' in TW Bechtler (ed), *Law in a Social Context: Liber Amicorum Honouring Professor Lon L Fuller* (Kluwer 1978) 84. Roger Cotterrell makes an essentially similar point in R Cotterrell, *The Politics of Jurisprudence: A Critical Introduction to Legal Philosophy* (Butterworths 1989) 112.

literally, Kelsen almost assigns *to* legal norms the task of 'conferring' legal meaning upon acts or events. The norm is 'made flesh', so to speak, and dwells among those who inhabit that autonomous legal universe that Kelsen strives diligently to construct in the *Pure Theory of Law*. The interpretive act of conferring legal meaning – which would ordinarily be seen as a task capable of performance only *by a human being* (eg by a judge) – is virtually usurped by the legal norm itself. By that reckoning Kelsenian legal meaning appears *not* to reside with a human being, remaining in some unspecified or metaphorical sense, bound up with the very material of the legal norm itself and analytically disjoined from human agency. The Reconstructed Legal Norm, as a *legal norm*, sits uncomfortably with this scenario becoming merely the *outcome* of a humanly mediated process, with the process itself and its human agent receding into the background. Just as legal norms in general 'confer' legal meaning (per Kelsen), so the Reconstructed Legal Norm 'confers' legal meaning, albeit (one assumes) as a mere end result of a human interpretive process.

On the other hand, and quite significantly (as has been noted),[35] Kelsen's pure theory does on occasion cede the interpretive process to the judiciary: for example, a judge's interpreting a fact as a delict by applying an appropriate legal norm to the fact.[36] When that happens – when, in other words, Kelsen's notion of legal meaning manifests itself as an integral part of the judicial role – the *Pure Theory of Law* becomes markedly 'Weberian'. If the judicial role involves interpreting human behaviour or other events by reference to legal norms – the norms being 'applied' to the relevant behaviour or events – then a judge acts subjectively meaningfully in so interpreting the behaviour or events.[37] Judges' interpretive acts – the subjective meaning of their action – contain as a component the evaluative legal meaning that they confer upon the events that are the object of the proceedings before the court. In that setting – and on a less literal reading of Kelsen – the Reconstructed Legal Norm holds out the possibility of embodying, albeit as a 'hypothesis', the interpretive judicial *activity* of conferring legal meaning on legally relevant facts and events. In short, a conclusion or judgment of the type 'If A commits an unlawful

[35] See this chapter at n 32.

[36] *Pure Theory of Law* (this chapter, n 4) 11.

[37] A judge acts 'subjectively meaningfully' in rendering a judgment and in carrying out the other duties and responsibilities entailed in the judicial role. The fact that judges are subject to a range of institutional demands and constraints, necessitated by judicial office, that require them to act in conformity with the norms and conventions of established judicial practice qualifies the judges' (judicial) behaviour no less as *subjectively* meaningful behaviour, and something that may be the subject of the techniques of 'understanding' applied by interpretive sociology. However, not only is the judge an actor within the collectivity that is the judiciary; the judiciary is itself an organ of the collectivity that is government (in the widest sense). The behavioural patterning, and regularities, to be found within these collectivities suggest the need for sociological analysis based not *only* on the (*genuinely* 'subjective') subjectively meaningful behaviour of individual role-occupants (eg of any given judge) looked at in isolation – in so far as it is possible to view such behaviour in 'isolation' – but of the *inter-subjectively* meaningful behaviour patterns prevailing within the collectivity in question (eg characteristic of any given *judiciary*).

act, A ought to be punished' – which the Reconstructed Legal Norm could exemplify in any hypothetical case – necessarily involves an attribution of legal meaning in the Kelsenian sense of *rechtliche Bedeutung* because the relevant unlawful act *means* (in law, and in the perception of the judge) that a punishment ought to be exacted against A.

By that account Kelsen's concept of the Reconstructed Legal Norm or *Rechtssatz* implies not only the *activity* of 'judging' or rendering a judgment – social action in Weberian sociology[38] – but hints at the presence of the *human being* lying behind this activity, ie the *judge*. Kelsen's concept of the Reconstructed Legal Norm thereby connects strikingly with his concept of legal meaning since the conferment of legal meaning is literally part and parcel of the activity of formulating a judgment such as one framed in terms of: 'A ought to be punished'. According to Kelsen the very idea of an 'unlawful act' takes on a new significance in the pure theory. The events constituting the unlawful act 'become' the condition, defined by the Reconstructed Legal Norm, for the imposition by the state of a coercive act:

> From the standpoint of immanence, which the Pure Theory of Law supplants, the concept of the unlawful act undergoes fundamental reinterpretation. What is dispositive for the concept of the unlawful act is not the legislator's motive, not the circumstance that a material fact is undesirable to the norm-issuing authority … Rather, what is dispositive is simply and solely the position that the material fact in question has in the reconstructed legal norm, namely, its position as the condition for the specific response of the law, for the coercive act (the action the state takes).[39]

[38] The concept of 'social action' is integrally related to the concept of 'sociology' in Weber's thinking: 'Sociology … is a science which attempts the interpretive understanding of social action in order thereby to arrive at a causal explanation of its course and effects. In 'action' is included all human behaviour when and in so far as the acting individual attaches a subjective meaning to it … Action is social in so far as, by virtue of the subjective meaning attached to it by the acting individual (or individuals), it takes account of the behaviour of others and is thereby oriented in its course'. See M Weber, *The Theory of Social and Economic Organization* (AM Henderson and T Parsons (trs and eds), The Free Press 1947) 88.

[39] *Pure Theory of Law* (this chapter, n 4) 26–27. The interpretive act involved in bringing an 'unlawful act' within the terms of the Reconstructed Legal Norm – by any common-sense account a judicial cognitive act of conferring legal meaning on, ie *interpreting*, the events constituting the act (assuming the matter has come before a court for judicial determination) – seems to *inhere in* the Reconstructed Legal Norm. Kelsen's pure theory thus maintains its focus on the legal norm (specifically the Reconstructed Legal Norm) whilst other phenomena equally worthy of consideration such as the nature of judicial reasoning and the interpretive mental processes involved in applying legal norms to factual situations are subordinated. The question is whether an overtly professed interest in (for example) 'mental processes' would cause the pure theory to slide inexorably towards psychology or sociology, thereby compromising its 'purity' and forcing it into 'syncretism'. Kelsen seems to think so when he maintains this: 'The Pure Theory of Law does not look to mental processes or physical events of any kind in seeking to cognize norms, in seeking to comprehend something legally. To comprehend something legally can only be to comprehend it *as* law'. (See *Pure Theory of Law* (this chapter, n 4) 11, emphasis added.) Yet the pure theory's manifest interest in such matters as the motivational force of legal norms, acts of legal interpretation (in the sense of legal meaning or *rechtliche Bedeutung*), human behaviour, judicial cognitive acts, and so on, surely creates difficulty for Kelsen in plausibly maintaining this 'purist' theoretical stance.

4.5. Sociological Repositioning of the *Rechtssatz*

The scene has been set for a sociological repositioning of Kelsen's Reconstructed Legal Norm (ie *Rechtssatz* in its quasi-technical sense)[40] as an 'artefact' of interpretive sociology.[41] The stimulus for this repositioning is twofold.

First, there is the connection maintainable between the Reconstructed Legal Norm and the specifically Kelsenian concept of legal meaning (*rechtliche Bedeutung*), taken with the tendency of *both* of those concepts to 'gravitate' towards interpretive sociology in ways already indicated. The Reconstructed Legal Norm operates as a link between Kelsen's somewhat behaviourally disengaged notion of legal meaning (*rechtliche Bedeutung*) and a behavioural environment in which the interpretive process inhering in the Kelsenian idea of legal meaning may be appropriately situated. Given that the Reconstructed Legal Norm represents a hypothetical judgment – that is, the outcome of the judicial interpretive process – it can be seen as the end result of an act of conferring legal meaning upon a particular factual situation. The Reconstructed Legal Norm incorporates the (ideal) form: 'if A is, then B ought to be'. So, imagining an example where 'A is' – such as a factual scenario where Max, say, drives through red traffic lights without stopping – the legal meaning of this is an act in violation of the criminal law or an offence to which a specific penalty is attached. The legal consequence, seen as the imposition of a penalty or 'coercive act', is represented by the words '… then B ought to be' in Kelsen's formulation, ie a penalty ought to be imposed on Max. The legal norm applicable to this factual situation thus provides a means of interpreting, or conferring legal meaning upon, relevant conditioning facts, ie facts A ('if A is …'). The act of conferring legal meaning on human behaviour is also social action in the Weberian sense of action (or human behaviour) that 'takes account of the behaviour of others and is thereby oriented in its course'.[42]

Secondly, Kelsen's stance that legal norms have a *motivational* dimension perhaps self-evidently carries the Reconstructed Legal Norm (as a legal norm in 'ideal' form)[43] towards the domain of sociology given the close connection

[40] See this chapter at n 6.

[41] Some elements of the thinking underlying the idea of the Reconstructed Legal Norm are treated as pointing towards, or serving as a point of departure for, a sociological (and basically *non-Kelsenian*) analysis of legal meaning. Essentially, what is proposed is the repositioning of the Reconstructed Legal Norm within a sociological theoretical setting. In the first place, the Reconstructed Legal Norm is taken to function as a kind of theoretical reconstitution of the acts of interpretation brought to bear by a judge on facts or events established by a court in the context of legal processes (which is tolerably consonant with Kelsen's analysis in the *Pure Theory of Law*). But, in the second place, the interpretive reconstitution in question *in its theoretically repositioned form* is taken to correspond not to the interpretive acts of just *any* hypothetical judge; but to those of a hypothetical judge sitting at – and conferring conclusive legal meaning from the standpoint of – the highest hierarchical level of a legal system: in other words, a theoretical construct such as *Iudex*, discussed in sections 3.2.3 and 3.3 (Chapter 3, above) and considered more generally at greater length in Chapter 8, below.

[42] See M Weber, *The Theory of Social and Economic Organization* (AM Henderson and T Parsons (trs and eds), The Free Press 1947) 88.

[43] See the Paulsons' observations in *Pure Theory of Law* (this chapter, n 4) 132–133.

between the idea of noncausal motivation and that of subjective meaning or *Sinn* in interpretive sociology.[44] Yet a cautionary note must be sounded here. The Reconstructed Legal Norm, as we know, takes the form of a hypothetical judgment that represents the 'norm' emanating from the judicial activity of – as Kelsen sees it – 'concretising' a general norm in its application to the facts of the case in hand.[45] In this context a legal norm is seen as a judgment or order of the court; a kind of judicial command: 'Party X ought to pay compensation to Party Y' or 'Pay compensation to Party Y' [addressed to Party X]. In taking this form the legal norm is always in a sense *ex post facto*: the end result of the institutional judicial activity of passing judgment. The difficulty here, of course, is that if the legal process necessitates the 'application' of a norm to a factual situation presented to a court, a legal norm that is imagined or hypothesised to be the outcome of judicial 'application' would require to have had some *antecedent* existence – or to have taken some form other than that of a judgment – in order to have been 'applied' in the first place. If a legal norm taking the 'ideal' form of the Reconstructed Legal Norm is actually constituted as an outcome of judicial 'application', what ideal form does the 'legal norm' take which pre-exists that 'application' – and which 'motivates' an actor to conform with it? Looked at another way, what form does a 'legal norm' take when it is seen as the reason, justification or basis for the hypothetical judgment of the court? It cannot surely *be* the judgment of the court.[46]

The combination of the notion of legal meaning or *rechtliche Bedeutung* and that of hypothetical judgment reflected in Kelsen's Reconstructed Legal Norm together suggest the possibility of the development of a unified theoretical construct whose principal function is to facilitate the ready identification, and sociological analysis, of any legal institutional structure that serves, among other things, as a repository of final, conclusive and authoritative legal meaning in a given legal system.[47] And that possibility suggests at least one sense in which a sociologically repositioned conception of the Reconstructed Legal Norm can be formulated as a model for 'a collectivist *verstehende* sociology' of law, towards the realisation of the implications of Richard Tur's observation, mentioned at the outset.

With a view to repositioning Kelsen's Reconstructed Legal Norm within a sociological frame of reference, then, a new question arises for consideration. If the Reconstructed Legal Norm represents a hypothetical judgment expressing the linking of a conditioning material fact with a conditioned legal consequence, *whose* judgment, albeit hypothesised, can it be said to represent? Kelsen is silent as

[44] Weber allows for the possibility of a necessary causal element to the things that motivate human behaviour whilst Kelsen resolutely denies this causal element in the legal context, promoting instead an explanation based around the notion of 'imputation'. See *Pure Theory of Law* (this chapter, n 4) 23–24.

[45] ibid 67–68.

[46] It is beyond the scope of this chapter to attempt a resolution of this conundrum.

[47] Given that the construct in question is *Iudex* (see this chapter at n 41), the sociological repositioning of Kelsen's Reconstructed Legal Norm attempted here serves, more accurately, to reinforce and validate the theoretical assumptions underlying that construct.

to the position in the judicial hierarchy occupied by the hypothetical judge whose task is to render the hypothetical judgment corresponding to the Reconstructed Legal Norm. Indeed, the demands of theoretical 'purism' – resulting in the kind of 'reductionism' of human behaviour to legal norms that has previously been mentioned – would no doubt count against the pursuit of that line of enquiry. In Kelsen's pure theory the 'god in the machine' is always a norm – or, in the context of the present discussion, the Reconstructed Legal Norm – not a person: a human being; an occupant of judicial office; a judge. The specifically 'judgmental'[48] dimension of the Reconstructed Legal Norm is thus given no special status in the pure theory.[49] As such, the hypothetical judgment represented by the Reconstructed Legal Norm may or may not *conclusively* dispose of hypothetical legal proceedings. Conceivably, then, if the hypothetical judgment is taken to be that of just *any* judge, sitting in *any* court, it may not *ex hypothesi* conclusively dispose of a case. In principle, a hypothetical judge sitting in a court at (say) the lowest level of the judicial hierarchy could render a hypothetical judgment capable of formulation in terms that *appear* to equate to a Kelsenian 'Reconstructed Legal Norm': ie 'A ought to be punished', or 'A ought to pay £10,000 to B'. But if that hypothetical judgment were thereupon *ex hypothesi* to be appealed to a higher court it may be overruled or modified by that higher court: eg 'A ought to be acquitted', or 'A ought to pay £5,000 to B'. Unless the judgment represented by the Reconstructed Legal Norm is taken to correspond to the hypothetical judgment of the *highest* court of a jurisdiction – ie a court beyond which no appeal is legally competent – the hypothetical judgment enshrined in the Reconstructed Legal Norm will always be contingent and potentially liable, albeit *ex hypothesi*, to revision (eg overruling, reversal, modification, etc) by a hypothetical higher court until the highest court is reached. This argument, of course, takes for granted that the hypothetical legal system applies a principle of *res judicata* whereby a disputed issue or judgment of a court that has been appealed to a supreme or final level in the court hierarchy is exhaustive of the disputed issue and legally conclusive of any issues of law or fact in dispute. (The criminal law equivalent is also assumed.)

Overall, the heuristic value of the Reconstructed Legal Norm is questionable in so far as the status of the hypothetical judgment that it represents is unspecified or is taken to be that of a court *other than* the highest court of the hypothetical legal system concerned. An acceptable conception of the Reconstructed Legal Norm, arguably, is one that hypothesises a conditioned legal consequence that is *not* liable to judicial revision, ie a consequence that is, for purposes of the hypothetical

[48] In this context 'judgmental' denotes 'cognitively judgmental' as opposed to evaluatively or normatively judgmental. In other words, if the legal norm (and by extension the Reconstructed Legal Norm) is, in Kelsenian terms, 'a hypothetical judgment that expresses the specific linking of a conditioning material fact with a conditioned consequence' (*Pure Theory of Law* (this chapter, n 4) 23) then it has a 'judgmental component' in so far as it represents or corresponds to the hypothetical judgment of a hypothetical judge.

[49] That is, in terms of the hierarchical position of the hypothetical judge who *ex hypothesi* renders a hypothetical judgment.

legal system in question, final and conclusive. Any other hypothesis implies a situation where the legal meaning of a fact – ie the 'conditioning material fact' of the Reconstructed Legal Norm – is not, or is not *necessarily*, its conclusive legal meaning for purposes of the hypothetical legal system in question. And such a hypothesis, if taken to be part of the Reconstructed Legal Norm, must surely rest the Reconstructed Legal Norm on a shifting and unstable foundation. To maximise its theoretical utility, arguably, the Reconstructed Legal Norm must be taken to correspond to the hypothetical judgment of a judge sitting in the *highest* court of a given legal system – an 'ultimate judge', a '*Iudex*' – because only such a judgment conveys a *legally settled* interpretation of the matters of fact and law hypothetically at issue. That, however, introduces into the Reconstructed Legal Norm a human element (ie the 'ultimate judge') that, by compromising the theoretical 'purity' of the theory, places it beyond the reach of that theory. Kelsen – possibly in order to avoid such a dilemma – engages in the kind of 'reductionism' of human actors to 'norms' already noted.[50] As the 'norm' is the pre-eminent concept in the pure theory – not human actors such as supreme court judges, hypothetical or otherwise – the pure theory's focus is fixed on 'the norm', and on normative constructs such as the Reconstructed Legal Norm. Yet despite Kelsen's insistence that the pure theory 'does not look to mental processes or physical events of any kind',[51] key concepts in the pure theory such as the Reconstructed Legal Norm do necessarily presuppose the human beings – and the human activities and attendant 'mental processes', eg interpreting, judging, engaging in legal reasoning, and so on – lying behind them.[52] Hence, certain of the characteristics of these human, institutional activities – and their attendant 'mental processes' – must, it is contended, be treated as part of – or, for that matter, part of a sociologically repositioned variant of – the Reconstructed Legal Norm. The fact that Kelsen predicates the Reconstructed Legal Norm upon a form of social action – the activity of judging – without literally analysing that activity[53] does not necessarily weaken the explanatory power of the Reconstructed Legal Norm. On the contrary, it furnishes a basis for the essentially different exercise of examining the implications of the idea that the embodiment of authoritative legal meaning – the final, most authoritative acts of legal interpretation in a given legal system – factually resides with a judge, or 'collectivity' of judges, sitting in the highest court of appeal of that legal system. For the purpose of the sociological repositioning of Kelsen's Reconstructed Legal Norm the conditioned legal consequence embodied in the Reconstructed Legal Norm is taken to represent the final, conclusive and authoritative legal meaning of relevant conditioning material facts and thus, in a sense, constitutes an 'emanation'

[50] This point is touched upon above, with support for the position being drawn from writings of Roger Cotterrell and Donald Galloway. See this chapter at n 34.

[51] See *Pure Theory of Law* (this chapter, n 4) 11; and this chapter at n 39.

[52] An essentially similar point is made in section 4.4 (this chapter, above).

[53] Presumably such an analysis might, in Kelsen's judgment, have carried the pure theory 'perilously' close to a 'contaminating' discipline such as sociology or psychology.

from, or hypothetical judgment of, a judge, or 'collectivity' of judges, sitting in the highest court of appeal of a given hypothetical legal system.[54]

The key point to emerge from the sociological repositioning of the Reconstructed Legal Norm suggested here – which has a bearing on the broader strategy of exploring the idea that Kelsen's pure theory represents a model for a 'collectivist *verstehende* sociology' (of law) – is this. The exercise of repositioning the Reconstructed Legal Norm in a sociological context prompts, among other things, consideration of where the final, most authoritative acts of legal interpretation in a given legal system factually reside. In other words, it prompts reflection upon what can be regarded as an 'ultimate repository of legal meaning' in a legal system. Yet the idea which has been advanced that a judge, or 'collectivity' of judges, sitting in the highest court of appeal of a legal system represents the ultimate repository of legal meaning in that system is merely a point of departure for consideration of the sense in which the definitive legal interpretation or legal meaning of material facts or events might be regarded as being in some sense within the domain of a *collectivity*.

Let us begin with the assumption that in theoretical terms the judge, or 'collectivity' of judges, sitting in the highest court of appeal of a legal system – and whose interpretive acts represent an ultimate repository of legal meaning for the system in question[55] – can be personified as a single, hypothetical, ultimate judge. Elsewhere, such a judge – styled '*Iudex*' – is constructed as a Weberian ideal type.[56]

[54] This theoretical position, though probably 'non-Kelsenian', does not derogate from the primary function of the Reconstructed Legal Norm to enable an analytical distinction to be made, on one hand, between legal norms and moral norms and, on the other, between (normative) laws of the legal world and (causal) laws of the natural world (ie of natural science). In fact it reinforces that function. In the first place, it emphasises the institutional basis of legal meaning – which is taken to reside in 'judgmental' processes underlying judicial action, albeit at the supreme hierarchical level: interpreting, judging, engaging in legal reasoning, and so on. There are probably few counterparts to this in the 'moral world'. Whilst in the second place, it preserves, or at any rate does nothing to undermine, the idea of the 'normativity' of laws of the legal world when contrasted with laws of the natural world. For there is no suggestion that laws of the legal world equate in any way to the causal laws of the natural sciences. Indeed the very opposite is implied by Kelsen's view that legal science is a 'human science' or *Geisteswissenschaft*, in so far as Kelsen consistently holds to that view.

[55] This is true in two senses. First, the collected judgments, opinions and decided cases in *written form* that emerge from the relevant court represent – at any given time, and to the extent not superseded – a set of definitive statements of the law on the issues of law and fact concerned. Secondly, if a matter is litigated or appealed to the highest hierarchical level of a legal system or system of courts the resulting interpretive acts of the judges at that level will represent – at least for a period of time after delivery of the judgment – the most legally definitive and conclusive resolution or disposal of the litigated or appealed issues of law and fact that the system is competent to produce.

[56] See H Ross, *Law as a Social Institution* (Hart Publishing 2001) 98–103. That a Weberian ideal type can incorporate behavioural characteristics of a *plurality* of actors – in this case, distilling the interpretive acts of (say) judges sitting as a final court of appeal (which could, in turn, incorporate the decisions and judgments of many judges at different hierarchical levels of the system, over many years) – is clear from Weber's methodological writings: 'An ideal type is formed by the one-sided *accentuation* of one or more points of view and by the synthesis of a great many diffuse, discrete, more or less present and occasionally absent *concrete individual* phenomena, which are arranged according to those one-sidedly emphasized viewpoints into a unified *analytical* construct (*Gedankenbild*)'. The possibility of a hypothetical actor (*Iudex*) – which 'telescopes' the interpretive acts of pluralities of judges – can readily

In short, in acting individually and personally *Iudex* acts subjectively meaningfully in the fullest sense of 'subjective', ie personal to that unique individual. But in *also* acting in the capacity of an ultimate supreme court judge *Iudex* conforms to institutional conventions that render judicial acts 'non-subjective' – or, in some sense, 'inter-subjective'. Thus, when *Iudex* has (say) an informal conversation about the weather with a newsvendor there is nothing that makes that an official or judicial act of *Iudex*.[57] Nor is there any sense in which that, or any similar, course of social action should necessarily be regarded as establishing any kind of pattern of conduct for any group of individuals constituting a 'collectivity'. Yet there are at least two particular senses in which the legal meaning conferred by *Iudex* on material facts established in legal proceedings might be regarded as being in some sense within the domain of a 'collectivity'.

First, and most obviously, a judgment may represent the collective legal opinion of a quorum of judges sitting in a legal system's highest court of appeal. For all legal purposes – regardless of the fact that each judge will normally differ in the precise terms on which a judgment is formulated – the judgment will represent the decision of the court and a unitary basis on which the case is to be disposed of. Secondly, and more importantly, judgments made at a supreme hierarchical level of a legal system – or judgments otherwise constituting the 'best authority' in the absence of a judgment of the hierarchically supreme court – usually, or at any rate in jurisdictions applying a *stare decisis* principle, represent a precedent for the disposal of new cases arising in the future that raise the same, or similar, issues of fact or law. That has the effect of generating what might be loosely termed a 'collective mindset' around the judgments in question, which may be discernible from an examination of the subjective component of the behaviours of individuals constituting particular interest groups or 'collectivities'. Examples of the groups in question include: lower court judges, court and other government officials, lawyers, police, prison officers, court enforcement officials, teachers of law, compliance officers in financial institutions and other large commercial organisations, charities – basically any individual, or any organisation, with a concern to comply with or advise on laws that affect their or others' interests or apply to their or others' areas of activity. The 'hypothesis of the ultimate judgment' arguably comes to be incorporated in the behavioural patterns of a variety of groups of actors.[58] (These groups may be regarded as discrete 'collectivities'.)

be accommodated in Weber's analytical construct. See M Weber, '"Objectivity" in Social Science and Social Policy' ['*Die 'Objektivität' sozialwissenschaftlicher und sozialpolitischer Erkenntnis*'] in M Weber, *Max Weber On The Methodology of the Social Sciences* (EA Shils and HA Finch (trs and eds), The Free Press 1949) ch II, 90 (Weber's emphasis).

[57] A similar argument is advanced in this chapter at n 37.

[58] See H Ross, *Law as a Social Institution* (Hart Publishing 2001) 102–103: 'Now *because* judicial action mobilises coercive and sanction-exacting forces in society, countless individuals, in attempting to imagine the legal consequences of their action and that of others "out of court" … may strive to adopt the same perspective as an "ultimate judge". In this way an individual may attempt to visualise what the legal result would be of a given course of action, or of *any* legally relevant "facts", based on the hypothesis of what the legal result would be *if* a dispute were to arise or criminal proceedings

Unless the 'mental processes' used by those involved in *definitively and conclusively* interpreting or judging relevant material facts by reference to the applicable laws of a given legal system (ie *Iudex*) are in some sense replicated by other groups with a vested interest in potential legal outcomes, those others may act – or may advise others to act – in a way that is unduly productive of legal, commercial or other risk; or that is unlawful or illegal; or that is civilly or criminally actionable, and so on. All such groups have an interest in attempting to visualise – in some cases by taking appropriate legal advice – what a hypothetical ultimate judge might hold the legal outcome to be, whether under criminal or civil law, if a particular course of conduct were to be pursued. The modes of behaviour predicated on the hypothesis of the ultimate judgment depend in turn on the factual reality of the higher appellate judiciary of a legal system acting consistently in the sense of conforming by and large to the conventions attending the senior judicial role, and acting within the general environment of the legal culture of that 'collectivity'. It is only through consistency of action through manifested, inter-subjective understandings and motivations that anything approximating to the actings of a judicial 'collectivity' can be inferred.

Empirically, the possibility of formulating 'a collectivist *verstehende* sociology' of law around the hypothetical judicial behaviour of a theoretical construct such as *Iudex* depends on whether 'collectivities' – pluralities of human actors from a variety of different interest groups – do *in fact* possess a 'collective mindset' that replicates the legal cognitive acts, and legal reasoning processes, of an ultimate supreme court judge: a judge with characteristics – when viewed in a theoretical context – of 'a *Iudex*'. That is a task that could be undertaken by interpretive sociology.[59] Often enough the evidence will simply lie in the fact that individuals

were to be brought following the occurrence of certain "events" and this dispute or those proceedings were to be litigated or tried to a point in the system where a final and authoritative determination was made. In other words, what would be the rights, duties, powers and liabilities of the litigants or, as the case may be, criminal suspects?'

[59] From the standpoint of traditional Weberian scholarship, the very possibility of a 'collectivist' – as opposed to a conventional 'individualist' – *verstehende* sociology of law might suggest on the face of it an unwarranted departure from that tradition and also, arguably, a contradiction in terms. What is being advanced in this chapter, however, is not a departure from any conventional Weberian position. Rather, this possibility merely elaborates on the idea that certain aspects of the behaviour of a 'collectivity', such as the higher appellate judiciary, constituted as a plurality of particular, office-holding individuals, is recognisably patterned, or oriented in consistent ways, and is in principle capable of theoretical reconstruction as an ideal type. And to that end Weberian methods are to be applied – methods that draw on the empirical data furnished by the many concrete individual phenomena derivable from the modes of behaviour characteristic of relevant pluralities of actors who constitute identifiable 'collectivities'. *Iudex* represents the beginnings of one such theoretical reconstruction and, as already indicated, this ideal type could be the product of (to use Weber's words) a synthesis of 'a great many diffuse, discrete, more or less present and occasionally absent *concrete individual* phenomena' – ie specifically, a distillation of the 'judgmental actings' of each of a plurality of individual judges who constitute the 'collectivity' of the higher appellate judiciary. Moreover, and more importantly, beyond *Iudex* there lies the possibility of developing *other* distinct ideal types that arguably incorporate a '*Iudexian* mindset' – one that, beyond legal theory, would seek to replicate the outlook and approach of an ultimate supreme court judge. (Examples include the typical defence lawyer, or typical prosecution lawyer, or typical court official, or typical tax inspector, and so on.) Those actors may be found to adopt '*Iudex*-like' modes of thought

and groups do factually seek, and act upon, legal or other professional advice that, consciously or otherwise, applies what would be recognisable as the hypothesis of the ultimate judgment: 'if I act in manner X, what would the legal consequence of that be, in the opinion of an 'ultimate judge' delivering a judgment in the highest court of appeal in the jurisdiction in question?' This is not vastly different from the formula built into Kelsen's Reconstructed Legal Norm: 'if A is, then B [legally] ought to be'; or, phrased as a question, 'if A is, what ought B [legally] to be?'.

4.6. Concluding Reflections

In this chapter an attempt has been made to demonstrate how Kelsen's concept of the Reconstructed Legal Norm or *Rechtssatz* (as formulated in the *Pure Theory of Law*), and the Kelsenian concept of legal meaning or *rechtliche Bedeutung*, gravitate in striking ways towards (Weberian) interpretive sociology despite Kelsen's apparent use of the Reconstructed Legal Norm, and the linked idea of 'imputation', to *resist* the gravitational pull of sociology (albeit 'sociology' in its Comteian or 'positivistic' form). As a point of departure for a discussion of where the final, most authoritative, acts of legal interpretation in a given legal system factually reside the Reconstructed Legal Norm was sociologically repositioned as an 'artefact' of interpretive sociology. The key question was what could be regarded as an 'ultimate repository of legal meaning' in a legal system? It was suggested that a judge, or 'collectivity' of judges, sitting in the highest court of appeal of a legal system represented an 'ultimate repository of legal meaning' of that system. And for purposes of sociological analysis, the suggestion was that that judge (or judges) could be personified as a Weberian ideal type – the theoretical construct, *Iudex*.

This line of argument, however, was merely part of a broader strategy to explore the sense in which Kelsen's pure theory could, in the words of Richard Tur, be regarded as a model for 'a collectivist *verstehende* sociology' of law. In its most focused form the contention here was that the Reconstructed Legal Norm – as a key concept of the *Pure Theory of Law* – assisted in the task of identifying, constructing or, for that matter, validating the theoretical strategy of constituting *Iudex* as an 'ultimate repository of legal meaning' in a hypothetical legal system. From that point of departure, it would become the task of interpretive sociology to investigate or explore whether, and the extent to which, discrete groups or 'collectivities' seek to replicate the standpoint, or some variant of the standpoint, of an ultimate supreme court judge: a judge with characteristics – when viewed in a

in certain areas of their activity. And likewise, discrete groups, or 'collectivities', of such actors could provide an empirical basis for the construction of ideal types associated with *their* behavioural modes, and modes of thought, applying Weberian principles of type-construct formation. The idea of 'collectivism' alluded to in this chapter is thus neither collectivism in the conventional sense nor is it intended to stand, in any sense, in opposition to methodological individualism. Generally on methodological individualism, see S Lukes, 'Methodological Individualism Reconsidered' (1968) 19(2) *British Journal of Sociology* 119.

theoretical context – of 'a *Iudex*'. Such a standpoint might be of practical utility when attempting to visualise what the legal outcome might be – whether under criminal or civil law – if any particular course of conduct were to be pursued. And these 'collectivities' could provide a basis for the construction of ideal types associated with *their* behavioural modes. In theoretical terms – and in the context of theorising – the task of 'visualising' legal outcomes from a '*Iudexian*' standpoint would take the form of the hypothesis of the ultimate judgment – 'if I act in manner X what would *Iudex* hold to be the legal consequence of that?'

More generally, has a basis been identified, or a case been made, for interdisciplinarity in the sense of the present discussion? If 'syncretism' (in the pejorative 'Kelsenian' sense) denotes the *uncritical mixing* of disciplines, or beliefs, or philosophies, then self-evidently no case for an attempted 'syncretism' of the theoretical part of jurisprudence (exemplified by Hans Kelsen's *Pure Theory of Law*) and interpretive sociology is a case worth making. A different proposition altogether is the development of a genuinely interdisciplinary approach to legal theory in which the insights of the theoretical part of jurisprudence and interpretive sociology can be combined in a way that better enhances the explanatory power of each of those fields of enquiry. If the outcome is an improved understanding of the social phenomenon of law then the case for that is probably too obvious to be worth making.

5

HLA Hart and the Gravitational Pull of Social Theory

5.1. Introduction

In Chapter 2 the quest for a theoretical context in which to accommodate HLA Hart's version of will theory – a context defined in his broader theoretical writings – proved inconclusive. It was recognised that, in an important chapter of *Essays on Bentham* (chapter VII),[1] focusing on the use of will theory to explain the core class of legal 'rights correlative to obligations', there was little evidence of Hart's deployment of his pioneering ordinary language approach. By contrast Neil MacCormick, when seeking to explain the nature of legal rights generally, appeared to integrate his version of interest theory more coherently with aspects of his institutional theory of law. In other words, MacCormick's institutional theory could be viewed as a viable theoretical context in which to accommodate elements of his distinctive version of interest theory.[2] In the result, MacCormick's institutional theory and his version of interest theory (in so far as they are separable and distinguishable) could be viewed as mutually supportive theoretical undertakings.

Yet if Hart, in what was undoubtedly an important essay outlining a version of his will theory of rights, appeared to neglect aspects of his ordinary language philosophical approach, it is clear that that approach had never been fully exhaustive of the possibilities for theoretical enquiry available to Hart in the wider context. These possibilities might have been realised either in Hart's more general investigations into the nature and key characteristics of legal phenomena (for instance, in *The Concept of Law*) or in his more particular analyses of core legal concepts such as legal rights and legal powers (for instance, in *Essays on Bentham*). Take Hart's famous description of *The Concept of Law* as an 'essay in descriptive sociology'.[3] This leaves little room for doubt that his social scientistic tendency – equating

[1] See HLA Hart, *Essays on Bentham: Jurisprudence and Political Theory* (Clarendon Press 1982) (hereafter, in this chapter, '*Essays on Bentham*').

[2] See generally DN MacCormick, 'Law as Institutional Fact' (1974) 90 *Law Quarterly Review* 102 (hereafter, in this chapter, 'Law as Institutional Fact'); and N MacCormick, *Institutions of Law: An Essay in Legal Theory* (Oxford University Press 2007) (hereafter, in this chapter, '*Institutions of Law*').

[3] HLA Hart, *The Concept of Law* (2nd edn, Clarendon Press 1994) (hereafter, in this chapter, '*The Concept of Law*') v.

to the 'gravitational pull' exerted by social theory in some shape or form – might have impacted in some way in the context of his most important theoretical and philosophical writings.

In this chapter, mirroring the parallel exercise undertaken in Chapter 4 in relation to Kelsen's *Pure Theory of Law*, it is proposed to examine a few aspects of the gravitational pull exerted by classical social theory – with the focus on Weber (or on the more generic philosophy of the social sciences) – on elements of *The Concept of Law*, with some consideration of the possible implications of that for approaching an understanding of Hart's analysis of legal 'rights correlative to obligations', as this is specifically presented in chapter VII of *Essays on Bentham*. Given that that analysis is grounded more in a particular version of will theory inspired by Bentham's writings than in social theory as such, that should not inhibit asking the question whether there is anything to be gained from viewing Hartian will theory in a context originating in, but extending perhaps beyond the narrower parameters set by, *The Concept of Law*, when viewed as an essay 'in sociology'. In other words, even if the outline of a sociological approach to law is discernible in one key writing – namely, *The Concept of Law* – it may still be possible to detect resonances of such an approach in other important writings if the evidence of such an approach is clear enough, or if (alternatively) a sociological reading of the relevant writings is tenable.

5.2. Social Theory and Tensions Around the Idea of 'Descriptive Sociology'

In her biography of Hart – as we have seen in Chapter 4 – Nicola Lacey comments speculatively on the possible influence of Weber on Hart's theoretical writings.[4] Later, in a lecture at the University of Texas,[5] Lacey returns to this theme – indeed, to the wider theme of whether *The Concept of Law* could be regarded as an 'essay in descriptive sociology', and the still wider question of whether, ultimately, sociology as an academic discipline (and its methods) might be regarded as being too fundamentally incompatible with Hart's philosophical world view – encompassing his Oxonian ordinary language philosophical approach – for Hart to have engaged more intensively with sociological analysis in his exploration of law and its conceptual and institutional structures. From her further 'excavations' of Hart's private papers – in fact, in a notebook from the late 1980s, on which she comments in both the Hart biography and the Leon Green (Texas) lecture – Lacey uncovers a startling admission. Nearly three decades after its publication Hart evidently acknowledged having been mistaken in describing *The Concept of Law* as an essay

[4] See N Lacey, *A Life of HLA Hart: The Nightmare and the Noble Dream* (Oxford University Press 2004) 230.

[5] See N Lacey, 'Analytical Jurisprudence versus Descriptive Sociology Revisited' (2006) 84 *Texas Law Review* 944 (hereafter, in this chapter, 'Analytical Jurisprudence').

in descriptive sociology, suggesting instead that he should have contented himself with the more modestly scaled claim that the book provided, as Hart puts it, the '*normative concepts required* for a descriptive sociology'.[6] But even if his position had shifted since writing *The Concept of Law* Hart had evidently not abandoned the idea that the book might have, or might still have, something to offer a 'descriptive sociology' of law – a primarily descriptive theory of law professing a sociological dimension.

Lacey undertakes a critical examination of the opposition maintainable between an enquiry grounded in analytical jurisprudence (analytic philosophy) and one grounded in descriptive sociology: the discussion being framed in terms of 'X versus Y' in the title of her lecture. In a key argument, Lacey highlights a tension between the perceived generality and universality of outcome implied by the former and the perceived particularity and empirical facticity of outcome implied by the latter. Viewing Hart's project as an attempt to produce 'a general, universally applicable and fundamentally descriptive theory of law',[7] Lacey argues in effect that that outcome would (or doubtless would in Hart's view) have been more readily realisable from an enquiry employing conventionally philosophical analytical techniques than from one employing conventionally sociological analytical techniques. The more 'sociological' an enquiry may be, the less universal it can be (so the argument goes). If philosophy and sociology are looked to to provide the best descriptive account of a phenomenon such as law that holds for all of its manifestations, any concession to the empirical particulars attending the sociological part of the enquiry may disrupt the imperative for universality. As Lacey comments: 'the richer the characterization of law's social basis – its institutional forms, its various types of rules, its role, and its functions – the less plausible is any theoretical claim to universality'.[8] In short, the more particular and empirically informed an analysis is – focusing, say, on historical, geographical or cultural particulars – the more likely it is to be derailed by inconvenient facts and truths: in other words, 'disruptive reality'. For it is precisely those particulars that move the analysis away from theoretical generalities.

Lacey concludes this line of argument by suggesting that, in seeking to maintain the claim to universality (through philosophy) as well as to empirical integrity (through sociology, for example), Hart ended up with 'the worst of both worlds'.[9] By identifying, and in some measure analysing, a number of the specific features characteristic of a 'centralized state legal order' in *The Concept of Law* Hart had compromised universality.[10] This may be because state law is only one type of law and may differ from other types such as (for example) customary law, Canon Law, international law, feudal law. The (philosophical) imperative for universality

[6] ibid 949 (emphasis added). (HLA Hart, *The Concept of Law* (this chapter, n 3) v.)
[7] ibid 955.
[8] ibid 957.
[9] ibid 957.
[10] ibid 957–958.

(arguably dictated by the conventions of a philosophically grounded analysis) seemingly prevented Hart from undertaking an empirically and sociologically adequate account of the institutional apparatuses of law, in the sense of the organised institutional structures that carry out specifically legal or law-related tasks, including courts of law and judiciary, police, lawmakers and legislatures, the legal profession, and so on. As Lacey points out, Hart 'failed to deliver any rich paradigm of law's institutional form'.[11]

We need only reflect upon the three 'remedies' that Hart promotes as 'curative' of the 'defects' that *ex hypothesi* beset so-called 'pre-legal' communities to appreciate the narrowness of this aspect of Hart's theoretical outlook.[12] Instead of pointing to the need to introduce relevant institutional structures – such as law-creating bodies and dispute-resolution and enforcement mechanisms (such as police and civil enforcement agencies) – Hart suggests that all that is necessary is that rules (*secondary* rules) should be brought into being. The implication is that, once the necessary rules have been established, everything else falls into place without more ado. But that analysis clearly offers an empirically impoverished account of social and institutional reality. The need for appropriate institutions and agencies – in other words, structures of organised and professionalised roles, offices and behaviours – is, for all practical purposes, left out of Hart's account.

Are these shortcomings necessarily accountable to the adoption of an approach that is more philosophically weighted than sociologically inclined; and is the imperative to pursue the former approach necessarily incompatible with the pursuit of the latter? The question of necessary incompatibility appears to take as an implicit premise that sociology generally lacks an adequate philosophical underpinning. Yet (for instance) Weberian sociology has deep philosophical roots in German Idealist philosophy (of which Wilhelm Dilthey was a significant exponent – see Chapter 4, above). Weber was also significantly influenced by adherents to the Southwest German School of Neo-Kantianism who included Wilhelm Windelband and Heinrich Rickert.[13]

Apart from the obvious fact that the foundations of Weberian sociology are by no means philosophically impoverished, it is possible that Hart held to the view that by focusing significant attention on *rules* in *The Concept of Law* he might avoid the need to engage with some of the empirical complexities surrounding organised institutional structures such as legislatures, courts, prosecutorial authorities,

[11] ibid 958.

[12] See HLA Hart, *The Concept of Law* (this chapter, n 3) ch V, especially 91–99.

[13] See generally HH Bruun, *Science, Values and Politics in Max Weber's Methodology* (expanded edition, Routledge 2016); and J Freund, 'German Sociology in the Time of Max Weber' in T Bottomore and R Nisbet (eds), *A History of Sociological Analysis* (Heinemann Educational Books Ltd 1978) ch 5. See also D Käsler, *Max Weber: An Introduction to his Life and Work* (P Hurd (tr), Polity Press 1988) ch 6. See further, A Bergstraesser, 'Wilhelm Dilthey and Max Weber: An Empirical Approach to Historical Synthesis' (1947) 57(2) *Ethics* 92, 102–110; and J Habermas, *Knowledge and Human Interests* [*Erkenntnis und Interesse*] (JJ Shapiro (tr), Heinemann Educational Books 1972) ch 7.

and so on, which might have precipitated a type of analysis that lay beyond the frame of reference he had set for his enquiry. The Hartian exploration of rules – seen essentially as a linguistic phenomenon – not only fitted readily and tidily with conceptual analysis characteristic of major branches of philosophy, but also happened to align with ordinary language philosophy of the kind practised by JL Austin and others in the mid-twentieth century. So, a reductivist approach to the complex phenomenon of law – where law and its framework of key concepts is reduced to rules – must have seemed, on the face of it, worth pursuing. And once committed to that outlook, Hart could make the confident, if exalted, claim that the idea of a union of primary and secondary rules, central to *The Concept of Law*, is the 'key to the science of jurisprudence'.[14] Yet if Hart's approach appears to have prevented him from giving a proper or fuller account of the institutional dimension of law,[15] Neil MacCormick was seemingly less inhibited in that regard, despite his writing being positioned within a tradition of philosophising not entirely dissimilar to that of Hart, which likewise eschewed any overtly sociological account of relevant phenomena.[16]

There are nonetheless features of Hart's general outlook, identifiable in *The Concept of Law* and elsewhere, that resonate with aspects of Weberian social theory. For instance, according to Lacey, Hart, writing in a private notebook in late 1985 – which is significantly later than the 1950s to early 1960s timeline for writing and publishing *The Concept of Law* – touches upon a debate which Weber had memorably explored in his essay, '"Objectivity" in Social Science and Social Policy'.[17] A key aspect of the debate centred on the perceived need for the social scientist to make selections from the infinite plurality of the observed or observable world – eg of data, factual matter, expressions of opinion, specifics of phenomena under investigation – making reference to guiding principles designed to inform those selections. John Finnis had commented on this (for instance) in *Natural Law and Natural Rights*,[18] though Hart, in his notebook, attributed the insights in question

[14] See HLA Hart, *The Concept of Law* (this chapter, n 3) 6, 81. (Hart was echoing John Austin's words.)

[15] As Lacey comments: 'The capacity of a fuller articulation of the institutional dimensions of law to compromise universality perhaps also explains Hart's notoriously under-developed account of adjudication: an under-development which allowed Dworkin, unencumbered by this particular methodological postulate, to provide a more textured account to which Hart had difficulty in responding'. See N Lacey, 'Analytical Jurisprudence' (this chapter, n 5) 958.

[16] In his characterisation of law as 'institutional fact', MacCormick does not, however, subject legal institutions *as such* to investigation. He acknowledges that the law operates through institutional entities such as courts and legislatures, which he recognises as structures of organised human behaviour; but his primary scholarly interest is in rule-clustered 'artefacts' or 'things' created out of rules – for example the 'institution' of marriage or of contract. This serves to reorient his enquiries along similar lines to Hart's. See sections 2.3.2, 2.3.3 and 2.4 (Chapter 2, above).

[17] M Weber, '"Objectivity" in Social Science and Social Policy' ['*Die 'Objektivität' sozialwissenschaftlicher und sozialpolitischer Erkenntnis*'] in M Weber, *Max Weber On The Methodology of the Social Sciences* (EA Shils and HA Finch (trs and eds), The Free Press 1949) ch II (hereafter, in this chapter, '"Objectivity" in Social Science').

[18] See J Finnis, *Natural Law and Natural Rights* (Clarendon Press 1980) ch I, especially 4–18. (Weber is mentioned at various points in that chapter.)

primarily to Joseph Raz.[19] What Weber had recognised – influenced in part by writings of Heinrich Rickert – was that in making selections, and abstracting particulars, from the boundlessness of reality, the investigator would be guided by values adapted to the nature of the subject matter under observation, informed by the type of problems being investigated and the questions requiring to be addressed. (This was the so-called 'value-relation' which preoccupied Weber in some of his most significant writings; and is to be contrasted with the idea of 'value freedom'.)[20]

On the basis of a few observations in one of Hart's notebooks can it be said that Hart (unlike Weber) in any sense *wrestled* or *struggled* with these concerns? It appears from Lacey's research that Hart simply and straightforwardly observes that the need for description in analytical writings '… will involve *selection* of some elements … and the selection will be *evaluative* (not morally) in sense of answerable to some criteria of *importance*'.[21] By contrast, as a practical proposition, Weber elevated the problem of selection to a methodological principle, one approach to this being the formulation of specially designed concepts that, in their most developed form, were not advanced as a description of reality but were intended to provide an 'unambiguous means of expression to such a description'.[22]

While it is clear that Hart, in his most significant writings, does not adopt an explicit approach to the task of selection, there is evidence of Hart's making use of techniques *facilitative of selection* that would not have seemed out of place in a Weberian analysis, or indeed that of other social theorists. For instance, Weber develops and utilises the analytical construct (*Gedankenbild* or 'mental construct') of the *ideal type* which, he argues, brings 'order to chaos'.[23] While Hart does not explicitly develop an abstract concept along the same lines, a resonance of the Weberian ideal type makes an appearance in *The Concept of Law* in the guise of an imaginary absolute monarch, Rex (alias Rex I) and his imagined successors, Rex II and Rex III. Hart employs the device of the 'Rex dynasty' (as he calls it)[24] towards critiquing a number of aspects of Austinian legal theory with the aim of outlining more credible and convincing theoretical positions than those attempted by John Austin. In the discussion to follow, it is instructive to give consideration to that and other resonances (intended or otherwise) of Weber's work in Hart's writings – with the particular focus on *The Concept of Law* – for the insight that this affords not

[19] Lacey points out that Finnis in fact covered the point more 'forcefully' than Raz. See N Lacey, 'Analytical Jurisprudence' (this chapter, n 5) 955.

[20] See T Parsons, 'Max Weber 1864–1964', (1965) 30(2) *American Sociological Review* 171, 173–174. See also HH Bruun, *Science, Values and Politics in Max Weber's Methodology* (expanded edition, Routledge 2016) 85. And see further, T Parsons, 'Value-Freedom and Objectivity' in O Stammer (ed), *Max Weber and Sociology Today: Explorations in Interpretative Sociology* (Basil Blackwell 1971) 33.

[21] N Lacey, 'Analytical Jurisprudence' (this chapter, n 5) 955 (Hart's emphasis). The same point is made in N Lacey, *A Life of HLA Hart: The Nightmare and the Noble Dream* (Oxford University Press 2004) 351.

[22] See M Weber, '"Objectivity" in Social Science' (this chapter, n 17) 90.

[23] ibid 78.

[24] See HLA Hart, *The Concept of Law* (this chapter, n 3) 63.

only into aspects of Hart's work generally, but salient aspects of the position that Hart develops on *rights* through his distinctive will theory.[25]

5.3. Resonances of Weber in Hart's Key Writings

In the discussion to follow, consideration is given to a variety of resonances of Weberian sociological analysis to be found in Hart's writing. These include the following. (A) Consideration is given to the possibility of viewing Hart's Rex archetype as – or as possessing at least some Weberian characteristics of – a social science ideal type. (B) An attempt is made to 'critically juxtapose' Hart's critical reflective attitude (the 'internal aspect' of rules) with Weber's concept of rule-following behaviour. (C) Consideration is given to Hart's key theoretical position that legal rules are to be viewed as *social rules*. (D) Consideration is given to the idea, and implications of the idea, that the (Hartian) legal right and the exercise of a legal right are to be viewed as an instrument or manifestation of *social power*. Finally, (E) brief consideration is given to Hart's apparent (limited and non-explicit) use of a device resembling a social science typology (principally the concept of the *municipal legal system*).

Needless to say, there is overlap between these topics so that, in places, unavoidably the discussion may appear somewhat artificially demarcated. Moreover, the fact that Hart makes no mention of Weber in *The Concept of Law* implies that elements of the discussion to follow are necessarily speculative and *developmental* in the sense that Hartian positions may in some cases be taken to be merely the starting point of a discussion that develops the core ideas further: such as, in the direction of social theory.

5.3.1. Rex Archetype Viewed as an Ideal Type

In the model of the original position which he outlines in *A Theory of Justice* John Rawls invites us to engage in a thought experiment where key characteristics are to be assigned to hypothetical 'contracting parties' – imaginary individuals who have the task of entering into a social contract with others similarly tasked.[26] Here,

[25] In 'Analytical Jurisprudence' (this chapter, n 5), Lacey comments that it is her intention to use her engagement with Hart's biography and intellectual legacy 'as the jumping-off point for a further examination of the relationship between the analytic and sociological approaches to legal theory, and of the relative contributions of philosophy, history, and the social sciences to our systematic understanding of the nature of law' (at 946). She maintains as one of her key conclusions that 'a view of analytic and sociological jurisprudence as mutually dependent would be more intellectually satisfactory than the philosophical imperialism that currently characterizes the field' (948).

[26] J Rawls, *A Theory of Justice* (Oxford University Press 1973) ch III. 'The intuitive idea of justice as fairness is to think of the first principles of justice as themselves the object of an original agreement in a suitably defined initial situation. These principles are those which rational persons concerned to

Rawls draws upon the social contractarian tradition of classical political philosophy, which reached a high point during the Enlightenment era.[27] The primary objective is for Rawls's hypothesised contracting parties to agree upon principles of justice that regulate the basic institutions of the society they inhabit. Among other things, the choice of principles is made from behind a 'veil of ignorance'.[28] The assigned characteristics of ignorance serve in part to define the position of the imaginary contracting parties. They are, for instance, blinded to factors such as class position and social status, personal wealth (or poverty), and intelligence and strength, and such like.[29] In short, they are taken to be oblivious to anything that could allow bias to enter into the choice of principles of justice.[30] In outlining relevant characteristics of contracting parties, Rawls concedes not only the influence of moral philosophy, but social theory as well.[31] And it is clear that, in so doing, Rawls perhaps edges several steps beyond any concession towards social theory that Hart would have been prepared to make. As we have seen, Hart readily embraces Oxonian analytic philosophy; but at the same time he expresses scepticism as to the value of sociological analysis.[32]

In advancing a scenario involving hypothetical contracting parties positioned behind a veil of ignorance while following 'a procedure familiar in social theory', Rawls aligns himself with an established tradition involving the use of abstractions in political philosophy, social theory, economics and other disciplines, some of which happen to resemble Weberian ideal types.[33] But just as, in the absence of an

advance their interests would accept in this position of equality to settle the basic terms of their association. … It is clear … that the original position is a purely hypothetical situation. Nothing resembling it need ever take place.' (ibid 118, 120)

[27] See, for instance, Jean-Jacques Rousseau, *Discourse on Political Economy and the Social Contract* (C Betts (tr and ed), Oxford University Press 1994); and T Hobbes, *Leviathan* (E Curley (ed), Hackett Publishing Co Inc 1994).

[28] J Rawls, *A Theory of Justice* (Oxford University Press 1973) 136–142.

[29] ibid 137.

[30] This, of course, is only the 'tip of the iceberg' of Rawls's hypothetical contracting parties. And those imaginary parties, in turn, are merely one constituent part of the more encompassing original position.

[31] J Rawls, *A Theory of Justice* (Oxford University Press 1973) 119–120: '[O]ne follows a procedure familiar in social theory. That is, a simplified situation is described in which rational individuals with certain ends and related to each other in certain ways are to choose among various courses of action in view of their knowledge of the circumstances … [T]he conception of the original position embodies features peculiar to moral theory … [The original position] … is a state of affairs in which the parties are equally represented as moral persons'.

[32] See generally HLA Hart, 'Analytical Jurisprudence in Mid-Twentieth Century: A Reply to Professor Bodenheimer' (1957) 105 *University of Pennsylvania Law Review* 953.

[33] For instance, in economics, there is the archetypal *homo economicus*: see J Persky, 'Retrospectives: The Ethology of Homo Economicus' (1995) 9(2) *The Journal of Economic Perspectives* 221. In sociology, Ralf Dahrendorf has written about the so-called *homo sociologicus*: see R Dahrendorf, *Homo Sociologicus* (Routledge & Kegan Paul 1973). See also AC Zijderveld, *The Abstract Society: A Cultural Analysis of Our Time* (Penguin Books Limited 1974) 31 who comments thus: 'Ralf Dahrendorf, one of the leading contemporary European sociologists, wrote an essay on role theory, *Homo Sociologicus*, in which he discusses the paradox that man, as he is experienced in everyday life, appears to be different from the artificial man as he is analysed and interpreted by the social scientist. … [The social scientist] … constructs an artificial creature that blindly obeys the rules and laws laid down by the social scientist in his theoretical models. Total man is thus divided by various social scientists into *homo economicus*,

explicit reference, one could no more assign the origin of Rawls's thought experiment directly to Weber (say), it would likewise be misguided, in the absence of an explicit reference to Weber in *The Concept of Law*, to attribute Hart's Rex archetype directly to Weber, or to any other social theorist, or indeed (following Rawls's lead) to some generic conception of social theory. Nonetheless, for reasons already mentioned, the exercise of identifying resonances of Weber in Hart's device of Rex and elsewhere is instructive.

Perhaps one of the most strikingly visible resonances lies in the general frame of reference that Hart outlines when first introducing Rex to the discussion in chapter IV of *The Concept of Law*. In the context of a critique of John Austin's claim that the populace renders habitual obedience to the commands of a sovereign, Hart posits his imaginary 'absolute ruler', Rex. The society ruled by Rex is characterised as 'probably far too simple ever to have existed anywhere, and it is certainly not a primitive one; for primitive society knows little of absolute rulers like Rex'. Hart describes this society as a 'constructed' world – the 'constructed … simple legal world of Rex I'[34] – and as something 'supposed' (or hypothesised): 'we shall suppose that there is a population living in a territory in which an absolute monarch (Rex) reigns for a very long time'.[35] In at least two respects Hart's archetypal Rex (and the society or kingdom associated with Rex) has an echo of the Weberian ideal type. Rex and his kingdom are first and foremost a *construct* – in other words, they are constructed in the mind of the theorist. In this respect Hart and Weber (or at any rate Weber's translators) use similar terminology. Thus, Weber maintains that an ideal type is the product of a synthesis in which phenomena are to be arranged into a unified 'analytical construct' (*Gedankenbild*). Secondly, in maintaining that Rex's kingdom is a 'simple' or simplified society, with no actual or historical counterpart in the real world, Hart appears to echo Weber's position that an ideal type is utopian, and cannot be found empirically anywhere in reality.[36] Also, by creating a model designed to simplify the real world, Hart may have been, knowingly or unknowingly, following Weber in attempting to bring order to chaos.[37] Hart, as we have seen, later explicitly acknowledges the need for the analyst to make selections from the boundlessness of reality, with the selections answerable to some criteria of importance.[38]

who fits the model of the economist and acts according to economic laws, *homo psychologicus*, who is part of the psychologist's model and obeys his causal laws, *homo sociologicus*, who belongs to a sociological model and acts in accordance with the laws established therein, and so on in all the social sciences'.

[34] See HLA Hart, *The Concept of Law* (this chapter, n 3) 54.

[35] ibid 52.

[36] Weber makes the point that the ideal type – constructed out of syntheses of multiple points of view and concrete individual phenomena (which may be present, or indeed *absent*: in other words supplied by the theorist); and organised as an integrated theoretical construct – 'cannot be found empirically anywhere in reality. It is a *utopia*'. See M Weber, '"Objectivity" in Social Science' (this chapter, n 17) 90.

[37] ibid 78.

[38] See N Lacey, 'Analytical Jurisprudence' (this chapter, n 5) 955; and N Lacey, *A Life of HLA Hart: The Nightmare and the Noble Dream* (Oxford University Press 2004) 351.

In key respects, however, Hart's Rex archetype falls short of a developed Weberian ideal type. Weber, as we have seen, emphasises that an ideal type calls for the distillation and assimilation of data that point to the need for significant empirical content.[39] What emerges from Hart's analysis is an empirically thin account both of the system of governance under discussion (a monarchy) and of a society in which that system might be installed. In constructing his archetype primarily to highlight the shortcomings of a rival analysis Hart binds himself to the limitations of that other analysis. Essentially, he appropriates the Austinian model of a commanding sovereign (in which the sovereign [Rex] 'controls his people by general orders backed by threats')[40] without significantly extending its reach – for instance, by seeking to capture historically or analytically authentic elements of a monarchical system of rule. Ultimately, that leaves Hart's Rex dynasty as a kind of shell whose overriding purpose is to provide a vehicle for subverting the position maintained by Austin. Hart is much less interested in describing and explaining the characteristics of a monarchical system as such than in refuting, critiquing, and in some sense caricaturing, a theoretical posture adopted by John Austin.

Taking stock of Hart's analytical construct, Rex, it is clear that this operates neither as a Weberian ideal type in the conventional sense (even if possibly exhibiting a few of its characteristics), nor as an archetype or thought experiment following the tradition of the writings of political philosophers such as Rawls. (Nor indeed is the Rex archetype any kind of *homo economicus*, *homo psychologicus* or *homo sociologicus*.) Instead, Rex represents a straightforward reimagining of the Austinian commanding sovereign designed to highlight the flaws (as Hart sees them) inhering in that model in terms of whether it represents a sufficiently insightful explanation of the law of a modern state. In the course of critically reconsidering the Austinian position Hart sets about exposing those flaws. Rex is thus a vehicle for Hart to advance an alternative explanation of both the 'material' of law (with the focus on legal rules) and the typical response of the populace when confronted with legal rules. Towards that end, a number of complementary positions are outlined, namely: (i) a rule-based, as opposed to a command-based, analysis, and (ii) a perspective on legal obligation based not on habitual obedience to sovereign commands, but rather on a critical reflective attitude (allied to the so-called 'internal aspect' of rules).[41]

This perhaps represents a significant step beyond the position adopted by Austin, but in some measure it is also a step beyond aspects of Weber's position, informed as it is by Hart's distinctive theoretical standpoint as a *legal* philosopher and jurist. Ultimately, Hart's critique of Austin's commanding sovereign – and the distinctively original analysis developed around that critique – could have been realised without the need for the Rex archetype. It would be possible to make the same analytical points without reference to a reworked, essentially Austinian,

[39] See this chapter, above, at n 36.
[40] HLA Hart, *The Concept of Law* (this chapter, n 3) 52.
[41] ibid 57.

model of a commanding sovereign. To that extent, the Rex archetype is perhaps extraneous; but undoubtedly its presence makes Hart's substantive analysis that much more compelling and accessible.

5.3.2. Critical Juxtaposition of Hart's Critical Reflective Attitude with Weber's Concept of Rule-Following Behaviour

We have seen that Hart's preparedness to acknowledge the influence of Weber's writings was restricted to private handwritten annotations in a Weber text in his personal library (to the extent that that represents any kind of acknowledgment).[42] In marginal notes written by Hart (discovered by John Finnis), Hart comments positively on Weber's idea that human behaviour may be oriented to 'maxims' within an order,[43] which calls attention not only to the possibility of behaviour being modified so as to conform to a 'maxim' (or rule, to use more familiar Hartian terminology), but to the idea of rules being configured as an 'order'.[44] The idea of human behaviour being modified – indeed consciously oriented – so as to conform to the demands of a legal rule is, of course, so universal as to overflow the limits of any (merely) theoretical frame of reference: in other words, it is far from being the exclusive preserve of a Weber or a Hart. So far as Hart is concerned, this seminal idea makes its appearance in *The Concept of Law* as a concomitant of Hart's critique of the Austinian habit of obedience in the context of his discussion of the Rex dynasty. At the same time, a number of considerations, necessarily implied by Hart's core expository theory, place this idea firmly within *both* the Hartian and Weberian analytical 'camps'.

In essence, for Hart, legal rules are guides to conduct.[45] In a similar vein, for Weber a rule can be viewed as a 'real determinant' of empirical action.[46] Weber

[42] See N Lacey, *A Life of HLA Hart: The Nightmare and the Noble Dream* (Oxford University Press 2004) 230 (especially the passage reproduced in Chapter 4, above, at n 1).

[43] One context in which the idea of orientation of behaviour to 'maxims' is to be found is that of the *social relationship*. Weber writes: 'The meaningful content which remains relatively constant in a social relationship is capable of formulation in terms of maxims which the parties concerned expect to be adhered to by their partners, on the average and approximately'. See M Weber, *The Theory of Social and Economic Organization* (AM Henderson and T Parsons (trs and eds), The Free Press 1947) 120.

[44] For instance, Weber makes reference to the concept of a '*legal* order': 'A "legal order" shall … be said to exist wherever coercive means, of a physical or psychological kind, are available; ie, wherever they are at the disposal of one or more persons who hold themselves ready to use them for this purpose in the case of certain events; in other words, wherever we find a consociation specifically dedicated to the purpose of "legal coercion"'. See M Weber, *Economy and Society: An Outline of Interpretive Sociology* [*Wirtschaft und Gesellschaft: Grundriss der Verstehenden Soziologie*] (G Roth, C Wittich and others (trs and eds), Bedminster Press Inc 1968) (hereafter, in this chapter, '*Economy and Society*') 317. Weber analyses other types of 'order' including 'legitimate order' (ibid 31–36); and 'economic order' (ibid 311–319).

[45] This point is made by Hart in a number of places. See HLA Hart, *The Concept of Law* (this chapter, n 3) 11, 36, 39, 40, 61. Law is also, for Hart, a means of 'social control': ibid (for example) 39–40, 91–92, 124, 170, 193; and a means of 'coercive control': ibid 41.

[46] See M Weber, 'The Concept of "Following a Rule"' in WG Runciman (ed), *Max Weber, Selections in Translation* (Cambridge University Press 1978) ch 5. See especially at 105.

explores the possibility that legal rules can become an integral part of the subjective meaning (*Sinn*) of law-oriented human behaviour. He outlines a type of social action – rationally regulated action (*Gesellschaftshandeln*) – characterised by behaviour that is 'meaningfully oriented toward rules which have been … established rationally with a view toward … [the] expected behaviour' of those to whom the rules apply.[47] (Clearly, *legal* rules are so established.) As we have seen, the more encompassing idea, in Weber's writings, that human beings act subjectively meaningfully had its origins in the work of (among others) the German idealist philosopher Wilhelm Dilthey, who emphasised the need for the human (or 'mental') sciences (*Geisteswissenschaften*) to focus attention on the world of the mind: for instance, motivations for action, goals and objectives, cultural values, morality, ideologies and (religious) beliefs. In a similar vein, but in the world of law and legal institutions, Hart advances the thesis that legal rules have an *internal aspect*, which is closely associated with the 'internal point of view'[48] and 'internal statements'.[49] When Hart refers to rules having an internal aspect it is not rules per se that have this dimension: the phrase 'internal aspect of rules' better describes an *attitude towards rules* – specifically *legal* rules – adopted by persons who are in some way affected (such as being bound) by the rules. Hart probably recognises this when he posits the closely related idea of the *critical reflective attitude*.[50] Inevitably law – whether viewed as a (Hartian) guide to conduct or as a (Weberian) real determinant of empirical action – must take its place within the structure of motivations, beliefs, goals and other mental content that define the interior world of the acting individual. Hart holds out the possibility of a jurisprudential exploration of the critical reflective attitude – focusing on the 'internal aspect' of legal rules – just as Weber holds out the possibility of making the subjective meaning of human behaviour generally an object of sociological enquiry.

For Weber, '[a]ction is social in so far as, by virtue of the subjective meaning attached to it by the acting individual (or individuals), it takes account of the behaviour of others and is thereby oriented in its course'.[51] Thus, legal rule-following

[47] See M Weber, *Economy and Society* (this chapter, n 44) 1376.

[48] See HLA Hart, *The Concept of Law* (this chapter, n 3) 89–123; and (for example) 137–138, 147, 201.

[49] ibid 102–112. (Hart sets up 'internal statements' in opposition to 'external statements'.)

[50] ibid mainly 57, 85, 91, 102. (Hart also refers (at 57) to a 'reflective critical attitude' and appears to intend the two phrases to be equivalent.)

[51] See M Weber, *The Theory of Social and Economic Organization* (AM Henderson and T Parsons (trs and eds), The Free Press 1947) 88. Weber also has a theoretical interest in the causes and effects – the causal dimension – of human behaviour. This impels him to a definition of sociology as a science that attempts 'the interpretive understanding of social action *in order thereby to arrive at* a causal explanation of its course and effects. In "action" is included all human behaviour when and in so far as the acting individual attaches a subjective meaning to it'. See M Weber, *Economy and* Society (this chapter, n 44) 4 (emphasis added). From the point of view of (Weberian) sociology, *causal* explanation is the *end result* of a process that starts with attaining an understanding of individual subjective meaning which in some cases will incorporate an idea (in the mind of the observed actor) of a legal rule viewed, in Weberian terms, as a 'real determinant' of empirical action. In other words, a legal rule will be viewed as being *causative* of a particular end result, such as behaviour that is aligned with (for example) a requirement imposed by the rule. See generally KH Wolff, 'Phenomenology and Sociology' in T Bottomore and R Nisbet (eds), *A History of Sociological Analysis* (Heinemann Educational Books Ltd 1978) ch 13, especially 501.

behaviour will often be social action in the Weberian sense if the individual engaging in such behaviour takes account of others,[52] or of the behaviour of others, in at least the following two senses. First, most laws – whether civil or criminal – will seek to guide or control behaviour that could have an impact upon others, or upon their interests. So if an actor, observing relevant legal rules, for instance consciously avoids behaviour that might result in the commission of a civil wrong (eg by driving carefully so as to avoid injuring others or damaging their property), then in some measure this takes account of others or of the expected *behaviour* of others – for example (in the latter case) where there is a possibility that an injured party might exercise a legal right to compensation for breach of a corresponding duty of care on the part of the party causing injury. But for any given actor, the primary motivating factor may simply be the imperative to avoid causing harm to others, regardless of the existence of legal rules, and regardless of considerations of how an injured party might respond in terms of seeking compensation, and so on. Secondly, as legal rules presuppose the existence of institutions involved in their administration, interpretation and enforcement, the individual engaging in legal rule-following behaviour may take account of the expected 'behaviour of others' in the sense of the likely responses of relevant institutions (eg police, courts, civil enforcement agencies) by, for example, assessing the likelihood of enforcement action being taken if (say) a criminal offence is committed.

Taking stock, it is possible to recognise in Weber's writings, a direct connection between the concept of social action and a rule-following state of mind coming within the subjective meaning of human behaviour. When Weber's seminal concept of social action is the adopted frame of reference the concept of legal rule-following behaviour perhaps represents one of its most characteristic forms. It is possible to assert an equivalent connection in Hart's writings. The question here is how, for Hart, is the social dimension of legal rule-following behaviour represented in ideas such as the internal aspect of rules, which is in turn allied to the critically reflective dimension of rules. The most promising point of departure is Hart's concept of the *social rule*, of which law is only one manifestation. If legal rules are (Hartian) social rules, and those (social) rules have an 'internal aspect' whose central characteristic is a critical reflective attitude, there is at least a resonance of Weberian sociological analysis in that position. (The assumption here is that there is some degree of correspondence between the Hartian internal aspect of rules and Weberian rule-following subjectively meaningful behaviour.) The more encompassing idea of viewing law as a (Hartian) guide to conduct or as a (Weberian) real determinant of empirical action is similarly resonant.

A brief consideration of Hart's concept of social rule – and corresponding resonances in Weber's writings – is therefore instructive.

[52] Taking account of the behaviour of others necessarily includes, in some sense, taking account *of others*.

5.3.3. Legal Rules Viewed as (Hartian) Social Rules

Hart does not attempt an explicit definition of the concept of 'social rule' in *The Concept of Law*. Instead, its key characteristics are identifiable from the broader analysis, mentioned above, where Hart critiques the Austinian habit of obedience using his archetype of the Rex dynasty as a frame of reference. In the course of this analysis Hart argues that the behaviour that social rules render obligatory must be 'general though not necessarily invariable; [meaning] … that it is repeated when occasion arises by most of the group'.[53] Deviations from a social rule – to be regarded as 'lapses or faults' – are open to criticism of the community, while threatened deviations result in pressure for conformity.[54] Such criticism, and demands for compliance, are to be seen as legitimate or justified by observers of non-compliant behaviour, and even by those engaging in such (non-compliant) behaviour.[55] In the broadest terms, Hart maintains that 'if a social rule is to exist some at least must look upon the behaviour [rendered obligatory by the rule] … as a general standard to be followed by the group as a whole'.[56] At the same time, according to Hart, a social rule has an 'internal aspect' which coexists with an 'external aspect' where the latter comprises regular uniform behaviour which an observer could recognise and record.[57] The idea that legal rules are social rules is complemented by the idea that law is, for Hart, a means of social control in that members of social groups accept and use rules (including legal rules) as guides to conduct.[58] Moreover, legal rule-following behaviour – ie orientation to legal rules viewed as (Hartian) social rules – has characteristics that are not dissimilar to 'social action' in the Weberian sense where (according to Weber's definition) the individual engaging in such behaviour takes account of others, or of the behaviour of others.[59] This would suggest that, for both Weber and Hart, legal rule-following behaviour is inherently social, both as a general proposition (given that legal rules are invariably designed to – and do in fact – impact persons *other than* the individual engaging in legal rule-following behaviour) and, more narrowly,

[53] HLA Hart, *The Concept of Law* (this chapter, n 3) 55.

[54] ibid.

[55] ibid. 55–56.

[56] ibid 56.

[57] ibid 56. See also Hart's more detailed analysis of the notion of the external point of view in his notes to p 86 of *The Concept of Law* (ibid 291). For Hart's apparent conflation of the external point of view seen as a methodological device (ie a viewpoint adopted by an observer, such as a sociologist, as a means of obtaining knowledge of the legal world) *and* as an aspect of a perceived reality (ie a viewpoint actually adopted in the legal world by law-affected actors such as private citizens) see N MacCormick, *HLA Hart* (Edward Arnold (Publishers) Ltd 1981) 32–40.

[58] As Hart observes: 'The principal functions of the law as a means of social control are not to be seen in private litigation or prosecutions, which represent vital but still ancillary provisions for the failures of the system. It is to be seen in the diverse ways in which the law is used to control, to guide, and to plan life out of court'. See HLA Hart, *The Concept of Law* (this chapter, n 3) 40.

[59] See section 5.3.2 (this chapter, above).

as an institutional phenomenon, in that social (institutional) structures are established for the administration, interpretation and enforcement of legal rules.

It is clear that on a number of levels – even if through the use of differing concepts and language – the Hartian and Weberian analyses converge. So it is instructive to take stock. First, in the Hartian idea of the internal aspect of (legal) rules there is a resonance of Weberian analysis where the subjective meaning of (legal) rule-following behaviour includes an element of conforming to (or otherwise taking account of) legal rules. Secondly, the idea of legal rule-following behaviour, in a context involving Hartian social rules, resonates with the Weberian idea of social action, where individuals engaging in legal (social) rule-following behaviour can be regarded as consciously modifying or orienting their behaviour: (i) directly by reference to others or the behaviour of others (for example, those protected or advantaged by law-compliant behaviour), or (ii) indirectly by reference to the presence of law enforcement and other institutional structures that law presupposes (where, for example, the individual anticipates institutional intervention for non-conformity with (say) a criminal law).

Any Weber-inspired reimagining of elements of Hart's expository writings inevitably comes up against the *sociological* shortcomings of Hartian analysis. Hart's concept of the social rule, in particular – and indeed the very idea of the realm of the social – is sketchy. Yet the task of outlining a workable conceptual framework is not insurmountable. For instance, Weber's concept of social action, as we have seen, captures the straightforward idea of the individual acting socially when orienting behaviour by reference to one or more others (or to their behaviour).[60] One individual acts with respect to another, rendering the behaviour intrinsically social in that it is other-directed: that is, directed to another human being as opposed to self-directed or directed towards a non-social end. Weber's concept of the *social relationship* is closely aligned with the concept of social action. For Weber, a social relationship equates to 'the behaviour of a plurality of actors in so far as, in its meaningful content, the action of each takes account of that of the others and is oriented in these terms'.[61] Weber, as we have seen, identifies an important further dimension – a *normative* dimension – noting that 'maxims' govern the constant or stable components of a social relationship.[62] In a legal context a social relationship might subsist between individuals acting subjectively meaningfully in consciously orienting their behaviour by reference to legal rules. It is the assigned characteristics of Hart's concept of the social rule (outlined and discussed above) that in effect serve to

[60] For Weber, as we have seen, '[a]ction is social in so far as, by virtue of the subjective meaning attached to it by the acting individual … it takes account of the behaviour of others and is thereby oriented in its course'. See M Weber, *The Theory of Social and Economic Organization* (AM Henderson and T Parsons (trs and eds), The Free Press 1947) 88.

[61] ibid 118.

[62] ibid 120.

define it. Hart does not attempt an explicit definition of 'social rule' or, indeed, of the expression 'social', in *The Concept of Law*, doubtless relying on the ordinary meaning. Yet Hart's notion of the critical reflective attitude probably marks the most promising step towards giving content to the idea that social rules (such as legal rules) have an 'internal aspect'.

5.3.4. The (Hartian) Legal Right Viewed as an Instrument of Social Power

We have seen that in *Essays on Bentham* Hart, towards outlining a version of the will theory of rights, views an important category of rights as conferring *power* on the right-holder.[63] Hart identifies a legal right – falling within the extensive category of 'rights correlative to obligations' – with a *power of control* over a correlative obligation residing in another.[64] It was suggested in Chapter 3 that in terms of Hartian will theory a legal right could be viewed as a power from a variety of *non-juridical* perspectives.[65] To that end it could be argued that an analysis of legal rights may be accommodated within a Weberian social power frame of reference that draws appropriately upon the Hartian version of will theory. One possible point of departure for such an analysis would be an exploration of the perceived overlap between Hartian and Weberian analyses, discussed in Chapter 1.[66] In that context, a point of intersection was briefly identified between Weber's concept of *Herrschaft* and Hart's notion of the right-holder as a 'small-scale sovereign'.[67] This idea echoes aspects of the discussion, earlier in the present chapter, centring on Hart's archetypal sovereign, Rex. Hart touches upon the *personal relationship* claimed to exist between ruler and ruled: 'on this account of the social situation under Rex, the habit of obedience is a personal relationship between each subject and Rex'.[68] Hartian will theory could perhaps be regarded as turning on the metaphor of the 'small-scale sovereign', even if Hart seemingly makes little of this beyond a passing comment in *Essays on Bentham*. It would appear that for both Hart *and* Weber the legal right is to be seen as a manifestation of a relationship of social power obtaining between a superordinate party (the right-holder, occupying the position of a 'small-scale sovereign') and a subordinate party (the duty-bearer). According to Weber, '*Herrschaft* … does not mean that a superior elementary force asserts itself in one way or another; it refers to a meaningful interrelationship between those giving orders and those obeying, to the effect that the expectations toward which

[63] See generally section 1.4 (Chapter 1, above) and sections 3.2.1 and 3.3 (Chapter 3, above). See, in particular, HLA Hart, *Essays on Bentham* (this chapter, n 1) 188.

[64] ibid (eg) 183, 188.

[65] See section 3.2.1 (Chapter 3, above) at n 20. See also section 1.4 (Chapter 1, above) and generally Chapter 5, below.

[66] See section 1.4 (Chapter 1, above).

[67] See HLA Hart, *Essays on Bentham* (this chapter, n 1) 183.

[68] See HLA Hart, *The Concept of Law* (this chapter, n 3) 52.

action is oriented on both sides can be reckoned upon ...'.[69] Guenther Roth, as we have seen,[70] develops this idea further, characterising the concept of *Herrschaft* ('domination') as a 'structure of superordination and subordination, of leaders and led, rulers and ruled'.[71] Alan Hunt makes an essentially similar point, observing that power in Weber's sense is to be viewed as a 'relational concept', centring upon the impact of one person upon another in so far as the behaviour of the one may be analysed as having been determined by the other.[72]

Weber makes explicit that this relational dynamic is manifested not only in exercises of social power centring upon 'leaders and led, rulers and ruled' (to use Roth's words), but at the level of economic (contractual) relations where (for example) an employee asserts a claim to wages from an employer. This theoretical position chimes with corresponding aspects of Hartian will theory in underlining how exercises of social power centred upon legal (and contractual) rights will often involve an imposition of *will* on the part of the right-holder:

> The concept of power is sociologically amorphous. All conceivable qualities of a person and all conceivable combinations of circumstances may put him in a position to *impose his will* in a given situation.[73]
>
> Domination [*Herrschaft*] in the quite general sense of power, ie, of the possibility of imposing one's own will upon the behavior of other persons, can emerge in the most diverse forms. If, as has occasionally been done, one looks upon the claims which the law accords to one person against one or more others as a power to issue commands to debtors or to those to whom no such claim is accorded, one may thereby conceive of the whole system of modern private law as the decentralization of domination in the hands of those to whom the legal rights are accorded. From this angle, the worker would have the power to command, ie, 'domination', over the entrepreneur to the extent of his wage claim.[74]

Paralleling positions outlined not only in Weber's writings but in his own writing both when alluding to the relational nature of Rex's rule in *The Concept of Law* and when making a passing reference to the idea of a 'small-scale sovereign' in *Essays on Bentham*, Hart identifies a connection between exercises of social power by a sovereign (on one hand) and exercises of social power attending the possession of a right (on the other). But given that Hart characterises the position obtaining

[69] See M Weber, *Economy and Society* (this chapter, n 44) 1378. See also 212–213. *Herrschaft* is also discussed in more detail in section 1.4 (Chapter 1, above).

[70] See section 1.4 (Chapter 1, above) at n 49.

[71] See M Weber, *Economy and Society* (this chapter, n 44) 61–62 n 31.

[72] A Hunt, *The Sociological Movement in Law* (The Macmillan Press Ltd 1978) 113.

[73] M Weber, *Economy and Society* (this chapter, n 44) 53 (emphasis added).

[74] ibid 942. Weber nonetheless points out that this terminology is 'rather forced'. Elsewhere he comments as follows: 'It is essential to include the criterion of power of control and disposal (*Verfügungsgewalt*) in the sociological concept of economic action if for no other reason than that an exchange economy involves a complete network of contractual relationships, each of which originates in a deliberately planned process of acquisition of powers of control and disposal'. See M Weber, *The Theory of Social and Economic Organization* (AM Henderson and T Parsons (trs and eds), The Free Press 1947) 163.

between ruler (Rex) and the ruled-over populace as personally relational in order to highlight perceived weaknesses in John Austin's account of the populace's claimed habit of obedience to sovereign commands, he would have no cause to seek to *strengthen* Austin's account towards an entirely different theoretical objective.[75] It is therefore not unexpected that he does the opposite. In rejecting the Austinian analysis Hart, crucially, substitutes for the idea of a habit of obedience (to a sovereign's command) the idea of a critical reflective attitude (to legal rules). Sovereign commands are thus in effect supplanted by legal rules. Essentially, Hart rejects the idea of bare obedience because of its association, in Austin's writings, with a *habit* of obedience, which Hart considers to be analytically flawed.[76] Weber, by contrast, has no such hesitancy in that he places the idea of obedience – and indeed the idea of *command* also – at the centre of one of his key definitions of *Herrschaft* (domination).[77]

Ultimately, neither in *Essays on Bentham* nor in *The Concept of Law* (when discussing Rex) does Hart refine to any significant extent either the idea of a sovereign, or the nascent idea of a 'small-scale sovereign', towards developing any kind of sociologically informed analysis of the social power element of the legal right. Arguably this missed opportunity leaves the way open for exploring and developing aspects of at least the *relational* nature of rights, whether that is done in the context of Hart's Rex archetype or otherwise. Aside from the Rex archetype, Hart's more generic characterisation of a right as a power undoubtedly offers the promise of a point of departure for an account that centres on the idea of a legal right as a locus of social power via the idea of social relationality (at the same time as

[75] Essentially, by characterising the relationship of command between Rex and his subjects as relational and personal Hart reinforces the Austinian position in order to erect what he considers to be a more compelling account of the nature of law centred upon *impersonal* legal rules. Hart's overriding argument is that the 'stuff' of law is rules and not transitory situational commands that are more or less spent the moment they are issued. Legal rules are enduring; and rules of succession (such as between Rex I and Rex II) govern the line of monarchical succession in a more effective way than a simple command ever could.

[76] Hart arrives at this position by way of an analysis of the *continuity* of the authority to make laws, and the *persistence* of laws, long after the original maker (ie Rex) 'and those who rendered him habitual obedience have perished'. According to Hart, neither the idea of continuity, nor the idea of persistence, is adequately explained either by the Austinian notion of a habit of obedience, or the idea of sovereign commands. It can only be properly explained, according to Hart, by *rules of sovereign succession*: in other words, rules governing the succession by one sovereign (Rex II) of his predecessor (Rex I). See HLA Hart, *The Concept of Law* (this chapter, n 3) 51–66.

[77] 'To be more specific, *domination* will thus mean the situation in which the manifested will (*command*) of the *ruler* or rulers is meant to influence the conduct of one or more others (*the ruled*) and actually does influence it in such a way that their conduct to a socially relevant degree occurs as if the ruled had made the content of the command the maxim of their conduct for its very own sake. Looked upon from the other end, this situation will be called *obedience*.' See M Weber, *Economy and Society* (this chapter, n 44) 946 (Weber's emphasis). What is of particular interest here is that even Weber does not appear to be entirely satisfied with the idea of command. According to Weber, the command of a ruler is treated by the ruled *as if* it were a 'maxim' (eg a rule or a principle or a norm). Essentially, for Weber, a command 'has become' a rule; just as for Hart the concept of a rule supplants the discarded Austinian concept of a [ruler's] command. The Weberian and Hartian analyses thus, in different ways, appear to mirror one another.

aligning with Weber's concept of *Herrschaft*). As we have seen, in Hartian terms, the social power inhering in a right – within Hart's extensive category of 'rights correlative to obligations' – takes the form of a right-holder's 'exclusive control, more or less extensive, over another person's duty'.[78] Following through the implications of the position outlined in Hartian will theory,[79] the control (or power) invested in the right-holder confers an ability – through an exertion of *will* on the right-holder's part – to exercise a choice to enforce a correlative duty or obligation (imposed on another), or to waive it, or to leave it unenforced. And, as we have seen (in this chapter, immediately above) in a legal context, for Weber, the exercise of a right – entailing an imposition of will – is to be viewed as a power to 'issue commands'.[80]

Viewing exercises of social power within a legal rights dynamic as an exertion of will, consistent with a Hartian will theory perspective on legal rights; or, more generally (and in Weberian terms) as an imposition of the will of one upon the behaviour of another are, needless to say, not theoretical positions unique to the writings of Hart or Weber. For instance, the American sociologist, Herbert Kelman, has written insightfully in this area.[81] Essentially, Kelman views social power, or social influence, in terms of socially induced behaviour change.[82] The influencing agent is a source of power, while the subject influenced is a target. (In a context involving legal rights, the influencing agent would be a right-holder while the target would be a duty-bearer.) Social influence – the impact of (for instance) a power exercise – occurs when targets modify their behaviour as a result of induction by the source.[83] Induction may involve the source offering or making available to the target some kind of behaviour and communicating something about the probable effects of adopting that behaviour. Induction may involve persuading, ordering or threatening.[84] Among

[78] HLA Hart, *Essays on Bentham* (this chapter, n 1) 183. Later in the same chapter Hart argues that we may recognise as a 'defining feature' of a right correlative to obligation 'the individual's legal powers of control, full or partial, over that obligation … The case of a right correlative to obligation then emerges as only a special case of legal power in which the right-holder is at liberty to waive or extinguish or to enforce or leave unenforced another's obligation'. (ibid 188)

[79] See section 1.4 (Chapter 1, above) and section 3.2.1 (Chapter 3, above).

[80] See M Weber, *Economy and Society* (this chapter, n 44) 942. See also M Weber, *Max Weber on Law in Economy and Society* (M Rheinstein (ed), Harvard University Press 1954) 323–324. What is striking here – both in Hart's idea of a 'small-scale sovereign' and Weber's concept of *Herrschaft* – is that both theoretical positions, overtly or by implication, pivot on the notion of 'command'. Needless to say, in *The Concept of Law*, Hart goes to great lengths to dissociate himself (theoretically) from John Austin's notion of law as the commands of a sovereign, substituting for the (Austinian) idea of a habit of obedience to commands the rival notion of a critical reflective attitude to rules (which, in turn, overlaps with the 'internal aspect' of rules). Yet it seems clear that Hart in *Essays on Bentham* concedes some ground to the notion of a command when viewing a right-holder as a 'small-scale sovereign'.

[81] See generally HC Kelman, 'Further Thoughts on the Processes of Compliance, Identification, and Internalization', in JT Tedeschi (ed), *Perspectives on Social Power* (Aldine Publishing Company 1974) ch 5.

[82] ibid 128.

[83] ibid 128–129.

[84] ibid 128.

other things, Kelman analyses influence under conditions of legitimate authority.[85] When the duly constituted administration of a legitimate political system makes certain demands, citizens are required to accept them regardless of their personal preferences.[86] The target therefore comes to accept, and to act upon without challenge, a legitimate request, command or order of the source. Kelman cites conditions of legitimate influence or authority where influencing agents are in a position to make demands, and exert control over targets, by virtue of their position in the social system.[87]

Where social influence, in the sense envisaged by Kelman, derives from the presence of laws – or of legal rights or duties – this implies a social power dynamic that can be analysed in terms of at least three discussion points, the first two of which have a bearing on social science methodology.

First, there may be an element of what Hart would refer to as externally 'observable regularities of conduct'.[88] Now, while isolated or one-off acts of compliance with legal rules or legal duties are clearly possible, they may not be readily identifiable as establishing any kind of *pattern*. In a context involving recurrent behaviour associated with performance of legal duties, an observer might record (say) vehicles stopping at red traffic lights, or regular monthly repayments being made by a debtor to a creditor in accordance with contractual obligations set out in a loan agreement. This may be viewed initially from the standpoint of Hart's 'extreme external' point of view – a standpoint from which empirically observable regularities can be identified but which do not serve to *explain* the regularities in question.[89] For such an explanation, it would be necessary to investigate motivations or reasons for action. Thus, an automated vehicle that stops at a red traffic light does so because it is digitally and mechanically programmed to do so, though that would still, ultimately, be traceable back to human agency (ie to those who initially programmed the vehicle). A Hartian 'extreme external' observer may record the *same* regularities (ie vehicles halting when the lights turn to red) regardless of whether the vehicle is automated or has a driver; and observers may be completely unaware of any difference when observing the events that confront them. However, in a situation where human agency is explicitly involved – eg literally a human being driving a car – it goes without saying that *thought processes* intervene. This may be manifested, for example, in the driver's desire to obey the (criminal) law governing compliance with traffic lights,[90] though it is equally conceivable that drivers may halt their vehicles purely for reasons of personal safety or in recognition that, by giving way to other users of a junction, equal access may be afforded to all users of the

[85] ibid 160–169.
[86] ibid 161.
[87] ibid.
[88] See HLA Hart, *The Concept of Law* (this chapter, n 3) 89.
[89] ibid discussion generally at 89–91.
[90] See Road Traffic Act 1988, section 36(1).

junction. These underlying motivations would necessarily remain impenetrable to an observer austerely adhering to a Hartian 'extreme external' point of view.

The need for an approach that, in explanatory terms, moves beyond Hart's 'extreme external' point of view leads to the second discussion point arising from Kelman's social influence model. Here, there is a need for what might be termed *hermeneutic* engagement with the events unfolding in the presence of the observer. In this aspect of the analysis, and viewed in Weberian terms, the observer has the task of discerning the *subjective meaning* (*Sinn*) of the observable regularities. This has been touched upon (above and elsewhere) when considering the predisposition of a given individual to engage in law-compliant behaviour.[91] This inclination may have diverse, indeterminate and even shifting, origins. Hart points out that private citizens may obey the law from any motive whatever, though they may *accept* legal rules as common standards of behaviour.[92] This acceptance may in turn be founded on an obligation to respect the constitution.[93] Some may literally *reject* legal rules but nevertheless obey them because they judge that unpleasant consequences are likely to follow violation.[94] Ultimately, a moral commitment to law may lie at the heart of the individual's acceptance of, and desire to obey, the law. In *The Concept of Law* one point at which moral commitment to law might be engaged is in Hart's discussion of the 'critical reflective attitude'.[95] This is an attitude towards patterns of behaviour viewed 'as a common standard' in a social group, evidenced in the use of normative and justificatory language. The behaviour in question – and indeed by extension, the legal rules governing such behaviour – may be considered 'right' or 'wrong'. Those subject to relevant standards or legal rules may believe that they 'ought' to, or 'must' observe them.[96]

In an investigative (social science) context, the range of motivations involved in legal rule-following – or indeed rule-rejecting – behaviour will be discernible only to an observer who adopts what Neil MacCormick refers to as Hart's 'non-extreme external' or hermeneutic point of view.[97] MacCormick identifies this point of view as 'the central methodological insight of Hart's analytical jurisprudence',[98] dovetailing as it does with classical social theory – in particular, Weber's *Verstehende* methodology, grounded in *Geisteswissenschaften*. The observer makes a connection between observed behaviour (or behavioural patterns) and the presence of legal rules, or of legal rights or duties, governing and to a greater or lesser extent impelling (in the mind of the actor) the behaviour in question. The observer, as MacCormick points out, is constrained by the need to describe legal rules (and their deployment in relevant circumstances) from the internal point of view of

[91] See also section 4.4 (Chapter 4, above).
[92] See HLA Hart, *The Concept of Law* (this chapter, n 3) 116.
[93] ibid 116–117.
[94] ibid 90.
[95] ibid 57.
[96] ibid.
[97] See N MacCormick, *HLA Hart* (Edward Arnold (Publishers) Ltd 1981) 36–40.
[98] ibid 38.

the individual impelled to act in the required way, necessarily disregarding any commitment the observer may have for or against those rules in their internal aspect.[99] Where, according to Hartian will theory, a legal right invests a right-holder, through an exertion of will on the right-holder's part, to exercise certain choices – specifically, to enforce a correlative duty or obligation imposed upon another person, or to waive it, or to leave it unenforced – the choices in question can be seen as corresponding in some measure to the content of the right-holder's will.

The idea that the possessor of a right is in a position to exercise the right through an exertion of will – when viewed from the point of view of Hartian will theory – leads to the third discussion point in our review of Kelman's social influence analysis. Taking the exercise of a legal right as precipitating behaviour change, an exertion of will may not in itself bring about a desired result – namely, performance of a correlative obligation. In a situation where the duty-bearer is reluctant to perform the obligations imposed, or unjustifiably delays performance, the strength of purpose of the right-holder may go some way towards bringing about performance. Indeed, if persuasion fails, the right-holder may escalate enforcement measures by engaging the services of a lawyer, or by using unlawful or unsavoury tactics such as intimidation or threats (eg of violence).

But what sets apart exercises of social power that are ancillary to rights – such as use of simple persuasion, say – from exercises of social power that are integrally related to the key characteristics of a legal right, is the institutional dimension of such a right. Deployments of social power attending the exercise of legal rights may involve right-holders in invoking centralised (state) judicial and enforcement mechanisms – in other words, (Weberian) *coercive apparatuses* – to secure performance of the given legal obligation.[100] Hart's claim, grounded in his version of will theory, that the exercise of a right engages the will of the right-holder in making a choice to enforce, waive or leave unenforced a corresponding obligation, in fact understates how little control the right-holder may actually have when invoking enforcement mechanisms, and how minimal may be the role of the right-holder's will, overall, when such mechanisms are engaged. If choices to enforce or waive a right, or to leave it unenforced, are more or less *exhaustive* of Hartian will theory in that such choices correspond to the content of the right-holder's will, then that seems theoretically constrained. But the fact is that, any analysis that seeks to advance beyond that to a more thoroughgoing exploration of the social power dimension of legal rights must recognise that legal rights can be as

[99] ibid 37.

[100] See M Weber, *Economy and Society* (this chapter, n 44) 313. Weber, as we have seen in section 3.3 (Chapter 3, below), refers to the existence of a 'coercive apparatus' consisting of 'one or more persons whose special task it is to hold themselves ready to apply specially provided means of coercion (legal coercion) for the purpose of norm enforcement'. In outlining the scope of the concept of a 'legal order', Weber refers to the need for the deployment of physical or psychological coercion. (ibid 317)

disempowering as they are empowering. More accurately, while legal rights are fundamentally empowering, nonetheless, within that context of empowerment, a right-holder's power is qualified in ways that are disempowering of the right-holder. As soon as a right-holder initiates legal proceedings against a duty-bearer (for example, in civil litigation), the right-holder is saddled with actual or potential risks, burdens, costs and responsibilities, some of which are unforeseen or unforeseeable, and which may become more problematic the longer the proceedings play out. A right-holder may thus suffer a drastic loss of control – a loss of power – as soon as the enforcement process is underway.

What factors, then, play into such a loss of control? Taking civil law proceedings as an example, one key factor centres on the fact that such proceedings are governed by complex procedural rules and rules of evidence. Litigants have no direct control over the content of those rules. From an ideal position where a right-holder simply requests and secures performance from the duty-bearer (where right-holder empowerment is maximal), the reality of pursuing civil litigation by way of an intricate rule-governed process represents, to mix metaphors, a shark-infested ocean replete with pitfalls for the unwary. The fact that the duty-bearer is faced with identical complexities may serve as a leveller in terms of the distribution of advantage and disadvantage between the parties. But the need to resort to an institutional process *at all* is plainly disempowering (at the same time as it may be empowering) when viewed against the ideal situation where such resort is avoidable and the right-holder is in a position to secure performance directly from the duty-bearer. At the same time, civil litigation involves co-ordinated activities of legal professionals – such as court officials and administrators, clerks, lawyers, civil juries and judges – some of whom (for example, judges) may have exceptionally wide powers and discretion, not least in terms of the operational minutiae around the conduct of proceedings. Furthermore, the overlaying of relevant adjective law over substantive legal rights can in some cases result in the challenge and defeat not of the substantive rights themselves but literally of the *proceedings*. For instance, proceedings may be time-barred by the operation of civil limitation laws.[101] The party initiating civil law proceedings also takes the risk that costs may be wholly or partially irrecoverable. Clearly, any costs awarded against a right-holder, or costs not assigned to the other litigant, will serve to diminish and devalue (for example) any compensatory award made by the court. This literally 'monetises' the right-holder's (partial) disempowerment.

[101] The removal of a statutory time-bar that has previously halted civil proceedings may pave the way for (later) unimpeded litigation in a situation where the underlying substantive rights have at all times remained intact. For instance, the Limitation (Childhood Abuse) (Scotland) Act 2017 disapplied (with effect from 4 October 2017) civil limitation laws in the context of personal injury claims in Scotland arising from allegations of childhood sexual abuse, physical abuse, emotional abuse and abuse in the form of neglect. The prevailing three-year time bar in such claims became inoperative (subject to qualifications). The substantive right – eg to the protection of the civil law from abuse (manifested, ultimately, in a right to compensation in respect of assault and other injury) – had never been extinguished in law.

Of special significance, moreover, is the fact that, generally in common law jurisdictions, civil law proceedings are an *adversarial* process. The imperative for litigants is to present to the court the most credible and persuasive account of their respective positions, having regard to limitations on availability, and indeed admissibility, of evidence. At the same time the court has the task of interpreting established facts in the light of applicable legal rules, doctrines and principles. All of this is designed to establish *and set up* rights that neither the parties nor the court can simply take for granted. Ultimately, the evidence presented, and argumentative positions adopted, by litigating parties must stand up to the scrutiny of the judicial process. The fact that, ordinarily, both parties enter the process with equally plausible positions that are often diametrically opposed, suggests that the empowerment afforded by a (claimed) right – especially a strongly contested one – is in some sense illusory. When civil law proceedings are concluded, the court could in principle make a decision that favours one or other of the parties; and this serves to increase the scope for uncertainty attending the possession of a right (or the perception of right-holders that they are in fact in possession of a right). All of this suggests that Hart's characterisation of a legal right – pursuant to his will theory – as a power of control (residing in the right-holder) over a correlative obligation (residing in a duty-bearer) stands in need of refinement.[102]

5.3.5. Social Science Typologies in *The Concept of Law*

Earlier in this chapter we touched upon Hart's use of Rex as an ideal type, possibly inspired by social or political theory or, possibly, writings of Max Weber – though there is no clear evidence of that in *The Concept of Law*. (Weber is not mentioned, even in the book's very substantial body of endnotes.) We concluded that while Hart's substantive discussion of the archetypal Rex dynasty made his pivotal critique of the Austinian notion of a commanding sovereign all the more compelling and accessible, the critique appeared to be neither analytically dependent on use of the archetype, nor was the archetype itself especially evocative of, say, a Weberian ideal type in a conventional sense. On the basis of that evidence alone, Hart could scarcely be seen as a committed exponent of social scientific – or, more narrowly, Weberian – analytical method. Yet, in another respect, he might be viewed as venturing upon the terrain of the Weberian 'pure type'. An example of this is Hart's acknowledgment, early in *The Concept of Law*, that a key task is to explore structural elements of the type of legal order that he refers to as a 'municipal

[102] See also the discussion of the *Iudexian* archetype in Chapter 8. A theoretical modifier of the Hartian position is arguably to be found in the hypothesis of the ultimate judgment ascribable to *Iudex* (representing a hypothetical determination of the content, scope, import and effect of any given legal right for the practical purpose of mobilising the coercive apparatuses of the legal system). In that context, distinctive modes of legal (judicial) reasoning and other considerations must be factored into any given characterisation of a legal right.

legal system'.[103] Hart makes clear his goal to 'advance legal theory by *providing an improved analysis of the distinctive structure of a municipal legal system* and a better understanding of the resemblances and differences between law, coercion, and morality, as types of social phenomena'.[104] This important demarcation of the theoretical reach of *The Concept of Law*, is consistent with an approach – elevated to a methodological imperative by Weber and others – that insists on the need for the investigator to make selections from boundless reality, guided by criteria of importance and (particularly in the context of Weber's writings) relevant *values*.[105] This, as we have seen earlier in this chapter, is an approach that Hart explicitly advocated.[106] Hart's theoretical focus upon a municipal legal system – narrowing the scope of *The Concept of Law* to an enquiry into the 'features of municipal law in a modern state',[107] which in turn equates to a 'centralized state legal order',[108] as Lacey terms it – appears to resonate not only at the most generic level in the idea of promoting what is essentially an ideal type; but, arguably, also at the level of the *specific*: Hart's centralised state legal order has echoes of Weber's pure type of *legal authority with a bureaucratic administrative staff*.[109] Superficially, a number of points of convergence can be identified between the respective Hartian and Weberian models. It is notable that Hart does not seek to promote his concept of a municipal legal system literally *as* an ideal type. It is left to the reader of *The Concept of Law* to reconstruct the elements of his municipal legal order from characteristics scattered randomly through the work.

First and foremost, the Hartian municipal legal system is expressed in the separation of powers model of the centralised state – originally developed in the writings of Montesquieu and Locke[110] – where governmental responsibilities are distributed across judicial, executive and legislative functions, reflecting (in part) Hart's claim that the 'key to the science of jurisprudence' lies in the combination of primary and secondary rules.[111] That dichotomy gives a central place to secondary rules of change and of adjudication corresponding respectively to the legislative and judicial functions of government. (An apparent omission from Hart's scheme

[103] See HLA Hart, *The Concept of Law* (this chapter, n 3) (eg) 5, 17, 79, 100, 122, 199. See also section 2.2 (Chapter 2, above) n 6.

[104] ibid 17 (emphasis added).

[105] See generally M Weber, '"Objectivity" in Social Science' (this chapter, n 17). See also HH Bruun, *Science, Values and Politics in Max Weber's Methodology* (expanded edition, Routledge 2016) 85. See further, T Parsons, 'Value-Freedom and Objectivity' in O Stammer (ed), *Max Weber and Sociology Today: Explorations in Interpretative Sociology* (Basil Blackwell 1971) 33.

[106] N Lacey, 'Analytical Jurisprudence' (this chapter, n 5) 955; and N Lacey, *A Life of HLA Hart: The Nightmare and the Noble Dream* (Oxford University Press 2004) 351.

[107] HLA Hart, *The Concept of Law* (this chapter, n 3) 79.

[108] N Lacey, 'Analytical Jurisprudence' (this chapter, n 5) 957–958.

[109] M Weber, *Economy and Society* (this chapter, n 44) 217–226.

[110] See generally Montesquieu, *The Spirit of the Laws* [*De L'Esprit des Lois*] (AM Kohler, BC Miller and HS Stone (trs and eds), Cambridge University Press 1989). See also J Locke, *Two Treatises of Government* (P Laslett (ed), Cambridge University Press 1988) 117–121, 364–374. See further A Cobban, *Rousseau and the Modern State* (2nd edn, George Allen & Unwin Ltd 1964) 81–91.

[111] HLA Hart, *The Concept of Law* (this chapter, n 3) 6, 81.

is the rules governing the executive function – administrative law.)[112] Weber, on the other hand, has little to say about the separation of powers doctrine in his analysis of the pure type of legal authority.[113] He is seemingly less concerned with that doctrine per se than with a related principle of separation, namely, the idea of the office-holder being separated from ownership of the 'means of production or administration'.

> Officials, employees, and workers attached to the administrative staff do not themselves own the non-human means of production and administration … There exists, furthermore, in principle complete separation of the organization's property … and the personal property … of the official …
>
> In the rational type case, there is also a complete absence of appropriation of his official position by the incumbent.[114]

Weber's ideal type envisages the separation of capacity associated with the holding of one office from capacities of other office-holders (eg president, prime minister, judge, civil servant). At the same time, office-holders in their respective official and private capacities are separated from both the (physical) infrastructure of governance (such as a parliament building or a court building or a police station or a prison; or files, papers, storage facilities, furniture etc.) and their personal property. As soon as these 'separations' are successfully realised in the type of governance structure suggested by Weber's pure type of bureaucratic legal authority, the possibility of separating one *power structure* from another (for instance, separating legislative from executive arms of government) appears to be more readily realisable. Elements of Weber's pure type of legal authority therefore go some way towards facilitating the idea – implicit in Hart's model of a municipal legal system – of a separation of powers model of the centralised state.

Hart's concept of a municipal legal system is also suggestive of the traditional Western rule of law paradigm that envisages the equal subjection to law of officials and citizens alike.[115] Hartian secondary rules, in the main, govern the responsibilities of officials, such as legislators and judges acting in that capacity; while primary rules apply to the entire citizenry, extending, of course, to officials in

[112] See R Sartorius, 'Positivism and the Foundations of Legal Authority', in R Gavison (ed), *Issues in Contemporary Legal Philosophy: The Influence of HLA Hart* (Clarendon Press 1987) ch 2.1 at 45. See also H Ross, *Law as a Social Institution* (Hart Publishing 2001) 48. Obviously, Hart is not unaware of the conventional tripartite division of governmental functions: see HLA Hart, *The Concept of Law* (this chapter, n 3) 28–29, where Hart makes reference to 'the three departments, judicial, legislative, and administrative, into which government is customarily though vaguely divided'.

[113] M Weber, *Economy and Society* (this chapter, n 44) 217–226. In a late essay, 'Politics as a Vocation', Weber comments only in passing on the separation of powers doctrine in the context of a discussion of presidential powers in the American political system. See M Weber, 'Politics as a Vocation' ['*Politik als Beruf*'] in HH Gerth and CW Mills (trs and eds), *From Max Weber: Essays in Sociology* (Oxford University Press 1946) 108.

[114] See M Weber, *Economy and Society* (this chapter, n 44) 219.

[115] See generally BZ Tamanaha, *On the Rule of Law: History, Politics, Theory* (Cambridge University Press 2004).

their *non-official* capacity.[116] An official, in other words, is expected to be no less obligated to refrain from criminal conduct (such as assault, theft, fraud) and to observe (for example) contractual obligations when acting as a private citizen than any 'ordinary' (non-official) private citizen. In Weber's pure type of bureaucratic legal authority the rule of law paradigm is manifested in the idea that the 'typical person in authority' (the 'official') is subject to an 'impersonal order' to which official actions are oriented. For their part, those who *obey* authority (otherwise, *the law*) occupy the role of citizen or 'private individual' in the context of both Hart's municipal legal system and Weber's ideal type of legal authority.[117]

According to Hart, the laws to which citizens and officials are subject are framed in general terms and have an 'open-textured' structure.[118] In other words, they are framed in terms that allow for application to specific cases, reflected in the way in which instances of factual scenarios (eg an alleged criminal offence) are presented to a court of law and adjudicated upon. The open texture gives scope for interpretational discretion exercisable by judges and others. In a similar vein, in his pure type of bureaucratic legal authority, Weber refers to legal precepts and principles that are capable of 'generalised formulation'.[119] In the context of a working bureaucracy – where governance is raised to the level of a (humanly) 'mechanised' operation – the generality of the governing norms lends itself to uniformity and consistency of approach. Indeed, every 'legal bureaucracy' – the institutions and apparatuses that operate to perform governmental functions of the centralised state in ways prescribed by law – needs to operate 'mechanistically' otherwise everyone will just 'do their own thing'. Inevitably, without some uniformity of approach, the institutions and apparatuses of legal authority will descend into dysfunctionality.

Taking stock, then, even if a few similarities are identifiable between Hart's model of a municipal legal system and Weber's pure type of bureaucratic legal authority, that in itself does not make Hart a 'Weberian'. It is undeniable that Hart's municipal legal system could be said to represent the product of a discriminating, if mainly unacknowledged, *selection* from the infinitude of reality; and that that model, when viewed as some kind of ideal type, progresses somewhat beyond Hart's archetypal Rex dynasty. In a number of respects the resultant model does go some way towards comprising, as Weber would put it, a one-sided accentuation of points of view and a synthesis of diffuse and discrete individual phenomena arranged, according to those points of view, into a unified analytical construct.[120]

[116] As Hart comments: '... a distinction may be made between the members of the society in their private capacity as individuals and the same persons in their official capacity as electors and legislators'. See HLA Hart, *The Concept of Law* (this chapter, n 3) 75–76.

[117] See M Weber, *Economy and Society* (this chapter, n 44) 217–218. See also HLA Hart, *The Concept of Law* (this chapter, n 3) 135, where Hart makes reference to rules of law that guide the actions of officials and private individuals alike.

[118] HLA Hart, *The Concept of Law* (this chapter, n 3) 124–136.

[119] Max Weber, *Economy and Society* (this chapter, n 44) 217.

[120] See Weber's outline of key characteristics of the ideal-type construct in M Weber, '"Objectivity" in Social Science' (this chapter, n 17) 90. See also section 4.5 (Chapter 4, above) at n 56.

Yet while Hart makes reference in *The Concept of Law* to a number of discrete characteristics that go to make up his model of a Western municipal legal system, the task of formulating the model as a 'unified analytical construct' is not something that Hart literally attempts. So while, arguably in some respects, Hart and Weber occupy a not dissimilar epistemological space, a number of the specific analytical tasks promoted in Weber's general social scientific writings are simply not undertaken in *The Concept of Law*.

5.4. Concluding Reflections

In this chapter we have explored the gravitational pull exerted by social theory on Hart's writing (principally *The Concept of Law*) against the background of Hart's much-scrutinised claim – even if, apparently, later privately retracted in part – that his major work was to be regarded as an 'essay in descriptive sociology'. The chapter also touched upon the possible implications of this tendency for approaching an understanding of Hart's analysis of legal 'rights correlative to obligations' viewed in a social theory context. It is worth briefly revisiting a few of the resonances that have been identified in Hart's writings that could be said to have their origin either in Weber's writings or more generally in social theory.

Arguably, the most compelling line of analysis to emerge from this exercise turns on the idea that the (Hartian) legal 'right correlative to obligation' may be seen as an instrument of social power. (Interestingly, the origins of this idea had emerged not in *The Concept of Law* – a claimed 'essay in descriptive sociology' – but in Hart's *Essays on Bentham*.) In essence – and representing a core tenet of Hartian will theory – Hart characterises a legal right as a power of control (residing in a right-holder) over a correlative obligation (residing in a duty-bearer). We saw that it is possible to identify echoes of such a social power dynamic in Weber's concept of *Herrschaft*, which Weber scholars have characterised as a structure of superordination and subordination, and as a relational concept centred upon the impact of one person upon another in so far as the behaviour of the one (for example, a duty-bearer) may be analysed as having been determined by the other (for example, a right-holder). We also found that Hart's concept of the social rule – outlined in *The Concept of Law* – in certain respects complemented his will-theory-based analysis of legal rights advanced in *Essays on Bentham*. The class of social rules subsumes *legal* rules and can perhaps be seen (in the context of Hartian theorising) as the substructure of legal rights. Furthermore, the social relationality of legal rights is mirrored in the inherently relational structure of Hartian social rules. (In particular, the idea of Hohfeldian relationality is explored in Chapter 3, above.) At the same time we saw that Hart's concept of social rule incorporates the idea of a critical reflective attitude which, as was also argued, may be grounded in socially directed behaviour of the rule-following subject. It was also possible to identify in the idea of a critical reflective attitude echoes both of Weber's idea of subjective meaning (embedded in social action) and of the related Weberian idea of rule-following behaviour.

We found, moreover, that the respective positions of right-holder and duty-bearer could be reimagined in the metaphor of the sovereign-subject relationship expressed in Hart's archetypal Rex dynasty. (Hart, of course, does not actually pursue that line of analysis – his use of the Rex paradigm is primarily as a means of critiquing the Austinian model of law as commands of a sovereign habitually obeyed by the populace.) In this context, a right-holder could be seen to occupy the role of – in Hart's words – a 'small-scale sovereign'. Again, this resonated with the idea of a command, and of a command-issuing right-holder, reflected in Weber's concept of *Herrschaft*.

The resonances of social theory identified in Hart's writings in this chapter – with entirely distinct echoes of social theory underlying Kelsen's writings outlined in Chapter 4 – point to a need, in the analysis to follow, to develop a theoretical position that synthesises these core insights and draws the disparate strands of analysis together. But there is also a need to factor in the institutional dimension of legal rights, as suggested in Chapters 2 and 3, given that the adoption of a perspective that accentuates the position of right-holder and duty-bearer *whilst playing down* or failing to have due regard to the standpoint of an institutional insider – such as an ultimate supreme court judge – will necessarily (so the argument goes) lead to an impoverished or distorted theoretical account of the legal rights subsisting within a Hartian so-called 'municipal legal system'. This general outlook and approach are therefore elaborated upon, and refined, in Chapters 7, 8 and 9.

6

Towards a Defence of Hartian Will Theory*

6.1. Introduction

In Chapter 3,[1] there was brief discussion of the critique of Hartian will theory developed by Neil MacCormick out of an analysis of the position of children viewed as a 'test case'.[2] MacCormick's critique, as we have seen, centres on the idea that – at least according to his interpretation of Hartian will theory – any given right-holder would need to have a certain degree of cognitive or volitional capacity before any claimed legal right (of the purported right-holder) could, as a practical proposition, be considered to exist. Needless to say, many children, particularly those in infancy or otherwise of a young age – and with, at least in principle, some claim to the possession of a particular legal right – might be considered to have significant shortcomings at the level of cognitive or volitional capacity; and this, so the argument goes, strikes against the idea (claimed to be critical to Hartian

* This chapter overlaps with (but progresses beyond) two previously published articles on a related theme: H Ross, 'Children's Rights and Theories of Rights' (2013) 21 *International Journal of Children's Rights* 679; and H Ross, 'Children's Rights – a Defence of Hartian Will Theory' (2014) 22 *International Journal of Children's Rights* 43. Hart does not tend to use the expression 'will theory' to describe what is referred to in this book as 'Hartian will theory'. Instead, he claims to provide 'a general theory in terms of the notion of a legally respected individual choice': see HLA Hart, *Essays on Bentham* (this chapter, n 3, below) 193. (He also describes his theory thus at p 189.) Yet, while Hart explicitly refers to his theory – when distinguishing it from interest (or 'benefit') theory – as 'the rival "choice" theory' (ibid 190), it is nonetheless clear that his theory can be viewed as being centred on the will of the right-holder inasmuch as an exertion of 'will' would be manifested in the right-holder's exercise of relevant choices – eg to take steps to enforce a right, or to waive it, or to leave it unenforced. For convenience, therefore, this book uses the expression 'Hartian will theory' to denote what Hart refers to as his 'choice theory'. Hart even makes a concession in the direction of 'benefit theorising', when he remarks that in some sense the 'notion of individual benefit' must be brought to bear in theorising about rights, albeit (as Hart points out) '*not* as the benefit theory brings it in': ibid at 189. He claims that this is with a view to 'supplement[ing] the notion of individual choice'.

[1] See, in particular, sections 3.2.1 and 3.2.3 (Chapter 3, above).

[2] See principally DN MacCormick, 'Children's Rights: A Test Case for Theories of Right' (1976) 62 *Archiv für Rechts- und Sozialphilosophie* 305. This article is also reprinted with modifications as chapter 8 of DN MacCormick, *Legal Right and Social Democracy: Essays in Legal and Political Philosophy* (Clarendon Press 1982) (hereafter, in this chapter, 'Children's Rights: A Test Case'). (In this chapter, references are to the article reprinted as a book chapter in 1982.) See also, more generally, DN MacCormick, 'Rights in Legislation' in PMS Hacker and J Raz (eds), *Law, Morality, and Society: Essays in Honour of HLA Hart* (Clarendon Press 1977) (hereafter, in this chapter, 'Rights in Legislation').

will theory) that the possession of a right is necessarily dependent on the ability of the right-holder – by way of an exertion of will – to choose to waive or extinguish the right, or to enforce it or leave it unenforced.[3] MacCormick's position, or its central arguments, have gained wide acceptance as a persuasive basis for holding Hart's version of will theory to be untenable and for rejecting Hartian will theory in favour of interest theory.

In this chapter it is proposed to revisit and examine MacCormick's critique of Hartian will theory with a view, ultimately, to outlining a possible *defence* of Hart's theoretical position against MacCormick's critique, taking in lines of analysis set out in Chapter 1 and also touching upon issues explored in Chapter 3. This will lay the groundwork for developing, in Chapter 9, an independent position on Hartian will theory arising out of the part of Chapter 5 (particularly section 5.3.4) that focuses upon the (Hartian) legal right viewed as an instrument of social power. The idea, in the final analysis, is to view Hartian will theory as a credible alternative to versions of the rival interest theory of legal rights, such as those of MacCormick and Raz. Nonetheless, in Chapter 9, consideration is given to the possibility of combining elements of Hartian will theory and traditional interest theory towards developing the beginnings of a 'third way' approach to rights theorising that reaches beyond the two rival approaches.

6.2. Core Aspects of MacCormick's Critique of Hartian Will Theory

As we have seen in Chapter 3, MacCormick gives credence to the idea that if we were to regard Hartian will theory as presenting, in principle, an accurate and analytically sound way of conceptualising legal rights, we would have to deny to children the possibility of their possessing any rights at all, legal or otherwise: given a child's relative inability to exert control over the behaviour of others, or to make the choices upon which the existence of rights are (according to Hartian will theory) *said* to depend.[4] Plainly, this is not so much a reflection of a 'real world' in which children do not have any legal rights to speak of; rather, it is a consequence of following through the implications of a theoretical position which, in the opinion of some, fails to accommodate the possibility of children possessing and exercising legal rights so as to enjoy the benefits of legal rights conferred upon them.

What, then, is the force of the arguments that underpin MacCormick's critique of Hartian will theory where the main focus is upon the position of the child

[3] See HLA Hart, *Essays on Bentham: Jurisprudence and Political Theory* (Clarendon Press 1982) (hereafter, in this chapter, '*Essays on Bentham*') generally ch VII, but particularly 174–189. See also, more specifically, 183–184, 185, 188.

[4] This point is made quite explicitly by Tom Campbell. See TD Campbell, 'The Rights of the Minor: as Person, as Child, as Juvenile, as Future Adult' (1992) 6 *International Journal of Law and the Family* 1, 2. See also the general discussion in section 3.2.1 (Chapter 3, above).

viewed as a 'test case'? A number of considerations are identified in the analysis to follow, with a brief outline of MacCormick's fundamental position being an appropriate point of departure.

6.2.1. Revisiting MacCormick's Fundamental Position

In Chapter 3 – in particular, sections 3.2.1 and 3.2.3 – MacCormick's basic position is briefly outlined. Examining this in further detail and, where appropriate, restating that position, we find that there is a key consideration – possibly above and beyond any other – that makes Hart vulnerable to the charge that the notion of children's rights is incompatible with Hart's version of the will theory of rights. As it happens, this is only marginally relevant to the position of children per se, deriving instead from a more fundamental proposition, residing at the core of Hartian will theory, which is that certain characteristics of a right identified by Hart are *necessary and sufficient* features – rather than being (as MacCormick would urge) merely ancillary or incidental features – of a right.[5] The implication of this, from a practical standpoint, is that if it is arguable that the characteristics in question are absent in a given case then it will follow that no right can be said to exist. Needless to say, as MacCormick has maintained, the presence or absence of the relevant features of rights, when Hartian will theory is applied in a given case, significantly impacts the position of children, extending to their claimed ability or inability to possess and exercise rights (legal or otherwise). In the extreme case, when relevant characteristics are considered to be absent, what is implied in terms of Hartian will theory is that legal rights cannot in any meaningful sense be ascribed to children. It is instructive, then, to give brief attention to the generic characteristics that Hart considers to be indispensable to – or to be defining features of – rights, and to the relevance that the presence or absence of such characteristics have when considering the status of children's rights (in *theory*, at any rate).

As discussed in Chapter 3,[6] Hart makes a point of highlighting, (in chapter VII of *Essays on Bentham*) that the power of control with which a right-holder is invested – principally in the sense of having the ability to enforce a right, waive it or leave it unenforced – is not only *necessary* for a right to exist in a given case, but is necessary *and sufficient*:

> [W]hat is sufficient and necessary [for a right to exist] is that [the right-holder] … should have at least some measure of the control, described above, over the correlative obligation.[7]

[5] As MacCormick notes: 'while conceding the truth, and the practical importance, of these points, I would strongly contend that powers of waiver or enforcement are essentially ancillary to, not constitutive of, rights (whether primary rights or remedial rights)'. See DN MacCormick, 'Children's Rights: A Test Case' (this chapter, n 2) 164.

[6] See section 3.2.1 (Chapter 3, above), n 11.

[7] See HLA Hart, *Essays on Bentham* (this chapter, n 3) 188.

We have seen at various points in the preceding discussion that the definitional dependence of a right on the concept of power of control – to say nothing of the need for such a power to ground the factual existence of a right – are two of the considerations that render the idea of children's rights especially problematic in Hartian will theory.[8] If we could dispense with the idea that power of control, with its attendant choices, is actually *constitutive* of a right – that being MacCormick's interpretation of Hartian will theory – the problematic issues surrounding children's rights, and identified by MacCormick, would surely disappear. In that situation, an absence of ability on the part of young children to exercise a relevant power of control, or to make relevant choices attending the possession of a right, would no longer be relevant to whether the claimed right does or does not exist (including whether in principle a child can be the possessor of a right). However, dispensing with power of control and related choices would mark a fundamental departure from Hartian will theory. It would be Hartian will theory stripped of its most essential characteristics. And, simply put, it would *not* be Hartian will theory.

6.2.2. MacCormick's Remedial Rights Thesis

In reflecting upon whether the presence of incapacities of children in principle renders important aspects of Hartian will theory untenable, it is instructive to have some regard to the practicalities of *agency*. Ordinarily, the powers of control and their attendant choices which, for Hart (following MacCormick) are actually constitutive of a legal right, would be exercised not by an incapacitous child as such, but on behalf of the child through persons who are not equivalently lacking in capacity. More often than not a child's parents, or a guardian, would become involved in taking steps to pursue or enforce a claimed right. At first sight this would appear to provide a convenient practical response to the theoretical difficulty inherent in Hartian will theory where a lack of cognitive or volitional capacity implies a (theoretical) inability on the part of a child to possess and exercise a legal right, and thus to enjoy the benefits thereby conferred. MacCormick, however, takes the view that the availability of a representative to pursue a claimed legal right on behalf of an incapacitous child does nothing to address the shortcomings of Hartian will theory that he has identified. According to MacCormick, the incapacities standing in the way of a child's pursuing and enforcing a right *that is claimed to exist at a substantive level* – thereby, in terms of MacCormick's understanding of Hartian will theory, 'dispossessing' the child of the substantive

[8] It should be recalled that Hart maintains that we may recognise as a defining feature of a right correlative to obligation the 'individual's legal powers of control, full or partial, over that obligation'. (ibid 188) For Hart, the idea of power of control appears to be synonymous with the notion of choice. Thus, anyone 'who has a right has a choice respected by the law', whilst (according to Hart) his theory is 'centred on the notion of a legally respected individual choice' (ibid 189) (mainly) to take enforcement action, or to waive the right, or to leave it unenforced.

right – are not in any sense compensated for at the same (ie the substantive) level when the representative steps in to act on the child's behalf. Rather, the representative's agency, according to MacCormick, operates at the level of *remedial rights*. So, if we seek to argue that the availability of agency relationships rescues Hartian will theory from the difficulties it faces our efforts will be misdirected – or so MacCormick would maintain. MacCormick takes the view that the mechanism of representation operates remedially – ie as a kind of 'remedy' – empowering (capacitous) adults to do what a child cannot do. Here, a child's representative is seen to exercise rights grounded in adjective law, not substantive law. According to this view, then, Hartian will theory would 'deny' rights to children at the substantive level, but not at the remedial level.[9]

But is MacCormick's position tenable? Ordinarily, when a legal right is exercised at a substantive level there will be some rudimentary recognition of the existence of the right, leading (if need be) to the right-holder's calling upon a duty-bearer to perform the relevant obligation – eg it may be a simple contractual (and therefore legally recognised) obligation to render performance under the contract. There may be little activity beyond that; though that in itself might be a preliminary to (for instance) enforcement action. Clearly, infants cannot begin to engage with even these most basic preliminaries, lacking, as they do, the necessary intellectual competence and maturity. The prerequisites of a valid substantive legal right that Hartian will theory would insist upon – the ability to exercise control over the obligations of others, and to make associated choices, such as enforcing or waiving the right – are simply absent in the case of an infant. Yet MacCormick appears to argue to a remarkable position, which is that the enforcement of a legal right by a child's representative, taking place at the 'remedial' level, does nothing to maintain or secure any claimed right of the child at the substantive level because, *at that [substantive] level* (on MacCormick's interpretation of Hartian will theory) the right literally does not exist. MacCormick's position implies that action taken by a representative on behalf of a child that is purely 'remedial' in nature – presumably involving some 'exercise' of remedial (adjective) rights – can be taken independently of the existence (or claimed non-existence) of any substantive right. The notion that one can possess a remedial right without at the same time possessing the substantive right that underpins it is surely fallacious. Remedial rights, falling within adjective law and entailing an ability (eg in a civil law setting) to instigate and prosecute legal proceedings including, if necessary, enforcement action, such as by officials or officers of the court, surely rest upon pre-existing substantive rights. The key question is how can 'remedial' action be taken on behalf of a child in relation to a (necessarily substantive) right that – following the logic of MacCormick's critique – never existed in the first place? The idea of exercising a remedial right in the context of (eg civil) court proceedings in the pursuit of some form of redress (a 'remedy') in respect of a matter that has no

[9] See DN MacCormick, 'Children's Rights: A Test Case' (this chapter, n 2) 156–157.

basis in any substantive right is surely untenable. Arguably MacCormick is forced to paint himself into this corner as, without some accounting for the possibility of 'remedial' or adjective interventions which the law provides for, he would have to deny the availability of an entire area of law – the law of agency – which operates (among other things) to enable legal rights to be exercised and enforced on behalf of those who are simply incapable of doing this for themselves.

In a conventional situation where a child's representative takes action pursuant to a substantive legal right claimed to be possessed by the child, the law will treat such action as being, for all practical and legal purposes, the action of the child. Anything that can be classed as an exercise of rights on behalf of a child – whether remedial or substantive – is deemed by law to be an exercise of rights possessed by the child. Mechanisms of agency are not incompatible with Hartian will theory: they complement it. Such mechanisms make it possible for a child – who lacks the cognitive or volitional capacity to exercise the power of control, or to make any of the choices, that Hartian will theory (or at least MacCormick's interpretation of that theory) might insist are necessarily entailed in the existence of a legal right – to be fully in possession of legal rights. We have seen that Hart explicitly acknowledges the special theoretical difficulties entailed in the idea of children's rights without any corresponding acknowledgment of this by MacCormick.[10] At the same time Hart recognises the possibility that rights can be possessed by a child in situations where the rights are exercisable not directly by the child but by a representative. Hart observes that the power of control over a corresponding obligation – this being a core feature of his version of will theory – is exercised by a representative on behalf of 'infants or other persons not *sui juris*' and may be subject to approval by a court. Hart points to a key constraint upon the power of representatives. What they can and cannot do is determined by what those whom they represent could have done if *sui juris*. But, critically, any legal rights exercised by a representative are regarded as belonging at all times to the child and not to the representative.[11]

It is not in doubt that Hart accommodates the possibility of children's rights even while failing to address more generally the theoretical conundrum to which MacCormick draws attention – namely, the problematic question whether a legal right can 'survive' an absence of cognitive and volitional capacity of the claimed right-holder. In framing his version of will theory in the way he does – in particular, making reference to necessary and sufficient existence conditions of rights – Hart perhaps unwittingly creates a (theoretical) 'rod for his own back'. But, at the same time, MacCormick arguably fails to make a convincing case that Hartian will theory is not in significant ways rescued by the availability of the agency relationship. In attempting to explain away agency as something that can operate exclusively at a 'remedial' (adjective) level, via remedial rights, without being in any way predicated upon rights that exist at the substantive level (ie at the level of the (purported) right-holding child) is questionable.

[10] See section 3.2.3 (Chapter 3, above) at nn 46 and 47.

[11] See HLA Hart, *Essays on Bentham* (this chapter, n 3) 184 n 86. See also 185 n 88.

Yet, the issues highlighted by MacCormick still leave Hart vulnerable to a criticism voiced by Tom Campbell who, perhaps more convincingly than MacCormick, identifies the real crux of the problem:

> The embarrassment for the power theorists of denying rights to children may seem to be avoided by allowing that a proxy, such as a parent, may exercise, on behalf of a child, the discretionary powers which constitute the rights in question. However, on the power theory, this must be *less than a full possession of a right* since the bearer's will, the exercise of which is definitive for the existence of the right, is not involved. Indeed, it would appear, on the assumptions of the theory, that the proxy is the right-holder … [C]hildren's rights exercised by proxies are certainly less than full rights as defined by the power theory.[12]

6.2.3. The Fallacy of the 'Sliding Scale'

MacCormick's critique of Hartian will theory, as we have seen, focuses upon the position of the child viewed as a 'test case'. Plainly, MacCormick's critique is worthy of attention, though we have seen in section 6.2.2 that some aspects of his analysis are open to question. A further reason to query the soundness of the critique, it is suggested, centres on what might be referred to as the *fallacy of the 'sliding scale'*. Underlying MacCormick's stance is an assumption that anyone who is *not* incapacitous,[13] and is therefore *ex hypothesi* unhindered by cognitive and volitional shortcomings, falls by default within a category of potential right-holders with (on the face of it) no constraints upon their ability to understand, exercise, enforce and ultimately possess, legal rights.[14] The assumption would be that persons in that category – with the power of control and associated choices that Hartian will

[12] See TD Campbell, 'The Rights of the Minor: as Person, as Child, as Juvenile, as Future Adult' (1992) 6 *International Journal of Law and the Family* 1, 4 (emphasis added). Note that Campbell refers to 'will theory' and 'power theory' interchangeably. It may be argued that Campbell, in interpreting Hartian will theory seemingly as literally as MacCormick, reaches a similarly uncompromising position that might have been mitigated by a more attentive (and sympathetic) reading of Hart's stated position. See, further, the discussion in section 6.3 (this chapter, below).

[13] In this context, (very broadly) someone might be viewed as incapacitous by reason of (for instance) infancy, immaturity, or some mental incapacity or disorder.

[14] See DN MacCormick, 'Children's Rights: A Test Case' (this chapter, n 2) 164: '[T]he central point which … [Hartian will] theory stresses is one which should not be denied. It is certainly true that *apart from such cases as those of children or the mentally incapacitated*, the holder of a legal right is normally permitted and empowered in law to choose whether or not on any given occasion he should avail himself of his right by insisting on performance by another party of the relevant duty'. (Emphasis added.) This passage makes clear that, in MacCormick's critique, children and the mentally incapacitated – where the latter category could extend to (mentally incapacitated) adults *and* children – are to be regarded as an *exception* to what might be regarded as the 'norm'; but it also demonstrates MacCormick's acquiescence in the core ideas of empowerment and choice residing within Hartian will theory. Towards reinforcing this position, MacCormick also argues that '… in all normal cases rights ought to carry with them powers of waiver or enforcement. That the legal system does in fact normally confer just that power of waiver or enforcement on right holders should accordingly be taken as implying no more than the unsurprising truth that the liberal principle is deeply embedded in our law'. (ibid 165)

theory, following MacCormick's interpretation, would identify as *constitutive* of a legal right[15] – are fully apprised of the existence, content, scope and effect of their legal rights and would ordinarily be in a position to take action to exercise and enforce them.[16] What would appear to make children (and children's rights) ideally suited to being treated as a 'test case' in terms of MacCormick's critique is the fact that children should be seen as an *exception*.[17] And it is the presence of such a problematic, and problematising, exception that, MacCormick would argue, fatally undermines Hartian will theory.[18]

Yet, if we follow through the logic of MacCormick's stance it is arguable that, ultimately, the *awareness* – or lack of awareness – that individuals have of their legal rights is as significant in this context as any cognitive incapacity that might be said to beset them. Without doubt, cognitive shortcomings adversely impact an individual's awareness of legal rights; but so also do such matters as ignorance of the law or a simple lack of knowledge of legal rights. Viewed in those terms, children may be no more a 'test case' for a critique of Hartian will theory than the immense category of potential right-holders who are not children and may be assumed to be fully capacitous *yet* are oblivious of their legal rights. So if, according to MacCormick's interpretation of Hartian will theory, legal rights 'do not exist' for children (or children of a certain age), then potentially they 'do not exist' for a very much wider category of possible right-holders for reasons connected with those right-holders' fundamental lack of awareness of the rights they are thought to possess.[19] If MacCormick is correct to hold that Hartian will theory is in error in *necessitating* (before the rights can be said to exist) a measure of cognitive capacity – including, by extension, awareness of legal rights – this suggests the need to incorporate within MacCormick's stance some kind of threshold beyond which rights are to be held to exist; and falling short of which rights must be held not to exist. Such a threshold might perhaps be viewed as a fixed point on a 'sliding scale'. This is not an idea that MacCormick explicitly entertains, of course; but it can reasonably be inferred from his critique. Indeed, pressing the matter further,

[15] See, for example, DN MacCormick, 'Children's Rights: A Test Case' (this chapter, n 2) 157, 164.

[16] Essentially, MacCormick opposes the idea, which he holds to be implicit in, and to be a corollary of, Hartian will theory, that if individuals have certain capacities it follows that they *can* be – and if they do not, they *cannot* be – the possessors of a legal right.

[17] See especially the passage cited above, this chapter, n 14.

[18] This point – when framed in terms of a child's lack of volitional capacity – is made more explicitly by Tom Campbell. See TD Campbell, 'The Rights of the Minor: as Person, as Child, as Juvenile, as Future Adult' (1992) 6 *International Journal of Law and the Family* 1, 2. See also the related discussion in section 3.2.1 (Chapter 3, above) at n 18.

[19] It might be objected that, unlike many adults, it is simply impossible for children of a very young age – at least until (eventually) they reach an appropriate level of intellectual maturity – to grasp the concept and implications of possessing a legal right. Many adults, on the other hand, will not be in that situation for as long as it is open to them to inform themselves of their legal position and they choose to do that. But there will always be a significant number of adults who, not unlike children of a certain age, will simply lack awareness of the legal rights they possess; and that will be the case even if there is no question of the adult having any kind of mental impairment or disability, and regardless of any advice they might have sought: eg from a lawyer or other adviser.

if children are a 'test case' and a problematic exception, the suggestion is that there is a category wider than, and lying beyond, children that MacCormick would regard as essentially *unproblematic*, because he would assume the members of that category to be cognitively competent and fully aware of their rights. The individuals in that (wider) category would be the 'classic case' that would make Hartian will theory, in MacCormick's estimation, tenable and workable. This would follow from MacCormick's acknowledgment that Hart is not entirely in error in holding that a right (at least for some) gives a right-holder not only control over a correlative obligation but choices associated with such control.[20]

But what is the force of MacCormick's critique if children are to be considered problematic (owing to shortcomings in their cognitive capacity) even while the position of individuals in a wider, supposedly unproblematic, category may in fact be *equivalently* problematic, not because of any existential lack of cognitive capacity but owing to a generalised lack of awareness (and frequent misunderstanding) of such matters as the content, scope and effect – and, indeed, the very existence – of their legal rights? On that basis, children may not, after all, be exceptional if many more (beyond children) are, for not unrelated reasons, in the same boat. If this fairly reflects the extended logic of MacCormick's critique, one might ask at what exact point on an imaginary 'sliding scale' would right-holders be deemed to have sufficient awareness of key aspects of their legal rights for those rights to be considered to have a 'fully-fledged' existence?[21]

At one end of the continuum, for instance, will be right-holders with an all-encompassing *unawareness* of important aspects of their rights with no ability personally to take the action necessary to enforce those rights: here we find, for example, infants or adults with certain types of mental impairment. For this purpose, it must be assumed, contrary to the implications of MacCormick's interpretation of Hartian will theory, but conformably to Hart's own stated position, that such persons *do* in fact have legal rights, and that the mechanism of agency operates entirely functionally to facilitate the exercise of those rights.[22] At the other end of the continuum are right-holders with a far-reaching awareness of the existence, content and significance of their legal rights and a knowledge and understanding of the steps necessary to enforce those rights: for instance, commercial entities with in-house counsel, or access to external advisers, responsible for ensuring

[20] This is certainly suggested by the passages reproduced above – see this chapter, nn 5 and 14. MacCormick accepts the general premise (of Hartian will theory) that rights confer power of control and choices. He disputes that power of control and choices are *constitutive* of a right, preferring to regard these as ancillary or incidental to a right.

[21] We might ask how *perfect* a knowledge one needs to have in order to meet the threshold for the existence of a right on a 'sliding scale'? Ultimately, the question might resolve to who, short of a '*Iudex*', would possess that perfect knowledge? (See, in particular, the discussion in section 3.2.3 (Chapter 3, above).) On the other hand, one might question whether, for all purposes of the day-to-day engagement with such rights as we might claim to have, a 'perfect' knowledge of such rights is ever a practical necessity.

[22] See, mainly, the discussion in section 3.2.3 (Chapter 3, above) at nn 46 and 47 and section 6.2.2 (this chapter, above).

compliance with contractual obligations or regulatory requirements applicable within the sector in which they operate. While there is relative certainty at the two extremes, the extensive area between the extremes (including the position of older children) is necessarily uncertain; and this makes a judgment that a right exists or does not exist – based on right-holder awareness; or, for that matter, cognitive or volitional (in)capacity – somewhat unsafe.

The extended logic of MacCormick's critique thus appears to suggest that Hartian will theory is unworkable in shedding light upon the position of all but a tiny minority of exceptionally well-informed individuals who are in the best position to exercise the very power of control and associated choices that – at least in terms of MacCormick's reading of Hart – *call into existence* any right they may be thought to possess. And while this may be an extended reading of the implications of MacCormick's critique, it must be seen to go hand in hand with a similarly outlying theoretical position (also suggested by MacCormick's critique) which is that Hartian will theory implies that legal rights 'metamorphose' into existence the more awareness individuals have of the rights they are thought to possess. This is the 'sliding scale' approach assignable to MacCormick's critique; and it is surely flawed. The key point here is that the problematic implications of viewing children as an (exceptional) 'test case' – and otherwise following through the logic of MacCormick's critique *beyond* children – *are more of MacCormick's, than of Hart's, making*, given Hart's explicit reliance on the mechanism of agency which, some might argue, goes some way towards rescuing Hartian will theory from the conundrum of the incapacitous child.[23]

In the final analysis, our awareness of the existence, content, scope, import and effect of those legal rights we may claim or suppose ourselves to have will always be a matter of degree, turning upon such considerations as the extent of our cognitive, volitional or intellectual capacity; or the extent of our actual knowledge of the rights in question; or the presence or absence of reliable legal advice; or our practical ability to exercise rights and pursue enforcement action. However, to believe, and to argue, that Hart rests an account of the existence of legal rights upon these considerations is surely a distortion of his version of will theory implying, as it does, a fallacious 'sliding scale' approach in which legal rights are to be regarded as somehow arbitrarily 'metamorphosing' in and out of existence mainly dependent upon elements of the consciousness of the right-holder. The recognition of this account of Hartian will theory *as* a distortion renders untenable key aspects of MacCormick's critique of that theory, and the extended logic of his critique.

6.2.4. The Problematic Position of 'Rights' Grounded in Criminal Law

A further plank of MacCormick's critique of Hartian will theory focuses attention on one of its central tenets – the idea that a legal right gives the right-holder,

[23] See above, this chapter, n 22.

among other things, the power and choice to *waive* the right in question.[24] MacCormick argues that there are situations where a power to waive a legal right is absent – for instance, the right may be, or may appear to be, legally incapable of waiver. MacCormick maintains that this is problematic for a theory in which the presence of such a power is to be seen as a prerequisite of the existence of the relevant rights. *Ex hypothesi* if the power of waiver is absent there can be no right.[25] There is a difficulty with this line of argument, however, which is that the right which MacCormick uses to illustrate his point appears to have its origin primarily in the *criminal law* (which is the branch of law least susceptible to personal waiver – as discussed below).[26] At the same time, the right in question is probably multi-layered, straddling criminal law and civil law: one layer may be incapable of waiver; another may not. Inevitably, this raises the question whether the type of right identified by MacCormick, in terms of its key characteristics, is best suited to validate this aspect of his critique.

MacCormick focuses upon a right not to be subjected to certain violations of one's physical integrity, claiming that rights of that kind are legally incapable of waiver: 'no [legally] valid consent can be given which releases the assaulting party from the duty of non-interference'.[27] He considers the situation where an invasive surgical procedure is performed by someone who is not a registered medical practitioner.[28] In the case of an operation carried out by an unqualified person, MacCormick supposes that the patient would be legally incapable of waiving the right to physical non-interference conferred by the law in that situation.[29] Moreover, it would matter nothing in MacCormick's view that the patient had in fact given consent to the unqualified surgeon to carry out the operation: the law would not recognise this purported waiver of the right. Under the criminal law, in particular, the surgical procedure performed by the unqualified surgeon might equate to an offence akin to an assault,[30] or wounding with intent to cause grievous bodily harm.[31]

[24] See HLA Hart, *Essays on Bentham* (this chapter, n 3), principally at 183–184.

[25] As MacCormick puts it: 'If there be no power to waive or assert the immunity, the claim, or whatever, upon some matter, upon that matter there is, *by definition*, no right either'. See DN MacCormick, 'Rights in Legislation' (this chapter, n 2) 196. This, of course, is based on quite a literal reading of Hartian will theory. See, further, the discussion at section 3.2.1 (Chapter 3, above); and the discussion in section 6.3 (this chapter, below).

[26] ibid 197. MacCormick refers explicitly to 'the law relating to assault' which could place his example within both (English) criminal law and the law of tort.

[27] ibid.

[28] ibid.

[29] Were it not for the 'medical exception' even lawful surgery carried out by a registered medical practitioner could be regarded as intentional wounding and in principle an offence under (for example) section 18 or 20 or 47 of the Offences against the Person Act 1861. See *R v Brown* [1994] 1 AC 212 (HL).

[30] See, for example, Offences against the Person Act 1861, section 47.

[31] See Offences against the Person Act 1861, section 18. See also, more generally, Alexandra Mullock, 'Surgical harm, consent, and English criminal law: When should "bad apple" surgeons be prosecuted?' (2021) 21(4) *Medical Law International* 343. As Mullock points out (at 355): '[t]he House of Lords in *Brown* [*R v Brown* [1994] 1 AC 212] confirmed that as a general principle, consent does not provide a defence to those who consensually inflict actual or serious (grievous bodily) harm on another. Certain

Even at first sight, it is obvious that the hypothetical situation presented by MacCormick is not as clear-cut as he appears to suggest. If a key aspect of his critique of Hartian will theory turns on whether certain rights are or are not capable of waiver, the class of rights that MacCormick highlights for discussion – towards comparing like with like – should correspond to the same class that Hart places at the centre of his analysis of will theory: namely, 'rights correlative to obligations'.[32] The focus of MacCormick's critique, therefore, should be (for example) on whether one individual, A, has a straightforward right under the law to demand physical non-interference from another, namely B: this being a 'classic' Hohfeldian claim-right–duty situation. Yet, as discussed below, MacCormick appears to go beyond that by encroaching upon the arena of criminal law where the question of susceptibility of waiver (of purported 'rights') is most acute.

Taking a (Hohfeldian) right as the point of departure – for example, A's right under the civil law of tort not to be subjected to physical harm by B – any potential liabilities arising in tort are necessarily overlaid (in MacCormick's hypothesis) by a criminal law dimension which, as discussed below, contrasts with the civil law dimension. Staying with civil law for the moment, in the case of an illegal surgical procedure – such as a 'backstreet abortion'[33] – are legal rights conferred under a *contract* if the abortionist claims a right to payment for the service rendered and the person seeking the abortion demands surgical intervention that is (for instance) reasonably skilful and does not cause 'collateral' injury, complications, infection, and so on? Arguably, in that situation the answer is in the negative, as not only is the surgical procedure (the abortion) and its execution unlawful but the contract itself is most likely illegal, and therefore void and unenforceable.[34] So, neither party to the arrangement would have the legally enforceable contractual rights (including the ability to waive such rights) that equate to the power of control and associated choices that Hartian will theory would identify as an integral part of – and of the possession of – legally enforceable (contractual) rights. This would follow from the fact that, from the outset, there is simply no legally recognised contract to speak of. It would thus seem that the contractual position neither reinforces, nor subverts, Hartian will theory.

consensual harms, however, may be regarded as legitimate if the harm occurs as a result of … reasonable surgery …' Mullock refers to at least one instance where surgery was regarded as not reasonable. A surgeon, Simon Bramhall, 'branded' a patient's transplanted liver with his initials using an argon gas coagulator and – quite apart from consequences in terms of his professional fitness to practise – was convicted of 'assault by beating' after pleading guilty. (No physical harm was caused by the 'branding'; though one patient reportedly suffered emotional trauma.) (ibid 351–352)

[32] See HLA Hart, *Essays on Bentham* (this chapter, n 3) 188. See also, generally, sections 3.2.1 and 3.2.2 (Chapter 3, above). This class of rights corresponds to the 'classic' Hohfeldian claim-right–duty nexus.

[33] Abortion-related offences are governed by the Offences Against the Person Act 1861, section 58; but an abortion carried out by a registered medical practitioner and otherwise complying with the Abortion Act 1967, section 1, is lawful.

[34] See Roger Brownsword and others, *The Law of Contract* (7th edn, LexisNexis Butterworths 2022) ch 5.

Maintaining the focus nonetheless on civil law, there are rights in tort that lie against an individual performing, say, an illegal surgical procedure which would in principle be waivable by a potential claimant even if, in actuality, that would probably never happen. The enforcement of such rights against the surgeon would represent an exercise of legal power of control as envisaged by Hartian will theory. At the same time, waiver of the rights in question aligns with choices identified by Hart. In a case in 2017 a qualified surgeon, Ian Paterson, was convicted of criminal offences under the Offences against the Person Act 1861 involving wounding and grievous bodily harm. Over many years he had carried out invasive and unnecessary, or inappropriate, surgery; in many cases for no medically justifiable reason.[35] Although multiple actions in tort have been pursued by former patients, and compensation funds have been established,[36] there would have been nothing to prevent any given claimant from waiving the right to pursue a claim in tort or from simply leaving the right unenforced.[37]

The presence of rights under contract or tort, existing alongside criminal laws (or criminal law 'rights', if such exist), and in relation to which the control and choices envisaged by Hartian will theory operate, does little to reinforce MacCormick's critique, predicated as it is upon the idea that certain rights are legally incapable of waiver. A focus on rights arising under contract or tort which may be waivable, obscures what the nature is of 'rights' that are (or to an extent are) derivable from the *criminal* law – if they are 'rights' in any conventional sense. Conceivably it is the criminal law component of the rights that MacCormick highlights for discussion that precipitates the best argument that the multi-layered rights in question are incapable of waiver. But this argument is only tenable: (A) if, in fairness to Hart, such 'rights' are 'Hartian' (Hohfeldian) 'rights correlative

[35] See Alexandra Mullock, 'Surgical harm, consent, and English criminal law: When should "bad apple" surgeons be prosecuted?' (2021) 21(4) *Medical Law International* 343, especially 348–351. Although MacCormick refers to the position where surgery is performed by someone who is not a registered medical practitioner, similar considerations would no doubt apply to someone who *is* a registered practitioner (such as Ian Paterson, as he was at the relevant time) but who nonetheless carries out unlawful surgical procedures in breach of the criminal law.

[36] See Andrew Gregory, '1,500 more patients of jailed breast surgeon Ian Paterson recalled' *The Guardian* (London: 1 February 2023): www.theguardian.com/society/2023/feb/01/1500-more-patients-of-jailed-breast-surgeon-ian-paterson-recalled (accessed 28 July 2025).

[37] It is unlikely that any consent standardly given by a patient in advance of receiving medical treatment would be considered to extend to a surgical procedure that was later established to be criminally unlawful. The terms of the consent would not ordinarily contemplate this possibility and probably could not operate as a waiver of liability in tort. On that basis it would be legally competent for a patient to consent in advance to the 'intentional wounding' entailed in a 'normal' (lawful) operation, thereby waiving relevant rights in tort. That said, the giving of consent, say, to an abortionist to carry out an illegal abortion (even if consent is only to be inferred from the circumstances – as opposed to being in writing) might operate as a waiver of liability in tort. However, it seems unlikely that patients in that situation – with knowledge of the intrinsic illegality of the abortion – would typically be minded to pursue remedies under the civil law: for instance, if they regretted opting for an abortion, or the abortion was bungled. But it remains a theoretical possibility that such patients could either expressly (in writing) waive such rights (if any) as may accrue to them under the law of tort, or otherwise be regarded as having waived such rights, having acquiesced in an intrinsically unlawful operation. The principle of *volenti non fit injuria* may have some relevance here.

to obligations' (to maintain MacCormick's critique within the scope of Hartian will theory); (B) if there are indeed 'rights' in the sense envisaged by MacCormick that are in fact grounded in criminal law; and (C) if the 'criminal law layer', ie an independent 'right' grounded in the criminal law, of the generic right to physical non-interference – which possibly subsists alongside a corresponding (Hohfeldian), and probably waivable, right (eg) in tort – is legally incapable of waiver. All three points bring to the fore the key question of the extent to which certain 'rights' can be grounded in the criminal law (at all). It is to this critical aspect of the discussion that we now turn.

Disregarding all concomitant civil law rights that may be waivable – such as contractual rights (if any), or rights arising in tort – any claimed 'right' not to be assaulted or subjected to harm or intentional wounding (or similar) must be viewed in the context of potential criminal liability in order to give credence to the relevant aspect of MacCormick's critique. On the face of it, a 'right' apparently grounded in criminal law – such as the 'right' not to be assaulted – doubtless has the appearance of a reflexive Hohfeldian right which in principle anyone could demand from anyone else. The criminal law imposes requirements that appear to be framed as duties – such as a duty to refrain from dangerous driving; a duty not to engage in insider trading; a duty to refrain from cruelty to animals, and so on. Certain of these 'duties' appear to confer 'rights' that correlate with them, such as a 'right' not to be assaulted. But does this accurately reflect how criminal laws, and criminal liability, actually operate? To what extent does the criminal law in fact confer 'rights,' such as to physical non-interference; and are the relevant 'rights' (particularly in the situation highlighted by MacCormick) legally incapable of waiver, thereby possibly (arguably) defeating one of the principal tenets – centred on power of control and choice – of Hartian will theory?

Our point of departure is to assert that a law establishing an offence under the criminal law does not confer anything that we would ordinarily consider to be a reflexive Hohfeldian claim-right *enforceable directly under the criminal law* such as in the generic situation where A has a right to demand that B refrain from violating A's physical integrity. It is true that criminal laws may have a superficial 'Hohfeldian' appearance, and that this might precipitate the question of how a purported 'right' might be enforced.[38] For instance, section 39 of the Criminal Justice and Licensing (Scotland) Act 2010 is framed in terms that define the respective positions of the offender and the target of the offence: 'A person ("A") commits an offence, to be known as the offence of stalking, where A stalks another person ("B")'. (The section goes on to define the main elements of the offence of stalking; and includes defences and punishments.) B does not, of course, have an enforceable legal right *conferred by section 39* availing directly against A, that A should refrain from activities falling within the definition of 'stalking' in that

[38] Even without that superficial (Hohfeldian) appearance of a right of A availing against B, most criminal laws – and criminal statutes in particular – are framed in terms of an 'offence'.

section.[39] But that does not exclude interpreting behaviour criminalised in this way as something to be avoided, even in the absence of explicit references to words of prohibition, or to the language of duty – ie a duty to refrain from the behaviour in question.[40]

An analysis of section 39 of the Criminal Justice and Licensing (Scotland) Act 2010 in terms of reflexive Hohfeldian claim-rights directly enforceable under the criminal law by B against A – for example, where A is suspected of 'stalking' B – is clearly problematic because section 39 does not confer the type of 'private' (or privately enforceable) rights that are to be found in the law of contract or tort.[41] Moreover, what we might take to be criminal law 'duties' (for instance, a duty not to 'stalk') are in reality an *interpretation* of criminal laws. Few of these, as we have seen, need make any explicit mention of 'duty', when use of the expression 'offence' is standard – an offence being something that is prohibited and to be avoided. In that situation even the use of prohibitive language is not essential. It may be unhelpful to view 'substantive' criminal laws – as opposed to procedural criminal laws that actually *do* explicitly confer rights, such as the right to silence – in terms of the 'rights' they purportedly confer upon (potential) victims of crime;[42] or of the 'duties' they purportedly confer upon (potential) perpetrators of offences.

Undoubtedly a shift of perspective is called for, in which there is less attention on the position of a perpetrator of crime vis-à-vis a victim (seen in terms of the victim's 'right' that the perpetrator refrain from committing criminal acts) and more on the position of a public official – eg a prosecutor – vis-à-vis an offender (or suspect). When the focus is on the position of (say) a public prosecutor, a promising line of enquiry emerges, centring on the relationship between legal power-holders and those subject to relevant powers. Seen in Hohfeldian terms, the emphasis moves from the Hohfeldian claim-right–duty nexus to the Hohfeldian power–liability nexus.[43] The criminal law confers legal powers upon a prosecutor

[39] See, in particular section 39(6): conduct constituting 'stalking'.

[40] As AM Honoré observes: 'Why are criminal statutes couched in terms such as "A person who does *X* is guilty of an offence" rather than "No one may do *X*"? … The form "No one may do *X*" is inherently imperfect. On the other hand the form "One who does *X* is guilty of an offence" implies the prohibition of *X*. It does so because it is self-evident that we should abstain from crime. To put the matter more formally there exists a rule or assumption of law to the effect that "no one may behave in a manner which constitutes an offence"'. See AM Honoré, 'Real Laws' in PMS Hacker and J Raz (eds), *Law, Morality, and Society: Essays in Honour of HLA Hart* (Clarendon Press 1977) ch 5, at 117.

[41] Nigel Simmonds contends that the criminal law, unlike the civil law, is not usually thought to be in the business of conferring rights: 'Of course part of the object of the criminal law is the *protection* of rights, but these rights are conferred either by morality (eg in the case of the right not to be assaulted) or by civil law (in the case of property rights)'. See NE Simmonds, *Central Issues in Jurisprudence: Justice, Law and Rights* (Sweet & Maxwell 1986) 138.

[42] The tendency to place the target of a criminal offence and the perpetrator at the centre of philosophical enquiry seems to be inevitable for a theoretical approach, such as the will or interest theory of rights, that attempts to view important dynamics within the legal world from the standpoint of a presumed 'right'-holder (or presumed 'duty'-bearer).

[43] The expression 'liability' is obviously appropriate when used in the context of legal terminology such as 'criminal liability' (or, in a slightly different context, 'tax liability'). But, by and large, 'liability' tends to be reserved for use in civil law where it is synonymous with 'duty' in the typical context of a

to take action in relation to a suspect when an offence has been committed.[44] These are legal powers in the sense of the Hohfeldian power–liability nexus; they are not 'rights' in the sense of Hohfeldian claim-rights (of a typically private nature) conferred personally upon the victim of a crime. This may cause us to identify a *prosecutor* – being the party invested with a *power* of prosecution – as a closer approximation to a party invested with a legal 'right' than a 'right'-holding crime *victim*. It is useful to adopt the standpoint of the prosecuting authorities because there is no mechanism readily available under the criminal law for a victim to claim and take enforcement action in relation to what we might conventionally regard as 'rights' grounded in criminal law that avail directly against an (alleged) offender.[45]

This prompts a reappraisal of MacCormick's fundamental position that certain 'rights' traceable ultimately to the criminal law – for example a 'right' availing against an unqualified surgeon not to be subjected to an invasive (potentially dangerous) surgical procedure – are incapable of waiver by the potential 'right'-holder (ie the patient) vis-à-vis the potential 'duty'-bearer (ie the unqualified surgeon). If MacCormick's position is valid, Hartian will theory would appear to be in error because *ex hypothesi* at least one significant power (or attendant choice) – that Hart would maintain is a prerequisite of the existence of the right in question:[46] namely, the ability to waive the right – is denied by law to the

Hohfeldian claim-right–duty nexus where a claimant may, for instance, assert a claim in tort against an alleged tortfeasor, such as a claim grounded in a right to compensation for personal injury. The resultant claim (say, to compensation) establishes a 'liability' in tort to make a payment to the claimant at a level determined by the court. In *Salmond on Jurisprudence*, the expression 'subjection' is used in preference to Hohfeld's 'liability'; but that is perhaps more descriptive of the effect of a power exercise than an instance of usage of standard legal terminology. See G Williams, *Salmond on Jurisprudence* (11th edn, Sweet & Maxwell 1957) 270, 275 n (c).

[44] This may also serve to explain the widespread use of the concept of *offence*, particularly in criminal statutes. Anything defined as an 'offence' immediately falls within the competence of a prosecutor or other public official to take enforcement action when relevant evidence emerges.

[45] Even where a so-called 'private prosecution' might seem appropriate, the party minded to pursue the prosecution (eg a crime victim or a family member with a relevant interest) is probably best seen as, in some sense, standing in for the prosecuting authorities in the exercise of a public power than as becoming involved in enforcing anything approximating a (privately enforceable) right against an alleged offender – for example, a right that the alleged offender should refrain from violating the victim's physical integrity (or should make restitution to the victim for having done so). Under Scots law, for instance, private prosecutions are extremely rare and proceed by way of an application to the High Court of Justiciary for a Bill for Criminal Letters. When granted, the Bill authorises the prosecution to be brought. Parties bringing a Bill must, among other things, establish a wrong that is personal to themselves. Relevant case law has repeatedly emphasised that the court's permission will only be granted in exceptional circumstances. See *McBain v Crichton* 1961 JC 25; and, more generally, *X v Sweeney* 1982 JC 70. For two relatively recent (failed) attempts to secure Bills for Criminal Letters see *Stewart v Payne; McQuade v Clarke* [2016] HCJAC 122; 2017 JC 155.

[46] In the context of his critique of Hartian will theory, MacCormick consistently maintains a stronger stance than Hart in relation to the prerequisites in question; and he interprets the theory in this way in order to subvert it. For his part, Hart argues that a right-holder need only have 'some measure' of control over a correlative obligation: '[W]hat is sufficient and necessary [for a right to exist] is that [the right holder] … should have at least some measure of the control, described above, over the correlative obligation'. See HLA Hart, *Essays on Bentham* (this chapter, n 3) 188. Part of this 'control', of course, is

'right'-holding patient. Patients in that situation would be thought to be incapable of divesting themselves of the relevant 'right'. However, the defect in MacCormick's position, it is suggested, is the assumption that in this situation the patient does in fact have a 'right' of physical non-interference – grounded in criminal law – directly maintainable against the unqualified surgeon. If the patient could in fact properly be regarded as possessing such a 'right', and the 'right' is correctly to be viewed as incapable of waiver, then MacCormick's critical stance against Hartian will theory might have force. But, crucially, the power and the choice as to whether to pursue legal proceedings under the criminal law against the unqualified surgeon – seen in terms of a Hohfeldian power–liability nexus obtaining between the prosecuting authorities and a suspected offender – simply do not lie with the patient.[47]

Given that, ordinarily, the relevant power and choice in fact lie with the prosecuting authorities, the patient is not possessed of anything – any *right* – that can be waived. MacCormick appears to take the view that an unwaivable Hohfeldian claim-right, grounded in criminal law – or at any rate the criminal law-based 'layer' of a multi-layered right that may have a wider grounding extending to (eg) the law of tort – obtains directly between the patient and the unqualified surgeon.[48] The prosecutor thus has a legal power to prosecute, whilst the unqualified surgeon is 'liable' to prosecution, with all that that entails as the process plays out – eg arrest, detention, questioning, charge, custody, trial, acquittal or incarceration (or other punishment). The discretion whether or not to prosecute – as with all criminal law prosecutions – will inevitably turn upon an assessment of matters such as availability and sufficiency

the ability (or choice) to waive a right. And MacCormick seeks to argue that if the ability to waive a right is not present in a given case then (according to Hartian will theory) a right cannot exist. However, it is clear that Hart does not adopt such an uncompromising position. (See the more extensive discussion of this point in section 6.3 (this chapter, below).)

[47] This line of argument adopts an essentially similar stance in relation to the Hohfeldian power–liability nexus as Hart (in the context of his version of will theory) explicitly adopts in relation to the Hohfeldian claim-right–duty nexus (which is the legal relationship corresponding to Hartian 'rights correlative to obligations'). See HLA Hart, *Essays on Bentham* (this chapter, n 3) generally ch VII; but particularly at 174–188. The position adopted here, in other words, is that power-conferring laws may often be seen to 'behave' in a not dissimilar way to duty-imposing laws in conferring a (usually quite extensive) power of control *and attendant choices* with, more often than not, wide discretion as to whether to exercise the power conferred (at all), and as to the manner in which the power exercise should proceed once the relevant decision has been made.

[48] If it is the case that the only non-waivable part of a multi-layered right – such as the right not to be assaulted – is the element of the right grounded in criminal law; and if that element of the (broader) right appears to be incapable of waiver precisely because it is partly grounded in criminal law, then MacCormick is surely in error in failing to recognise this or make it explicit. To the extent that the (broader) right in question is not grounded in criminal law (eg being grounded in the law of tort) it is probably waivable; to the extent that it is grounded in criminal law, it is simply not the 'right' of the presumed 'right'-holder; it is, instead, a power of prosecution with which a public official is invested. It is interesting that *Hart* explicitly recognises that criminal law 'behaves' in this way, particularly when differentiated from civil law; yet MacCormick perseveres with his (evidently criminal law 'rights'-based) critique of Hartian will theory. Thus Hart observes that a 'person protected only by the criminal law has no power to release anyone from its duties … [H]e has no unique power to determine whether the duties of the criminal law should be enforced or not'. See HLA Hart, *Essays on Bentham* (this chapter, n 3) 184.

of evidence; whether or not a prosecution is in the public interest; what the prospects of a conviction are, having regard, among other things, to the need for proof beyond reasonable doubt, and so on. If a prosecutor waives the power of prosecution in a given case, it is the decision of the prosecutor, not that of any alleged victim of a (suspected) criminal offence.[49] If the patient in MacCormick's hypothetical scenario does not, from the outset, possess any criminal law-based 'right' availing directly against an unqualified surgeon not to be subjected to an unlawful surgical procedure, the question whether the 'right' is legally capable of waiver by the patient simply does not arise. One cannot waive a 'right' that one never had, or never could have had, from the outset. In the criminal law context, rights of waiver (and the conferment of immunity from prosecution) tend to lie with a public official, not a private individual.[50]

To take stock, MacCormick maintains that patients may have no 'choice' (in the sense envisaged by Hartian will theory) to waive, among others, a purported criminal law-based 'right' not to be subjected to an unlawful surgical procedure that, he claims, avails directly against an unqualified surgeon. This is because (so the argument goes) the law has selectively denied the patient the ability to waive any such 'right'. However, a more accurate reading of the situation would conclude that patients have no more control over, nor choice in the matter of, the criminal law consequences of an unqualified surgeon's actions than any crime victim would have over *any* criminal proceedings. They simply do not have the (criminal law-based) 'right' that MacCormick appears to claim for them.[51] Instead, a power of

[49] Waiver of (or immunity from) prosecution is competent, for instance, under section 71(1) of the Serious Organised Crime and Police Act 2005 which empowers a prosecutor to 'offer any person immunity from prosecution' by way of an immunity notice. The effect of the notice (section 71(2)) is that 'no proceedings for an offence of a description specified in the notice may be brought against that person'.

[50] MacCormick's point could perhaps have been made more effectively by making reference to a possible Hohfeldian claim-right that is genuinely incapable of waiver. For example, the Unfair Contract Terms Act 1977, section 2(1), provides that a person 'cannot by reference to any contract term … exclude or restrict his liability for death or personal injury resulting from negligence'. In this situation, one of the contracting parties (B) is denied the possibility of introducing into the contract a limitation of liability that B might seek to found upon at a later time; while the other contracting party (A) – who would ordinarily be the party considered to be in a weaker bargaining position – is denied the possibility of acceding to the introduction of that limitation into the contract. The result is that, once the contract is entered into – and focusing on a possible future personal injury claim by A against B – A will in principle have an unrestricted right to pursue such a claim, such right being legally incapable of waiver *by the terms of the contract entered into with B*. Any purported contractual waiver of that right would be void under the Unfair Contract Terms Act 1977. In other words, section 2(1) preserves a right to pursue a claim under the law of negligence in particular circumstances by ensuring that waiver of the right, by way of an express contract term undertaken by the weaker contracting party, is legally incompetent. MacCormick might argue that the right in question is incapable of waiver *by contractual means* in a question arising between the contracting parties. The right is therefore lacking a power of waiver – at least in the relatively narrow contractual context envisaged by section 2(1) – that Hartian will theory (at any rate according to MacCormick's interpretation) would hold to be necessary to its existence.

[51] The alleged victim of a crime may occasionally be given an option to 'press charges' by prosecuting authorities, giving the impression that a private individual has some control (albeit limited) over the prosecution process. However, in that situation the alleged targets of crime are given an opportunity to indicate whether they might be prepared to provide key evidence to the authorities, and to co-operate as a witness, without which any prosecution may fail due to a lack of evidence. Viewing this in terms of 'rights', or of a waiver of 'rights', would be misconceived.

prosecution lies with a public official; and that power is legally capable of waiver if the law has determined that to be so. Hartian will theory is therefore neither displaced nor falsified in the situation under discussion.

6.3. Defending Hartian Will Theory

Our consideration of selected aspects of MacCormick's critique earlier in this chapter represents only a step towards a more extensive defence of Hartian will theory. MacCormick undoubtedly raises matters of significance; and many of his criticisms have dominated responses and approaches to Hart's version of will theory for several decades. We have seen that MacCormick's most enduring criticism has been the alleged failure of Hartian will theory to give a convincing account of the position of the rights of the child – children being viewed as a 'test case'. This is, of course, part of a more acute difficulty, highlighted in MacCormick's critique, which is the idea that a given individual (at least according to MacCormick's interpretation of the theory) requires a certain degree of cognitive or volitional capacity before any claimed legal right of that individual can be said to exist. This interpretation of Hartian will theory holds that a given legal right effectively owes its existence to the ability of a right-holder, by way of an exertion of will, to exercise powers of control and attendant choices that are said to go hand in hand with the possession of the right – including the choice to enforce a right, or waive it, or leave it unenforced.

As we discovered, a key stumbling block to MacCormick's critique is that, in singling out children as a special case – or as a source of particular difficulty viewed from the standpoint of Hartian will theory – MacCormick implicitly endorses the idea that sectors of the population *other than children* are *not* a source of similarly acute difficulty when viewed from the same standpoint. In other words, the position of children renders Hartian will theory problematic while that of other sectors of the population by implication does not. Yet we have seen that, in terms of the core idea of rights awareness – which is related to the problem of cognitive or volitional (in)capacity – a significant sector of the population may be in a position not entirely dissimilar to that of (for instance, *older*) children. Some people will be more aware than others of such matters as the existence, content and scope of their legal rights; though few will have anything approaching a 'perfect' awareness or knowledge of a claimed right. In the result MacCormick may be thought to be unwittingly supportive of the inherently questionable idea that legal rights 'metamorphose' into existence the more awareness individuals have of the rights that they believe they possess. What is implied is that once an individual reaches a 'tipping point' of rights awareness, a claimed 'nascent' right crystallises into a 'fully-fledged' right. This position was manifested in the 'sliding scale' fallacy discussed in section 6.2.3 (this chapter, above).[52]

[52] There is a parallel discussion, at section 3.2.2 (Chapter 3, above), where a not dissimilar conundrum attends an aspect of Joseph Raz's version of interest theory (the 'second difficulty').

But if this represents a valid objection to MacCormick's critique of Hartian will theory then should it not serve as a basis for a yet more convincing rejection of the idea – central to Hartian will theory – of placing the will or consciousness of the right-holder at the centre of the explanatory process? The point is that if the problematic issues attending children's rights are potentially *more far-reaching* even than MacCormick suggests, is this not more problematic as an issue for Hartian will theory than as an issue for MacCormick's *critique* of that theory: in other words, more theoretically intractable to the former than to the latter?

It is suggested that that is not the case, and that we need to refocus attention upon Hartian will theory, reflecting carefully upon what Hart actually writes, rather than viewing the theory, with all of its alleged shortcomings, through the lens of MacCormick's critique. The point is that MacCormick's interpretation of key aspects of Hartian will theory is, at times, selectively strict and literal. For instance, as previously noted,[53] MacCormick asserts that if some aspect of the power of control that is said to characterise a legal right (such as the ability to exercise a waiver) is absent Hartian will theory would hold that 'there is, *by definition*, no right'.[54] But when, following MacCormick's adoption of a literal approach to important aspects of Hartian will theory, *we adopt the same approach in attempting a defence of the theory* – in other words, attending to the detail of the relevant theoretical writings – something quite surprising emerges. What we find is that Hart's assertion of the existence conditions of a legal right is not inflexible. In fact, it appears to be more accommodating than MacCormick allows for. Hart claims that for a right to exist it is sufficient and necessary that the right-holder should have *at least some measure of control* over the correlative obligation.[55] He does not claim that *all* elements of power of control, and attendant choices, must be present together at the same time for a given right to exist.[56] He also argues that a defining feature of a right correlative to obligation is 'the individual's legal powers of control, full *or partial*, over that obligation'.[57] Hart, in other words, apparently builds a greater degree of flexibility into his version of will theory than MacCormick appears – or is prepared – to acknowledge. In consequence, it is clear that key theoretical positions that MacCormick attributes to Hart (in what is not the most sympathetic interpretation) in some way run counter to Hart's own expressly stated positions.

[53] See above, this chapter, n 25.

[54] DN MacCormick, 'Rights in Legislation' (this chapter, n 2) 196. It was earlier observed that Hart appears to create a 'rod for his own back' when framing elements of legal rights in terms of necessary and sufficient existence conditions. See section 6.2.2 (this chapter, above).

[55] See HLA Hart, *Essays on Bentham* (this chapter, n 3) 188.

[56] So, in a given case where a right is incapable of waiver, it should remain possible to take enforcement action. And it will *always* be possible to leave a right unenforced, though an infant will not *consciously* leave the right unenforced – it will be purely by default if there is no representative on hand to make the decision on the infant's behalf.

[57] See HLA Hart, *Essays on Bentham* (this chapter, n 3) 188.

If, according to Hart, a right-holder requires only *some* measure of control over a correlative obligation, and if the right-holder's legal powers of control in a given case need only be *partial*, then MacCormick's conclusion (originating in his narrow interpretation of Hartian will theory) that there can be 'no right'[58] – such as in a situation where a power of waiver is absent, or a degree of cognitive or volitional capacity on the part of a right-holder is lacking – does seem unnecessarily drastic.[59]

6.4. Concluding Reflections

It is clear from a number of lines of discussion pursued in this and other chapters that the route to a reassessment of Hartian will theory does not lie in a straightforward refutation of aspects of MacCormick's critique. That only takes us so far. MacCormick's critique has often had the effect of narrowing the parameters of productive critical enquiry and debate. Rather, the suggestion is that not only should any reassessment of Hart's theory move beyond the relatively narrow frame of reference set by MacCormick's critique; it must exploit more fully the possibilities inhering in a theory of rights that places the will of the right-holder at the centre of the explanatory process: as Hartian will theory does, where the will of the right-holder is expressed in the exercise of relevant choices (eg to enforce or waive the right). This in turn points to the need for a realistic assessment of the explanatory power of – and the necessary limitations attending – such a theory.

One of the key difficulties with Hartian will theory and MacCormick's critique of that theory is that both theoretical positions too readily lend themselves to the idea that criteria for the existence of rights operate in an all or nothing fashion. Hart frames his general theoretical position in terms of necessary and sufficient existence conditions (of rights) yet admits of exceptions that qualify his general position – such as the absence of a power of waiver in the case of welfare rights; and the need for representatives to exercise relevant choices on behalf of children with limited cognitive or volitional capacity. The latter point nonetheless leaves Hart vulnerable to Tom Campbell's objection that, in the case of the exercise of rights by a proxy, at least some children will inevitably enjoy 'less than [the] … full

[58] DN MacCormick, 'Rights in Legislation' (this chapter, n 2) 196. See further, above, this chapter, n 25.

[59] Hart occasionally recognises that not all 'legal rights correlative to obligations' will be accompanied by the 'kind of control … which according to the view suggested above, is a defining feature'. For instance, in the context of welfare rights – such as to 'unemployment relief' [unemployment benefit] that avail against a public official – he comments that the right-holder, among other things, lacks the ability to extinguish or waive such rights. See HLA Hart, *Essays on Bentham* (this chapter, n 3) 185–186. He thus acknowledges that 'defining features' of rights that he has identified may not be exceptionless. Of course, this may be a step too far for MacCormick, who appears to hold to the erroneous position that *all* of the defining features are *in terms of Hartian will theory* always and necessarily 'constitutive' of rights.

possession of a right since the bearer's will, the exercise of which is definitive for the existence of the right, is not involved'.[60] At the same time, MacCormick seemingly disregards Hart's concessions to the idea that there can be exceptions to his general position, holding Hart strictly to that position without admitting of, or making allowances for, exceptions that Hart is prepared to recognise. In his critique of Hartian will theory MacCormick uses versions of those exceptions as a 'stick to beat' Hart with, despite Hart's factoring those exceptions into his thinking. Yet MacCormick appears to make significant concessions to the bigger picture in acknowledging core principles inhering in Hartian will theory 'which should not be denied'.[61] One result of this, which merits further attention, arises from the idea that in conferring relevant choices, legal rights are *empowering*. Hart clearly articulates that position, while MacCormick is supportive of it, albeit contending 'strongly' that certain powers – such as of enforcement and waiver – are *ancillary to*, not constitutive of, primary and remedial legal rights.[62]

In the result, *both* theorists concur at a key point where it matters: namely, that legal rights are *empowering* or they *confer* power. Inevitably, Hart adopts a stronger position, which is that legal rights *are* powers (ie powers of control over a correlative obligation), giving Tom Campbell grounds for recognition that Hartian will theory is a theory of legal rights viewed as powers. It is, in other words, a 'power theory'.[63]

This theme is revisited and developed further in Chapter 9.

[60] TD Campbell, 'The Rights of the Minor: as Person, as Child, as Juvenile, as Future Adult' (1992) 6 *International Journal of Law and the Family* 1, 4.

[61] See especially the passages cited above, this chapter, nn 5 and 14.

[62] DN MacCormick, 'Children's Rights: A Test Case' (this chapter, n 2) 164 (especially the passage reproduced above, this chapter, n 5).

[63] See TD Campbell, 'The Rights of the Minor: as Person, as Child, as Juvenile, as Future Adult' (1992) 6 *International Journal of Law and the Family* 1, 4. (See above, this chapter, n 12.)

7

Ronald Dworkin's 'Herculean' Approach to the Judicial Role

7.1. Introduction

We have seen that Rawls, in outlining his hypothetical contracting parties as a feature of his original position, makes passing reference to the influence of moral philosophy and social theory.[1] The imaginary parties originate in the social contractarian tradition of classical political philosophy to which *A Theory of Justice* is in some measure indebted. Rawls's theory represents in part a modern take on strands of thought underlying that tradition. More critically in the present context, the hypothesised contracting parties – 'rational individuals with certain ends and related to each other in certain ways' – are positioned within a simplified situation (a hypothesised 'original position') that, as Rawls points out, 'need [not] ever take place'.[2] By contrast, Ronald Dworkin, when formulating his model of the Herculean judge in his 1975 *Harvard Law Review* article, 'Hard Cases',[3] admits to no similarly explicit leanings towards social theory, though his credentials as a moral – indeed pre-eminently a legal – philosopher are never far from the surface of his writing. In the discussion that precedes the introduction of his 'Hercules' archetype, Dworkin famously sets the scene by outlining the task faced by a judge presiding over a so-called 'hard case': namely, a case where 'no settled rule dictates a decision either way'.[4]

Not unlike the unheralded appearance of the Rex archetype in *The Concept of Law*, Dworkin's similarly unannounced Herculean judge – 'a lawyer of super-human skill, learning, patience and acumen'[5] – simply 'materialises' at quite an advanced stage in his analysis of the judicial treatment of 'hard cases'. There

[1] John Rawls, *A Theory of Justice* (Oxford University Press 1973) 119–120. See discussion at section 5.3.1 (Chapter 5, above) generally, and at n 31.

[2] ibid 120. Rawls stresses that the original position is a purely hypothetical situation that need not have any counterpart in the real world: 'it does not follow at all that there are actual situations that resemble it'. (ibid 120)

[3] Ronald Dworkin, 'Hard Cases' (1975) 88 *Harvard Law Review* 1057 (hereafter, in this chapter, 'Hard Cases'). Dworkin's essay is in fact a revised form of his inaugural lecture at Oxford University delivered in 1971 on taking up the Chair of Jurisprudence as immediate successor to HLA Hart.

[4] ibid 1060.

[5] ibid 1083.

is a compelling sense that Hercules is designed to reflect Dworkin's own idea of the judicial consciousness. This archetypal judge is no mere draftsman of workaday judicial opinions; he is a 'philosophical judge' whose labours extend to the development of *theories* both of legislative purpose and of legal principles; and also to constitutional and political *theories*.[6] It may be going too far to suggest that the Herculean archetype represents a straightforward projection by Dworkin *of himself* into that archetype. Yet, at the same time, to *deny* that elements of Dworkin-the-philosopher are integral to Hercules acting in the role of 'philosophical judge' or judicial 'theorist' would surely oversimplify the Dworkinian project. So, while it may be a step too far to maintain that Hercules is just Dworkin by another name – a kind of 'egocentric projection' – nonetheless the critical importance of Dworkin's writing to post-war Anglo-American jurisprudence necessitates a serious examination of Dworkin's Herculean archetype, recognising the (probably undeniable) embeddedness of the consciousness of Dworkin-the-philosopher in that archetype.[7]

Questions abound (though not all are within the scope of this book to address). Can Hercules be *universalised*, albeit as a judge of the common law (rather than, say, the civilian) tradition; or do most key elements of the archetype fit only the judicial traditions of the USA? Can Dworkin's archetype be inserted into the frame of reference of a Weberian ideal-type construct?[8] Is Dworkin's archetype *empirically* adequate – for instance, do judges really (or routinely) *theorise* and are they especially *philosophical*? If empirical adequacy is the touchstone, and if Hercules is found to be in any sense empirically inadequate, does this point to the need to construct a rival, explicitly *empirically* informed, judicial archetype that does not necessitate disentangling its author from his creation?

In this chapter it is proposed to reconsider Dworkin's Herculean archetype in the light of a few of these questions, but ultimately with a view to progressing to the development, in Chapters 8 and 9, of a *Iudexian* perspective on legal rights, building upon positions outlined in earlier chapters. To an extent, that (*Iudexian*) perspective is empirically grounded in UK higher appellate court decision-making. For now, our point of departure is a brief descriptive and critical assessment of some of the more important elements of Dworkin's Herculean archetype.

[6] See, for instance, Dworkin's references to: 'philosophical judge' (ibid 1083); 'constitutional theory' (ibid 1084); 'political theory' (ibid 1083, 1084); and theories of 'legislative purpose' and of 'legal principles' (ibid 1083).

[7] There may be an echo of Plato's philosopher king in Dworkin's Hercules: '[u]nless … philosophers bear kingly rule in cities, or those who are now called kings and princes become genuine and adequate philosophers, and political power and philosophy are brought together … there will be no respite from evil … for cities, nor, I fancy, for humanity'. See Plato, *The Republic* (AD Lindsay (tr), JM Dent & Sons Ltd 1976) book V, 473–474 (at p 166).

[8] See M Weber, '"Objectivity" in Social Science and Social Policy' ['*Die 'Objektivität' sozialwissenschaftlicher und sozialpolitischer Erkenntnis*'] in M Weber, *Max Weber On The Methodology of the Social Sciences* (EA Shils and HA Finch (trs and eds), The Free Press 1949) ch II (hereafter, in this chapter, '"Objectivity" in Social Science') 90. See also section 4.5 (Chapter 4, above) at n 56.

7.2. The Herculean Archetype and Dworkin's Anti-Positivist Stance

We might ask at the outset why Dworkin's Herculean judge is – indeed *needs* to be – 'superhuman'? Of course Hercules is in some sense 'idealised', though that is not to suggest that Dworkin's archetype is an 'ideal-typification' in the special sense maintained in social theory. Yet the recognition that Hercules has philosophical and theoretical inclinations over and above his 'superhuman' qualities probably removes him from any notion of a judge in an everyday institutional setting. But would a judge in the *highest* appellate court of, say, a common law jurisdiction (in contrast to a judge of a lower court) need to exhibit 'superhuman' qualities? This raises the question of verisimilitude, mentioned in passing in Chapter 3.[9] What, if anything, does the Herculean archetype tell us about the 'real world' of judges and judicial decision-making? Plainly, there may be elements of the Herculean archetype that fit with observable institutional reality; just as others may not.

While it is instructive to identify elements of the Herculean archetype that do and do not fit with some conception of (institutional) reality, a useful preliminary step is to explore briefly Dworkin's fundamental point of departure – his influential critique of legal positivism – which, albeit indirectly, draws him towards the idea of the Herculean judge.[10] One of the key aims of Dworkin's critique is to examine the implications for legal positivism of the idea that – often in so-called 'hard case' judicial decision-making where there is said to be no pre-established legal rule straightforwardly applicable – judges may exercise *discretion* in arriving at a decision. Dworkin frames this position in terms of the idea, claimed to be a core tenet of legal positivism, that discretionary judicial decision-making 'means reaching *beyond* the law for some other sort of standard to guide … [the judge] in manufacturing a fresh legal rule or supplementing an old one'.[11] The implication is that while exercises of judicial discretion involve the quest for a 'standard' – ie they are not wholly unfettered: grounded

[9] See section 3.3 (Chapter 3, above) at n 73. In *Seven Theories of Human Society*, Tom Campbell reminds us of the need for a theory to meet the test of empirical adequacy: '[P]ersistent failure to produce empirical statements which correspond with observed social phenomena in areas of central concern to a theory undermines the credibility of a whole approach'. See T Campbell, *Seven Theories of Human Society* (Clarendon Press 1981) 46. In the case of Dworkin's Hercules, clearly nothing so drastic as 'persistent failure' in correspondence with social reality, or any attendant undermining of credibility, is suggested here.

[10] Our initial focus in this chapter is with 'early Dworkin', culminating in the publication of *Taking Rights Seriously*, where the implications of key arguments outlined in republished essays – including 'Hard Cases' (see below) with its discussion of the Herculean archetype – are (first) outlined. In later writings the archetype is developed to a more advanced level than attempted in relevant earlier writings. See generally R Dworkin, *Taking Rights Seriously* (Gerald Duckworth & Co Ltd 1977).

[11] R Dworkin, 'The Model of Rules' (1967) 35 *University of Chicago Law Review* 14 (hereafter, in this chapter, 'The Model of Rules') 17 (emphasis added). Dworkin also maintains at p 34 that 'the positivists' doctrine of judicial discretion … argues that if a case is not controlled by an established rule, the judge must decide it by exercising discretion'.

in nothing – this, according to Dworkin's characterisation of legal positivism, would necessarily be a standard lying 'beyond' or outside the law.[12] Developing his position further, Dworkin allows for the possibility that the invocation of non-rule standards by judges – such as 'principles, policies and other sorts of standards'[13] – is itself not far removed from the judicial act of exercising discretion in that in some cases it may be on a par with reaching somehow 'beyond' the law.[14]

On the face of it, Dworkin's stance that judges routinely reach beyond positive or posited law in making decisions is surely a challenge to *any* legal positivistic position regardless of the theorist selected as a target of critical attention. However, Dworkin chooses to focus on the main tenets of the *Hartian* version of legal positivism. In particular – linking his analysis to the question of judicial discretion and the judicial tendency, on occasion, to invoke principles or policies (as opposed to pre-established legal rules) in decision-making – Dworkin's strategy is to identify what he perceives as a key limitation in the scope and applicability of Hart's ultimate criterion of legal validity: his *rule of recognition*.[15]

[12] ibid 17. Dworkin apparently misstates Hart's position, attributing to Hart the view that when a 'judge's discretion is in play, we can no longer speak of his being bound by standards, but must speak rather of what standards he "characteristically uses"'. See 'The Model of Rules' (this chapter, n 11) 35. Dworkin references *The Concept of Law* (1961) at 144, but Hart does not maintain that position there, making reference instead to the use of judicial discretion necessitated by the open-textured nature of law. Hart speaks of the need to show 'the varied types of reasoning which courts characteristically use in exercising the creative function left to them by the open texture of law in statute or precedent'. Hart is clearly committed to the idea that legal rules are binding on a judge even where the rules in question, being open-textured in nature, require to be interpreted as an integral part of an exercise of judicial discretion. Although Dworkin identifies the idea of a judge 'reaching beyond the law' as one of the 'key tenets' of legal positivism (in the context of what develops into a critique of HLA Hart's version of positivism), Hart states largely *constrained* positions on judicial discretion such as where he envisages discretionary processes that are clearly *immersed* in law and do not necessarily lie *beyond* law: 'In every legal system a large and important field is left open for the exercise of discretion by courts and other officials in rendering initially vague standards determinate, in resolving the uncertainties of statutes, or in developing and qualifying rules only broadly communicated by authoritative precedents … [T]hese activities … must not disguise the fact that both the framework within which they take place and their chief end-product is one of general rules'. See HLA Hart, *The Concept of Law* (2nd edn, Clarendon Press 1994) (hereafter, in this chapter, '*The Concept of Law*') 136. Elsewhere (ibid 272) Hart does speak of judges in certain cases exercising discretion in such a way as to 'make law'. That, perhaps, edges closer to Dworkin's idea of the judge reaching beyond the law for a standard to be applied in the instant case.

[13] R Dworkin, 'The Model of Rules' (this chapter, n 11) 22.

[14] Dworkin suggests that if we deny that legal principles are binding in the same way that legal rules (clearly) are we might assert that the use of legal principles – such as in two specially highlighted cases, namely, *Riggs v Palmer* (115 NY 506, 22 NE 188 (1889)) and *Henningsen v Bloomfield Motors, Inc* (32 NJ 58, 161 A 2d 69 (1960)) – actually involves judges in reaching beyond legal rules ('beyond the "law" … for extra-legal principles'), in the same way that judges might do when exercising judicial discretion. Dworkin makes a more explicit connection between exercises of judicial discretion and the use of principles when, later in the analysis (at 31), he considers two competing, but in his view equally tenable, approaches to principles, the first of which acknowledges that certain principles may have a binding quality that is equivalent to that of legal rules. The second approach, which Dworkin goes on to discuss in some detail, expressly equates the judicial use of principles to exercises of judicial discretion, such as where the deployment of a principle, for instance in the cases of *Riggs* and *Henningsen*, was to be seen as 'an act of judicial discretion applied *ex post facto*'. See R Dworkin, 'The Model of Rules' (this chapter, n 11) 30–31.

[15] For the main thrust of Dworkin's critique of the rule of recognition, see 'The Model of Rules' (this chapter, n 11) 40–46.

If we begin with the premise that legal positivism, among other things, promotes a belief in the possibility of clearly differentiating law from non-law (for instance, law and morality),[16] the presence of 'non-law' – or, at least, any *claimed* 'non-law' standard such as principles or policies or a standard that (Dworkin might claim) lies within discretionary judicial decision-making – must present a challenge to any positivist theory (such as Hart's) that promotes a criterion of legal validity or identity that would operate to place any (claimed) non-law ground of judicial decision-making decisively outside the legal domain, whilst identifying those standards that lie unequivocally within its domain.[17] According to Dworkin's reading of Hart, valid legal rules must have a clear 'pedigree',[18] enabling their origin to be traced (for example) to reported case law or to the act of an authoritative body such as a legislature. This process makes it possible, in Dworkin's words, 'to distinguish valid legal rules from spurious legal rules (rules which lawyers and litigants wrongly argue are rules of law) and also from other sorts of social rules (generally lumped together as 'moral rules') that the community follows but does not enforce through public power'.[19]

Dworkin's position suggests that the possibility of drawing a clear dividing line between law and non-law could be illusory if cases coming before the courts – especially so-called 'hard' cases – are decided on the basis of standards lying 'beyond' the law, such as standards formulated in the context of exercises of judicial discretion or entailed in the judicial use of (for example) policies or principles – eg in a case such as *Riggs v Palmer* (where a general principle excluded the application of otherwise strictly applicable legal rules).[20] In their quest to differentiate law from non-law, legal positivists would be inclined to point to the existence of a law-identifying criterion of legal validity such as Hart's rule of recognition. But if, as Dworkin argues, some judicial decision-making is grounded in standards that originate purely in acts of discretion or (which may come to the same thing for Dworkin) derive from (claimed) non-law standards such as principles, the rule of recognition would tend to be ineffectual as a means

[16] See, for example, HLA Hart, *The Concept of Law* (this chapter, n 12) 302.

[17] As soon as the standards (or grounds of judicial decision-making) are incorporated into published case reports do they 'become law' (case law)? As Dworkin concedes: 'True, if we were challenged to back up our claim that some principle is a principle of law, we would mention any prior cases in which that principle was cited, or figured in the argument. We would also mention any statute that seemed to exemplify that principle (even better if the principle was cited in the preamble of the statute …)'. See 'The Model of Rules' (this chapter, n 11) 41.

[18] See R Dworkin, 'The Model of Rules' (this chapter, n 11) 17, 18, 29, 32.

[19] ibid 17.

[20] Dworkin (as previously mentioned) would maintain that applying a principle such as in the case of *Riggs v Palmer* is in itself equivalent to an exercise of judicial discretion. In the Postscript to *The Concept of Law*, Hart frames the issue highlighted by Dworkin (which is one of the key points of contention between Dworkin and Hart) in this way: '[I]n any legal system there will always be certain legally unregulated cases in which on some point no decision either way is dictated by the law and the law is accordingly partly indeterminate or incomplete. If in such cases the judge is to reach a decision … he must exercise his *discretion* and *make* law for the case instead of merely applying already pre-existing settled law. So in such legally unprovided-for or unregulated cases the judge both makes new law and applies the established law which both confers and constrains his law-making powers'. See HLA Hart, *The Concept of Law* (this chapter, n 12) 272.

of assisting a judge to identify such standards in advance of rendering a decision ultimately grounded in the standards in question.

Following through the Dworkinian argument, if a criterion such as Hart's rule of recognition is ineffectual in identifying those (claimed) *non*-law standards that are grounds of judicial decision-making (such as principles or policies or any non-law standard lying within exercises of judicial discretion), but is instead restricted to the identification only of explicitly posited law, such as legal rules with a plainly identifiable 'pedigree', then such a criterion must fail.[21] And that (claimed) failure inevitably infects legal positivism in the wider context: in other words, the failure of the rule of recognition must fatally undermine the idea of legal positivism. In essence, Dworkin maintains that the very idea of a criterion of legal validity must be misconceived because, with its apparent narrow focus on the identification of explicitly posited law, it will always come up against the problem of accurately identifying what Dworkin would consider to be the fullest range of standards – both 'law' and 'non-law' (or 'beyond' law) – that are, so the argument goes, grounds of judicial decision-making. If this position is valid, it must be anathema to a legal positivist with the task of differentiating law from non-law. At the same time, the recognition of Dworkin's position that some grounds of judicial decision-making are indeed, as Dworkin claims, standards lying 'beyond the law' – in other words, they have the appearance of *non-law* – must also in principle be incompatible with the very idea of legal positivism.

It is instructive, taking forward this synoptic account of points of contention between (early) Dworkinian theory and Hartian theory, to seek to identify connections between Dworkin's more general anti-positivist stance and his Herculean archetype. This is in order to determine the extent to which the archetype might play into Dworkin's critique of Hartian legal positivism – such as, for example, by reinforcing it or taking it in a new direction. One key point to emphasise is that Dworkin apparently does not make an *explicit* connection between elements of his Herculean archetype and his linked critiques of legal positivism and of the rule of recognition. But if we follow through the logic of those critiques – where Dworkin identifies characteristics of judicial decision-making which, he claims, render the rule of recognition inutile or problematic – we might ask whether his idealised ('Herculean') characteristics possibly represent an *exacerbation* of that position.

7.2.1. Dworkin's (Earlier) Herculean Archetype and Hart's Rule of Recognition

The key question is whether the Herculean archetype embodies, and indeed goes some way beyond, those problematic aspects of judicial decision-making which Dworkin would argue *already* lie beyond the reach of a rule of recognition to

[21] Dworkin makes the point that '[p]ositivism … is a model of and for a system of rules, and its central notion of a single fundamental test for law forces us to miss the important roles of these standards that are not rules'. See R Dworkin, 'The Model of Rules' (this chapter, n 11) 22.

identify (eg principles, policies). And if so, does the archetype render Hart's rule of recognition – and the seminal idea of legal positivism – that much more problematic when viewed from Dworkin's critical standpoint?

It may be that the Herculean archetype in some measure represents more a distillation than an idealisation of the characteristics of judicial decision-making outlined in 'The Model of Rules' and in the early sections (I to III) of 'Hard Cases'. So if, for example, the judicial decision-making efforts of Hercules engage any of the diverse roles of the 'typical Dworkinian' judge – acting, for instance, as a 'philosophical judge' or as a constitutional theorist, or as a political theorist or a theorist of 'legislative purpose' or theorist of 'legal principles'[22] – then (so the argument goes) 'Herculean' decision-making could be that much more problematic for the functioning of a Hartian rule of recognition designed, on the face of it, to identify only the most straightforward grounds of judicial decision-making, such as legal rules with a 'pedigree'. The point here is that if, as Dworkin argues, the rule of recognition already faces an uphill task accommodating ('mere') legal principles (and similar standards), how much more intractable will that task be when judicial *philosophies* or *theories* (or, indeed, other 'standards' or *modi operandi* that may be unique to Hercules) are factored in as possible grounds of judicial decision-making? What tests of 'pedigree' can be applied to the 'political theory' of a judge, for example?[23] Certainly, a rule of recognition might be deployed in identifying the *ratio decidendi* of a precedent expressed in the opinion of judge A in reported case: *X v Y*. This would clearly identify a 'source' of the standards enshrined in the precedent – here, one need only cite *X v Y*. But Dworkin might argue that the rule of recognition is deficient as a means of precisely identifying any 'political theory' or judicial philosophy (say) that underpins the precedent in question, thereby rendering problematic the legal positivist imperative to differentiate 'law' and 'non-law'.

Against that background, it might be thought that any uniquely 'Herculean' characteristics that Dworkin introduces over and above those of the 'typical Dworkinian' judge – assuming Hercules to be, fundamentally, such a judge – might render the rule of recognition, and by extension the idea of legal positivism, even more acutely problematic. This would depend not only upon whether Dworkin's critiques of legal positivism and of the Hartian rule of recognition are tenable on the terms that Dworkin frames them (as discussed in more detail below) but on how key characteristics of the Herculean archetype might be imagined to impact those critiques. (On the question of impact, a line of argument is briefly pursued (below) that is *not* one that Dworkin himself pursues in his discussion of Hercules, even if it is a natural extension of his critical position.) In the context of the developing discussion, it is useful to explore a

[22] See above, this chapter, n 6. The judicial decision-making of Hercules does appear to engage these diverse roles.

[23] The notion that the Herculean archetype 'exacerbates' the Dworkinian attack on the idea of the rule of recognition is implicit in Dworkin's analysis. Dworkin does not expressly maintain that line of argument, however.

few of the characteristics of the Herculean archetype that, we may speculate, could serve to reinforce Dworkin's critiques of (Hartian) legal positivism and the Hartian rule of recognition. Once done, we can take a step back to assess whether the critical Dworkinian approach is in fact tenable. Beyond that, we can consider the role of the Herculean archetype in the context of (early and later) Dworkinian theory and assess whether it might serve as a point of critical comparison for the further development (in Chapter 8) of a *Iudexian* archetype, discussed at various points in earlier chapters.

According to Dworkin, then, Hercules is first and foremost a 'philosophical judge', or (using Dworkin's game-construction analogy) a 'philosophical referee', tasked with developing '*theories* of what legislative purpose and legal principles require' in order to reach decisions on 'controversial issues about legal rights'.[24] Obviously this fits with the idea of the 'hard case', where no settled rule dictates a decision either way.[25] When legislation is at the centre of the decision in hand, Hercules theorises about the rationale of the legislation; and when the common law is the focus of the decision, Hercules theorises about common law principles. Moreover, on one hand, Hercules accepts 'that statutes have the general power to create and extinguish legal rights'; while, on the other, he accepts that judges 'have the general duty to follow earlier decisions of their court or higher courts' whose rationale extends to the case in hand.[26] These respective approaches are (in Dworkin's words) 'devices' for applying a 'general political theory' to 'hard cases' (assuming 'hard cases' approximately equate to 'controversial issues about legal rights'). To facilitate his judicial decision-making, Hercules is imagined to be a lawyer of superhuman skill, learning, patience and acumen.[27] Given that a judge, in the more general sense, would (in Dworkin's view) adhere to the settled practices of the legal system – accepting 'the autonomy provided by its distinct constitutive and regulative rules'[28] – Hercules doubtless conforms to that pattern of behaviour. Likewise, Hercules is to be regarded as possessing other general characteristics of a (Dworkinian) judge. In particular, Dworkin considers a judge to be a 'political official' – occupying a pivotal position within the institutional structures of the state – whose decision-making is governed by the 'doctrine of political responsibility'.[29] Adherents to that doctrine, according to Dworkin, must make 'only such political decisions as they can justify *within a political theory* that also justifies the other decisions they propose to make'.[30]

[24] R Dworkin, 'Hard Cases' (this chapter, n 3) 1083 (emphasis added).
[25] ibid 1060.
[26] The idea of binding precedent (or *stare decisis*) is as much an accepted feature of Dworkinian, as it is of Hartian, thinking – see HLA Hart, *The Concept of Law* (this chapter, n 12) 135, 153–154 – yet it is neither theorist's innovation: it is simply an approach to judicial decision-making that is characteristic of the common law tradition.
[27] See R Dworkin, 'Hard Cases' (this chapter, n 3) 1083.
[28] ibid.
[29] ibid 1064.
[30] ibid (emphasis added).

From the above account it can be seen that Hercules – sharing characteristics of Dworkinian '*non*-Herculean' judges – is seemingly immersed in the ethos of what it is to be a philosopher and a theorist: and one, moreover, with 'political' leanings, revealed in 'political decisions' (which Dworkin considers judicial decision-making to be). At the same time, and in similar fashion to 'non-Herculean' judges, such 'political decisions' as Hercules makes can be justified only to the extent that they accord with a 'political theory' applied consistently across the span of his decision-making.[31] Now it may be that since Hercules is explicitly a judge 'in some representative American jurisdiction',[32] his archetypality does not, factually, resonate through the entire common law world. In particular, the idea that common law judges, even in 'hard cases', are typically in the business of philosophising, theorising and making 'political decisions' may not accord with the self-perception of many judges practising within that tradition. That is not to deny that common law judges are 'political' – in other words, like anyone else they have a political outlook, whether manifested publicly or privately[33] – without necessarily having their judicial decision-making *given over* to political decision-making. But it is probably inescapable that Herculean adventures in philosophy, theory, politics and indeed morality,[34] if this is an authentic representation of judicial decision-making in common law jurisdictions, must render the operation of a rule of recognition less straightforward, thereby *potentially* reinforcing Dworkin's critique.

If Dworkin is correct and judicial decision-making in 'hard cases' (or even straightforward cases) is indeed in some measure an affair of 'politics' (or of philosophy, or of theory, or of morality, in any combination) and not largely one based around law seen as an 'affair of rules', as Hart maintains,[35] then the (Hartian) legal positivist imperative to draw a sharp dividing line between 'law' and 'non-law' through the deployment of a rule of recognition would appear vulnerable to Dworkin's scepticism.[36] This follows from the suggestion that in judicial (Herculean) decision-making those standards that a rule of recognition might identify as 'law' (such as relatively strictly delimited legal rules) become intermingled with what might similarly be identified as 'non-law' standards. For Dworkin, it seems, the standards relied upon in making a decision, and the judicial decision itself, are 'all law' – a seemingly undifferentiated amalgam. In a given case, a Dworkinian might say that there is 'politics' in the mix; or that a moral principle,

[31] ibid.

[32] ibid 1083.

[33] The classic work on the political world view of members of the judiciary in the UK is JAG Griffith, *The Politics of the Judiciary* (5th edn, Fontana Press 1997).

[34] In *Law's Empire* Dworkin maintains that judges (which would include Hercules) as adherents to the idea of law as integrity must regard as law what morality would suggest to be the best justification of past judicial decisions. See R Dworkin, *Law's Empire* (Fontana Paperbacks 1986) (hereafter, in this chapter, '*Law's Empire*') 119–120.

[35] See, generally, HLA Hart, *The Concept of Law* (this chapter, n 12); and particularly at 13.

[36] See R Dworkin, 'The Model of Rules' (this chapter, n 11) 45: '[W]e must reject the positivists' first tenet, that the law of a community is distinguished from other social standards by some test in the form of a master rule'.

say, underlies the judge's thinking (or is actually determinative of the decision, as in *Riggs v Palmer*). Or if Hercules is especially philosophically inclined, he might have arrived at a decision based to some extent on a commitment to a particular philosophical outlook.

Yet if we follow the trajectory of Dworkin's more general position, there is at least one significant instance where Dworkin incorporates into his Herculean archetype features which Hart explicitly regards as key characteristics of the rule of recognition. In fact, the instance in question could be regarded as a point of theoretical crossover – where Dworkin's Herculean archetype literally reflects (and even in a sense replicates) an important aspect of the very theoretical device that Dworkin seeks to undermine: ie the rule of recognition (a 'master rule'). To this extent Dworkin could be said to endorse the rule of recognition, if only tacitly. At the relevant point of crossover, writings of both theorists appear to converge, while the actual point of convergence bears some similarity to the version of the doctrine of hierarchical ordering of norms outlined in Kelsen's *Pure Theory of Law*.[37] Hart argues that the rule of recognition (among other things) identifies characteristics of rules of law so that 'where more than one of such general characteristics are treated as identifying criteria, provision may be made for their possible conflict by their arrangement in an order of superiority, as by the common subordination of custom or precedent to statute, the latter being a "superior source" of law'.[38] Dworkin, for his part, attributes the principle of hierarchy – the hierarchical ordering of legal standards that Hart would say inheres in the rule of recognition – to judicial tasks that Hercules consciously carries out as part of his role. In fact this appears to be a defining task of the Herculean judge. It is literally (in Dworkin's words) 'why I called our judge Hercules'.[39] The first task of Hercules is to construct a 'scheme of abstract and concrete principles that provides a coherent justification for all common law precedents and, so far as these are to be justified on principle, constitutional and statutory provisions as well'.[40] It is unclear where this Sisyphean act of synthesis would ordinarily play out. It might be a task more suited to a glossator or (in the context of Scots law, for instance) an institutional writer.[41] Even a supreme court judge *might* attempt something akin to that, though

[37] See H Kelsen, *Pure Theory of Law* (published as Hans Kelsen, *Introduction to the Problems of Legal Theory* [*Reine Rechtslehre. Einleitung in die rechtswissenschaftliche Problematik*]) (BL Paulson and SL Paulson (trs and eds), Clarendon Press 1992) (hereafter, in this chapter, '*Pure Theory of Law*') 63–75.

[38] See HLA Hart, *The Concept of Law* (this chapter, n 12) 95. Hart restates essentially the same position at 101: 'In a modern legal system where there are a variety of "sources" of law, the rule of recognition is correspondingly more complex: the criteria for identifying the law are multiple and commonly include a written constitution, enactment by a legislature, and judicial precedents. In most cases, provision is made for possible conflict by ranking these criteria in an order of relative subordination and primacy. It is in this way that in our system "common law" is subordinate to "statute"'.

[39] See R Dworkin, 'Hard Cases' (this chapter, n 3) 1094.

[40] ibid.

[41] For instance, see James Dalrymple of Stair, *The Institutions of the Law of Scotland* (1681); and GJ Bell, *Principles of the Law of Scotland* (1829). See also JW Cairns, 'Institutional Writings in Scotland Reconsidered' (1983) 4 *Journal of Legal History* 76.

on a significantly more modest scale such as in the context of a single act of judicial decision-making that settles a relatively narrow point of law. But at least this seems closer to what judges do in the 'real world' than, say, the idea of judges philosophising or theorising or making overtly 'political decisions'.

The next task of Dworkin's Hercules aligns most closely with elements of both Kelsen's doctrine of the hierarchical ordering of norms and aspects of Hart's rule of recognition highlighted above,[42] but raises the question whether the task is genuinely a part of the judicial role or resides, say, in the constitutional make-up of a legal system to be identified or 'discovered' by a rule of recognition, or indeed a (Hartian) rule of adjudication. As Dworkin explains, there lies 'within the vast material of legal decisions that Hercules must justify' vertical and horizontal ordering. The *vertical* ordering involves distinguishing 'layers at which official decisions might be taken to be controlling over decisions made at lower levels'.[43] This echoes Hart's position – which the rule of recognition is said to capture – that relevant standards may be arranged or ranked in order of superiority and subordination. So, statute would take precedence over custom or case law; while a decision made at a lower level of the courts hierarchy may be overruled by the decision of a higher court.[44] For Dworkin, *horizontal* ordering entails a need for consistency between and among standards arranged at the *same* level. Again, this straightforward principle could readily be captured in a rule of recognition or a rule of adjudication (or both).

Taking an overview, we should not underestimate the implications of the apparent theoretical interpenetration of Hartian and Dworkinian theory at the point where the rule of recognition 'meets' the Herculean archetype. The significance of this lies in the obvious fact that some features of one theoretical device (namely, Hart's rule of recognition – which Dworkin subjects to adverse critical scrutiny) coincide with equivalent features of a contrasting theoretical device (Dworkin's Herculean archetype) that Dworkin (stressing their importance) had proclaimed to be precisely the features that had made its eponym 'Herculean'. Clearly, this makes it more difficult for Dworkin – or Dworkinians – to argue that there is an irreconcilable gulf between the theoretical positions adopted respectively by Hart and Dworkin; and it surely lessens the force of Dworkin's critique of the rule of recognition and the impact of that critique in undermining the idea of legal positivism – in particular, *Hartian* legal positivism. For, much of the

[42] See above, this chapter, nn 37 and 38.

[43] R Dworkin, 'Hard Cases' (this chapter, n 3) 1095.

[44] There may be a question whether, in terms of Hartian theory, some aspects of this analysis would be more appropriately brought within a Hartian rule of adjudication than the rule of recognition, or within part of a rule of adjudication that operates in the same way as a rule of recognition. Commentators on Hart have remarked upon the tendency for the rules of recognition and adjudication to overlap or behave circularly. See, for instance, N MacCormick, *HLA Hart* (Edward Arnold (Publishers) Ltd 1981) 109: 'Are we to say that the rule of adjudication is a "valid" rule or not? It can be so only if it satisfies some criterion set in the rule of recognition. But the rule of recognition presupposes "judges" and "judges" presuppose a rule of adjudication. Which member of this logical circle of rules is the ultimate rule of a legal system?'.

force of Dworkin's critique of Hartian legal positivism lies in his critique of the rule of recognition.

Be that as it may, Dworkin's more fundamental ground for rejection of the rule of recognition centres on its so-called tests of 'pedigree', where certain (on the face of it 'non-law') standards that judges may refer to in their opinions, particularly when exercising discretion in 'hard cases', may not be readily traceable, say, to a source that the rule of recognition would ordinarily identify as a conventional 'law-based' source. For instance, a reference in a judicial opinion to a moral principle that appears to be determinative of the decision in a 'hard case' may, so the argument goes, ordinarily lie beyond the reach of the rule of recognition to identify – at any rate before the principle has taken on the character of 'law' through publication in a case report.[45] This is what Dworkin appears to suggest in his analysis of *Riggs v Palmer*, and in other contexts.[46] It is notable that when Dworkin critiques the rule of recognition for this claimed inadequacy, he invariably locates his analysis within *judicial practice* – in the reasoning and decision-making processes of judges. Clearly, this ties the practical use of the rule of recognition, and its purported failure, narrowly to the practice of the *institution of the judiciary* and to decision-making within that institution. The implication is that Dworkin would have little interest in possible failure of the rule of recognition outside of that institutional context because in that setting – eg a textbook writer's speculations about a 'non-law' standard – neither a moral precept nor any other (on the face of it) 'non-law' standard can have the status of 'law' in advance of formal (institutional) recognition such as in a later case report. For that, the standard in question must, ultimately, become an integral part of a judicial decision. This may suggest tacit acknowledgment that judicial acts of decision-making are *transformative* in a special way that Hart's rule of recognition and rules of adjudication assist us to understand more clearly. (This is briefly discussed below.)

When we examine Dworkin's critique more closely, following through the logic of his stated positions, we find that the point at which the rule of recognition is said to fail occupies such a narrow frame of reference that it might be thought to be of vanishing significance. And since the critique of the rule of recognition is equally central to Dworkin's broader critique of Hartian legal positivism we might ask if the same accusation (of narrowness) extends to that critique as well.

[45] See *Donoghue v Stevenson* [1932] AC 562, 580 (Lord Atkin): 'The rule that you are to love your neighbour becomes in law, you must not injure your neighbour: and the lawyer's question, Who is my neighbour? receives a restricted reply. You must take reasonable care to avoid acts or omissions which you can reasonably foresee would be likely to injure your neighbour.' For 'pedigree', and prior to publication of the case report, one might have looked to *Matthew* 22:39 or *Leviticus* 19:18.

[46] Dworkin appears to acknowledge that standards that may have had no grounding in law prior to a decision rendered in the instant case – he refers specifically to *principles* – become authoritative as soon as (if not before) the case is reported. Once reported, it becomes possible to cite a case in which a given standard (or principle) has figured in the argument. See 'The Model of Rules' (this chapter, n 11) 41. See also *Law's Empire* (this chapter, n 34) 91 where Dworkin refers to decisions of institutions (that include courts of law) being reported 'in a canonical way'.

It is instructive to take stock of this narrow frame of reference. It can be captured in five propositions. First (as indicated above), the context for any supposed failure of the rule of recognition is an institutional setting in which a judge decides a so-called 'hard case', being a case where 'no settled rule dictates a decision either way'.[47] Secondly, the judge in the case in question is minded to exercise discretion which, according to Dworkin, 'means reaching *beyond* the law for some other sort of standard to guide … [the judge] in manufacturing a fresh legal rule or supplementing an old one'.[48] Thirdly, the judge is only at a certain point in time – literally when engaged in the task of deciding the case – unable to deploy the rule of recognition effectively in identifying an appropriate 'non-law' standard that will ultimately determine the case. Fourthly, any claimed gap or uncertainty in the law – arising from the fact that no settled rule dictates a decision in the case (impelling the judge to reach 'beyond the law') – will in some cases endure only from the point in time when the judge gives expression to the existence of a gap or uncertainty in the law until the moment a decision in the case is officially rendered. The 'window' of uncertainty, in other words, may be relatively short-lived. (Outside the judicial setting there may be, at best, a consensus within informed opinion that the law on the question is unsatisfactory; but often it will be only when a judge defines this in a suitably precise way in a judicial opinion that the scope of the law's shortcomings in the relevant area becomes clear.) Finally, when a decision is rendered in the case (sometimes accompanied by publication in a case report) the case ceases to be a 'hard case'. It is now a decided case – a precedent. At the same time, any hitherto 'non-law' standard relied upon in the decision (such as a moral principle, say) – which Dworkin might have argued was initially beyond the reach of the rule of recognition to identify – will now have become absorbed into a precedent (in effect, becoming 'law') as a basis for future decision-making. The case, and its rationale (including any standard underpinning it previously regarded as 'non-law') is now a fully-fledged precedent, identifiable by the rule of recognition in no less a way than a legal rule whose status as law may never have been in doubt.[49] *Riggs v Palmer* and *Donoghue v Stevenson* are examples of such precedents.

If this properly represents the scope of Dworkin's perception of failure of the rule of recognition, then, it is failure within a strikingly narrow 'window'. Arguably in every situation lying beyond that 'window' – where there is no failure – there will often be (at least qualified) success in deploying a 'master rule'. There will be instances where something akin to a rule of recognition is successfully deployed outside the 'window' of failure. For instance, in the judicial setting, there will be instances of the use of a rule of recognition or similar criterion that reinforce its *general* relevance and effectiveness. Is the deployment of such a criterion alien to

[47] See R Dworkin, 'Hard Cases' (this chapter, n 3) 1060.

[48] R Dworkin, 'The Model of Rules' (this chapter, n 11) 17 (emphasis added). Dworkin also maintains (at 34) that 'the positivists' doctrine of judicial discretion … argues that if a case is not controlled by an established rule, the judge must decide it by exercising discretion'.

[49] See texts cited above, this chapter, n 46.

the Herculean archetype? Unless Hercules is entirely unconcerned with routine judicial decision-making, there would be a need to identify what counts as a legal standard relevant to the case being decided. This would extend to uncontentious standards – statutes, precedents, secondary legislation, principles, doctrines – to which any common law judge would be expected to have regard when deciding a case: 'hard case' or otherwise. In each case before the court a judge will also need to be conversant with laws that have no bearing on the relatively narrow *ratio decidendi* that may have qualified it as a 'hard case'. A wide range of laws, identifiable by reference to an appropriate criterion, may come into play in the case before the court – eg straightforward rules or principles with no special claim to difficulty or novelty; routine rules of evidence; rules of criminal or civil procedure; laws having only 'persuasive' force; precedents where only *obiter dicta* are relevant to the court's decision-making; judgments of lower courts that can safely be disregarded.

Inevitably, this counts against Dworkin's critique of the rule of recognition and his closely-related critique of Hartian legal positivism. Occasional 'failure' does not imply that the criterion is untenable across the board (ie encompassing both 'hard cases' and non-'hard cases'). And beyond the judicial setting, such as in the domain of practising lawyers, prosecutors, tax officials – even private individuals – there will be many instances of the use of a criterion that serves to identify 'the law' applicable to the situation in hand.

Even so, to what extent is Dworkin's position tenable *within* his 'window' of (purported) failure? If this is correct, the rule of recognition occasionally fails because 'non-law' standards, featuring in judicial decision-making, do not meet any of the so-called tests of 'pedigree' residing within the rule of recognition. This in turn is said to defeat the (Hartian) legal positivist's imperative to identify and describe 'law' using the rule of recognition and, in so doing, to differentiate 'law' from 'non-law'. But, for Dworkin, the Hartian project appears to fail at a more profound level in that when the rule of recognition is said to be ineffectual as a means of identifying valid law within the narrow 'window' outlined above, the judge is 'thrown upon' exercising discretion and reaching 'beyond the law' in making a decision: those tasks being identified by Dworkin – according to his characterisation of the *Hartian legal positivist's* outlook – as being integral to judicial decision-making.[50] If a judge does not ultimately make a decision that applies pre-existing law this, according to Dworkin, highlights a major weakness of the Hartian legal positivist outlook in that that (outlook) appears to affirm the sacrificing of an important principle that legal philosophers, such as Lon Fuller for instance,[51] have imagined to be essential for Western state law to uphold. That is the fundamental principle outlawing retroactive laws,[52] which is related to the principle usually

[50] Dworkin highlights use of a rule of recognition (and tests of 'pedigree'), exercises of judicial discretion and the resulting need to reach 'beyond the law' as characteristics or key tenets of Hartian legal positivism. See R Dworkin, 'The Model of Rules' (this chapter, n 11) 17–18; and 41.

[51] See LL Fuller, *The Morality of Law* (rev edn, Yale University Press 1969) generally ch II.

[52] ibid 51–62.

formulated in terms of the maxim *nulla poena sine lege* (or *nullum crimen sine lege*).[53] Now while these connected principles are usually seen as applying in the criminal law context,[54] the Dworkinian critique could apply equally to *any* area of law. As Dworkin puts it, 'if a judge makes new law and applies it retroactively in the case before him, then the losing party will be punished, not because he violated some duty he had, but rather a new duty created after the event'.[55] The rationale for avoidance of retroactive or *ex post facto* law-making, as Dworkin explains, is that the law needs to give explicit notice of the existence of a legal duty to enable duty-bearers to arrange their affairs and modify their behaviour accordingly.[56] Dworkin believes this to be impossible when a judge 'legislates' retroactively.

However, does that necessarily hold for the narrow 'window' of judicial decision-making outlined above? Hart thinks not. Initially Hart endorses Dworkin's stance that retroactive law-making may be considered unjust in disappointing the expectations of those who, in acting, 'have relied on the assumption that the legal consequences of their acts will be determined by the known state of the law established at the time of their acts'.[57] But when viewed in the narrow context of the judicial consideration of 'hard cases', even the principle outlawing retroactive laws appears to lose some of its impact. As Hart points out, Dworkin's objection to the possibility of judges retroactively 'legislating' when exercising discretion in so-called 'hard cases' '... even if it has force against a court's retrospective change or overruling of clearly established law, seems quite irrelevant in hard cases since these are cases which the law has left incompletely regulated and where there is *no known state of clear established law to justify expectations*'.[58]

Ultimately Dworkin's critical position – within the ever-narrowing 'window' of supposed failure of the rule of recognition and attendant weakening of the idea of Hartian legal positivism – attempts to cast doubt on the notion that judges decide cases by exercising discretion in the sense of reaching beyond 'law' (identifiable by a rule of recognition) into the terrain of 'non-law' (not so identifiable). But because the Hartian legal positivist's characterisation of judicial decision-making supposedly fails within its narrow 'window' one would expect any corrective theory advanced by Dworkin to be restricted in its scope to addressing only the claimed shortcomings found within that 'window' and not elsewhere. However, Dworkin's 'solution' is designed not merely to address those shortcomings but to establish an alternative characterisation of judicial decision-making; and this

[53] See J Hall, 'Nulla Poena Sine Lege' (1937) 47(2) *Yale Law Journal* 165. Dworkin also notes that judges 'should apply the law that other institutions have made; they should not make new law. That is the ideal, but for different reasons it cannot be realized fully in practice'. See R Dworkin, 'Hard Cases' (this chapter, n 3) 1058.

[54] See US Constitution prohibiting *ex post facto* legislation: Article I, Section 9, Clause 3.3.

[55] See R Dworkin, 'Hard Cases' (this chapter, n 3) 1061. Dworkin ties this to the idea that judges, being unelected, should not be making law as they are not accountable to the electorate in the same way as legislators are. It follows from this that adjudication needs to be 'as unoriginal as possible'. (ibid)

[56] ibid 1062.

[57] HLA Hart, *The Concept of Law* (this chapter, n 12) 276.

[58] ibid (emphasis added).

appears to operate generically, not merely as a response to theoretical difficulties posed by 'hard cases' within their narrow frame of reference. And this slightly subverts the far-reaching purpose of Dworkin's attack on Hartian legal positivism. Dworkin had set out to attack what turns out to be a relatively narrow aspect of Hart's perspective, mischaracterising this as generally fatal to Hartian legal positivism.[59] What is surprising is that that appears to be the basis for advancing a new *general* theoretical outlook on adjudication – with the groundwork being laid in earlier writing and more developed positions appearing in later writing. In particular, when Dworkin comes to write *Law's Empire*, his assault on Hartian legal positivism is tacitly presupposed as it is seemingly, by then, an accepted fact. The advancement of a new theory of adjudication is no longer explicitly dependent on, or grounded in, the success of that assault.

Nonetheless it is appropriate to ask to what extent Hart's idea of judges applying legal rules and deploying (something resembling) a rule of recognition as an identifying criterion when so doing – and indeed, pursuing that approach in innumerable routine cases (*non*-'hard cases') – would need to be modified, if at all, in the light of Dworkin's alternative characterisation of judicial decision-making.

It may also be asked how credible is the Herculean archetype if Hercules would have little cause to deploy a criterion akin to a rule of recognition in any of the multiplicity of non-'hard cases' where the possible use of such a criterion might be appropriate. Is the Hartian rule of recognition *entirely* misconceived in Dworkin's opinion? And is Hercules a judge of 'hard cases' only; or a judge 'for all seasons'?

Key elements of Dworkin's approach to adjudication outlined in *Law's Empire* incorporate the perspective of a more fully developed version of his Herculean archetype than is to be found in earlier writings. Dworkin returns to, and in effect reconfigures, his Herculean archetype in chapter 7 of *Law's Empire*. Given the focus of this Chapter 7 (of this book) on the Herculean archetype – and its possible use in facilitating the further development of a *Iudexian* archetype (taken up again in Chapter 8) – it is useful to explore briefly, in the remainder of the chapter, Dworkin's more developed Herculean archetype.

7.2.2. Dworkin's (Later) Herculean Archetype

By the time of *Law's Empire*, Hercules has become 'an imaginary judge of superhuman intellectual power and patience', where previously Dworkin had imagined him to be a lawyer of 'superhuman skill, learning, patience and acumen'.[60] The

[59] Regardless of Dworkin's position, there will always be judges who decide some, or *many*, cases on the basis of legal rules; and the rules in question will be identifiable through the deployment of a criterion resembling a Hartian rule of recognition.

[60] Respectively, R Dworkin, *Law's Empire* (this chapter, n 34) 239; and 'Hard Cases' (this chapter, n 3) 1083.

fundamental point of departure, therefore, changed little between Dworkin's earlier and later writings.

It is worth briefly reflecting on the 'space' that the 'earlier' Herculean archetype comes to occupy before Dworkin resumes discussion of it in chapter 7 of *Law's Empire*. It seems clear that, in terms of Dworkin's thinking, 'earlier' Hercules would have no role in engaging in the type of 'Hartian' forays into discretionary 'non-law' decision-making that Dworkin so decisively rejects. This stance is continued more explicitly in *Law's Empire* where – so the argument goes – judges should have little need for decision-making that is purely discretionary and not securely grounded in *law* given that, being on a (Dworkinian) quest for coherence, their decision-making in cases coming before them is designed to achieve the best possible 'fit' with the entire body of precedents and other applicable legal standards relevant to those cases.[61] Hercules, however, as a *superhuman* judge, is idealised beyond ordinary imagination. If the archetype were to be modelled, say, on a Weberian conception of ideal type construction, it would doubtless be considered more 'utopian' than Weber would allow for when formulating an ordinary ideal type that is merely and largely reflective of empirical reality.[62]

Is a judgment of 'a Hercules' (as a theoretical proposition) any more or less credible than that of a 'Hartian' judge which (in the latter case) might occasionally involve use of judicial discretion, extending to the use of supposedly 'non-law' grounds of decision-making: at least for a brief 'window' in advance of the judgment becoming a recognised legal precedent in its own right (whereupon it becomes *law*)? Even if the core decision – its *ratio decidendi* – is not traceable to any conventionally 'legal' source,[63] the formal (as opposed to substantive) validity of the decision (its 'pedigree'), once the decision is officially handed down, would be straightforwardly traceable to an empowering rule of adjudication which is, in turn, validated by a rule of recognition, following Hart. And that would hold for both a 'Herculean' and a 'Hartian' judge.[64] The rules, equivalent to Hartian rules of adjudication, that empower identifiable individuals to carry out the judicial role – regardless of any exercise of discretion, or the (supposed) grounding of a decision in 'non-law'[65] – confer formal, if not necessarily substantive, validity on judges'

[61] See (for example) R Dworkin, *Law's Empire* (this chapter, n 34) 250–254, 265. Judgments of 'fit' also underlie Dworkin's 'chain novelist' model of adjudication. (ibid 228–238, especially at 230–231)

[62] Weber makes the point that as a constructed ideal type 'cannot be found empirically anywhere in reality' it is a 'utopia'. But there must be degrees of utopianism. An ideal type that significantly parts company with perceived reality may not be especially illuminating; nor indeed would it be *Weberian*. See M Weber, '"Objectivity" in Social Science' (this chapter, n 8) 90.

[63] In the earlier example of *Donoghue v Stevenson*, the seminal 'rule that you are to love your neighbour' (as Lord Atkin puts it) has its substantive origin in biblical or theological texts, rather than in 'strictly legal' sources.

[64] Hercules, even if 'superhuman', is still in the final analysis a judge: as an institutional actor, he must be properly and validly appointed. A judge is not just 'anyone'. And judicial decision-making occurs only in the setting of a properly convened court.

[65] And indeed, this is regardless of the Dworkinian principle of 'integrity' and 'fit'. A judgment will be formally valid whether or not a judge such as Hercules has embarked on the 'superhuman' Dworkinian exercise of fitting the decision into the seamless web of legal authorities and other standards that have a bearing on the case.

official decision-making.[66] The decisions of persons with relevant qualifications, meeting all applicable appointment criteria in a properly constituted court of law, count as *judicial* decisions; and in any system that recognises the principle of *stare decisis*, those decisions have the status of 'law', unless and until subsequently overruled by a court or superseded by statute. Kelsen argues that the normative output of a judge's deliberations – the judicial decision – is itself a 'norm', an order of a court.[67] Anyone not qualified or appointed may express an opinion, but it is no more than that. It has no formal status, unlike a judicial decision which disposes of the instant case at the same time as it establishes a precedent.

Turning to the 'later' Hercules, Dworkin's archetype approaches its fullest expression in *Law's Empire* perhaps because, unlike in 'Hard Cases' where Hercules had simply emerged from 'nowhere' (resembling a sketch), Dworkin appears to acknowledge that a more developed version of the archetype is actually a good idea. Thus, in later writing, Hercules is harnessed towards recreating, in an idealised form, elements of judicial decision-making that serve to advance key tenets of his broader theoretical outlook. So, critically, the 'later' Hercules 'accepts law as integrity' as his defining judicial philosophy.[68] Further into chapter 7 (of *Law's Empire*), Dworkin focuses on the judicial reasoning involved in reimagining the decision-making in the English tort case of *McLoughlin v O'Brian*,[69] assigning to Hercules a sequence of six hypothetical arguments that he is tasked to analyse and reconcile. The assumption is that, in capturing the best interpretation of the body of standards – eg judicial precedents, doctrines, rules, principles, and so on – relevant to the reimagined *McLoughlin* case, Hercules is as engaged with those standards as it is possible to be. Hercules's interpretation of the applicable body of

[66] In terms of substantive validity, legal commentators (Dworkin, even) may argue endlessly over whether the substantive 'pedigree' of the *ratio decidendi* of a given judicial decision is properly traceable, for instance, to an earlier authoritative decision of another (in some cases, higher) court, or represents the best 'fit' with the accumulation of laws, legal rules, principles, doctrines and other standards relevant to the case in hand. But a decision's seeming lack of substantive 'pedigree' may count for little against the executive force – the 'institutional heft', one might say – of a judgment of a properly constituted court. Whatever the derivation of the *ratio decidendi* of a judgment may happen to be substantively – whatever its 'fit' or lack of 'fit' – a judgment is still a judgment. It is an authority; a precedent to be observed and followed (and even if distinguished or overruled it still represents a 'hurdle' to be scaled in future judicial decision-making). In terms of formal validity, rules of adjudication are exemplified in the Constitutional Reform Act 2005, establishing the Supreme Court in the UK. Sections 24 to 27 govern qualifications for appointment of members of the court, selection of its members and the selection process. Anyone *not* appointed or selected in accordance with those provisions is not a member of the Supreme Court. Only an individual properly appointed has the competence by law to engage in an act of decision-making that has any claim to validity as a judgment of the UK Supreme Court.

[67] See H Kelsen, *Pure Theory of Law* (this chapter, n 37) 57. According to Kelsen, in tracing the various norms of a legal system back to a basic norm it is necessary to show that a particular norm was created in accordance with the basic norm: 'For example, one may ask why a certain coercive act is a legal act and thus belongs to a certain legal system – the coercive act of incarceration, say, whereby one human being deprives another of liberty. The answer is that this act was *prescribed by a certain individual norm, a judicial decision*'. (Emphasis added.)

[68] R Dworkin, *Law's Empire* (this chapter, n 34) 239.

[69] [1983] 1 AC 410, reversing [1981] QB 599. See R Dworkin, *Law's Empire* (this chapter, n 34) 240–275.

standards is tested 'by asking whether it could form part of a coherent theory justifying the network as a whole'.[70] However, in the final analysis the assigned judicial tasks are (for Dworkin) inescapably 'Herculean', and that may be both a strength and a weakness of Hercules as an archetype. Dworkin (again) urges us to '[imagine] … a Herculean judge of superhuman talents and endless time'.[71] Yet, given that what is demanded of Hercules is 'a full interpretation of all of his community's law at once' it is clear, as Dworkin recognises, that '[n]o *actual judge* could compose anything approaching' this.[72] Such a judge can only hope to 'imitate Hercules in a limited way'.[73] Thus, on one hand, we are asked to assume that there is no judicial task that would be beyond Hercules to undertake; while, on the other, the approach to decision-making adopted by any ordinary (or 'actual') judge will only ever represent a shadow of a Herculean approach, which a real judge cannot begin to replicate. If 'later' Hercules is so detached from 'reality' (ie from 'actual' judicial decision-making), what is the *point* of this archetype? This is a question taken up in the next section.

7.2.3. What is the Point of Dworkin's Herculean Archetype?

Dworkin's immediate response is that an ordinary judge can 'allow the scope of his interpretation to fan out from the cases immediately in point to cases in the same general area … of law, and then still farther', provided this offers a promising way ahead. This is compatible with imitating the Herculean approach to judicial decision-making.[74] So far so good. But there is nothing especially 'Herculean' about that approach to judicial reasoning or decision-making, whether adopted by Hercules or by an 'actual' (ordinary) judge. Even Dworkin's six hypothetical arguments exploratory of the *McLoughlin* case (which Dworkin assigns to Hercules) appear unexceptional when reckoned beside a task of judicial exegesis calling for superhuman talent and endless time. Moreover, the idea of Hercules (or indeed any ordinary judge) reviewing an ever-expanding body of case law, to determine coherence or 'fit', leaves unanswered the question – held over from earlier Dworkinian critiques of Hart's rule of recognition – of the nature of the identifying criterion used by a judge to track down instances of valid case law. There are multiple references in *Law's Empire* to 'past decisions', 'past judicial decisions'

[70] To that end (and at the risk of over-simplification) Hercules might ask whether a judicial decision made in the instant case is fair and just because one that fails in that respect would undermine the rationale of a system that, *as a whole*, seeks to ensure fair and just decision-making. See R Dworkin, *Law's Empire* (this chapter, n 34) 245.

[71] R Dworkin, *Law's Empire* (this chapter, n 34) 245.

[72] ibid (emphasis added).

[73] ibid.

[74] ibid. Literally the same approach is adopted by Hercules whose 'judgments of fit expand out from the immediate case before him in a series of concentric circles'. (ibid 250)

and similar expressions,[75] but no mention of the need for a basic test or criterion that can be used to identify what counts as valid law, such as a Hartian rule of recognition: an idea rejected by Dworkin in earlier writings.[76] For Dworkin, valid law – including 'past decisions', 'past judicial decisions' and so on – is simply something that 'we have *no difficulty* identifying'.[77] A claimed lack of 'difficulty', however, does not imply the absence of an identifying criterion. Plainly questions of 'pedigree' still arise and Dworkin appears to acknowledge this when he observes that 'the decisions … [that] institutions [such as legislatures, courts and administrative agencies] make *are reported in a canonical way*'.[78] What (for Hercules, say) would count as a valid precedent; or an authoritative or trusted 'canonical' report? Is there 'no difficulty' in identifying sources of law when those sources are readily identifiable, even if tacitly, by a mechanism resembling a rule of recognition? Or are the identifying criteria simply absorbed into the consciousness of legal professionals (including judges) through training and professional experience, without the need for an explicit rule of recognition?

In order to strengthen the (later) Herculean archetype, Dworkin applies a series of 'stress tests', focusing on its possible weaknesses. The danger here, of course, is that the weaknesses may prove more resilient than the archetype itself. Thus, Dworkin (acting as critic of Hercules – in effect, as 'devil's advocate') points to supposed Herculean failings, a few of which are simply reflective of a wider judicial reality. (So, to the extent that Hercules might act in the same way as any ordinary judge, it may be questionable to view those situations as failings.) Take, for instance, the Dworkinian critic's challenge that Hercules relies on 'his own opinion'. Here, Hercules's decision is based around a choice of one of the six *McLoughlin* case arguments he is tasked to reconcile in chapter 7 of *Law's Empire*.[79] And while that, at first sight, seems an acceptably neutral stance, Dworkin in

[75] For example, at various places, Dworkin also refers to 'decisions'; 'cases'; 'earlier cases'; 'precedents'; 'precedent cases'.

[76] The position outlined earlier in this chapter is that much of the law, save to the extent that standards fall within the so-called narrow 'window' of judicial decision-making mentioned above, is routinely capable of identification in this way. Dworkin's outright rejection of such a test or criterion – eg see 'The Model of Rules' (this chapter, n 11) 45 – seems questionable, particularly if the argument that there is a measure of theoretical interpenetration of the rule of recognition and the Herculean archetype has force. See section 7.2.1 (this chapter, above).

[77] (Emphasis added.) As Dworkin observes more fully: 'In fact we have no difficulty identifying collectively the practices that count as legal practices in our own culture. We have legislatures and courts and administrative agencies and bodies, and the decisions these institutions make are reported in a canonical way. In the United States we have the Constitution as well. Each lawyer has joined the practice of law with that furniture in place and with a shared understanding that these institutions together form our legal system'. See *Law's Empire* (this chapter, n 34) 91. For his part, Hart maintains a position that is not far removed from this: 'For whereas a subordinate rule of a system may be valid and in that sense "exist" even if it is generally disregarded, the rule of recognition exists only as a complex, but normally concordant, practice of the courts, officials, and private persons in identifying the law by reference to certain criteria. Its existence is a matter of fact'. See HLA Hart, *The Concept of Law* (this chapter, n 12) 110.

[78] R Dworkin, *Law's Empire* (this chapter, n 34) 91 (emphasis added).

[79] ibid 240–275.

the role of critic maintains that Hercules's decision *ignores* 'the actual law'; and, instead, substitutes Hercules's 'own views about what the law should be'.[80] This causes the (Dworkinian) critic to ask whether Hercules's decision has survived the proper threshold test of 'fit'; and whether Hercules ought to have expanded the range of his study of precedents further. Dworkin as critic even considers that Hercules has possibly 'misapplied his own methods'.

But if the (Dworkinian) critic is correct then it would indeed be remarkable if a judicial archetype with a Dworkinian world view – whose first instinct is to eschew the possibility of discretionary judicial decision-making – reimagined the decision in the *McLoughlin* case in terms of an exercise of ('strong') discretion that disregards 'the actual law'. Yet in the 'real world', judicial culture and tradition are not necessarily inimical to that approach, regardless of Dworkin's theory of adjudicatory 'fit'. The reimagined Herculean decision in *McLoughlin* – indeed *any* judicial decision, whether of a 'Hercules', and whether or not it applies or departs from pre-established law – serves to reinforce the presence of judicial powers that may be far-reaching enough to allow for pre-established law to be disregarded or, at any rate according to the perception of most common law judges, distinguished.[81] Whether or not a departure from pre-established law constitutes a genuine exercise of judicial discretion may be arguable; but the reimagined *McLoughlin* decision would nonetheless be validated, in a 'real life' situation, by legal powers coming within the scope of (Hartian-type) rules of adjudication.[82] And it is to rules of adjudication – in an exercise of judicial decision-making that would usually, but may not in every case, involve a *parallel exercise* of tracing substantive validity or 'pedigree' to one or more pre-established laws: eg statute or precedent – that any examination of the 'pedigree' of a judicial decision will always, ultimately, lead back. This could entail a question as elementary as: 'is person X, who purports to be a judge sitting in a duly convened court of competent jurisdiction in [district] Y, properly and validly appointed as such a judge in terms of a relevant [statutorily] defined process, Z?' Once X's credentials as a judge are properly established – in the normal situation this would merely be assumed – X can be viewed as possessing an appropriate range of legal powers that validate decision-making (including discretionary decision-making) within the scope of X's judicial authority. This is the sense – alluded to earlier in this chapter – in which judicial decision-making is transformative. A judicial decision – such as one made within the narrow 'window' of 'hard case' decision-making – that substantively originates in a standard that has no discernible 'pedigree' following the (unproductive) application of a rule of recognition will nonetheless

[80] ibid 258–259.

[81] See R Cross, *Precedent in English Law* (Clarendon Press 1961) 245–246.

[82] See, for instance, section 40(5) of the Constitutional Reform Act 2005 which defines, in the broadest terms, the powers of the UK Supreme Court: 'The Court has power to determine any question necessary to be determined for the purposes of doing justice in an appeal to it under any enactment'.

have a rule of adjudication to fall back on as the basis of its validity. (For their part, rules of adjudication, one assumes, are readily identifiable by an appropriate rule of recognition.) Once the decision is handed down – particularly if it is published in official law reports – the decision then becomes straightforwardly identifiable in its own right by the rule of recognition.

The rationale behind Dworkin's (later) Herculean archetype perhaps emerges more clearly when we contrast Dworkin's particular approach to his Herculean archetype with Weber's approach to generic ideal-type construction (touched upon briefly in Chapters 1, 4 and 5, above). Weber argues that '[s]ubstantively, this construct [the ideal type] … is like a *utopia* which has been arrived at by the analytical accentuation of certain elements of reality … It is not a *description* of reality but it aims to give unambiguous means of expression to such a description'.[83] Dworkin, of course, is not primarily in the business of providing means of expression to 'descriptions' of judicial reality – unlike Hart with his espousal of a 'descriptive sociology'.[84] However, acting again in the role of critic of Hercules, Dworkin points to a few of the more 'utopian' elements of the Herculean archetype, emphasising that no 'real judge' possesses the legal powers of a Hercules.[85] Moreover, 'real' judges tend to be more instinctive when deciding 'hard cases': '[t]hey do not construct and test various rival interpretations against a complex matrix of intersecting political and moral principles'.[86] But importantly, Dworkin *as critic* denies that there is anything to be gained by holding Hercules out as a model for other judges to follow, implying that in a 'real world' context 'actual judges' would have no practical use for the archetype: it would neither guide nor influence their decision-making. Yet, continuing

[83] See M Weber, '"Objectivity" in Social Science' (this chapter, n 8) 90.

[84] As briefly discussed in Chapter 5 (see section 5.2), Hart ultimately held to the idea that *The Concept of Law* might have something to offer a 'descriptive sociology' of law: in other words, a descriptive theory of law professing a sociological dimension. By contrast, in *Law's Empire* and other writings, Dworkin is not *generally* in the business of description; and indeed this seems to be underscored by the fact (and to the extent) that his Herculean archetype fails to reflect the perceived reality of what 'real judges' do. Hart describes Dworkinian theory as 'evaluative justificatory jurisprudence'. (See HLA Hart, *The Concept of Law* (this chapter, n 12) 241.) Nicola Lacey reinforces the same point when alluding to Hart's denial that *The Concept of Law* is a branch of 'justificatory moral or political theory'. Further, as Lacey argues, 'while *Law's Empire* advances an ideal vision and a legitimating argument for a certain conception of law, it neither engages in, nor undermines the validity of, the project of producing a general, universally applicable and fundamentally descriptive theory of law such as Hart himself had sought to provide'. (See N Lacey, 'Analytical Jurisprudence versus Descriptive Sociology Revisited' (2006) 84 *Texas Law Review* 944, 955.)

[85] R Dworkin, *Law's Empire* (this chapter, n 34) 264. In this context, Dworkin may be referring to the unique 'Herculean' powers of a judge of superhuman talent and endless time who can undertake a full interpretation of all of a community's law at once before arriving at a decision. Hercules even goes as far as doing what 'real judges' would do 'if they had a career to devote to a single decision' (at 265). This image of the judicial role, inevitably, is many steps removed from professional and institutional reality. The availability of an 'eternity' alone implies that the emergent written judgment may be of such extreme length and exhaustiveness that it is unwieldy and for all practical purposes (for future users) unmanageable.

[86] ibid 264–265.

his 'Socratic' dialogue (after reverting (back) to theorist from critic), Dworkin argues that his own (self-generated) 'critic misunderstands our exercise':

> Hercules is useful to us just because he is more reflective and self-conscious than any real judge need be or, given the press of work, could be. No doubt real judges decide most cases in a much less methodical way. But Hercules shows us the hidden structure of their judgments and so lays these open to study and criticism.[87]

On that basis, Dworkin's Herculean archetype appears to be designed for a practical, yet 'reflective', purpose: namely, to represent best judicial practice for 'real world' judges. Dworkin's (later) Herculean archetype is therefore probably as 'Weberian' and utopian as it needs to be to provide a benchmark (albeit unattainable) for ordinary judicial decision-making. Yet the Weberian ideal type is designed to facilitate *theoretical* enquiry. Perhaps recognising this limitation, the (Dworkinian) critic observes that if 'real judges' 'decided to imitate Hercules, trying in each case to secure some general theory of law as a whole, they would be paralyzed while their docket choked'.[88] The part of *Law's Empire* which discusses Hercules as 'myth'[89] plays up this dilemma so much that, *at the hands of Dworkin himself acting in the role of critic*, Hercules arguably mutates from a 'heroic' to a 'tragic' figure – 'tragic' because effectively redundant. Dworkin wishes for the impossible: that Hercules, in some sense representing the pinnacle of judicial decision-making, should be a great hands-on judge and master of 'fit' (and integrity), at the same time as he is a great theorist and philosopher; possibly a great jurist. But to the extent that judges of the 'real world' in their day-to-day activities may have little time for theory or philosophy they probably have little or no time for the deliberations of a Dworkinian Hercules. Dworkin as both hostile critic and champion of Hercules appears to succeed in drawing attention to Hercules's disengagement both from practical judicial decision-making and theoretical or philosophical enquiry.

As we have seen, Dworkin makes a case for Hercules as a significant exponent of the idea of law as integrity.[90] Later, in the role of champion of the Herculean archetype, he *resists* the Dworkinian critic's suggestion that 'law as integrity, with its elaborate and top-heavy structure, is at best a conception for hard cases alone',[91] arguing instead that that seminal idea works for 'hard cases' and 'non-hard cases' (or 'easy cases') alike:

> Law as integrity explains and justifies easy cases as well as hard ones; it also shows why they are easy. It is obvious that the speed limit in California is 55 because it is obvious that any competent interpretation of California traffic law must yield that conclusion. So easy cases are, for law as integrity, only special cases of hard ones and the critic's

[87] ibid 265.
[88] ibid.
[89] ibid at 263–266.
[90] ibid 239.
[91] ibid 265.

> complaint is then only what Hercules himself would be happy to concede: that we need not ask questions when we already know the answer.[92]

This goes some way to providing an answer to the question, framed earlier in this chapter, as to whether Hercules is a judge of 'hard cases' only; or a judge, as it were, 'for all seasons'. On the basis that for Dworkin 'easy cases' are a special instance of 'hard cases',[93] Hercules, as an adherent to integrity-based judicial decision-making, is arguably a judge for both types of case. Though we might ask why have a 'Herculean' judge performing the most ordinary of routine judicial tasks, if that is indeed part of the role Dworkin envisages for him. In that situation it would be difficult to discern what distinguishes Hercules's judicial decision-making role from that of any 'real judge' faced with both 'hard cases' and 'easy cases'; and all the more difficult to see why, particularly in the latter (if not in the former) case, Hercules would need the powers that Dworkin assigns to him, namely (to summarise): (i) the powers of a lawyer of 'superhuman skill, learning, patience and acumen' *or* (ii) the powers of a judge of 'superhuman intellectual power and patience'; who can (iii) undertake a full interpretation of all of a community's law at once before arriving at a decision; (iv) possessing 'more powers than any actual judge could' in working 'so much more quickly' and having 'so much more time available', so that: (v) 'he can explore avenues and ideas they cannot'; and (vi) 'he can pursue, not just one or two evident lines in expanding the range of cases he studies but *all the lines there are*'.[94] (It may be that Dworkin offers a straightforward answer to the question why a 'Herculean' judge might have no involvement in deciding 'easy cases'. He (Dworkin) hints at the presence of *obviousness* – if an 'easy case' is an obvious one, why involve Hercules?)

7.3. Concluding Reflections

The Herculean archetype in the final analysis works best not as part of a theory that sees itself on a quest for the most accurate descriptive account of law as a social institution (encompassing a similarly descriptive account of the role of the judge and of judicial decision-making). Such a project is plainly more Hartian than Dworkinian. The archetype is probably at its most effective operating within its

[92] ibid 266.

[93] ibid. We have seen that Dworkin defines 'hard cases' as cases where 'no settled rule dictates a decision either way'. (See 'Hard Cases' (this chapter, n 3) 1060.) It seems remarkable that Dworkin appears to dissolve what, for him, is a critical distinction between 'hard cases' and 'easy cases' such that the latter are subsumed by the former. In the example that Dworkin gives, centring on the California speed limit, the 'easy case' in question cannot become a variant of a 'hard case' because the 'easy case' is simply that – it does not, in other words, fit with Dworkin's definition of 'hard case' precisely because a 'settled rule dictates a decision'.

[94] R Dworkin, *Law's Empire* (this chapter, n 34) 265 (emphasis added).

own characteristic 'Dworkinian' frame of reference. As we have seen, this equates to a philosophical outlook that Lacey has described as 'an ideal vision and a legitimating argument for a certain conception of law'.[95] We have also seen that Hart has similarly described Dworkinian theory as 'evaluative justificatory jurisprudence'.[96] It therefore comes as no surprise when elements of the Herculean archetype part company with credible perceptions of what counts as empirical (judicial) reality. Dworkin itemises key 'Herculean' characteristics – including those outlined immediately above – that contribute to the realisation of that vision. Not only does the archetype idealise *personal* characteristics of Hercules (eg superhuman intellect or skill or patience); it idealises key aspects of the practice of 'Herculean' judicial decision-making (eg the task to undertake, in a single act, the fullest examination of all of a community's law). In embracing law as integrity as his core judicial philosophy,[97] a 'Herculean' judge adheres to a position where 'judges must conceive the body of law they administer as a whole rather than as a set of discrete decisions that they are free to make or amend one by one'.[98] At the same time, law as integrity 'directs' a judge – therefore *Hercules*, as an adherent to law as integrity – 'to regard as law what morality would suggest to be the *best justification* of … past decisions'.[99]

Hercules's detachment from judicial reality narrows, but does not remove, the scope for constructive theoretical engagement. In the next chapter, a few elements of the Herculean archetype are adapted towards the further development of a *Iudexian* archetype. Dworkin's archetype is arguably not so idealised or utopian that it entirely fails to capture what 'real judges' do, or that it is of precisely *no* assistance to 'real judges' seeking guidance in real-life decision-making. Yet, as we will find in the next chapter, one of the key differences between a Herculean and a *Iudexian* archetype is that the former, it would appear, represents a 'superhuman' judge *with no special status* within the judicial system.[100] In other words, Hercules is not explicitly an *ultimate* judge, or judge sitting in a final court of appeal issuing conclusive, unappealable judgments. But while his decisions may represent the best moral justification of past decisions – or the best 'fit' with all of those decisions (pursuing, as he does, not just one or two evident lines in expanding the range of cases he studies but all the lines there are) – that may not be enough to prevent Hercules's decisions (hypothetically) being appealed to, and overturned by, a higher court (assuming Hercules sits in a lower court). The fact that Hercules

[95] N Lacey, 'Analytical Jurisprudence versus Descriptive Sociology Revisited' (2006) 84 *Texas Law Review* 944, 955.

[96] See HLA Hart, *The Concept of Law* (this chapter, n 12) 241.

[97] See R Dworkin, *Law's Empire* (this chapter, n 34) 239.

[98] ibid 167.

[99] ibid 119–120 (emphasis added).

[100] It will be recalled that, according to Dworkin, Hercules is not a judge of, say, the (federal) US Supreme Court but a judge 'in some representative American jurisdiction'; though that would not necessarily rule out the possibility of Hercules being a justice of a US *state* supreme court. See R Dworkin, 'Hard Cases' (this chapter, n 3) 1083.

ex hypothesi has expended limitless time and effort in producing the decision may not 'save' the decision from reversal. The hypothetical parties litigating a civil case, for instance, may have little interest in whether a 'Herculean' decision scales heights of moral perfection, or coheres with the most extensive body of precedents imaginable, when deciding to appeal, if the decision appears to be adverse to their interests. The integrity of the decision will count for nothing to litigants intent on securing a result that furthers their (eg personal or commercial or professional) objectives. Hypothetically, they may be minded to appeal the 'Herculean' decision; and there is an ever-present possibility it will be overturned.

8

Constructing *Iudex* as an Ideal Type*

8.1. Introduction

One key question to emerge from Chapter 7 turns on the idea that if Dworkin's Herculean archetype is disengaged from the 'polar opposites' of practical judicial decision-making and theoretical or philosophical enquiry, is Dworkin's offering effectively too idealised and utopian to resonate with 'real judges' and theorists alike? In other words, does it fail to capture what 'real judges' do; and (fail) to offer anything to those judges if they should look to Hercules for a steer on real-life judicial decision-making? At the same time, is the archetype – as first and foremost a theoretical device that happens (in certain respects) to fit Weberian parameters of ideal-type construction – instructive for *legal theorists* in search of a proper theoretical basis for understanding the place of the institution of the judiciary, and judicial decision-making, in Western jurisprudential thought (specifically in a common law context)?

These are challenging questions for the Herculean archetype; yet they probably do not rule out the possibility of elements of the archetype being reoriented or appropriated towards a closely related theoretical purpose. In particular, it seems possible to look to Dworkin's Herculean judge for inspiration in constructing or reframing the archetypal *ultimate judge* referred to at various points in earlier chapters – namely, *Iudex*. But in moving towards a more developed *Iudexian* archetype in this chapter, Hercules's predicament, highlighted at the end of Chapter 7, remains unresolved. Even if the Dworkinian archetype represents a 'superhuman' judge, he is apparently not endowed with any special judicial status. In particular, whatever his personal qualities and enhanced decision-making powers may be, Hercules is not configured – for instance, in *Law's Empire* – as a supreme court judge sitting in an imaginary final court of appeal, handing down unappealable judgments. So while 'Herculean' decisions are imagined to cohere as closely as possible with the entirety of a community's past judicial decisions – representing at the same time the best moral justification of those decisions – that is no guarantee that ('Herculean') decisions will survive review by a higher court. By contrast, the decision-making of the hypothetical *Iudex* is, by explicit design, definitive and conclusively declaratory of the law of the community in question.

* Lord Hope of Craighead kindly read and commented on an earlier version of this chapter.

Towards developing a rudimentary *Iudexian* perspective on legal rights that incorporates a few of the insights of the Herculean archetype, a useful point of departure is to consider whether it makes sense to view *Iudex* as being in any (Dworkinian) sense 'Herculean' or to consider whether 'a *Iudex*' would need to be 'Herculean' in any respect. One hypothesis worth touching upon is whether the most rigorous possible 'fit' of a judicial decision with past judicial decisions, and the moral authority of the decision, might be relevant considerations in making a judgment – especially one that approximates to a 'Herculean' one – proof against review by a higher court such as in a situation where Hercules is a lower-court (appellate) judge. But even if Hercules is considered to occupy the role of an ultimate judge, what then? It may not especially matter that a *Iudexian* judgment is strictly speaking unappealable if the substantive judgment – encapsulating, or approaching, the 'Herculean' ideal in key respects – is 'unassailably' sound, both legally and morally (the latter being perpetually disputable). In that situation would the legal or moral 'power' of a judgment have a bearing on its resilience – in other words, its capacity to withstand later scrutiny and review, whether by the (same) supreme court, or by the legislature? The point is that the 'power' of the judgment – for instance, whether it might be considered doctrinally 'unassailable' – may serve to render its finality irrelevant for practical purposes.

This and other questions are taken up in the next section before we move, later in the chapter, to a more general discussion of possible characteristics to be assigned to a hypothetical *Iudexian* archetype.

8.2. 'Herculean' Decision-Making (Case Study)

What do we already know about Dworkin's Hercules that assists the task of constructing a workable *Iudexian* archetype – that of an imaginary ultimate judge – assuming Dworkin's Herculean archetype to be a productive point of departure?

At the end of section 7.2.3 (Chapter 7, above), we noted that, by Dworkin's own account, a 'Herculean' judge could be synoptically described as a judge, and lawyer, of superhuman skill, learning, intellectual power, patience and acumen who possesses greater power than any 'actual judge' in working more speedily on the decision-making task in hand (despite the hypothetical availability of infinite time to devote to that task). Dworkin, as we have seen, imagines that Hercules – but not any 'actual judge' – undertakes among other things 'a full interpretation of all of his community's law at once'.[1] Ordinarily, Hercules has the capacity to explore avenues and ideas that no 'actual judge' could; and he pursues not just one or two lines in expanding the range of cases he studies but all the lines there

[1] R Dworkin, *Law's Empire* (Fontana Paperbacks 1986) (hereafter, in this chapter, '*Law's Empire*') 245.

are. So, he literally leaves no stone unturned. Dworkin's Herculean judge – whose 'judgments of fit expand out from the immediate case before him in a series of concentric circles'[2] – reviews an ever-expanding body of case law to determine coherence or 'fit' of key elements of that case with the entire body of precedents and other applicable legal standards relevant to the case. Hercules's commitment to the idea of law as integrity moreover impels him (and also 'actual judges') to regard as law what morality would suggest is the best justification of past decisions.

Against that background, is the Herculean archetype sufficiently anchored in the 'real world' for any of its elements to be applied towards outlining a *Iudexian* archetype (a constructed imaginary ultimate judge)? Do any aspects of the Herculean archetype translate into a (hypothesised) image –'a *Iudex*' – of how an ultimate 'real judge' might approach judicial decision-making? Developing a point made in Chapter 7,[3] it may be that 'real judges' occasionally demonstrate a 'Herculean' capacity to undertake, in a single act, the fullest examination of the law of a community, albeit on a scale that reflects not only the relatively narrow parameters of the case before the court, but institutional and practical realities also. One compelling line of enquiry turns on possibly identifying instances where 'real judges' appear to replicate some of the more realistic 'Herculean' avenues of approach to decision-making. This may be in the quest for a doctrinally 'unassailable' decision; and that in turn may be more a matter of a judge's adopting a rigorous approach to judicial method than any conscious attempt to imitate the attributes of an imaginary judge such as Dworkin's Hercules.[4] The Herculean archetype, as we have seen, appears to be centred on non-ultimate (and not necessarily appellate) US state-level (as opposed to federal-level) judges occupying that imaginary role. Yet Dworkin does not appear to rule out ultimate (eg supreme court-level) judges as 'Herculean candidates'.

The task of constructing a *Iudexian* archetype – which is purely a hypothesis[5] – finds inspiration in 'real life' instances of behaviour where ultimate *or indeed non-ultimate* judges appear to adopt what can be described as a 'Herculean' approach to decision-making, assuming that this approach reflects what is practically and humanly realisable. It is helpful to deploy a case study that explores aspects of the practice of 'real judges' in the UK based upon

[2] ibid 250. This might take the form of a 'chain novelist' approach to the adjudicatory task. (ibid 250–254, 265)

[3] See section 7.2.2 (Chapter 7, above).

[4] For an Australian perspective on judicial method, see generally The Hon Justice MH McHugh, 'The Judicial Method' (5 July 1998), accessible under the title 'The Australian Bar Association Conference, London, 5 July 1998, Democracy and the Law, "The Judicial Method"' here: https://www.hcourt.gov.au/resources-and-publications/speeches/michael-hudson-mchugh-ac-qc (accessed 28 July 2025).

[5] It is worth recalling that, according to Weber, an ideal type – which *Iudex* would be – is formed by accentuating one or more points of view and synthesising a range of concrete individual phenomena. A 'unified analytical construct' emerges from this process. See M Weber, '"Objectivity" in Social Science and Social Policy' ['*Die 'Objektivität' sozialwissenschaftlicher und sozialpolitischer Erkenntnis*'] in M Weber, *Max Weber On The Methodology of the Social Sciences* (EA Shils and HA Finch (trs and eds), The Free Press 1949) ch II, 90.

decision-making at the higher appellate level. To that end, a 'real life' example of appellate judges exhibiting elements of a 'Dworkinian Herculean' approach to judicial decision-making is to be found in the Scots law setting, in a remarkable series of judicial decisions (in the same case) made between 1994 and 1997 in the civil courts. In *Sharp v Thomson*[6] the appellate process commenced with an appeal at first instance.[7] This was followed by an appeal before the Inner House of the Court of Session (First Division).[8] The case culminated in a notably controversial appeal decided in the House of Lords.[9] *Sharp* appears to exemplify a situation where a pre-ultimate judicial decision, which encountered later adverse judicial treatment at the hands of a superior (in fact, ultimate) court, was nonetheless thought to have in some sense 'prevailed' over the later decision.[10]

In essence, and slightly simplifying the key facts, an incorporated company, A (Albyn), granted a floating charge to B (Bank of Scotland), and at a later time sold a house in Aberdeen to C (the Thomson siblings). A had a recorded title to the house. A received the sale proceeds and delivered an executed disposition (conveyance) to C's agent. However, a delay occurred in C's recording the disposition in the Register of Sasines.[11] Recording of the disposition would have given C a full, publicly recognised and indefeasible right and title to the house. But C's agent's delay in recording the disposition left the matter sufficiently in doubt for a declaratory action to follow later, initiated by the joint receivers of A (Sharp and Souter). On the day after delivery of the disposition to C's agent (10 August 1990) the floating charge 'crystallised' – ie it was deemed to have become a fixed security.[12] It

[6] A Scottish Law Commission discussion paper comments that '*Sharp v Thomson* [has] provoked more debate and discussion than possibly any case in modern times'. See Scottish Law Commission, *Discussion Paper on* Sharp v Thomson (Discussion Paper No 114, The Stationery Office July 2001) 2. See also KGC Reid, 'Equity Triumphant: *Sharp v Thomson*' (1997) 1 *Edinburgh Law Review* 464, 464: '[N]o decision in modern times has attracted more attention'.

[7] 1994 SLT 1068 (Lord Penrose).

[8] 1995 SC 455 (Lord President Hope, Lord Sutherland, Lord Coulsfield).

[9] 1997 SC (HL) 66 (Lord Browne-Wilkinson, Lord Keith, Lord Jauncey, Lord Steyn, Lord Clyde): reported in some contexts as *Sharp and Others v Woolwich Building Society*.

[10] See Lord Hodge (PS Hodge), 'Property Law, Fiduciary Obligations and the Constructive Trust' in F McCarthy, J Chalmers and S Bogle (eds), *Essays in Conveyancing and Property Law in Honour of Professor Robert Rennie* (Open Book Publishers 2015) ch 6, at 98: '[The] magisterial judgment … [of] Lord President Hope in the First Division on the structure of the Scots law of property … [is] an opinion which will stand the test of time.' The implication here – Lord Hodge commenting two decades after delivery of the Inner House judgment (in 1995) – is that Lord Hope's opinion had prevailed intellectually and doctrinally even if it had not prevailed *institutionally* (the decision having been reversed in 1997). Also, the subsequent Inner House (Extra Division) decision, *Burnett's Trustee v Grainger* (2002 SC 580) and House of Lords decision (2004 SC (HL) 19) (discussed further, below), went some way towards reinforcing (reinstating, even) – and therefore leaving to an extent intact – Lord Hope's judgment in *Sharp*.

[11] For centuries this was a public register for the registration of deeds transferring title to land in Scotland. With the closure of the register (in accordance with the Land Registration etc (Scotland) Act 2012) its functions have now largely been taken over by the Land Register of Scotland which gives effect to a more sophisticated cadastral system of registration of title to land going somewhat beyond a register of deeds.

[12] Insolvency Act 1986, section 53(7).

was argued that the floating charge 'attached' to (among other property) the house that A had sold to C, with the result that, assuming that that argument had force, B would become the holder of a fixed security over all of A's property such as to include the house – conferring on B (or, at any rate, the joint receivers of A) a wide range of legal advantages and privileges in relation to the house, extending to a right to sell or dispose of it notwithstanding the earlier sale to C. Two overriding questions that arose were: (i) whether, on the 'crystallisation' of the floating charge, A had already been *divested* of its right to the house such that the house had ceased to be comprised in A's 'property and undertaking' (in the sense of the Companies Act 1985 section 462), thereby falling outside the scope of the property secured by the 'crystallised' charge; and (ii) whether C had correspondingly been *invested* with a right to the house as bare holder of an executed disposition, despite not having at that time taken the step of recording the disposition in the Register of Sasines.

At first instance and on appeal the Inner House of the Court of Session, applying long-established principles of Scots land law, answered both questions, (i) and (ii), in the negative: A had not been divested of its title to the house; so that C correspondingly had not been invested with a right sufficient to escape the 'attachment' (charging effect) of the floating charge. The Court of Session thus upheld the orthodox principle of Scots law that ownership of land is transferred only on the recording of a disposition or other conveyance in the Register of Sasines (or equivalent registration in the Land Register of Scotland).[13] The mere delivery of an executed (and for the time being unrecorded) disposition by A to C did not alter that fundamental position. For as long as A was owner of the house, with a publicly registered title, C was not. There was no middle position.[14] It was held that – in the absence of the recording of C's disposition in the Register of Sasines – A remained owner of the house, so that the floating charge on the occurrence of a relevant 'crystallising' event (namely, appointment of the joint receivers by B) became a fixed security in relation to the house. Had this decision not been appealed to the House of Lords its consequence would have been to give A's receivers (and the bank, B) the benefit of the original sale proceeds (on the sale to C) and at the same time the benefit of A's continuing ownership of the house (duly 'attached' by the floating charge).[15]

Before briefly considering the position that emerged from the appeal to the House of Lords, it is useful to reflect for a moment on the leading judgment of

[13] At the relevant time (1990) the County of Aberdeen had not become an operational area for land registration purposes. That occurred on 1 April 1996.

[14] 'Scots law does not recognise a right which lies between the personal right on the one hand and the real right on the other … [T]here is no such thing as a real right which is imperfect or incomplete.' See *Sharp v Thomson* 1995 SC 455 at 468 F–H (Lord President Hope).

[15] As Kenneth GC Reid puts it: 'Albyn's receiver got both the price and the house; the Thomsons got nothing (other than, presumably, a claim against their solicitors)'. See KGC Reid, 'Equity Triumphant: *Sharp v Thomson*' (1997) 1 *Edinburgh Law Review* 464, 465.

the Lord President,[16] described in 2015 by the (now) Deputy President of the UK Supreme Court as 'magisterial'.[17] The judgment perhaps represents a classic attempt to define a *doctrinally* 'unassailable' position; and, despite being at the pre-ultimate rather than ultimate stage of the judicial process (making it vulnerable to reversal or other adverse judicial treatment) engages the more humanly attainable tasks associated with Dworkin's 'Herculean' archetype: such as drawing upon extensive historical and contemporary authorities,[18] at the same time as distinguishing or questioning a range of contrary authorities.[19] The judgment could be said to achieve the best possible 'fit' with the most extensive body of authoritative sources bearing on the dispute under discussion.[20] While it appears to be as doctrinally sound as an authoritative exposition of the law could be, there is the residual question whether the decision also mirrors the Dworkinian ideal of a judgment that morality would suggest to be the 'best justification' of past decisions. The Lord President observed in passing that the outcome was 'unsatisfactory' and likely to occasion 'hardship'. It was the result of the introduction by way of statute of a type of security (the floating charge) which was considered to be 'alien to Scots law'.[21] Lord Hope's observation is perhaps as close to a moral reading of the likely impact of the Inner House decision as it was appropriate for him to venture. However, Lord Coulsfield pressed the 'moral' viewpoint slightly further:

> I also recognise that there are grounds for saying that the result in the present case is unfair, if the respondents' property based argument prevails, and that it is not a happy situation to be holding that the requirements of a coherent system of property law defeat what appears to be a fair claim in an individual case.[22]

[16] 1995 SC 455, 457–481.

[17] See above, this chapter, n 10 (Lord Hodge).

[18] For instance, there is an extended discussion of historical authorities represented by the Scottish institutional writers, Stair, Erskine and Hume who – as the Lord President makes clear – centuries earlier had articulated the paradigmatic view of Scots land law as a unititular system whereby 'only one title of ownership is recognised in any one thing at any one time' (ibid 469 F–G, citing KGC Reid). This key historical and doctrinal insight effectively set the highest hurdle for the judges in the House of Lords to scale when later seeking (in terms of practical outcome) to subvert that paradigm. Lord Coulsfield in the later case of *Burnett's Trustee v Grainger* (2002 SC 580 at 586 C) observes that Lord Clyde in *Sharp* (House of Lords, 80 B–C) pointed out that no challenge was being made to the decision of the Court of Session (*Sharp*, Inner House) that no hybrid right between real right and personal right was recognised by Scots law and that that decision was not being questioned. As Lord Coulsfield remarks: 'It is not altogether easy to see how that unchallenged principle can be reconciled with the [other apparently contradictory] observations [from Lord Clyde's speech] just quoted'.

[19] *Sharp v Thomson* 1995 SC 455, 468–475.

[20] According to the Scottish Law Commission, the underlying issues were 'examined in considerable detail, and with *an almost exhaustive citation of authority*'. See Scottish Law Commission, *Discussion Paper on* Sharp v Thomson (Discussion Paper No 114, The Stationery Office July 2001) 2 (emphasis added).

[21] *Sharp v Thomson* 1995 SC 455, 481 C–E. This idea had originally been expressed in emphatic terms by Lord President Cooper in *Carse v Coppen* 1951 SC 233, 239.

[22] *Sharp v Thomson* 1995 SC 455, 504 F–H. Lord Coulsfield nonetheless points out that bankruptcy and insolvency proceedings are always inherently unfair: 'The supplier who has provided goods or services for which he has not been paid suffers a loss every bit as great as that of the person who has paid for property which he does not receive …' (ibid 504 G–I)

Judgments of fairness can be both moral and legal, though Lord Coulsfield inclined towards *contrasting* the notion of unfairness (possibly seen as a moral criterion) with the notion of coherence: that is, the coherence of a system of property law, seen as a juridical ideal. If a moral test of fairness of outcome is a factor to be weighed in the balance, yet systemic coherence is to be given primacy, the two may be in conflict. Indeed, to some, they may be irreconcilable. Thus, in some cases (viewed in Dworkinian 'Herculean' terms) the doctrinal 'unassailability' of a judicial decision might be achievable only in circumstances involving some (perceived) sacrificing of moral principle.[23] That was the dilemma with which the Law Lords doubtless thought themselves to be confronted in making a choice between doctrinal coherence of Scots property law (entailed in upholding the earlier Court of Session decision) and avoidance of hardship to individuals of undoubtedly limited means.[24] As the Scottish Law Commission points out, when the case arrived in the House of Lords the imperative was seemingly 'to correct what it perceived as an obvious wrong'.[25] The decision of the Court of Session had been, in the words of Lord Clyde, 'unattractive and unfair'.[26] According to Lord Jauncey it had produced 'a most inequitable result'[27] and 'a most unjust result'.[28] The approach of the House of Lords was to develop lines of analysis mainly centring around statutory construction. A key question was what 'property' (comprised in the 'property and undertaking' of the grantor of a floating charge)[29] could be regarded as being 'attached' or secured by the charge on 'crystallisation'? In addressing this question, the court found it necessary to maintain a distinction between property in which the grantor company (Albyn) held a *beneficial interest* (an idea mainly derived from the law of trusts) and property to which the company – albeit possessed of a real right via a deed recorded in the Register of Sasines – had retained only a 'bare' title following delivery to the Thomsons or

[23] But see the discussion of John Stuart Mill's harm principle – this chapter, below. (The emerging position is one in which a utilitarian moral principle is upheld (not sacrificed); whilst that principle is not necessarily seen to be in conflict with the aim of maintaining the coherence and doctrinal integrity of a system of property law.)

[24] We may speculate about what might have played out in the absence of a successful appeal to the House of Lords and in the event of a failed claim centred on the delay, on the part of the Thomsons' solicitors, in recording the disposition (if that amounted to professional negligence). One result would have been for the Thomsons to remain (legally) liable to make monthly repayments to their lender for the monies borrowed to pay for the house (subject to deduction of monies (if any) recovered in ranking alongside other unsecured creditors). To the Thomsons the loan would have been a financial millstone enduring doubtless for decades. And they would ultimately have had nothing to show for it, having been ostensibly 'dispossessed' of the house at the outset.

[25] Scottish Law Commission, *Discussion Paper on* Sharp v Thomson (Discussion Paper No 114, The Stationery Office July 2001) 3.

[26] 1997 SC (HL) 66 at 82 G.

[27] ibid 70 D.

[28] ibid 70 E.

[29] See Companies Act 1985, section 462. See also Insolvency Act 1986, section 53(7).

their agent of an executed (and as yet unrecorded) disposition. As the Scottish Law Commission puts it:

> The starting point was the proposition that a person who has made delivery of a conveyance and accepted payment of the price can no longer be said to have any beneficial interest in the property. Until the conveyance is registered he remains owner in the technical sense of that word, but he holds only on a bare title and the beneficial interest is in the purchaser.[30]

Following this through, the House of Lords (reversing the decision of the Inner House) held that when (on the appointment of the joint receivers) the floating charge 'crystallised', Albyn, despite having a recorded title, had ceased to have a beneficial interest in the house (a consequence of having delivered the executed disposition to the Thomsons or their agent). The result of that was that the floating charge did *not* 'attach' to, or become a fixed security in relation to, the house. The decision largely turned on an approach which (Lord Clyde observed) was confined to '[looking] … to a definition of property for the purpose of the terms of the floating charge which relates to the substantial beneficial interests of the purchaser as opposed to the bare title retained by the seller'.[31] This approach, according to Lord Clyde, did not need to venture into the problematic terrain of an 'analysis into real or personal rights or formal title',[32] though this claim has of course been disputed.

Critics have suggested that the House of Lords decision subverted historical and orthodox Scots law perspectives on ownership of land – in particular, the rationale underpinning a system of public registration of interests in land where the beginning and end of ownership lie (or ought to lie) in what appears on the face of the public record, not what is contained in private (non-registrable) arrangements made 'behind the scenes', such as delivery of a disposition that necessarily, for however short or lengthy a period of time, would not have the benefit of public registration.[33] Such private arrangements, when they become allowable exceptions, would tend to erode the fundamental principle that the public registration of important land rights should be a definitive, if not the exclusive, 'badge' of ownership. (Obviously, the House of Lords decision in *Sharp v Thomson* sought to mitigate what was seen as a 'draconian' consequence of non-registration – or,

[30] See Scottish Law Commission, *Discussion Paper on* Sharp v Thomson (Discussion Paper No 114, The Stationery Office July 2001) 3.

[31] 1997 SC (HL) 66 at 80 D.

[32] ibid.

[33] 'Lord Jauncey proposes uncertainty in place of certainty, and secrecy in place of publicity. The standard view is that ownership is indivisible and passes only with the public act of registration. Lord Jauncey divides ownership into two, in the English fashion. *Legal* ownership passes only with registration but *beneficial* ownership passes at some indeterminate earlier stage not vouched for by public act.' See KGC Reid, 'Equity Triumphant: *Sharp v Thomson*' (1997) 1 *Edinburgh Law Review* 464, 466. In the late nineteenth century, the decision of the House of Lords in *Heritable Reversionary Company Limited v Millar* (1892) 19R (HL) 43 had perpetrated what some might regard as 'doctrinal apostasy' of a not dissimilar kind. The House of Lords decision in *Sharp* was therefore not entirely ungrounded in precedent of the highest authority.

at any rate, non-timely registration – of a disposition.) The more non-registrable transactions and dealings qualify or undermine what is explicitly on the public register the less certainty there is and the more dispensable registration becomes.[34]

George Gretton makes an essentially similar point. Reflecting on the aftermath of the House of Lords decision, he emphasises that Scots law has always highly valued a registration system in which the register reflects reality.[35] He partly frames his position in terms of the 'slippery slope' involved in doing away with 'unpleasant consequences' of non-registration – in other words, the consequences that go to make registration a legal practical necessity and which (incidentally) serve to 'incentivise' registration. The more those consequences are removed, the more pointless registration becomes.[36] But that is not Gretton's most fundamental argument. In the context of noting an unwelcome trend towards 'unregistered conveyancing', Gretton observes that 'property law' – embracing the requirement for public registration – exists in Scotland to produce commercial certainty and to protect the rights not only of the immediate parties (such as the seller and purchaser of a house, say) but also 'the rights and legitimate expectations of third parties, and the public information interest'.[37] So while the Inner House acknowledged that the consequences of its decision might be unfortunate, the resulting difficulties would need (in Lord Hope's opinion) to be addressed by corrective legislation, not, as Gretton puts it, 'by changing the fundamentals of property law'. The solution put forward, on appeal to the House of Lords, appeared to be precisely that, however, involving, in Gretton's view, 'the destruction of property law and the subversion of the distinction between personal and real rights'.[38] This was something that (Gretton believes) '[t]he Inner House in *Sharp* [had] understood' only too well when it made its decision.[39]

> *Sharp* posed a problem. The House of Lords came up with a solution. But the cure was worse than the disease.[40]

[34] The need for public registration to address the risks attending non-registration had been identified nearly 400 years before *Sharp v Thomson* by the Registration Act 1617: 'Oure Souerane Lord Considdering the gryit hurt sustened by his Maiesties Liegis by the fraudulent dealing of pairties who haveing annaliet thair Landis and ressauit gryit soumes of money thairfore Yit be thair vniust concealing of sum privat Right formarlie made by thame rendereth subsequent alienatioun done for gryit soumes of money altogidder vnproffitable whiche can not be avoyded vnles the saidis privat rightis be maid publict and patent to his hienes liegis … ordanis That thair salbe ane publick Register'. ('Our Sovereign Lord considering the great hurt sustained by his Majesty's lieges by the fraudulent dealing of parties who having alienated their lands and received great sums of money therefor yet by their unjust concealing of some private right formerly made by them render subsequent alienations done for great sums of money altogether unprofitable which cannot be avoided unless the said private rights be made public and patent to his Highness's lieges … ordains that there shall be one public register'.)

[35] GL Gretton, 'The Integrity of Property Law and of the Property Registers' (2001) 15 *Scots Law Times* 135, 136.

[36] ibid 136.

[37] ibid 137.

[38] ibid.

[39] ibid.

[40] ibid 135.

This conveniently frames the discussion in terms of what was seen by the House of Lords as (possibly) a moral imperative to rescue a single litigant (the Thomsons) from the seemingly inequitable and unjust effects of a law designed as a safeguard against fraud, which comes to be weighed against the (implied) moral imperative of a judgment of a lower court (that of the Inner House of the Court of Session) to ensure the preservation of precisely that law from 'destruction' or erosion *possibly for the greater good of the wider community*. There is, of course, a utilitarian aspect to this which would prioritise the interest of the wider community over that of the individual.[41] To that end John Stuart Mill provides a compelling philosophical context, enabling us to view the public registration of land rights as a means of protecting the public generally from economic harm. As we have seen,[42] the Registration Act 1617 was designed to address the 'great hurt sustained by his Majesty's lieges by the fraudulent dealing of parties'[43] who had wrongfully profited from 'unjust concealing of some private right formerly made by them'.[44] In the modern era the rationale underlying the protection of society by law is traceable to Mill's highly influential, if not uncontentious, tenet of political theory, the so-called *harm principle*. This is outlined in Mill's essay *On Liberty*. According to this, 'the only purpose for which power can be rightfully exercised over any member of a civilized community, against his will, is to prevent harm to others'.[45]

The scope of Mill's harm principle has been debated and contested for well over a century. One of its earliest critics was James Fitzjames Stephen,[46] while more recently HLA Hart has argued that there may be grounds justifying the legal coercion of the individual other than the prevention of harm to others.[47] In a monumental study, Joel Feinberg reawakened scholarly interest in Mill and the harm principle, by extending and redefining the principle so as to encompass (among other things) the causing of *offence* to others, harmless wrongdoing, and

[41] It is worth recalling that Dworkin envisages that Hercules's interpretation of the body of standards relevant to a given case may be tested 'by asking whether it could form part of a coherent theory justifying the network as a whole'. (See R Dworkin, *Law's Empire* (this chapter, n 1) 245.) When Lord Coulsfield in the Inner House argues [*Sharp v Thomson* 1995 SC 455, 504 F–H] 'that the requirements of a coherent system of property law [might] defeat what appears to be a fair claim in an individual case' he appears to justify the instant decision by an appeal to a 'coherent theory' that upholds doctrinal integrity (ie general property law and the requirement for public registration of titles to land), whose overriding moral basis could be said to be protection of the wider community from harm (eg fraudulent dealings with land). Against that Dworkinian position, the mid-twentieth century Law Lord, Lord Macmillan, points out (citing Lord Wright) that a judge must neither speculate *nor theorise*. (See Lord Macmillan (HP Macmillan),'The Writing of Judgments' (1948) 26(3) *The Canadian Bar Review* 491, 498.)

[42] See above, this chapter, n 34.

[43] '... gryit hurt sustened by his Maiesties Liegis by the fraudulent dealing of pairties.'

[44] '... vniust concealing of sum privat Right formarlie made by thame.'

[45] JS Mill, 'On Liberty' in J Gray (ed), *On Liberty and Other Essays* (Oxford University Press 1998) 13–14.

[46] See JF Stephen, *Liberty, Equality, Fraternity* (RJ White (ed), Cambridge University Press 1967).

[47] HLA Hart, *Law, Liberty and Morality* (Oxford University Press 1963) 5.

harm *to self*.[48] By contrast, Bernard Harcourt has argued that the harm principle is collapsing under the weight of its own success – becoming meaningless.[49]

Be that as it may, it is clear that the harm principle remains resonant in moral, legal and political philosophy even while debates over scope and content show no sign of abating. On one hand the principle is framed so as to set, in the broadest terms, the conditions upon which law-making powers may be rightfully exercised by government – thereby serving to define the scope of legitimate government encroachment upon individual liberty. On the other hand, however, and more critical to the present discussion, the principle can be viewed as a moral precept such that (recasting Mill's harm principle with a slightly different emphasis) if it is never right for a lawmaker to exercise power over a community unless to prevent harm to others – 'gryit hurt', in the words of the 1617 Act – then the moral integrity of law-making acts will be the more secure to the extent that the laws introduced do in fact safeguard the community from harm. On this view laws, including civil laws, can be seen as morally justifiable on the basis of an appeal to the need to protect the community from certain kinds of harm.[50] It follows that anything (including a judicial decision) that undermines the legal protection thus afforded – such as a judicial decision that imperils a broadly conceived statutory protection – might be considered harmful to the community.

If we take a step back from Mill it is clear from the foregoing analysis that a *modified* Dworkinian position is the only realistic one to adopt in the context of the present discussion – particularly towards outlining a workable *Iudexian* archetype. Clearly, there is no judge on earth who is truly 'Herculean' in Dworkin's sense – that is, '*super*human', with *infinite* time to devote to decision-making and the ability to pursue *every possible avenue* of approach. Needless to say, those aspects of Dworkin's archetype – even as a theoretical conjecture – contribute little to our understanding of 'real life' ultimate (or appellate-level) judicial decision-making. Following through their implications, such an expenditure of effort by a judge, even if humanly possible, would surely generate impossibly unwieldy, impossibly exhaustive, written judgments. Judges do not need to hand down

[48] See Joel Feinberg, *The Moral Limits of the Criminal Law. Vol 1, Harm to Others* (Oxford University Press 1984); *The Moral Limits of the Criminal Law. Vol 2, Offense to Others* (Oxford University Press 1985); *The Moral Limits of the Criminal Law. Vol 3, Harm to Self* (Oxford University Press 1986); *The Moral Limits of the Criminal Law. Vol 4, Harmless Wrongdoing* (Oxford University Press 1988).

[49] See BE Harcourt, 'The Collapse of the Harm Principle' (1999) 90 *Journal of Criminal Law and Criminology* 109, 113. It is beyond the scope of this chapter to engage more than in passing with the extensive scholarship on the harm principle. It is only necessary to outline a straightforward position on harm that accommodates the modest purposes of our enquiry.

[50] For the applicability of JS Mill's harm principle in the context of *civil* law (eg law of libel and contract law) see D van Mill, 'Freedom of Speech' in *The Stanford Encyclopedia of Philosophy* (Spring 2015 Edition), EN Zalta (ed) http://plato.stanford.edu/archives/spr2015/entries/freedom-speech/ (accessed 28 July 2025). It should also be recognised that Mill's *On Liberty* was published a full ten years before steps were first taken, by way of the Debtors Act 1869, to abolish imprisonment for debt. So, penal methods of enforcement of civil law were as much a part of the landscape of legal coercion and 'interference with liberty of action' (as Mill puts it) as were methods of enforcement of criminal law.

judgments designed for 'deific consumption'. Their decisions have a practical orientation, often targeting the ordinary and everyday circumstances of the 'real world', though inevitably resonating within the world of professional legal practice.

Yet there are two highly instructive insights that emerge from Dworkin's Herculean paradigm, touched upon at various points earlier in this chapter. First, there is the idea of doctrinal 'unassailability' implicit in the Dworkinian notion of a judge who determines coherence or 'fit' of elements of a case by undertaking the most expansive and systematic review of available case law, to say nothing of the *wider* law of the community – taking in statute law and other legal standards. Even if a 'real judge' cannot (unlike the mythical judge Hercules) consider every conceivable avenue of approach, the emergent judgment may still be 'exhaustive' without being humanly unattainable.[51] The labours of a 'judicial Hercules' may be impracticable for any 'real judge', but something falling short of that may still satisfy the need for competent decision-making. Secondly, there is the Dworkinian ideal of law as integrity, to which Hercules is an adherent, where one of the judicial imperatives is to regard as law what morality would suggest to be the best justification of past decisions.[52] It has been suggested earlier in this chapter that *Sharp v Thomson* (the Inner House decision) was a case where a non-ultimate judgment aspired to doctrinal 'unassailability' at the same time as advancing, if largely by implication rather than explicit design, a position that upheld the moral (Millian and utilitarian) rationale of laws designed to protect the community from economic harm. For its part, the House of Lords, doubtless with the best intentions, attempted something similar, with a moral outlook more narrowly focused on the potential for its decision-making (if it chose to follow the Inner House decision) to visit perceived injustice and inequity upon individual litigants. They did this seemingly without regard to the potential (in *not* following the Inner House decision) to undermine or erode laws safeguarding the wider community from harm. And therein lay the moral trade-off. Academic and scholarly opinion – to say nothing of the later Inner House and House of Lords decisions in *Burnett's Trustee v Grainger*[53] – have in effect inclined to the view that the decision of the House of Lords in *Sharp* largely failed to define a position that could be described as cohering with 'a full interpretation of all of … [the] community's law at once', to use Dworkin's words (descriptive of the approach adopted by the Herculean judge).[54]

[51] See above, this chapter, n 20.

[52] R Dworkin, *Law's Empire* (this chapter, n 1) 119–120.

[53] 2002 SC 580 (Inner House decision, Extra Division: Lord Coulsfield, Lord MacLean, Lord Hamilton); 2004 SC (HL) 19; [2004] UKHL 8 (House of Lords decision: Lord Bingham, Lord Hoffmann, Lord Hope, Lord Hobhouse, Lord Rodger). For academic and scholarly opinion, see the extensive literature cited in Scottish Law Commission, *Discussion Paper on* Sharp v Thomson (Discussion Paper No 114, The Stationery Office July 2001) 2 nn 10 and 11; 4 nn 21 and 23.

[54] Ronald Dworkin, *Law's Empire* (this chapter, n 1) 245. In his opinion in *Burnett's Trustee v Grainger* in the Inner House decision (referring to *Sharp* in the House of Lords), Lord Coulsfield remarks that he is 'persuaded that Scots law does not recognise any right of property intermediate between a real and a personal right. I am also persuaded by counsel for the appellant *that to hold otherwise would create incoherence and uncertainty in the Scots law of property* … If I might say so, the coherency of that system was

Gretton's opinion that the House of Lords decision had ensured the 'destruction of property law'[55] now seems startling; but he and others were prescient in anticipating the raft of corrective legislation (including statutory innovations) that would be introduced post-*Sharp* to address the difficulties precipitated by that case, among other things.[56]

A 'postscript' to the discussion of *Sharp v Thomson* is suggested by the later House of Lords case, mentioned above, that in some sense marked the 'denouement' of the judicial progress of the earlier, more 'eventful', *Sharp* case. By the time of *Burnett's Trustee v Grainger*[57] the academic and (legal) professional 'fallout' from *Sharp* had settled down and law reform, on the back of specific Scottish Law Commission proposals, was by then under consideration.[58] Indeed, against the background of a 'tsunami' of legislative reform of Scottish land law from the first into the second decades of the new century, the controversy around the *Sharp* case subsided. Essentially, *Burnett's Trustee* ensured that for the time being, pending later statutory developments, the impact of *Sharp* would be restricted in that the decision would be confined to its own facts and also limited to floating charges (and to receivership – a statutory mechanism that was, in any event, largely swept away by statute, to be replaced by corporate administration). However, from the point of view of the present discussion centred on (Dworkinian) 'Herculean' decision-making, what is perhaps remarkable about *Burnett's Trustee* is that the leading judge in the Inner House decision in *Sharp* – then the Lord President of the Court of Session (Lord Hope) – was later elevated to the House of Lords where he had the opportunity to (colloquially speaking) 're-try' – or, more accurately, revisit – the House of Lords decision in *Sharp*, a situation doubtless of the rarest

fully discussed and amply set out in the opinions of the judges of the First Division in *Sharp*. Indeed, the Lord President's opinion in that case might be regarded as an *exegesis of the system*. As counsel for the appellant pointed out, the court in seeking to do justice between individuals may create uncertainty in the realm of property law, and that should be avoided.' (Emphasis added.) (2002 SC 580, 592 E–G).

[55] GL Gretton, 'The Integrity of Property Law and of the Property Registers' (2001) 15 *Scots Law Times* 135, 137. Commenting extra-judicially at a much later time (2018) in his published House of Lords diary, Lord Hope makes clear his personal opinion as to the destabilising impact of the decision of the House of Lords in *Sharp*: 'Instability to this system [ie the orthodox position on transfer of ownership of land under Scots law] was introduced by the decision of the House of Lords in *Sharp v Thomson* in which Lords Jauncey and Clyde, for reasons not wholly consistent with each other, delivered speeches overruling the decision of the Inner House in that case in which I was sitting as Lord President'. See Lord Hope of Craighead, *Lord Hope's Diaries: House of Lords 1996–2009* (Avizandum Publishing Ltd 2018) 201–202.

[56] For instance, Part 4 of the Land Registration etc (Scotland) Act 2012 has introduced a system of advance notices which provides protection to a purchaser of land (and buildings) against the possibility of adverse interests being publicly registered during the vulnerable period up to the date of registration of the purchaser's title following settlement of the transaction – after the price has been paid in exchange for an executed but (for the time being) unregistered disposition. The primary aim of the advance notice is to protect the purchaser's disposition. Also, section 50(2) of the same Act provides that '[r]egistration of a valid disposition transfers ownership'. This is explicitly reinforced by section 50(3) which provides that '[a]n unregistered disposition does not transfer ownership'.

[57] See above, this chapter, n 53.

[58] Scottish Law Commission, *Discussion Paper on* Sharp v Thomson (Discussion Paper No 114, The Stationery Office July 2001).

occurrence. As it happens, the House of Lords in *Burnett's Trustee* left it to a fellow (modified) 'Herculean', Lord Rodger of Earlsferry, to deliver the leading speech.[59]

In the final analysis, this was a situation where a non-ultimate judge, exhibiting modified 'Herculean' tendencies (see discussion earlier in this chapter), returned as an ultimate judge (a '*Iudex*') to reconsider a previously overruled decision of his court whose core rationale had largely been vindicated in judicial, academic, scholarly and professional circles; and was ultimately vindicated (in the wider property law context) by way of legislative endorsement. Superficially, the doctrinal *but not institutional* 'unassailability' of the earlier decision (*Sharp* in the Inner House) gave way to the institutional *and doctrinal* 'unassailability' of the later decision (*Burnett's Trustee* in the House of Lords) which effectively reinforced the decision-making in *Sharp* (in the Inner House), reaching back to before the 'interstitial' House of Lords decision in *Sharp*. The later ultimate decision (*Burnett's Trustee*), also significantly restricted the judicial and doctrinal impact of the earlier ultimate (House of Lords) decision in *Sharp*.

8.3. *Iudex* and Modified 'Herculean' Decision-Making

When *Burnett's Trustee* was litigated in the Sheriff Court – that being the lowest civil court in Scotland – perhaps not unexpectedly the sheriff principal considered the House of Lords decision in *Sharp* to be not only binding (therefore, in the sense of the present discussion, *institutionally* 'unassailable'), but to extend to an *analogous* position which, strictly speaking, *Sharp* had not addressed: namely, the position of the trustee in sequestration.[60] Plainly, this was the 'danger' that Gretton had in mind when warning of the 'destruction' of Scots property law;[61] and indeed

[59] Lord Rodger's speech covers similar ground to Lord Hope's earlier Inner House opinion (effectively endorsing it) but with perhaps more emphasis on the legal status of an executed disposition which has been delivered by a disponer to a disponee. (This proved to be a central question in both *Sharp* and *Burnett's Trustee*.) The distinction between real rights and personal rights, the concept of the 'personal fee' and the position of the disponee before infeftment (*Earl of Fife v Duff* (1862) 24 D 936) are only a few of the issues excavated in this wide-ranging opinion, which likewise counts as a masterly exposition of the historical development of the law, to say nothing of doctrinal orthodoxy, attending ownership of land under Scots law.

[60] *Sharp*, as we have seen, had been concerned with the position of the receiver of an insolvent company that had granted a floating charge which had subsequently 'crystallised' and become a fixed security in relation to the property comprised in the 'property and undertaking' of the company. See *Burnett's Trustee v Grainger* 2002 SC 580, at 594 A (Lord Hamilton commenting on the sheriff principal's earlier consideration of the effect of the House of Lords decision in *Sharp*). That the Inner House also considered itself bound by the House of Lords decision in *Sharp* is clear from further dicta of Lord Hamilton: 'This court is bound, as was the sheriff principal, by the decision of the House of Lords in *Sharp*. It is also bound by the ratio, as properly construed, of that decision. In so far as the views expressed in their Lordships' speeches go beyond that ratio these views are not, as a matter of judicial precedent, binding on this court but they are entitled to be afforded the greatest respect.' (*Burnett's Trustee v Grainger* 2002 SC 580, 594 B)

[61] GL Gretton, 'The Integrity of Property Law and of the Property Registers' (2001) 15 *Scots Law Times* 135, 137.

was the 'danger' which Lord Coulsfield in *Burnett's Trustee* appeared to highlight (in the context of the appeal from the Sheriff Court to the Inner House) when commenting that Lord Jauncey's approach in *Sharp* (the House of Lords decision) was potentially 'one which was easily capable of generalisation … [such that] his speech could bear an interpretation' that could have application to a wider variety of cases.[62] In fact, in the Sheriff Court (via the decision of the sheriff principal), the position of the trustee in sequestration was in effect regarded as equivalent to that of the receiver of an insolvent company that had granted a floating charge (as happened in *Sharp*).

The key issue to which our case study on *Sharp v Thomson* calls attention is that ultimate judicial decision-making is not 'Herculean' in the full Dworkinian sense and may indeed fall short of being 'Herculean' in the *modified* sense, as illustrated by the cases of *Sharp* and *Burnett's Trustee* where an 'interstitial' decision of the House of Lords was effectively sidelined in the service of a perceived need to preserve the integrity and coherence of orthodox principles of Scots property law. We have seen that judicial decision-making of the latter kind (ie modified 'Herculean' and therefore humanly attainable) is by no means the exclusive preserve of ultimate judges. (Dworkin, of course, does not seek to tie the Herculean archetype to *ultimate* judicial decision-making.) The difficulty, then, in terms of the theoretical position outlined in earlier chapters, is that when, on the doubtless rare occasions where there is a perceived mismatch between the institutional and doctrinal 'unassailability' of judicial decision-making, the decisions of *Iudex* may not represent an *enduringly* legally conclusive position on declared legal rights in a given case. Likewise, a (modified) 'Herculean' decision of an inferior court that is thought to be doctrinally 'unassailable' may be short-lived if it encounters later adverse judicial treatment in a superior court. Worse still, an ultimate court may saddle a legal system with a decision acknowledged to be doctrinally 'destructive' of legal orthodoxy. Such a decision may cry out for legislative, or later supreme judicial, corrective intervention.

In adopting a *Iudexian* perspective on legal rights – applying the hypothesis of the ultimate judgment (assignable to *Iudex*)[63] – we might choose to imagine what a modified 'Herculean' *Iudex* would make of the situation before the court at any given time: for instance, it might be a potential claim under a contract or in tort. In that situation, how are legal rights to be defined or enunciated? The idea of doctrinal and institutional 'unassailability', envisaging among other things some degree of persistence through time of decision-making (ie whether a judgment is likely to stand the test of time), may form part of this thought experiment. But of course there is a risk that the institutional (judicial) imagination encompassed within our experiment would mark a decisive shift from the realm of *descriptive theory* to that of *ideal theory*, the latter being especially characteristic of Dworkin's theoretical

[62] *Burnett's Trustee v Grainger* 2002 SC 580, 585 G–H (Lord Coulsfield).
[63] See section 1.1 (Chapter 1, above) and section 4.5 (Chapter 4, above).

world view.[64] In continuing to adhere to a broadly Hartian (descriptive) theoretical outlook in this book, however, we merely acknowledge that the two realms exist as possible approaches to understanding the legal (judicial) world while recognising that the boundary between the two is difficult to define with precision. The use of an empirical case study (centred on *Sharp v Thomson*) to facilitate building an outline of a *Iudexian* archetype has served to underpin the *descriptive* approach to the theoretical task in hand. Towards extending beyond that case study in the remainder of this chapter, continuing our exploration of judicial experience principally in the UK setting, two further areas of discussion are suggested for brief coverage. These areas necessarily overlap.

First, we touch briefly upon perceptions of the 'imperatives' of judicial ultimacy, addressing the question whether ultimate judicial decision-making is in any sense distinctive and set apart from non-ultimate decision-making.

Secondly, the idea that ultimate judicial decision-making might be, essentially, a *social activity* consisting of 'dialogues' between each judge and a range of interested parties,[65] is contrasted with the idea – perhaps more suited to the notion of an acmatic (modified) 'Herculean' version of a *Iudexian* judge – that such decision-making may also be viewed as in some sense a creative (even solitary) process. Lord Hope (and other *Iudexian* judges in the past, such as Lord Macmillan) have rightly drawn attention to this aspect of decision-making:

> [W]riting judgments … [is] a kind of craft that comes with experience. … Writing a very big judgment is like designing a painting on a blank canvas. The beginning of it is very important, how it is phrased and broken up and so on. It is a very special skill which I have very much enjoyed.[66]

8.3.1. Imperatives of Ultimacy

Is ultimate judicial decision-making qualitatively different from decision-making in inferior – in particular, inferior *appellate* – courts? It may be, for instance, that (viewed hypothetically) ultimate judges aim, among other things, to achieve legal and doctrinal 'unassailability' on the assumption that, if *institutional* 'unassailability' *is a given*, the emphasis may turn to intrinsically 'right' decision-making – ie what is intrinsically doctrinally right. (We have already seen that, even if that is the aim, ultimate judges (arguably) may fail in this task.)

Judges in the highest appellate courts of a judicial system almost certainly consider themselves to have a special responsibility to get their decision-making 'right' if no further judicial intervention is systemically possible beyond the decisions

[64] See section 7.3 (Chapter 7, above) at n 95, citing N Lacey, 'Analytical Jurisprudence versus Descriptive Sociology Revisited' (2006) 84 *Texas Law Review* 944, 955.

[65] See A Paterson, *Final Judgment – The Last Law Lords and the Supreme Court* (Hart Publishing 2013) (hereafter, in this chapter, '*Final Judgment*').

[66] (Lord Hope of Craighead.) See J Forsyth, 'Lord Hope reflects on his life in law' *The Scotsman* (10 June 2013) www.scotsman.com/news/lord-hope-reflects-on-his-life-in-law-1571963 (accessed 28 July 2025).

that they make. This is demonstrated compellingly in capital cases coming before the higher judiciary in the UK in the modern era – such as those originating in Commonwealth countries and appealed to the Judicial Committee of the Privy Council.[67] We have seen from *Sharp v Thomson* how decision-making that is widely considered to have erred in some sense can play out in terms of adverse academic and scholarly attention and 'pendular' judicial interventions (extending to the use of interpretive techniques designed to limit the impact of earlier decisions). Corrective law reform may follow. In the UK this can mean Law Commission proposals that precipitate legislative change. In some cases, and in certain jurisdictions, an earlier ultimate decision may be reviewed by the same supreme-level court, sitting at a later date.[68] Thus, judges and lawmakers alike may review or limit the impact of earlier decisions that appear to have erred; and in that way they could be said to be involving themselves in 'damage limitation' measures, or straightforward reform of the law, though some may argue that law reform (beyond incremental judicial development of the law) is always the preserve of the legislature.

A decision may be thought to be the 'right' one because, apart from other considerations, it meets the two main tests of the modified 'Herculean' approach outlined earlier in this chapter: (i) it is doctrinally 'unassailable' in that the decision – following rigorous, systematic and expansive analysis – coheres or 'fits' with the seamless web of available case law, statute and other applicable standards (being reinforced, in the case of an ultimate judicial decision, by *institutional* 'unassailability'),[69] and (ii) it achieves what morality would suggest to be the best justification of past decisions.[70]

[67] See *Watson v The Queen (Attorney General for Jamaica intervening)* [2005] 1 AC 472. For a capital case originating in Trinidad and Tobago see *Ian Seepersad and Roodal Panchoo v The Attorney General of Trinidad and Tobago* [2012] UKPC 4.

[68] See (for the House of Lords) the Practice Statement (Judicial Precedent) [1966] 3 All ER 77 (26 July 1966). This statement, made by Lord Gardiner (on behalf of the Appellate Committee of the House of Lords), signalled that the House would treat former decisions of the House as normally binding but that it would depart from a previous decision when it appeared right to do so. The Supreme Court has endorsed the Practice Statement: see *Austin v Mayor and Burgesses of the London Borough of Southwark* [2010] UKSC 28 at paras 24 and 25 (Lord Hope) commenting that the Practice Statement is 'part of the established jurisprudence relating to the conduct of appeals' and 'has as much effect in … [the Supreme] Court as it did before the Appellate Committee in the House of Lords'.

[69] This is the simple fact that the decision is unappealable, but it may be more than that in the opinion of some. Lord Macmillan, writing in 1948, quotes the view of Lord Sands (in *Assessor for Aberdeen v Collie* [1932] SC 304, at 311–312) where Lord Sands speaks of ultimate judicial decisions (of the House of Lords) as being 'infallible': '[T]he House of Lords is an infallible interpreter of the law … Accordingly, if the House of Lords says "this is the proper interpretation of the statute," then it is the proper interpretation. The House of Lords has a perfect legal mind. Learned Lords may come or go, but the House of Lords never makes a mistake'. This probably reflects the unarguable fact that a decision of an ultimate court – whether or not it is substantively right or wrong or, for that matter, doctrinally 'unassailable' – is final and unappealable: therefore institutionally 'unassailable' in the sense of the present discussion. In a slightly different context (referring to the rule of recognition), HLA Hart observes in effect that the standard metre bar (as it then (1961) existed in Paris) could never be more, nor less, than a metre because it was infallibly constituted as the definition of a metre. See HLA Hart, *The Concept of Law* (2nd edn, Clarendon Press 1994) 109. (See also Lord Macmillan, 'The Writing of Judgments' (1948) 26(3) *The Canadian Bar Review* 491, 494–495.)

[70] R Dworkin, *Law's Empire* (this chapter, n 1) 119–120.

Many judges would dispute that a judicial decision needs to satisfy the second test, though the test may be tacitly satisfied in the mind of a judge whilst remaining inexplicit in the emerging judgment. In a case before the UK Supreme Court – *Elgizouli v Secretary of State for the Home Department*[71] – a question arose as to the lawfulness of responses to requests for co-operation from a foreign state aimed at facilitating criminal proceedings that might have resulted in the imposition of the death penalty on the person who was the subject of the requests. The Supreme Court considered whether it was unlawful for the Secretary of State to provide legal assistance in the form of evidence to the USA, or for law enforcement authorities in the UK to provide personal data or information to their counterparts in the USA. Lady Hale, as one of seven judges, declared: '[I]t is not enough to think the death penalty immoral and unacceptable … What is immoral and unacceptable *is not necessarily unlawful.* As judges, our role is to uphold the law.'[72] Clearly, in the mind of 'a *Iudex*' (Lady Hale), a distinction was of necessity to be drawn between what is lawful or unlawful and what is moral or immoral. The moral dimension of the human condition, however, is ineliminable just as the infiltration of a judge's moral perspective into decision-making is unavoidable. Paul Wagner argues that the idea of the 'moral person', whose elements may be looked upon as universal human character traits, is 'embedded in the daily life of ordinary people' and 'deeply a part of every person's social life'. Wagner points out that ordinary language analysis may be an invaluable tool in understanding the idea of the 'moral person'.[73] Following the approach that HLA Hart would likewise adopt, we might see characteristic uses of language in a particular judgment – for instance, expressions such as 'fair', 'unfair', 'just', 'unjust', 'right', 'wrong', 'moral', 'immoral' – as signalling the possibility that the moral outlook of a judge as a 'moral person' may guide or precipitate a particular judicial decision, even if the appearance is that legal doctrinal argument has outweighed other considerations.

Whereas at non-ultimate stages of the appellate process there is the possibility of putting right perceived errors in the legal doctrinal grounds of a judicial decision – which may or may not sit coherently with a 'moral reading' of that decision – it is not especially straightforward to correct errors that occur at the ultimate level. The mindset of the ultimate judge must be that supreme-level decision-making presents a final opportunity to make the 'right' decision and ensure that perceived errors from earlier stages in the judicial process are corrected. So, while the driver for an ultimate judge to meet the *first* of the two main tests of the modified 'Herculean' approach outlined above (broadly, doctrinal 'unassailability') probably seems obvious, it is less obvious that an ultimate judge would

[71] [2020] UKSC 10.

[72] ibid at 2 (emphasis added). Lord Dyson MR is cited here. In *R (Sandiford) v Secretary of State for Foreign and Commonwealth Affairs* [2013] EWCA Civ 581; [2013] 1 WLR 2938: 'the death penalty is (in my view) rightly regarded by the Government as immoral and unacceptable' (para 61).

[73] PA Wagner, 'The Idea of a Moral Person' (1983) 18(2) *Journal of Thought* 85, 85.

seek to meet the *second* test – where the instant judicial decision is to cohere with the best moral justification of past decisions. Judicial decision-making at the ultimate level inevitably encounters greater critical scrutiny in the public domain than decisions of inferior appellate courts. So we might ask whether ultimate judges 'look over their shoulder' to ensure that their decisions do not sit awkwardly with, or do not offend, some perception of public morality or of the prevailing moral climate.[74] Certainly, ultimate judges tend to encourage trends that appear to be welcome (eg acting in the public interest; promoting the idea of good faith and so on); while discouraging seemingly unwelcome trends (eg avoiding 'opening the floodgates' to litigation; (avoiding) creating categories of liability that are too wide; (avoiding) legal 'slippery slopes', and so on). In all these respects there is a tendency to judicial conservatism. Supreme-level decision-making may be aligned with some conception of public morality, or public opinion, or the public interest, at the same time as appearing to be doctrinally coherent and sound. Inevitably, though, this carries a risk highlighted by HLA Hart when he observes:

> It seems fatally easy to believe that loyalty to democratic principles entails acceptance of what may be termed moral populism: the view that the majority have a moral right to dictate how all should live. This is a misunderstanding of democracy which still menaces individual liberty, and I shall devote the remainder of this lecture to identifying the confusion on which it rests.
>
> The central mistake is a failure to distinguish the acceptable principle that political power is best entrusted to the majority from the unacceptable claim that what the majority do with that power is beyond criticism and must never be resisted.[75]

Nothing perhaps better serves to constrain Dworkin's suggestion that decisions of a 'Herculean' judge should achieve what morality suggests is the best justification of past judicial decisions than Hart's warning about trends that menace individual liberty. The generality of Western state law serves to ensure that arbitrariness and subjectivity implied by the personal beliefs or preferences of individual judges is kept in check.[76]

[74] Alan Paterson argues that the Supreme Court is more accountable than the House of Lords was 'through the Supreme Court's greater transparency and their consequent willingness to engage with the public'. But at the same time he points out that 'when asked which audiences they wrote their judgments for, the Justices are little more inclined than their predecessors in the House of Lords to consider that the public is an audience for whom they write'. (See A Paterson, *Final Judgment* (this chapter, n 65) 318, 320.)

[75] HLA Hart, *Law, Liberty and Morality* (Oxford University Press 1963) 79.

[76] Roberto Unger argues that a 'legal order differs from politics and administration precisely because of its attachment to the aims of generality in legislation and of uniformity in adjudication'. He observes that laws are 'expected to address broadly defined categories of individuals and acts and to be applied without personal or class favoritism'. This leads to his overriding point, centring on the notion of the rule of law, that the generality of law 'establishes the formal equality of the citizens and thereby shields them from the arbitrary tutelage of government. Administration must be separated from legislation to ensure generality; adjudication must be distinguished from administration to safeguard uniformity. These two contrasts represent the core of the rule of law ideal'. See RM Unger, *Law in Modern Society: Toward a Criticism of Social Theory* (The Free Press 1976) 53–54.

Moving beyond the moral coherence of judicial decision-making as a possible imperative of ultimacy, Lord Reed, in his Bentham Association Lecture of 2019,[77] identifies practical imperatives, some of which may be better described as *constraints*, that apply in the context of the UK Supreme Court. These assist our understanding of how ultimate judicial decision-making in the UK setting may be qualitatively different from non-ultimate decision-making.

In the first instance Lord Reed points to the restricted context of ultimate judicial decision-making in which appeals – historically to the House of Lords and more recently to the Supreme Court – are permitted in only a fraction of cases 'where the appeal raises an arguable question of law of general public importance which the court ought to consider at that time'.[78] It is clear that non-ultimate appellate courts (such as the Court of Appeal) in a majority of cases must function de facto as 'final' courts of appeal; though when judges in those courts decide a case they may not have the mindset of ultimate judges. They are not to know at that stage whether the case before them will proceed to a higher appellate court.[79] Their decision will often dispose of the case. In the highest court, *Iudex*, deciding questions of law of public importance, will be acutely conscious of how decision-making at that level may be received in the public domain. So, even if ultimate judges are not 'looking over their shoulder' to ensure their decisions are not out of alignment with some perception of the prevailing *moral* climate, they clearly must work within some conception of public importance to be deciding a case at that level at all.

Lord Reed highlights another imperative of ultimacy which points to ways in which a *Iudexian* mindset might differ from that of lower appellate court judges. In an echo of a modified 'Herculean' approach, he observes that supreme-level judicial decision-making 'requires a sense of the coherence of the law as a whole, an awareness of how it has developed over time, and an understanding of how it needs to develop now so as to respond to the evolving needs of our society'.[80] Venturing upon the terrain of 'unmodified' Dworkinian 'Herculean' judges – albeit without infinite time or superhuman powers at their disposal – Lord Reed identifies other key points of differentiation between the functions of ultimate and non-ultimate courts:

> [T]he first function of the Supreme Court is to enable important questions of law to be considered with a degree of depth, time, combined intelligence, and breadth of

[77] Lord Reed (RJ Reed, Lord Reed of Allermuir), 'The Supreme Court Ten Years On' (The Bentham Association Lecture 2019, University College London, 6 March 2019) https://supremecourt.uk/speeches/lord-reed-at-the-bentham-association-lecture-2019-university-college-london (accessed 28 July 2025).

[78] ibid 4.

[79] We can only speculate whether the judges of the Inner House of the Court of Session in *Sharp v Thomson* (1995 SC 455, discussed above) – where, according to the Scottish Law Commission, the underlying issues were examined 'with an almost exhaustive citation of authority' (see above, this chapter, n 20) – approached the case effectively with the mindset of ultimate judges in the expectation that, despite being a case of some public importance (and a likely 'candidate' for appeal), it might not in fact be appealed to the House of Lords.

[80] Lord Reed, 'The Supreme Court Ten Years On' (see above, this chapter, n 77) 4.

> legal experience, *which the intermediate courts of appeal cannot normally be expected to devote to them*.[81]

So, an aspect of what appears to separate ultimate from non-ultimate judicial decision-making is *resourcing*. Faced with a relatively narrow disputed point of law to decide upon, the *Iudexian* judge has the time, space, skill and experience to undertake the task in hand.

Against the background of an outline of imperatives of ultimacy – mainly based on the experience of the UK judicial system – we might ask whether the constraints implied by those imperatives give way to the possibility of judicial *creativity* and *individuality*: for instance, at the point where an ultimate judge frames a judgment shaped by what Alan Paterson (referring to the UK Supreme Court) has described as the 'social activity' of judgment construction: involving 'dialogues' with interested parties. This is explored briefly in the next section.

8.3.2. Ultimate Judicial Decision-Making as a Creative Process

Human creativity in its highest expressions can sometimes appear 'Herculean', and this makes Dworkin's allusion to 'superhuman' in some contexts not entirely inappropriate. There is space for the transcendent, albeit still recognisably human, manifested in the work of 'properly human' titans: such as of literature (Shakespeare, Homer, Austen); music (Bach, Beethoven, Mozart, Byrd); fine art and sculpture (Michelangelo, Raphael, Picasso); natural sciences (Newton, Curie, Einstein); architecture (Brunelleschi, Wren).[82] (Our choice of 'titans', of course, may be selective and subjective.) Lewis Lockwood comments on how Beethoven's boundless creativity represented an all-consuming force in his life:

> For Beethoven, creative necessity dominated everything else. It utterly determined his outer life, constantly interfered with it, and rendered it perpetually erratic, as it does for most artists on his level …
>
> Yet … the theory of an absolute separation [of 'life' and 'art'] is self-defeating and will not hold. Works do not materialize out of nothing. They are created, and always by

[81] ibid 4–5 (emphasis added).

[82] Take JS Bach's monumental Ciaccona (or Chaconne) from his Partita No 2 in D minor for solo violin (BWV 1004). This masterpiece seemingly arrives 'from nowhere' as the finale of an otherwise relatively 'ordinary' – at any rate as 'ordinary' as Bach can ever be – set of pieces that go to make up the Partita. However the Ciaccona, forming the tiniest part of Bach's oeuvre, has been described by violinist Joshua Bell as 'not just one of the greatest pieces of music ever written, but one of the greatest achievements of any man in history'. See G Weingarten, 'Pearls Before Breakfast: Can one of the nation's great musicians cut through the fog of a DC rush hour? Let's find out.' *The Washington Post* (8 April 2007) www.washingtonpost.com/lifestyle/magazine/pearls-before-breakfast-can-one-of-the-nations-great-musicians-cut-through-the-fog-of-a-dc-rush-hour-lets-find-out/2014/09/23/8a6d46da-4331-11e4-b47c-f5889e061e5f_story.html# (accessed 28 July 2025). (See also www.youtube.com/watch?v=DBJPVnJ8m-Y (accessed 28 July 2025) (Gidon Kremer).)

> individuals carrying out specific imaginative purposes … Accordingly, we can acknowledge that deeply rooted elements in the creative individual's personality, angle of vision, speech habits, interactions with people, and ways of dealing with the world find resonance in many of the artist's works. Such elements combine to create what one writer calls the artist's 'creative character', the inner being that leaves an indelible personal imprint on works that in some way seems unmistakable, even if we cannot define it in detail. This idea comes close to what Flaubert meant when he wrote, 'The author in his works should be like God in the universe: always present, but nowhere visible'.[83]

Wherein, then, lies *Iudex's* 'creative character' – the 'inner being' that leaves an 'indelible personal imprint' on works, to use Lockwood's words? Part of this, as we have seen, lies in the idea of the judge as a 'moral person'. Ineliminable aspects of judges' humanity may come to inhabit their decision-making. The German Idealist philosopher, Wilhelm Dilthey – whose work influenced Weber in the development of his *Verstehende* methodology – calls attention to the notion of the acquired structure of a person's mental life which encompasses states of the mind including values, prejudices, moral outlook, reasoning, political orientation, preferences and religious or other beliefs. The intellect governs the ways in which these states are organised, processed and ordered. 'Only in the world of the mind which creatively, responsibly and autonomously, stirs within us, has life its value, its goal and its meaning.'[84] Dilthey promoted the idea that manifestations of mental content – or 'expressions' – were the key to entering the mindset of the observed subject.[85]

For a judge, judgments, speeches, opinions, are 'expressions' outwardly revealing the intellectual process involved in adjudication. But adjudication has an inner dimension. As Lord Hope has suggested, judicial decision-making, manifested in the writing of judgments, must be a creative process that starts with a 'blank canvas'. Superficially, the judicial task may appear to be constrained in some of the ways identified by Hart (engaging in rule-following and rule-applying behaviour predetermined by a master rule of recognition and judicial practice); or by Dworkin (eg seeking 'integrity' in judicial decision-making; aiming for the best 'fit' with past decisions or precedents). But, within those constraints – and the imperatives mentioned in section 8.3.1 (see this chapter, above) – there is undoubtedly a measure of freedom where judges might assert their 'creative character'. How does a judge's individuality and character shine through those 'expressions'? Lord Macmillan has referred to the deliverances of the judges of England in the leading cases of the law as being distinguished by the 'highest qualities of literary craftsmanship'.[86] He asks us to witness the historic judgments in which Lord Mansfield enunciated the principles of the common law in their application to

[83] L Lockwood, *Beethoven – The Music and the Life* (WW Norton & Company 2003) 18–19. Lockwood cites G Flaubert, *Correspondance* (1852), 2:155.

[84] See HP Rickman (tr and ed), *W Dilthey Selected Writings* (Cambridge University Press 1976) 170–171, 172.

[85] ibid 218, 221–222.

[86] Lord Macmillan, 'The Writing of Judgments' (1948) 26(3) *The Canadian Bar Review* 491, 493.

commerce; he speaks of the 'commanding brevity of Jessel, Master of the Rolls'; and he refers to the 'elegant irony' of Lord Bowen 'and those delightful passages in which Lord Macnaghten contrived to illumine with humanity and humour the most accurate exposition of the technical doctrines of the law'.[87]

Since a judgment of a court of law is primarily an argumentative medium, literary elegance and craftsmanship should not stand in the way of clarity of expression, forensic accuracy or explanatory power. Nor for that matter would brevity, irony, humanity or humour. In fact those attributes surely facilitate the judicial purpose to engage with and convey the factual and legal issues arising for determination and the applicable standards relevant to the issue. This may involve some 'judicial engineering' to make the instant decision 'fit' with past precedents and cohere (often inexplicitly) with the judge's moral and political outlook.[88] All of this is in the service of the delivery, ultimately, of a convincing judgment that stands the test of time. But does this not count for *every* judicial decision, especially higher appellate ones? Is there anything to differentiate judicial creativity, where *ultimate* decision-making is concerned, from judicial creativity in inferior courts? The question, put another way, is whether judicial creativity is manifested in an ultimate decision (of *Iudex)* in a way that would not be manifested in a lower court decision.

Arguably a higher plane of creativity is reached when the focus of *Iudex's* attention is on relatively narrow disputed points of law. Judicial reasoning at the ultimate stage in the process is normally unencumbered by (previously) chaotic and disputed facts. By the point at which the issues and salient facts are presented to *Iudex*, many questions around the ascertainment of facts – though not all questions of interpretation of the facts – will have been ironed out. In a similar way, important matters of legal principle and doctrine will often have been carefully analysed in lower courts. So, when a case arrives at the level of a supreme court the exposition of *law* has already attained a more advanced level of refinement and specificity that can only assist such a court. *Iudex* may choose to 'ride on the back' of positions previously articulated in lower, especially appellate, courts. But even when *rejecting* those positions the (rejected) positions may have taken *Iudex* 'halfway up the mountain', so to speak, either clarifying precisely what it is that *Iudex* now rejects, or casting a new light on a hitherto undiscovered angle which the earlier decision-making had only just begun to reveal.

[87] ibid.

[88] In *The Catholic Child Welfare Society and others v Various Claimants (FC) and The Institute of the Brothers of the Christian Schools and others* [2012] UKSC 56, Lord Phillips, deciding a question of vicarious liability, appears to express genuine (moral) concern at the plight and vulnerability of boys who had experienced abuse at the hands of the Brothers of the Christian Schools in a residential institution: 'Living cloistered on the school premises were vulnerable boys. They were triply vulnerable. They were vulnerable because they were children in a school; they were vulnerable because they were virtually prisoners in the school; and they were vulnerable because their personal histories made it even less likely that if they attempted to disclose what was happening to them they would be believed'. (para [92])

This, of course, does not reckon with the very few appellate-level judges whose contributions to the development of the law, and their creativity and adventurism, appear unconstrained even in historical hindsight. For instance, Lord Denning, in the Court of Appeal, pursued a creative agenda that is probably unrivalled in English legal history. Though he sat in the House of Lords from 1957 to 1962, he was not strictly 'a *Iudex*' when occupying the office of Master of the Rolls from 1962 to 1982, and faced the ever-present risk of his judgments being overturned by the House of Lords – which came to pass not infrequently.[89] Even disregarding his non-*Iudexian* status (as Master of the Rolls), it is questionable whether a judge with his adventurist attributes, in a judicial system otherwise adhering faithfully to the principle of *stare decisis*, represents anything other than a judicial outlier whose general approach lies somewhat beyond typification.

Attending to judicial approaches that *do* lend themselves to typification, it is perhaps useful to attempt the briefest synoptic account of strategies underlying ultimate judicial decision-making referencing, once again, the position in the UK Supreme Court. According to one view, judicial decision-making takes the form of a 'social activity' centring on judicial engagement with a range of interested parties: this being the central thesis of Alan Paterson's study, *Final Judgment: The Last Law Lords and the Supreme Court*.[90] Paterson argues that the 'key optic through which to understand judicial decision-making in the final court of appeal in the UK is the study of the *dialogues* which take place between the Justices and others. On this view judicial decision-making is a social activity'.[91] Paterson explores the nature of these dialogues, uncovering the multi-dimensionality of the *Iudexian* task.[92] He finds that a few of the more significant dialogues include those between Justices and lower appellate courts such as the Court of Appeal;[93] between Justices and judicial assistants;[94] and between Justices and government.[95] The pre-eminent dialogues, however, appear to be (first) those between Justices *and each other* (ie with their

[89] See generally MD Kirby, 'Lord Denning: An Antipodean Appreciation' (1986) 1 *Denning Law Journal* 103. Justice Kirby comments at length on aspects of Lord Denning's eventful career as Master of the Rolls. But perhaps the comments (both positive and negative) of the judges who were Lord Denning's contemporaries, highlighted in Justice Kirby's article, offer the most telling insight into the scale of Lord Denning's unorthodoxy and singularity as one of the highest appellate judges in postwar Britain. For instance, Lord Justice Kerr, while conceding that Lord Denning could go 'a little bit too far' (necessitating being put right by others), acknowledged (in effect) that this supreme ability and visionary quality could help lead the way to those content merely to follow. For his part, by contrast, Lord Hailsham pointed to what – in terms of the developing narrative of this and the preceding chapter – would amount to a distinctly non-'Herculean' approach to judicial decision-making, namely, a 'want of coherence in his approach to things. He has a highly subjective view of the world, I think'. (ibid 115, citing BBC interviews with Hugo Young)

[90] A Paterson, *Final Judgment* (this chapter, n 65) ch 1.

[91] ibid 9 (emphasis added).

[92] We can only briefly touch upon this in the present modestly scaled chapter.

[93] A Paterson, *Final Judgment* (this chapter, n 65) 209–213.

[94] ibid 247–257.

[95] ibid ch 7.

colleagues – in other words inter-judicial dialogues); and (secondly) those between Justices and counsel.[96]

The latter dialogues (with counsel) turn to a significant extent on the question whether it would be thought appropriate for the court to decide appeals on points of law which have not been argued by counsel or at least put to them for comment.[97] Needless to say, a practice of this kind would operate not as a straightforward imperative of ultimacy, but as a *constraining* imperative, reining in judicial creativity and judicial freedom. In the case touched upon in sections 8.2 and 8.3 (this chapter, above) – namely *Burnett's Trustee v Grainger*[98] – Lord Hobhouse observes that (at least in terms of the then prevailing practice of the House of Lords) the fact that the points he was about to discuss in his opinion had not been argued by counsel meant that what he said would necessarily be 'obiter and without the benefit of having heard argument'.[99] As Paterson makes clear, a not dissimilar practice continues to operate in the Supreme Court, as successor body to the Judicial Committee of the House of Lords. Paterson concludes (writing in 2013) that 'the constraining effect of the expectation that the Justices should stick to points of law that they have at least put to counsel has not greatly diminished'.[100]

When judicial decision-making is contextualised such as within Alan Paterson's 'social activity' frame of reference we might have cause to imagine that an ultimate judgment is reducible to the end-product of a 'process' in which the personality and individuality of *Iudexian* judges are *subjugated* – for instance, subjugated to a collegiate judicial consensus, or (subjugated) to interactions with key 'stakeholders' such as counsel, or hierarchically lower appellate courts or branches of government. We may conclude that it is *the process* that is determinative of outputs that come in the form of Supreme Court judgments. If so, then the implication may be that individual creativity is all but erased from ultimate judicial decision-making. Yet, based on observations of Lord Reed, there is a suggestion that the point of departure for Supreme Court judgment-preparation appears to be not so far removed from what might once have been regarded as the *end-point* of House of Lords decision-making – the preparation, through an individual creative process, of initially independent judgments ('speeches'). This does now appear to be embedded in the practice of the Supreme Court but, significantly, it is the *starting point* of judgment-preparation, not the end-point:

> As another matter of deliberate policy, judgment writing is not allocated [in the Supreme Court] in advance. So every member of the panel prepares every case with more or less

[96] Paterson devotes no fewer than three chapters to inter-judicial dialogues – chapters 3, 4 and 5. He also emphasises at the beginning of chapter 6 that 'the most significant dialogues in relation to judicial decision-making in the final court are those which take place between its judges, and between the judges and counsel'. (See A Paterson, *Final Judgment* (this chapter, n 65) 209.)

[97] ibid 20.

[98] 2004 SC (HL) 19.

[99] ibid 36 (para [55]).

[100] See A Paterson, *Final Judgment* (this chapter, n 65) 23.

equal thoroughness, and is expected to be equally engaged, whatever their previous experience may have been.[101]

Thus an interesting contrast appears to have emerged in the transition from judicial decision-making in the House of Lords to performance of the same function in the Supreme Court, turning on the nature of the decision-making medium: that is, *speech* as distinct from *judgment*. And this may have impacted unexpectedly on the very *possibility* of ultimate judges being more – or less – individually creative. In short, the contrast, highlighted by Lord Reed, is between speech-writing, reflecting the practice in the House of Lords (on one hand), and 'dialogue'-based and collegiate judgment-writing (on the other) which, as we have seen, reflects the practice now observed in the Supreme Court. On the face of it, it would seem that there may once have been greater scope for creative individuality in the House of Lords where each judge prepared a speech – that being the means by which any member of (and in) the House publicly communicates a position, line of argument or opinion to the other members.[102] Crucially, 'each member of the … [Judicial Committee] had to deliver his own speech: there could not be joint speeches, since members of the House speak one at a time'. Moreover, 'members of the … [Judicial Committee] worked on their speeches largely independently of one another, and circulated their drafts in hard copy. The degree to which they commented on each other's draft speeches, and responded to comments on their own draft, appears to have been relatively limited'.[103] As Lord Reed observes (writing in 2019), Justices of the Supreme Court, being no longer tied to speech-writing, have the flexibility to participate in the preparation of individual and joint judgments, and majority or unanimous (single) judgments of the entire court.[104] One advantage of majority or unanimous judgments is 'that the reasoning of the majority is expressed in a single text, so as to assist lower courts and legal practitioners'.[105] When judges repeat each other's reasoning with 'unintended subtle distinctions' academics and legal professionals can fasten onto this 'with unfortunate consequences for legal certainty'.[106]

Yet if, as Paterson appears to suggest, the primary 'social activity' at the heart of ultimate judicial decision-making in the UK consists of dialogues *conducted between and among the ultimate judges themselves*,[107] then it would follow that

[101] Lord Reed, 'The Supreme Court Ten Years On' (see above, this chapter, n 77) 4. Lord Reed also points out (ibid 10) that draft judgments, are circulated to all Justices. At a later time, comments on those drafts are similarly circulated. There are frequent conversations about the draft judgments and lively exchanges of ideas. This results in preparation of revised drafts which are re-circulated, prompting further discussion and revision. So, 'the preparation of a judgment becomes an iterative process, to which other Justices besides the author will usually make a significant contribution'.

[102] ibid 8.

[103] ibid.

[104] ibid 9.

[105] ibid.

[106] ibid.

[107] It is assumed, rightly or wrongly, that these dialogues take precedence over earlier dialogues with counsel (which become secondary in this scheme of things). And it is further assumed that wider-ranging dialogues will have been absorbed earlier within the overall decision-making process.

a composite judgment imputable to 'a *Iudex*' – for example, a single majority or unanimous judgment – represents a *concentration of creativity* that is more '*Iudexian*' than not given that, by this end-point in the process, *Iudexian* judges are (one assumes) exclusively engaged in authorship or co-authorship of the emergent judgment(s). Looked at another way, creativity at the ultimate level – and at the final stage of the process: ie preparation of judgment(s) – is probably accountable more to the 'inner being' or 'creative character' of *Iudexian* judges as a whole (whether viewed individually or collectively), than to any external 'stakeholder' or agency or (earlier) participant in the process with whom the *Iudexian* judges have previously entered into dialogues.

It may be safe to assume that, in the final analysis, a *single* majority or unanimous judgment of the UK Supreme Court represents a synthesised decision of a collectivity of *Iudexian* judges who 'own' their decision regardless of the prior process. And even if the judgment has been arrived at in some sense through 'compromise' or 'concession' to, or 'absorption' of the views of, both judicial and non-judicial actors, perhaps that is to be seen largely as a 'feeding-in' or 'informing' process that leaves judicial discretion and ultimate responsibility undisturbed. Of course, we need to attend to those 'compromises', 'concessions' and 'dialogues' in order to understand the totality of the process – in other words, to understand the process holistically. (That is the position suggested by Paterson.) But individual and collective *Iudexian* creativity, arguably, stands as the animating principle at the heart of ultimate judicial decision-making.[108]

8.4. Concluding Reflections

In this chapter we have explored, among other things, the possibility of drawing upon Dworkin's Herculean archetype for inspiration in outlining some elements of an archetype of an ultimate judge, *Iudex*, to whom there is imputed a hypothetical composite judgment of a collectivity of ultimate judges sitting in the highest appeal court of an imaginary common law judicial system – a system that adheres to the principle of *stare decisis*. The judgment represents the final, unappealable, decision of such a court. As mentioned in section 1.1 (Chapter 1, above), the hypothesis of the ultimate judgment ascribable to *Iudex* is taken to represent a final determination of the content, scope, import and effect of any given legal right for the practical purpose of mobilising the coercive apparatuses of the legal system in question towards enforcement of that (judicially declared) right. The judicial decision-making of *Iudex* could be said to represent a legally conclusive position on the rights – and obligations and powers and liabilities, and so on – of the parties in a hypothetical case.

[108] Clearly the presence of significant individual creative input extends *a fortiori* to any dissenting opinion.

In developing a *modified* 'Herculean' version of *Iudex* in this chapter the aim has been, on one hand, to abandon those aspects of the Herculean archetype that are simply not humanly attainable. So, *Iudexian* judges would not be considered to be superhuman; nor would they be thought to have infinite time at their disposal when deciding a case. Further, unlike Dworkin's Hercules, *Iudex* would not be expected to consider literally *every* possible avenue of approach when preparing (drafting) a judgment. On the other hand, Dworkin postulates the idea of a judge who – in seeking to emulate a 'Herculean' judge – determines coherence or 'fit' of elements of a case through systematic and expansive engagement with the seamless web of applicable case law, statute and other standards relevant to the case in hand. Such a judge also sets out to align the decision-making in the case then before the court with the judge's conception of morally right decision-making. According to Dworkin (as we have seen) law as integrity 'directs' a judge 'to regard as law what morality would suggest to be the best justification of … past decisions'.[109] In the resulting modified Herculean position outlined in this chapter, primacy has been given to the idea of *Iudex* (including 'real life' higher appellate-level judges) striving to achieve *mainly doctrinal* 'unassailability' in their decision-making. (Only the decisions of *Iudex* in the highest appellate court have *institutional* 'unassailability' in that, ordinarily, they are unappealable – even if there are later changes in the law.) A few of the limitations attending the alignment of higher judicial decision-making with a judge's moral outlook were outlined in section 8.3.1 (this chapter, above). There was some exploration of imperatives of, and the creative processes attending, ultimate judicial decision-making (sections 8.3.1 and 8.3.2). An attempt was made to suggest ways in which ultimate judicial decision-making might be qualitatively different from non-ultimate decision-making. A particular question addressed was whether judicial creativity is manifested in an ultimate decision (of *Iudex)* in a way that would not be manifested in a lower court decision.

Perhaps the most striking insight to emerge from the analysis, however, centres on 'lessons' to be drawn from the case study on *Sharp v Thomson*. We concluded from this – perhaps not surprisingly – that ultimate judicial decision-making is not 'Herculean' in the full Dworkinian sense and may indeed on occasion fall short of being 'Herculean' in the modified sense. It was seen from the case study that a later ultimate judicial decision (*Burnett's Trustee v Grainger* in the House of Lords) sought to limit the legal impact of an earlier decision (*Sharp v Thomson* in the House of Lords) in the service of a perceived need to preserve the integrity and coherence of orthodox principles of Scots property law. This appeared to point to the idea that non-ultimate judicial decision-making in some instances might come to be regarded – with the passage of time and by virtue of a later ultimate

[109] See R Dworkin, *Law's Empire* (this chapter, n 1) 119–120.

decision – as having achieved doctrinal, (probably) moral and (certainly) institutional 'unassailability'.

A theoretical dilemma was highlighted which remains unresolved in this chapter, which is that on the probably rare occasions where there is a perceived misalignment between the doctrinal, and the institutional, 'unassailability' of judicial decision-making, the decisions of *Iudex* may not represent an *enduringly* legally conclusive position on declared legal rights in a given case. At the same time, even a (seemingly) modified 'Herculean' decision of an inferior court, that is thought to be in some sense doctrinally 'unassailable', may be merely transient if it encounters later adverse judicial treatment in a superior court. The presence of both of these possible outcomes in the context of 'real life' higher appellate judicial decision-making is potentially disruptive of theory construction, serving as they do to draw attention to limitations in the explanatory power of a *Iudexian* archetype.[110]

The question remains whether there may be enough legal certainty in a common law legal system for anyone to make an 'educated guess' about how a *Iudex* might decide a case or rule on a point of law – this with a view to imagining the possible content and scope of legal rights at the centre of some real or hypothetical case or enquiry. If the case is a genuinely 'hard case' (in the Dworkinian sense) such a thought experiment may present something of a challenge. And it may be a still greater challenge if the judicial decision-making efforts of *Iudex* encompass the mindset of a (Dworkinian) 'philosophical judge'; or a theoretically inclined judge who espouses 'constitutional theory' or 'political theory' or theories of 'legislative purpose' or of 'legal principle'.[111] An attempt, via the hypothesis of the ultimate judgment, to second-guess a decision of *Iudex*, where the decision-making is refracted through a 'theory' or some philosophy or moral preference – aspects of which may be thought to be largely of *Iudex's* own making and subjective – is probably akin to an exercise in crystal ball gazing.

[110] A possible 'tidy' theoretical resolution of the apparent problem of 'transience' – the idea that as soon as a judgment of *Iudex* is handed down it is immediately (potentially) vulnerable to change despite its ultimacy – might be provided by Joseph Raz's concept of a *momentary legal system*: 'A momentary legal system contains all the laws of a system valid at a certain moment'. (See J Raz, *The Concept of a Legal System: An Introduction to the Theory of Legal System* (2nd edn, Clarendon Press 1980) 34. See also 189–197.) If we regard a judgment of *Iudex* as occurring at one 'snapshot in time' in the life of a legal system then it becomes possible to treat such a judgment as final and (at least *theoretically*) invulnerable to change. In a sense, then, final can be taken to 'mean' final. The difficulty with this approach, however, is that it is all too easy to lose sight of the fact that legal systems (including judicial decision-making at every level) are in a constant state of change and flux. If we cleave too closely to an idea such as Raz's momentary legal system we may be inclined to overlook the dynamic 'forward thrust' that lies at the heart of cases such as *Sharp v Thomson* in their progress through the judicial system. The significance of *Sharp* derives from viewing the case in terms of the 'historical sweep' of its 'pendular' decision-making – culminating, in fact, in a later case, *Burnett's Trustee v Grainger*. Adopting the point of view of a momentary legal system – where the focus may be on a series of discrete 'snapshots in time' – would obscure that significance.

[111] See R Dworkin, 'Hard Cases' (1975) 88 *Harvard Law Review* 1057, variously, 'philosophical judge' (at 1083); 'constitutional theory' (at 1084); 'political theory' (at 1083, 1084); and theories of 'legislative purpose' and of 'legal principles' (at 1083).

Even so, Dworkin's idea of the theoretically inclined judge is not so unorthodox that common law judges (even *Iudexian* ones) would reject it out of hand. Ultimate appellate judges such as Justice MH McHugh, formerly of the High Court of Australia, have embraced the notion of the 'theorising' judge in a limited way. Commenting on novel cases where precedents yield competing premises, he argues that '[t]he competing arguments, drawn from those premises, may be supported by the processes of deduction and induction. The choice between those arguments can only be made, however, by applying a *theory*, principle or value, representing some policy, which persuades the reader that one choice is better than [the] other'.[112] Even a judge who applies analogical reasoning must have 'an organising *theory* that explains why the facts of the instant case are similar or dissimilar to the facts of the precedent cases'.[113]

It goes without saying that we would be on safer ground where the relevant aspects of a given (disputed) legal right and key issues in dispute (actual or hypothetical) – when viewed from a hypothesised *Iudexian* perspective – are apparently not so intractable, particularly where they turn on the interpretation of known *law*, of legal doctrine and of (straightforwardly) *legal* standards. It was argued in Chapter 7 that Dworkin's 'window' of purported failure of a criterion such as a rule of recognition – which is designed to identify precisely those laws, doctrines and legal standards – is conspicuously narrow. As if to reinforce such an argument, Justice McHugh reminds us of Lord Devlin's observation that 90 per cent of the time of English judges is spent in the 'disinterested application of known law'.[114] In constructing *Iudex* as an ideal type with an essentially practical mindset, it is to the image of a *Iudex* involved in the disinterested application of known law that primacy is to be given, not the image of a *Iudex* whose typical caseload consists of the most unyielding of 'hard cases', or cases with an unforeseeable 'theoretical' dimension, or cases that might engage an imaginary appellate judge's undeclared moral or political beliefs. Our preferred approach, needless to say, maximises the scope for typification and seeks to anchor *Iudex* firmly in the world of 'real judges'. Even if an ultimate judge (as Lord Reed points out, referring to the position in the UK Supreme Court) handles only those cases where an appeal raises an arguable yet narrow question of law of general public importance, it is necessary to regard *Iudex* – and the hypothesis of the ultimate judgment – as being theoretically 'on hand' to engage with the widest possible range of cases. The decision-making of *Iudex*, in other words, is not (according to our hypothesis) to be confined to cases of exceptional difficulty or novelty, or those rarest of cases that meet the criteria applied by an ultimate court in deciding which cases should be made the subject of judicial decision-making at that level.

[112] See The Hon Justice MH McHugh, 'The Judicial Method Revisited' (17 January 2007) www.hkcfa.hk/filemanager/speech/en/upload/75/20070117%20McHugh%20-%20The%20Judicial%20Method%20Revisited.pdf (accessed 28 July 2025) at 18 (emphasis added).

[113] ibid (emphasis added).

[114] ibid 12. Justice McHugh cites Lord Devlin (PA Devlin, Baron Devlin), *The Judge* (Oxford University Press 1979) ch 1, 3; Lord Devlin, in turn, citing LL Jaffe, *English and American Judges as Lawmakers* (Clarendon Press 1969) 13.

9

Ontological Questions Around Legal Rights

9.1. Theoretical Tensions

This chapter addresses ontological questions around legal rights arising from enquiries pursued in earlier chapters. Later in this chapter we consider whether the overarching argument of the book could form the basis of a 'third way' approach to understanding legal rights beyond Hartian will theory and interest theory (as expounded by Raz and MacCormick, among others). To this end there is brief consideration of Gopal Sreenivasan's position as a representative of contemporary, so-called 'third way', literature.

The exploration of the Dworkinian Herculean archetype and of the *Iudexian* archetype in Chapters 7 and 8 has called attention to a wider tension existing between the sphere of the 'ideal' and the sphere of the 'real' or 'actual'. In Chapter 3 we saw an echo of this tension underlying Nigel Simmonds's characterisation of the analytical reach of the classical theories of rights – will theory and interest theory. The focal concern of the theories, in Simmonds's view, had been with the grounds of legitimacy of rights.[1] In the context of legal rights, for instance, a question we might ask is how their deployment, ultimately, of coercive means of enforcement might be justified. In an ideal world how would we imagine legal rights to be framed? What would make the claims of holders of legal rights legitimate in the eyes of the members of a community – those subject to and, ordinarily, benefiting from, its laws? Viewed from that perspective, the leading theories of rights would be less concerned with (in Simmonds's words) 'austerely analytical clarifications' of the concept of the right.[2] The pursuit of those clarifications would impel the theorist to investigate the nature and fundamental characteristics of rights – in particular (in the present context) discovery of what legal rights *are*, and what it is for such rights to exist.

Resonances of the same tension were to be found in Hart's characterisation of Dworkin's general theoretical approach as 'evaluative justificatory jurisprudence'.[3]

[1] See NE Simmonds, 'Rights at the Cutting Edge' in MH Kramer, NE Simmonds and H Steiner, *A Debate Over Rights* (Oxford University Press 1998) 113.
[2] ibid.
[3] See HLA Hart, *The Concept of Law* (2nd edn, Clarendon Press 1994) (hereafter, in this chapter, '*The Concept of Law*') 241.

Pressing Hart's observation further, Nicola Lacey, as we saw in Chapter 7, emphasises Dworkin's idealising preoccupation, arguing that the sphere of the 'ideal' (seeking, as *Dworkin* does, a 'legitimating argument for a certain conception of law') and the sphere of the 'real' or 'actual' (seeking, as *Hart* does, a 'universally applicable and fundamentally descriptive theory of law') are not necessarily incompatible.[4] According to Lacey, neither general approach need undermine the validity of the rival approach: indeed, they might be complementary. If, like Matthew Kramer,[5] we were inclined to rearticulate the 'analytical clarifications' to which interest theory and will theory naturally lend themselves, such an approach would be more characteristic of Hartian descriptive theorising than Dworkinian idealising theory. At the same time, we would necessarily oppose Simmonds's rejection of 'Kramer's austerely analytical approach'.[6] To that end we would be doing nothing more than aligning our enquiry with theorists on *both* sides of the will theory–interest theory debate (not merely Hart, but others such as Raz and MacCormick) who have made extensive use of analytical clarifications and conceptual refinements to shed light on the nature and fundamental characteristics of rights (in particular, *legal* rights) when pursuing lines of enquiry within their respective theoretical positions.

As we have seen, Lacey has highlighted a further tension – closely associated with those under discussion – that appears to render problematic an important aspect of Hart's 'universally applicable and fundamentally descriptive theory of law': specifically, Hart's claim that *The Concept of Law* represents an 'essay in descriptive sociology'.[7] Viewed in terms of the opposition maintainable between an approach grounded in analytical jurisprudence (originating in Oxonian analytic philosophy) and one grounded in descriptive sociology, Lacey has pointed to the perceived generality and universality entailed in the former and the perceived particularity and empirical facticity entailed in the latter. The key argument, as we have seen, is that the more 'sociological' an enquiry is, the less universal can it be. Such an enquiry is seemingly on an interminable quest to uncover and dissect empirical particulars such as law's institutional forms, its various types of rules, its role and its functions.[8] And this, so the argument goes, appears to conflict with the natural tendency of an approach that seeks generality and universality: for

[4] N Lacey, 'Analytical Jurisprudence versus Descriptive Sociology Revisited' (2006) 84 *Texas Law Review* 944 (hereafter, in this chapter, 'Analytical Jurisprudence') 955.

[5] See section 3.1 (Chapter 3, above) n 1. Theorists such as Kramer have been engaged in rights theorising which places 'analytical clarifications' at the centre of their efforts, while the interests of theorists such as Nigel Simmonds lie elsewhere. Kramer notes in the Introduction to *A Debate Over Rights* that in contrast to his own (ie Kramer's) approach, Simmonds believes that a conception of the formal aspects of rights should turn on moral or political values. Simmonds therefore (according to Kramer) perceives Kramer's austerely analytical approach to be arid. See Kramer's Introduction to MH Kramer, NE Simmonds and H Steiner, *A Debate Over Rights* (Oxford University Press 1998) 3.

[6] ibid.

[7] HLA Hart, *The Concept of Law* (this chapter, n 3) v. This is discussed more fully in section 5.2 (Chapter 5, above).

[8] N Lacey, 'Analytical Jurisprudence' (this chapter, n 4) 957.

instance, analytical jurisprudence which, in the case of Hart's writing, originates in Oxonian analytic philosophy. It would follow that the more an enquiry is mired in detail and empirical particulars *because* it is sociologically grounded (as Lacey would argue), the less universalisable will its key findings and conclusions be. That, according to Lacey, was the dilemma faced by Hart in at least partly delimiting the analytical scope of *The Concept of Law* as an 'essay in descriptive sociology'.[9]

Yet, as we have also seen to emerge from Lacey's examination of unpublished writings,[10] Hart apparently scaled back that claim when acknowledging, in a notebook dating from the late 1980s, that *The Concept of Law* provided, as Hart put it, (only) the 'normative concepts required for a descriptive sociology'.[11] On that basis Hart's more modest aim might have been to harness the generalising conceptual analysis characteristic of Oxonian analytic philosophy towards providing (merely) the tools facilitative of a descriptive sociology. By implication, the analytical core of *The Concept of Law* would only assist in the development of such a sociology, while all the time (arguably) falling some way short of that.

In order to inform and frame the discussion of a perspective on legal rights drawing on lines of enquiry from earlier chapters, it is worth examining more closely Lacey's suggestion that Hart's 'descriptive sociology' might have been caught between the demands of a particularising (sociological) approach and those of a generalising (philosophical) approach. Those positions were, according to Lacey, incompatible and (in combination) the 'worst of both worlds'.[12] At one level, Hart's subsequent scaling back of his 'descriptive sociology' claim might serve to lower the expectations of readers of *The Concept of Law* in search of a work that seriously engages with sociology (or, say, classical social theory). At another level, it may be possible to view Lacey's position as manifesting an older debate that greatly exercised Weber and others; and it may be that we can reappraise Hart's approach more sympathetically when reflecting upon the wider context provided by that earlier debate.

Influenced by the Baden Neo-Kantian philosophers Heinrich Rickert and Wilhelm Windelband, Weber attempted to bridge the perceived divide between methods appropriate to the study of human behaviour (broadly, human sciences) and those appropriate to natural phenomena (natural sciences).[13] The *nomothetic* or *generalising* approach of the natural sciences, seeking to formulate general scientific 'laws' – for example, Boyle's Law, Kepler's Laws, Newton's First Law of Motion, and so on – could be harnessed in a human context where there were

[9] ibid. See HLA Hart, *The Concept of Law* (this chapter, n 3) v.
[10] See section 5.2 (Chapter 5, above).
[11] See N Lacey, 'Analytical Jurisprudence' (this chapter, n 4) 949.
[12] ibid 957.
[13] See generally G Oakes, *Weber and Rickert: Concept Formation in the Cultural Sciences* (MIT Press 1988); also HH Bruun, *Science, Values and Politics in Max Weber's Methodology* (expanded edition, Routledge 2016). For a sceptical view on the influence of Rickert on Weber, see C Adair-Toteff, 'Why Rickert? Regarding the Dogma about Heinrich Rickert's Influence on Max Weber' (2023) 53(2) *Journal for the Theory of Social Behaviour* 127.

observable regularities of behaviour and recurrences of such behaviour. (The behaviours associated with a general election, for instance, would provide not only a clear instance of patterned human activity, but activity on a very significant and statistically measurable scale.) Such states of affairs came to be expressed in terms of probability in Weber's writings – this being the specifically *causal* dimension of Weberian sociology.[14] In the case of so-called *idiographic* sciences, the approach was to *particularise* the subject matter. For instance, the cultural sciences (*Kulturwissenschaften*) – history being an obvious instance – would focus on the uniqueness of historical actors or events, capturing the *meaningful* content of individual instances of human behaviour, such as through the application of Dilthey's *Verstehende* (interpretive understanding) method.[15] Weberian sociology thus held out the possibility of studying and explaining human behaviour by drawing not only upon the generalising methods of natural science but on the particularising approach characteristic of *Kulturwissenschaften*.[16] It demanded a synthesis of both approaches – being, in effect, a 'hybrid'.[17]

Without ruling out the possibility of sociology, or any given sociological approach, exclusively concerning itself with empirical particulars, *Weberian* sociology is not, as it happens, constrained in that way. It is possible that Hart, in characterising *The Concept of Law* as 'an essay in descriptive sociology' had a Weberian sociological approach in mind. (This is difficult to know for certain, given Hart's reticence about the influence of Weber on his writing.)[18] In places, Hart's writing resonates with Weberian sociology, as we have seen.[19] *The Concept of Law* need not fail as an 'essay in descriptive sociology' – or as a synthesis of

[14] For instance, Weber ties the idea of [social] power – often translated as 'domination', which is equivalent to *Herrschaft* in his writings – to a 'probability' of behaviour that is compliant to 'commands': 'The concept of power is sociologically amorphous. All conceivable qualities of a person and all conceivable combinations of circumstances may put him in a position to impose his will in a given situation. The sociological concept of domination must hence be more precise and can only mean the probability that a *command* will be obeyed'. See M Weber, *Economy and Society: An Outline of Interpretive Sociology* [*Wirtschaft und Gesellschaft: Grundriss der Verstehenden Soziologie*] (G Roth, C Wittich and others (trs and eds), Bedminster Press Inc 1968) (hereafter, in this chapter, '*Economy and Society*') 53 (Weber's emphasis).

[15] See HP Rickman (tr and ed), *W Dilthey Selected Writings* (Cambridge University Press 1976) 170–171, 172, 218, 221–222. See also section 4.3 (Chapter 4, above) and section 8.3.2 (Chapter 8, above).

[16] '[The distinction maintained] between nomothetic and idiographic (Windelband), or generalizing and individualizing (Rickert), sciences remains entrenched … [T]he distinction as an antinomy … holds true … only in a very limited sense: in the case of mechanics, the most fundamental natural science, and history, insofar as it is concerned with personalities. All other disciplines, from physics, chemistry, biology, and psychology to the social sciences, the cultural sciences, and many of the historical sciences, are defined as hybrid forms, located in a continuum between these poles.' See G Wagner and C Härpfer, 'Neo-Kantianism and the Social Sciences: from Rickert to Weber' in N de Warren and A Staiti (eds), *New Approaches to Neo-Kantianism* (Cambridge University Press 2015) ch 8, at 171.

[17] ibid.

[18] See generally section 5.2 (Chapter 5, above).

[19] See generally section 5.3.4 (Chapter 5, above); and see, in particular, Neil MacCormick's extolling of Hart's 'non-extreme external' or hermeneutic point of view as 'the central methodological insight of Hart's analytical jurisprudence', resonating as it does, and on a number of levels, with classical (Weberian) social theory: N MacCormick, *HLA Hart* (Edward Arnold (Publishers) Ltd 1981) 38.

philosophical and sociological approaches to legal phenomena – merely because *all* sociology is assumed or claimed (rightly or wrongly) to be particularising. There are recognisably 'sociological' parts of *The Concept of Law* that appear to edge towards generalisation: for instance, the generic concept of the social rule; the idea of the internal aspect of rules; the critical reflective attitude (to rules); and aspects of the Rex archetype (echoing Weberian ideal-type construction).[20] The idea of the legal right reimagined in sociological terms as an instrument or manifestation of social power – though alluded to in Hart's will theory of rights (outlined in *Essays on Bentham*) rather than specifically in *The Concept of Law* – also has a generalising dimension, and undoubtedly has resonances of classical social theory.[21] If Hart's approach to sociology such as it is, like Weber's, is indeed both particularising *and* generalising then – so far as it is generalising – there may be no necessary conflict between Hartian sociology, as manifested primarily in *The Concept of Law*, and the generalising dimension of Hartian (Oxonian) analytic philosophy.

Sizing up the tensions briefly outlined in this section, we find that they are perhaps more 'permissive' than they are restrictive – facilitating more than they impede and, to that extent, perhaps they are more in the nature of antinomies than tensions. The first tension, emphasising Dworkin's preoccupation with the realm of the 'ideal', did not appear to stand in the way of a Hartian 'universally applicable and fundamentally descriptive theory of law'.[22] Each could co-exist independently of the other; while each theorist could pursue positions best suited to his own theoretical and philosophical vision without those positions necessarily being in conflict. At the same time, an approach to understanding legal rights centring around the 'analytical clarifications' to which interest theory and will theory naturally lend themselves – albeit considered 'arid' to some – nonetheless could readily be accommodated within Hartian universal descriptive theorising. The use of conceptual analysis was to be found on both sides of the will theory–interest theory debate, deeply embedded in a tradition of theorising of significant explanatory power represented by theorists such as Hart, Raz, MacCormick and, more recently, Matthew Kramer and Gopal Sreenivasan. Arid or not, conceptual analysis was (and is) facilitative of, and indispensable to, a proper understanding of legal and social phenomena.

We also touched upon a related tension, centring upon the idea that the synthesising approach adopted by Hart in *The Concept of Law* was doomed to (qualified) failure because it was irretrievably caught between the demands of a particularising (sociological) approach and those of a generalising (philosophical) approach – the two positions being (as Professor Lacey has maintained)

[20] See generally section 5.3 (Chapter 5, above).

[21] See generally section 1.4 (Chapter 1, above) and section 5.3.4 (Chapter 5, above) touching upon Hart's notion of the right-holder as a 'small-scale sovereign'.

[22] See N Lacey, 'Analytical Jurisprudence' (this chapter, n 4) 955.

incompatible and representing the 'worst of both worlds'.[23] Despite the cogency of Lacey's stated position, it was maintained that Hart's sociological approach, mirroring the approach pioneered by Weber, was not exclusively particularising and (crucially) was sufficiently generalising for there to be no necessary incompatibility between a Hartian 'descriptive sociology' approach to phenomena and the largely generalising approach that was characteristic of Hartian (Oxonian) analytic philosophy.

Viewed as a whole, then, these tensions do not represent an impediment to an approach to understanding legal rights founded on conceptual analysis as an aspect of a 'universally applicable and fundamentally descriptive theory of law'. Such an approach need not rely on an 'ideal vision and a legitimating argument for a certain conception of law' (Lacey on Dworkin)[24] or on 'evaluative justificatory jurisprudence' (Hart on Dworkin).[25] To that end we can also, like Hart, draw on sociology and social theory – whether generalising or particularising (or both) – while at the same time adopting a generalising approach to explaining and understanding phenomena that is characteristic of Hartian (Oxonian) analytic philosophy. This provides a context in which, in the remainder of this chapter, we can attempt to reach a more considered view on a theoretical approach to exploring the nature of legal rights, drawing and building upon key strands of analysis from earlier in the book.

9.2. Ontological Questions Around Legal Rights

A useful point of departure towards outlining an image of the legal right informed by theoretical positions developed in earlier chapters is the critical discussion, mainly in Chapter 1, of important aspects of the two leading theories of rights – will (or choice) theory and interest (or benefit) theory. Chapter 1, among other things, touched upon some of the developments in this area since the early 1960s. A key aim of the emerging discussion was to challenge the conventional image of the legal right as something to be viewed strictly (and often exclusively) from the perspective of the *right-holder* – such as in terms of *right-holder* empowerment (originating in will theory) and protection of *right-holder* interests (originating in interest theory).[26] Without denying the importance of those perspectives – including broader theoretical perspectives such as a Dworkinian one centring (for example) on evaluative questions around the legitimacy of legal rights – it was argued in Chapter 1 that the institutional and coercive character of legal enforcement necessitates a view of legal rights as a repository of social power residing to

[23] ibid 957.
[24] ibid 955.
[25] See HLA Hart, *The Concept of Law* (this chapter, n 3) 241.
[26] See section 1.1 (Chapter 1, above). There is also coverage of this theme in section 2.3.2 (Chapter 2, above) and section 3.2.3 (Chapter 3, above: examining 'Constraining Factor III').

a significant degree in the decision-making of institutional actors such as judges and, ultimately, supreme court judges of a legal system's highest appeal court. This would hold despite the relatively small number of cases in which legal rights are actually litigated in the courts, the overwhelming majority of exercises of legal rights occurring without formalised institutional intervention. Arguably a theoretical outlook that adopts the narrow perspective of the right-holder (to the exclusion of relevant institutional perspectives) cannot on its own reliably reproduce the social power dynamic underlying the possession of a legal right. Of course we must still speak of 'A's right' and 'B's right', recognising that (when viewed in terms of Hartian will theory) legal rights invest the right-holder with a special kind of power: 'exclusive control, more or less extensive, over another person's duty'.[27] But the control in question is predicated on the availability, ultimately, of institutional (coercive) enforcement mechanisms. In the final analysis – such as in a situation where the duty-bearer is resistant to rendering performance – the control exercisable by the right-holder may be realised only through exercises of social (legal) power that guarantee the right: literally taking the form of institutional enforcement action. When we take a step back, we find that the social (legal) power entailed in 'A's right' is partly vicarious: it owes much of its potency to the actual or anticipated prospect of institutional intervention. Such intervention may need to happen in a given case if a right-holder takes enforcement action against a duty-bearer; or it may never need to happen.

Taking stock of this position, legal rights come to be viewed from a standpoint integral to the 'institutional imagination' or, more narrowly, the 'judicial consciousness'.[28] This standpoint, outlined mainly in Chapters 1 and 3, and further developed in Chapters 7 and 8, is theoretically captured in a (Weber-inspired) ideal type which hypothesises a supreme court judge, *Iudex*, whose decision-making is recognised as legally conclusive for the jurisdiction in question.[29] The animating principle here is that exercises of significant social power occur where state institutions such as the judicial system become involved, frequently as a last resort, in mobilising specifically coercive agencies – for instance civil enforcement agencies – towards enforcing legal rights. As noted in earlier chapters, in their decision-making, institutional entities (mainly of the state) with significant social power – for instance, tax authorities, prosecuting authorities, regulatory authorities, police, the legal profession and so on – fall in behind the stance taken by the courts. They generally seek to *replicate* the ultimate judicial point of view and its reasoning and decision-making processes. Private sector (commercial) organisations – eg pension funds, retailers, life assurance companies, and so on – follow suit. This is especially characteristic of common law jurisdictions which adhere to the principle of *stare decisis*. Because courts of law, as institutional structures,

[27] See HLA Hart, *Essays on Bentham: Jurisprudence and Political Theory* (Clarendon Press 1982) (hereafter, in this chapter, '*Essays on Bentham*') 183.

[28] See section 3.1 (Chapter 3, above) n 3.

[29] A number of possible characteristics of a *Iudexian* perspective are outlined in Chapters 7 and 8.

are an important locus of legal and social power – acting (in a sense) as 'gatekeepers' who hold legal enforcement apparatuses in check or otherwise act to mobilise those apparatuses – it makes sense, sociologically, to explore relevant *institutional* perspectives without necessarily neglecting other perspectives such as those centred narrowly on (for instance) the position of the right-holder or of the duty-bearer.

It is noteworthy that Weber, in defining the 'sociological point of view' to be adopted when seeking to understand law as a social and societal phenomenon, emphasises the idea of capturing some conception of empirical reality, framing this causally, in terms of probability:

> What *actually* happens in a group owing to the *probability* that persons engaged in social action (*Gemeinschaftshandeln*), especially those exerting a socially relevant amount of power, subjectively consider certain norms as valid and practically act according to them, in other words, orient their own conduct towards these norms?[30]

A focus on 'what actually happens' resonates more effectively with a Hartian descriptive project than with, say, a Dworkinian idealising project: what actually happens and what (ideally) ought to happen are obviously different questions. At the same time, an emphasis on the viewpoint of 'those exerting a socially relevant amount of power' directs our attention towards the activities of institutional structures such as the judiciary and (non-judicial) enforcement apparatuses. Weber's focus on social power in defining a sociological point of view for law complements his idea of what is entailed in the possession of a legal right. For Weber, this has both a causal dimension – framed in terms of 'chance' (often expressed, in the alternative, as 'probability') – and a social power dimension which presupposes the possibility of invoking institutional structures (for example, via legal proceedings) to make an appropriate enforcement intervention.[31] Weber's perspective (as we saw in Chapter 1) also represents, on the face of it, a synthesis of (Hartian) will theory on one hand and interest theory on the other. Social power is presupposed when the aid of a 'coercive apparatus' is invoked by the right-holder. That invocation (of assistance) advances the 'ideal or material interests' of the right-holder.

> Sociologically, the statement that someone has a right by virtue of the legal order of the state thus normally means the following: He has a chance, factually guaranteed to him by the consensually accepted interpretation of a legal norm, *of invoking in favor of his*

[30] See M Weber, *Economy and Society* (this chapter, n 14) 311 (Weber's emphasis).

[31] Weber's framing of a sociological position on the possession of a legal right in terms of 'chance' is in line with his methodological dualism which synthesises approaches that are characteristic of both the human sciences (*Geisteswissenschaften*) and natural sciences (*Naturwissenschaften*). A 'positivistic' explanation (in the Comteian sense) centred on 'chance' or 'probability' (characteristic of natural sciences) – such as the 'chance' of the right-holder's invocation of the aid of a 'coercive apparatus' – has the role of empirically 'verifying' the interpretive process (characteristic of human sciences) residing in the application of a legal norm to relevant facts that points to the conclusion that a legal right exists. See further the discussion in section 4.3 (Chapter 4, above).

> *ideal or material interests* the aid of a 'coercive apparatus' which is in special readiness for this purpose.[32]

Weber argues that, typically, the 'aid' in question consists in the readiness of certain persons to support the right-holder 'in the event that they are approached in the proper way', such support being guaranteed by 'a legal norm'.[33] Thus as we have seen in Weber's writings, the idea (traceable to interest theory) that legal rights are protective of interests converges with the idea (traceable to Hartian will theory) that a right-holder exercises a right through an exertion of will (directly by the right-holder or indirectly by a recognised representative) so as to control another person's (duty-governed) actions; and is *empowered* to the extent of the control exercisable. It is possible to maintain this position because (as discussed in Chapter 1) there is no contradiction in the idea of legal rights operating both protectively (relative to right-holders' interests) and in an empowering way. In Chapter 1 this is framed as a convergence of positions expressed in the principle: *that which protects also empowers*. A legal right, embodying the principle of protective empowerment, transcends the limited capacity of the individual right-holder to take effective action towards exercising 'control' (in Hartian terms) over another person's duty. In other words, it transcends the idea, narrowly focused on the viewpoint of the right-holder, that the (exercised) will of the right-holder and the right-holder's control, satisfactorily account for the social power inhering in a legal right. Arguably, in this context Hart is merely analytically less explicit than Weber. Protective empowerment approximates to the Weberian idea of social power or *Herrschaft*, reflecting 'the possibility of imposing one's … will upon the behavior of other persons',[34] where, in the context of a legal right, the will of the right-holder is imposed with the support of, and protection afforded by, relevant institutional structures.[35] The exercise of a legal right, then, envisaging institutional intervention or, minimally, the *threat* of institutional intervention, can be seen as an expression of social power; while the legal right itself may be viewed as an instrument of social power.

In Chapter 2 this fundamental position is developed with a more explicitly ontological outlook. As we have seen, in his early writings Neil MacCormick promotes a conception of a legal right that appears to integrate his version of interest theory with his institutional theory of law.[36] According to this account a legal right is an institution of law and, by reason of that, an institutional fact, or

[32] See M Weber, *Economy and Society* (this chapter, n 14) 315 (emphasis added).

[33] ibid.

[34] ibid 942.

[35] As mentioned in Chapter 3 – see section 3.3 (Chapter 3, above), n 71 – Weber outlines the idea of 'guaranteed law' which is a system where there exists a 'coercive apparatus' comprising 'one or more persons whose special task it is to hold themselves ready to apply specially provided means of coercion (legal coercion) for the purpose of norm enforcement. The means of coercion may be physical or psychological, they may be direct or indirect in their operation'. See M Weber, *Economy and Society* (this chapter, n 14) 313.

[36] See generally section 2.3 (Chapter 2, above).

constellation of institutional facts. MacCormick's primary focus (in this relatively narrow context) is on the facticity of legal rights (as institutions of law) and the conditions of their existence at their inception through the operation of institutive laws.[37] At the same time, legal rights and other institutions of law are to be seen as capable of reification: in other words, they are to be viewed as incorporeal 'things'. (This position emerges, in its fullest expression, in MacCormick's later writings.)[38] The idea that these 'things' (specifically *legal rights*) can promote the interests of, at the same time as empowering, a right-holder, is not incompatible either with (Hartian) will theory or any version of the interest theory of rights. Also, in distinguishing 'brute fact' from 'institutional fact', MacCormick suggests that these types of 'fact' exist on different planes. So, 'brute fact' (the world of physical objects) occupies the plane of 'shoes and ships and sealing wax' (as MacCormick puts it); while 'institutional facts' (such as legal rights) exist in a normative world as mental constructs – artefacts of the mind.[39] We can discern a simplistic parallel between physical things that both protect our interests and empower us, and 'things' of the mind that do likewise, albeit in a way that is purely behavioural – modifying or constraining human behaviour mediated by thought processes. In the gunman situation famously developed across writings of John Austin and HLA Hart, the physical object at the centre of the analysis – the gun – can be seen to represent an irresistible compulsitor (naked physical, yet also social, psychological, power) which is used to advance and protect the nefarious interests of the gunman intent on armed robbery. We can remove 'nefarious' from the equation where a gun is used – or its use is threatened – in a situation of legitimate self-defence. Here, the interest protected is that of self-preservation.

A legal right, then, occupies the institutional world in two senses framed (in Chapter 2) in terms of *philosophical institutionality* and *sociological institutionality*.[40] Each of these is now reconsidered in turn.

On one hand, the idea of *philosophical institutionality* (adapted from MacCormick) invites the possibility of 'confronting' aspects of factual reality with applicable legal rules so as to bring into existence, or permit the recognition of, an institution of law. MacCormick follows the position adopted by John Searle (in turn influenced by writings of GEM Anscombe) where – taking banknotes as an example – a five-dollar bill when stripped of its institutional character becomes

[37] See DN MacCormick, 'Law as Institutional Fact' (1974) 90 *Law Quarterly Review* 102, generally 106–107.

[38] See the discussion in section 2.3.3 (Chapter 2, above) citing N MacCormick, *Institutions of Law: An Essay in Legal Theory* (Oxford University Press 2007) 118. Hart also gives recognition to the reifying dimension of legal rights: '[D]uties with correlative rights are a species of *normative property* belonging to the right holder, and this figure becomes intelligible by reference to the special form of control over a correlative duty which a person with such a right is given by the law'. See HLA Hart, *Essays on Bentham* (this chapter, n 27) 185 (emphasis added).

[39] See DN MacCormick, 'Law as Institutional Fact' (1974) 90 *Law Quarterly Review* 102, 105.

[40] See Chapter 2, above, respectively sections 2.3.1 and 2.3.2.

a mere 'piece of paper with various gray and green markings'.[41] The application of legal rules governing the status of such a 'piece of paper' is transformative.[42] Hans Kelsen, as also noted in Chapter 2 (section 2.3.1) and more generally in Chapter 4, articulates a not dissimilar position in relation to the inferences to be drawn from the 'confrontation' of aspects of factual reality with legal norms. In this context Kelsen views a key judicial function in terms of acts 'of intellect' where relevant acts or events are 'confronted' with relevant laws, with the aim of conferring 'legal meaning' (*rechtliche Bedeutung*) upon them.[43] An example would be the legal meaning of marking 'X' on a piece of paper, where that is equivalent to voting using a ballot paper. There are resonances between Kelsen's notion of 'legal meaning' and his concept of the Reconstructed Legal Norm (or *Rechtssatz*), both as formulated in the *Pure Theory of Law*. These are discussed more fully in Chapter 4 – and are also briefly revisited below.

On the other hand, the idea of *sociological institutionality* (adapted from MacCormick) allows for the possibility – discussed in Chapter 2 but not significantly developed by MacCormick in his own writings – of viewing entities such as courts, tasked with interpreting and applying laws and (court-mobilised) enforcement agencies (including police, bailiffs, prisons etc), as institutions in a sociological sense: in other words, empirically identifiable structures of organised human behaviour. MacCormick refers to these as 'social institutions' but develops this idea little beyond that in his lecture 'Law as Institutional Fact'.[44] For MacCormick, institutions of law such as legal rights (their nature, existence and so on) appear to be a matter for philosophical enquiry; while the characteristics of social institutions as a constituent part of the social world appear to be a matter for sociological enquiry.

A key question, however, is whether (certain) social institutions play such a significant role in determining the type of questions that MacCormick would see as being the preserve of philosophical enquiry – essentially, the existence conditions of institutions of law – that the need for sociological enquiry in some shape or form becomes imperative. Law courts, in particular, discharge functions that may be literally *constitutive* of institutions of law. We saw in Chapter 2 that a court's intervention – this being a factually ascertainable human activity – may be critical in determining the existence (or non-existence) of an instance of an institution of law: a contract, for example. While MacCormick emphasises that instances of

[41] See section 2.3.1 (Chapter 2, above) and JR Searle, *Speech Acts: An Essay in the Philosophy of Language* (Cambridge University Press 1969) 51. See also, generally, GEM Anscombe, 'On Brute Facts' (1958) 18 *Analysis* 69.

[42] For instance, in the UK context, see section 1(1) and (2) of the Currency and Bank Notes Act 1954: 'The Bank of England may issue bank notes of such denominations as the Treasury may approve. All bank notes issued under this section shall be legal tender in England and Wales'.

[43] See H Kelsen, *Pure Theory of Law* (published as Hans Kelsen, *Introduction to the Problems of Legal Theory* [*Reine Rechtslehre. Einleitung in die rechtswissenschaftliche Problematik*]) (BL Paulson and SL Paulson (trs and eds), Clarendon Press 1992) 8–10.

[44] See DN MacCormick, 'Law as Institutional Fact' (1974) 90 *Law Quarterly Review* 102, 110.

institutions of law 'are properly said to exist over a period of time, from the occurrence of an institutive act or event until the occurrence of a terminative act or event',[45] the idea that courts might need to exercise a constitutive function in giving recognition to the (earlier) occurrence of institutive acts – such as where the existence of a legal right is in question – seems more suited to sociological enquiry (or legal doctrinal enquiry) than to philosophical enquiry. Of course, MacCormick might respond that a court ruling is merely one more 'institutive act or event' with a 'reconstitutive' effect and nothing more, thereby avoiding the need to engage with an aspect of the ontology of institutions of law that inclines explanation more towards sociological enquiry than philosophical enquiry. MacCormick's instinct would appear to be to locate questions around the existence of institutions of law 'safely' within philosophical enquiry.[46]

A court declaration of the existence of a 'real life' example of an institution of law in MacCormick's sense – such as a finding that a will is valid (in contrast to a finding of nullity, say) – may represent an instance of 'secondary institutionalisation', as discussed in Chapter 2. Here, sometime after the (earlier) occurrence of relevant institutive events, a court in its judgment retroactively endorses and 'reconstitutes' the will as a valid institution of law. Meantime in other settings, such as an informal one removed from the adversarial theatre of court proceedings, an expert reviewer of relevant precedents and other applicable legal standards (eg a solicitor or barrister) – consciously or otherwise applying the hypothesis of the ultimate judgment so as to approximate some conception of doctrinal 'unassailability'[47] – attempts to reach a similar conclusion to one that an ultimate court might be expected to reach. In that situation sociological enquiry or legal doctrinal enquiry, not philosophical enquiry, are more appropriate in understanding and explaining those factual decision-making processes and their 'real world' consequences. (Superficially, this would mark a return to Weber's focus upon what 'actually happens' when someone engages in rule-following behaviour.) The presence of institutional structures (courts, enforcement agencies etc) is to a significant extent creative of the conditions of protective empowerment inhering in legal rights and other legal mechanisms such as legal powers (or, to cite a random example, a 'Hohfeldian' immunity, treated as a type of right). Protective empowerment largely resides in the *potential* for such structures to be engaged. The actuality of such engagement is often less important.

The idea of sociological institutionality is nascent in MacCormick's lecture, 'Law as Institutional Fact' where primacy is instead given to philosophical institutionality. As we have seen earlier in this chapter and in Chapter 2, MacCormick

[45] ibid 108.

[46] This is reminiscent of Lacey's opinion that, in the mainly philosophical world that Hart occupied, any conspicuous indebtedness to the work of Weber would have been unlikely to win Hart approval. See section 4.1 (Chapter 4, above); and see N Lacey, *A Life of HLA Hart: The Nightmare and the Noble Dream* (Oxford University Press 2004) 231. Arguably, MacCormick inhabited the same world.

[47] See at various places in Chapter 8, above, but at section 8.3.1 in particular.

pursues a line of approach that resonates in important ways with a key position enunciated in Kelsen's *Pure Theory of Law*: notably, Kelsen's doctrine of legal meaning (*rechtliche Bedeutung*).[48] This points to (hitherto) unexplored ontological possibilities residing within the common ground identifiable in versions of philosophical institutionality and sociological institutionality that lie beyond MacCormick's (narrower) outlook. As we have seen, MacCormick in effect maintains that the act of 'confronting' relevant aspects of factual reality with applicable legal rules brings into existence (or enables recognition of the existence of) an institution of law such as a legal right.

Viewed in Kelsenian terms, the institution of law so identified (for example, a legal right) equates to the legal meaning of an occurrence which for MacCormick would be a relevant 'institutive act or event'. MacCormick, however, stops short of suggesting *who* engages in these acts 'of intellect'. Who, in other words (following Kelsen), does the 'confronting'? It is clear that while literally anyone can do this, the acts of intellect of judicial (and other institutional) actors will often, in the 'real world', carry greater sociological significance than those of others. Kelsen's achievement, or special insight, is to transform this into a convenient conceptual device: the Reconstructed Legal Norm (*Rechtssatz*), which represents a hypothetical *judgment* or order of the court expressing the linking of a conditioning material fact with a conditioned legal consequence.[49] This places judges at the centre of the activity of assigning legal meaning to events in the 'real world'. Using Kelsen's formulation of the Reconstructed Legal Norm – 'if A is, then B ought to be' – and contextualising this to reflect (in MacCormick's terminology) institutive acts or events attending the creation of a legal right, a judge would declare the legal meaning of the occurrence of (facts) 'A' to be that a legal right exists. And the consequences of that (that 'B ought to be') would legally follow – for instance, that the right-holder would be in a position to insist on performance by a duty-bearer of a specified act. That B ought to be given effect to would be reflected in an order of the court (literally a 'Reconstructed Legal Norm' – 'do B') where the judge ordains that a certain course of events should follow. Enforcement or implementation would be guaranteed by interventions by relevant enforcement agencies, if necessary.[50]

[48] This is extensively discussed in Chapter 4 – mainly at section 4.4.

[49] See H Kelsen, *Pure Theory of Law* (this chapter, n 43) 23.

[50] An extended version of the Reconstructed Legal Norm could take the form: 'If A is then B is; and if B is then C ought to be'. In that situation the court determines that institutive facts A have occurred, bringing an instance of an institution of law, B (eg a legal right), into existence (or at any rate conferring judicial recognition upon its existence). The consequence that ought to follow, ie C, would be literally what the court orders to be done as a result of B, a legal right, having been judicially declared to exist. This could be that an identified duty-bearer is required to perform an act – eg pay £100,000 to the right-holder. A further elaboration could incorporate a finding that the duty-bearer has failed to comply with the relevant imposed duty: 'If A is [judicial determination of institutive facts] then Bi is [judicial determination of a legal right] and Bii is [judicial determination of a corresponding legal duty]; and if C is [judicial finding of non-compliance with duty, Bii], then D ought to be [court order enforcing right, Bi].

In Chapter 4, Kelsen's position is taken a step further such that a Kelsenian Reconstructed Legal Norm becomes the authoritative order of an *ultimate* judge, or takes the form of an otherwise unappealable order of a *non*-ultimate judge. (For instance, in the UK the latter situation could correspond to a final order of a non-ultimate appellate court where the possibility of an appeal to a higher court has been denied.) In this way the Reconstructed Legal Norm hypothetically incorporates a principle of finality so that the legal consequences (that 'B ought to be') may be treated as *definitively and conclusively* following on from the occurrence of (facts) 'A' whose legal meaning is taken to be (for example) that a legal right exists. The legal validity of any 'real life' instance of a Reconstructed Legal Norm – essentially a final, unappealable order of a court – follows an earlier analysis where a judge might need to address a 'hard case' (to use Dworkin's terminology). It was noted in Chapter 7 that, within the constraints of 'hard case' decision-making, it may on occasion prove to be impossible to ground a decision directly in any pre-existing legal standard with a 'pedigree' identifiable by a Hartian rule of recognition. Nonetheless, in that situation it would always be possible (indirectly) to fall back on a rule of adjudication as the basis of validity of the decision: the relevant rule of adjudication being itself identifiable by the rule of recognition.[51] The point is that even a judicial decision appearing to lack substantive 'pedigree' is still, by virtue of a rule of adjudication, a decision of a duly appointed, duly authorised, duly empowered, judge whose decision-making is in effect self-validating regardless of the doctrinal 'pedigree' of the *ratio decidendi* of the decision.[52] As discussed in Chapters 7 and 8, however, ideally the decision of an ultimate judge should approximate to doctrinal 'unassailability',[53] in order that such decision-making approaches substantive, rather than merely formal, validity.

So, according to the ontological principles outlined in this chapter – which represent a synoptic account of the same principles discussed at greater length in earlier chapters – a legal right is a 'thing' or 'commodity' (essentially a mental construct) and an institution of law. This follows in part from MacCormick's reifying account of institutions of law where an institution such as a legal right is to be viewed as an institutional fact or cluster of institutional facts. A legal right operates to protect interests of a right-holder at the same time as investing the right-holder with significant social power, exercisable if necessary, and vicariously, through institutions in the sociological sense of structures of organised human behaviour such as courts and enforcement agencies. (Their intervention is usually at the instance, and discretion, of the right-holder, which Hartian will theory would recognise as acts of choice.) Protection of interests and empowerment are interpenetrating, indivisible and mutually reinforcing principles – what

[51] The example was given of the UK Supreme Court – see section 7.2.3 (Chapter 7, above) at n 82 – where section 40(5) of the Constitutional Reform Act 2005 defines the broad appellate powers of the court.

[52] See generally the discussion in section 7.2.3 (Chapter 7, above).

[53] See section 8.3.1 (Chapter 8, above).

protects empowers; while the ensuing power itself has an intrinsically protective effect. Viewed in Hartian terms, legal power deriving from the presence of a legal right and equating to a form of social power (in terms of controlling human social behaviour), is exercisable over another person's legally assigned obligation or duty. As we have seen, this amounts to, as Hart puts it, 'exclusive control, more or less extensive, over another person's duty'.[54]

Likewise, legal power is seen in Weberian terms as equivalent to social power captured in the concept of *Herrschaft*, reflecting 'the possibility of imposing one's ... will upon the behavior of other persons' (evocative of classical will theory).[55] As some right-holders will have a fundamentally unsafe grasp of matters such as the existence, content, scope, import and effect (etc) of their (claimed) legal rights – in some cases owing to a lack of cognitive or volitional capacity – the theoretical perspective from which legal rights are to be viewed is that of an ultimate judge, *Iudex*, whose decisions are given expression in the hypothesis of the ultimate judgment. This is (hypothesised to be) an unappealable judgment of an ultimate (or lower) appellate court that has the (imagined) practical consequence of mobilising the coercive apparatuses of the legal system towards enforcement of the right – a result that in the 'real world' would represent a significant manifestation, and deployment, of social power. The emerging hypothetical judgment can be imagined to take the form of a modified (extended) Kelsenian Reconstructed Legal Norm: 'If A is then B is; and if B is then C ought to be'. The legal meaning of facts 'A' (institutive of an institution of law) is that a legal right, 'B', is called into existence, or recognised to exist; and from the presence of that right certain consequences ('C') ensue. These are ordained by the order of the ultimate judge, *Iudex*: eg an identifiable duty-bearer must render performance to the right-holder of a specified act, 'C'.

Against the background of the preceding examination of ontological questions around legal rights (drawing upon lines of enquiry pursued in earlier chapters), the emerging image of a legal right, is one in which the insights of Hartian will theory, modified by elements of (Weberian) social theory, predominate, such that a legal right may be viewed, essentially, as an instrument of social power. Legal rights, fundamentally, operate to empower an identifiable right-holder in a situation where, by way of an exertion of the will of the right-holder or of a representative, the right-holder controls the behaviour of an identifiable duty-bearer, if need be

[54] HLA Hart, *Essays on Bentham* (this chapter, n 27) 183. Hart is referring to the extensive class of legal 'rights correlative to obligations' (ibid (eg) 168, 186, 188), corresponding to Hohfeld's claim-right–duty nexus. See also sections 3.2.1 and 3.2.2 (Chapter 3, above).

[55] M Weber, *Economy and Society* (this chapter, n 14) 942. It is worth recalling Guenther Roth's characterisation of *Herrschaft* as a relational 'structure of superordination and subordination, of leaders and led, rulers and ruled' (ibid 61–62 n 31). It is equivalent (according to Weber) to 'power to command' (ibid 942) in the sense of a 'meaningful interrelationship' (ibid 1378). As we have seen, a similar point is made by Alan Hunt in observing that power in the Weberian sense is to be understood as a *relational concept* focused upon the impact of one person upon another in so far as the behaviour of the one may be analysed as having been determined by the other. See A Hunt, *The Sociological Movement in Law* (The Macmillan Press Ltd 1978) 113.

with assistance from institutional structures duly mobilised towards enforcement of the rights. The emergent approach at the same time attempts the barest outline of a synthesis in which a key aspect of interest theory – which (it is maintained) is not incompatible with this book's dominant theoretical position – is harnessed towards reinforcing that position overall. This is captured in the principle of protective empowerment: *that which protects also empowers*. The possibility that this straightforward principle has the makings of further development towards a 'third way' approach to legal rights – beyond will theory and interest theory – is touched upon briefly in the discussion to follow. That, however, has not been an overriding aim of this book nor, in the remainder of this chapter, can it be realistically attempted. It will be enough if a few pointers for future consideration emerge from the brief discussion of 'third way' rights theorising in the penultimate section of this chapter.

9.3. 'Third Way' Rights Theorising

A 'third way' position that might be thought to come close to, or to complement, the theoretical position outlined in this book – located as it is somewhere between will theory and interest theory, albeit with an emphasis (in this book) towards the former – is an approach, suggested by Gopal Sreenivasan, in which he proposes an explicitly 'hybrid' theory, drawing upon elements of will theory and interest theory.[56] Sreenivasan takes as his starting point two of the standardly cited challenges to (Hartian) will theory, combining this with discussion of some recognised challenges to versions of interest theory, this being the stimulus for urging the adoption of a tenable 'third way' approach to theoretical enquiry unburdened by perceived shortcomings of the two mainstream theories. Sreenivasan's points of departure are familiar territory.

Early in his discussion of will theory Sreenivasan addresses important aspects of Neil MacCormick's familiar critique, which is commented on at various points in earlier chapters (see above).[57] A key part of that critique, it will be recalled, centres around two problematic situations: first, the position of inalienable or unwaivable rights and, secondly, the seeming inability of will theory to account for the possibility of incapacitous persons possessing rights. Essentially, Sreenivasan's opening position, broadly reflecting MacCormick's critique, is that the supposed failure of Hartian will theory turns on cases where

[56] See G Sreenivasan, 'A Hybrid Theory of Claim-Rights' (2005) 25(2) *Oxford Journal of Legal Studies* 257 (hereafter, in this chapter, 'A Hybrid Theory'). As mentioned below and elsewhere (eg see this chapter, section 9.4), this book attempts an elaboration of Hartian will theory (contextualised within Weberian social theory) in which a core aspect of interest theory – the idea that legal rights protect interests – serves to strengthen the overall theoretical position. The assumption is also made, following Raz, that the protection of interests by legal rights justifies their existence.

[57] See especially Chapter 6, above.

a (purported) right-holder lacks (in Sreenivasan's words) the 'full measure of control' over a correlative duty.[58]

On one hand, the lack of control may be because certain rights, being inalienable, leave the right-holder with no ability to waive the right, the power of waiver being – recalling MacCormick's strict reading of Hart – indispensable if the right is to exist. (Here, no power of waiver equals no right.) On the other hand, a right-holder's relative lack of control may be due to the (purported) right-holder (an infant, for example) lacking cognitive or volitional capacity.[59] This, so the argument goes, undermines the (purported) right-holder's ability to engage a proper understanding of the (claimed) right or, by way of an exertion of will, to take action to control the behaviour of the (purported) duty-bearer such as by insisting on performance, or by enforcing the (claimed) right, say, by raising a court action. (Here, no capacity equates to no right.)[60]

Sreenivasan maintains that, in the case of inalienable rights, while right-holders denied the possibility of waiving such rights may have, in some sense, a diminished measure of control in relation to the exercise of the rights, they nonetheless retain a significant measure of control over the (narrower) duties imposed upon the corresponding duty-bearers: '[I]t seems intuitive to regard the person disabled from waiving the relevant duties as still holding the correlative

[58] G Sreenivasan, 'A Hybrid Theory' (this chapter, n 56) 259.

[59] In this context MacCormick, as we have seen – for instance, at section 6.2.2 (Chapter 6, above) – relegates the law governing agency, including the law governing the acts of court-appointed representatives, to a marginal position. An agent or representative exercising or enforcing legal rights on behalf of an incapacitous person, according to MacCormick, relies on 'remedial' rights that, *so the argument goes*, are not predicated on, nor grounded in, substantive rights: in other words, 'remedial' powers exercisable by an agent are somehow freestanding and independent, and not reliant upon the prior existence of any substantive right invested in the incapacitous right-holder. (According to MacCormick's reading of Hartian will theory the substantive right may be non-existent.) Key principles of the law governing agency relationships, however, emphasise that the acts of an agent or representative, are in effect those of the principal. This operates at the level of substantive legal rights. An agent or representative will either step in to enforce a pre-existing substantive legal right of the incapacitous principal, or will create such a right *de novo* on behalf of the principal. It seems puzzling that a theoretical account of the nature of (legal) rights – concerned as it must be to reflect and explain something of the practical legal reality attending the state of possessing a legal right – should misdescribe this aspect of the legal position. If the holding of a right by an incapacitous person in the 'real world' is something falling short of the full possession of a right – entailing, in a given case, something less than the 'full measure of control' over a correlative duty – a theory of rights (including a critique of such a theory) should reflect that situation 'warts and all'. Agency can be seen as a legal mechanism that addresses practical difficulties around the exercise, and indeed creation, of *substantive rights*, facilitating their exercise.

[60] It will be recalled from earlier discussion that MacCormick rests his account of the shortcomings of (Hartian) will theory on what appears to be an inflexible reading of that theory. See generally sections 6.3 and 6.4 (Chapter 6, above). For instance, Hart admits of at least one exception, in the case of welfare rights, to the general theoretical requirement that a power of waiver should be seen as a defining characteristic of a right. (See HLA Hart, *Essays on Bentham* (this chapter, n 27) 185–186.) Hart also, as we have seen, makes allowances for the problematic position of (incapacitous) children (ibid 184 n 86). Moreover, Hart admits of the general possibility that the control exercisable by a right-holder over the obligations that may be demanded from a duty-bearer may be full or only *partial* (ibid 188). MacCormick thus holds Hart to significantly stricter positions on key aspects of will theory than those to which Hart holds himself.

claim-right'.[61] Following a line of argument advanced by Nigel Simmonds,[62] Sreenivasan highlights the distinction between partial and complete inalienability where, in the case of the former, the right-holder lacks the power to waive the corresponding duty but retains both the power to sue for enforcement and the power to waive compensation (if the court were minded to make such an award). In the case of the latter (complete inalienability), the right-holder has 'no control over the duty whatever', drawing attention to Simmonds's argument based around 'rights' grounded in criminal law. (It may be recalled that these 'rights' are problematic as straightforward instances of (claim-)rights for the reasons suggested in section 6.2.4 (Chapter 6, above).)

Despite mounting a credible (if brief) defence of will theory, including an apparently credible refutation of key positions adopted by its leading detractor (Neil MacCormick), Sreenivasan maintains – for reasons that come across as fragile – that will theory remains sufficiently unconvincing to necessitate seeking an alternative approach that addresses will theory's shortcomings, the rival interest theory being the most obvious setting in which the beginnings of a solution may lie. (Except that this is with a view to progressing ultimately towards a 'hybrid' theory that partially rejects, and partially embraces, aspects of both theories.) To this end, Sreenivasan turns his attention to one or two key aspects of interest theory.

Sreenivasan's characterisation of interest theory is immediately beset by the familiar issues identified in earlier chapters of this book (in particular, Chapter 3, above). There is an overriding focus on what rights are *for*; with less to say about what rights *are* (in contrast to will theory). Conferring some kind of benefit is central to this. The basic formulation of the core principle (a 'rough statement', as Sreenivasan describes it) makes this clear.[63] The starting point for Sreenivasan – not the end point – is that we are to suppose that X has a duty to φ. The origin of this duty is unclear. Crucially, the duty is the reflex of the claim-right, with which Y is invested, to demand performance of φ from X. This situation obtains 'just in case Y stands in a sanctioned relation to benefiting from X's φ-ing'. Much is predicated on the idea that if X is found in the peculiar circumstance of being burdened with a duty to φ, Y – standing in a 'sanctioned relation' to X and benefiting from performance of φ by X – will be invested with a claim-right. A number of critical pre-theoretical assumptions are made here: that a duty to φ has *materialised*; that the duty in question can be associated with a duty-bearer, X, while the corresponding claim-right can be associated with right-holder, Y; and that a sanction can be exacted for non-performance of φ by X implying, in the case of legal rights,

[61] G Sreenivasan, 'A Hybrid Theory' (this chapter, n 56) 260.

[62] ibid 260 citing NE Simmonds, 'Rights at the Cutting Edge' in MH Kramer, NE Simmonds and H Steiner, *A Debate Over Rights* (Oxford University Press 1998) 225–232.

[63] 'Suppose X has a duty to φ. Y has a claim-right against X that X φ just in case Y stands in a sanctioned relation to benefiting from X's φ-ing.' (G Sreenivasan, 'A Hybrid Theory' (this chapter, n 56) 261.)

the presence of institutional structures whose function includes applying sanctions; or, in the case of moral rights, probably something less formalised – eg social pressure. Armed with an array of pre-theoretical assumptions and with little inclination to speculate about the nature, origin or impact of any given duty or right beyond the floating of '*in medias res*' hypotheses largely unanchored in any wider context (beyond a passing reference to 'sanctioned relation'), this outlook lies very securely within the territory of classical interest theory. To his credit, this is reflected in Sreenivasan's analysis. (Sreenivasan has little choice but to take interest theory as he finds it, unmodified and unadorned.) Possibly (in part) because the main focus of interest theory is upon an abstraction – the conferment of a benefit upon right-holders towards the advancement of their interests – Sreenivasan seems able to conclude early on that interest theory, in seemingly avoiding such pitfalls as inalienability of rights and (mental) incapacity or incompetence of potential right-holders, is not beset with will theory's supposedly fatal shortcomings.

One key advantage of interest theory identified by Sreenivasan lies in its ability to account for the *justification* of claim-rights viewed in terms of the benefits conferred, by and large, upon right-holders. Will theory is by implication more limited in that the possession of a right is justified in terms of the powers (eg of waiver, of enforcement) conferred by rights – giving the right-holder a measure of 'autonomous choice'. As Sreenivasan points out, a right conceived from the point of view of will theory serves an interest: which is the 'interest in autonomous choice'.[64] Of course, this justification is apt to be eroded or defeated the less choice a right-holder enjoys in a given case. It follows that if all elements of choice are removed, any justification of a right (at any rate, according to this reading of will theory) is removed as well. Unlike will theory, interest theory is not beset by the limitations that would arise – when rights are viewed from a will theory perspective – from the availability (or non-availability) of choices. Nonetheless, Sreenivasan hints at the possibility of the kind of theoretical interpenetration touched upon in section 1.3 (Chapter 1, above). The right-holder, given the choices that will theory associates with rights, has an *interest in those choices*.[65] A right-holder also *benefits* from the availability of the choices in question. The possibility that will theory is reined in by limitations centring around the availability of autonomous choice, however, makes no allowance for the idea that a *legal* right viewed 'institutionally' from the perspective of will theory – where an exercise of a right may potentially engage mechanisms of (legal) social power – confers obvious benefits on a right-holder whose interests are clearly advanced by such protective and (ultimately) coercive arrangements. When interest theory's critique of will theory is overly focused on choices viewed narrowly from the perspective of a right-holder, institutional power is rather lost sight of or is tacitly reduced to a simplifying choice on the part of the right-holder to engage institutional processes in order to 'make

[64] ibid 262.
[65] ibid.

them do' what the right-holder requires. In Sreenivasan's example, this is a duty to φ. And the implication is that when X has a legal duty to φ, φ-ing is *precisely* what a court would order X to do if legal proceedings were to run their course. (This is Sreenivasan's 'sanctioned relation', one assumes.)

Reality is never that straightforward, however. In truth, many aspects of the playing out of institutional interventions (such as in a court of law) are not within the control, or necessarily the imagination, of the right-holder. On the other hand, if the perspective of will theory appears to leave open the possibility of viewing (legal) social power and associated choices in terms of both interests and benefits it might be objected that this is simply a reaffirmation of interest theory, or a position advanced by interest theory that will theory might seek to appropriate. A will theory-based account of legal rights that borrows from interest theory may be thought by some to be as unsatisfactory as a version of interest theory that insists on playing down, or denying, the relevance of the element of social (institutional) power inhering in legal rights to which will theory gives primacy. Arguably will theory provides *ontological* insights that surpass those of interest theory but perhaps fall short in terms of advancing credible justifications of rights or plausible insights into what rights are for. The question is less one of whether aspects of *both* theories can be harnessed towards providing a more rounded explanation of rights, but whether adherents to the theories genuinely need to inhabit mutually exclusive theoretical silos of their own making. After all, it can surely be acknowledged, first, that neither theory provides a wholly satisfactory account of rights; and, secondly, that a number of aspects of each theory better explains what the other theory does not.

The latter position readily indicates why Sreenivasan might be minded to pursue a hybrid 'third way' approach to theoretical enquiry. And that is what he attempts after analysing the recognised difficulties that interest theory encounters in satisfactorily accounting for *third party rights* (or 'third party beneficiaries').[66] In short, as Sreenivasan explains, third-party rights have presented a problem for interest theory because interests can appear to be assignable in situations where the benefits of being a right-holder seemingly extend to those who, by any conventional reckoning, lie outside the parameters of proximity implied by the possession of a right. Ultimately, this is because, as Sreenivasan puts it, 'for many duties, there is an intuitive limit to the number of people to whom the duty [corresponding to a right] is owed'.[67] If an indeterminate number of potential right-holders were

[66] ibid 262–264.

[67] ibid 263. In a dissenting speech in *Junior Books Ltd v Veitchi Co Ltd* [1983] 1 AC 520 Lord Brandon referred to 'important considerations which ought to limit the scope of the duty of care' in delict [tort] obtaining between parties who were not in a contractual relationship with one another (in a context where, had there been such a relationship, the contract – and not the law of delict [tort] – would have been decisive in determining the rights, obligations and liabilities subsisting between the parties). (This case originated in Scotland.) He took the view that, in the situation under consideration, the law should not create, as between two persons who are not in any contractual relationship with each other, obligations of one of those two persons to the other which are only really appropriate as between persons who

the beneficiaries of a right – their interest in the right being partly based on such benefit – the idea of an 'interest' in the context of right-holding would become meaningless.[68]

Sreenivasan points to a defence of interest theory (that, in his eyes, still fails to rescue that theory) which relies on a position adopted by Kramer, which in turn represents an adaptation of a Hartian position (itself inspired by Bentham).[69] According to Kramer's test, 'if detriment to X is *sufficient* to establish a breach by the duty-bearer, then X holds a correlative claim-right'.[70] This serves to limit the right in terms of the scope of the interest of potential right-holders in the benefit conferred by the right – detriment being the negation (or absence) of the right's benefit. Yet, even if this position is claimed to assist in addressing some of interest theory's shortcomings, arguably it continues to suffer from interest theory's intrinsic *ontological* shortcomings. What Kramer's position (reinterpreted by Sreenivasan) seems to imply is that a judgment about assigning a right to someone who can properly be regarded as the right-holder, touching on the question of what it takes for the right to exist, rests – via the identification of the benefit in which the right-holder has an interest (albeit a *negated* benefit or *detriment*) – on *what can be inferred from the breach of the right*. In ontological terms this is not especially informative. The existence or creation of a right must pre-date any instance of its breach. Yet this analysis of a right, predicated in part upon its breach, appears to suggest, necessarily *ex post facto*: (A) that something ('a right') has continuously existed from some *earlier* moment in time and (B) that one of the parties to the right (the 'right-holder') is identifiable with certainty if the consequences of a breach (of the correlative duty) are detrimental to that right-holder. If this accurately states Kramer's position it appears to turn ontology on its head in that

do have a contractual relationship. This dissenting opinion came to define the subsequent direction of English law on the matter and remains an important case in setting the boundary between the law of contract and the law of tort. Essentially Lord Brandon was cautioning against a situation where the law of delict [tort] might have created rights, obligations and liabilities that were potentially boundless in their incidence and reach, where the circumstances ordinarily attending entry into contractual relationships – invariably involving a restricted number of contracting parties – would have served to impose *natural* limitations on such incidence and reach.

[68] In the situation of third party right-holding, the identification of a third-party beneficiary will often (to a lawyer) be unproblematic: eg where A contracts with B to confer a benefit on C, all parties being explicitly identified in the contract. (In construction law and practice collateral warranties are usually tripartite in this way.) At the same time, the parties have varying, co-existing interests. Beyond third-party rights, however, a challenging situation for interest theory could arise where, for instance, all 500 workers in a factory have an interest in, and stand to benefit from, the owner of the factory successfully securing an order that will keep the factory in production, and the workers in secure employment, for five years, say. The order (a contract) plainly creates contractual rights and duties between the factory owner and the contracting party placing the order (the 'customer'). But can we infer from the presence of the multiplicity of interests (assignable to the workers) a corresponding multiplicity of rights (eg to enforce the contract between the factory owner and the customer)? Probably not.

[69] See G Sreenivasan, 'A Hybrid Theory' (this chapter, n 56) 263, citing MH Kramer, 'Rights Without Trimmings' in MH Kramer, NE Simmonds and H Steiner, *A Debate Over Rights* (Oxford University Press 1998) 66–68, 79–84.

[70] MH Kramer, 'Rights Without Trimmings' in MH Kramer, NE Simmonds and H Steiner, *A Debate Over Rights* (Oxford University Press 1998) 81.

we assert the existence of a right and the identity of the right-holder by discerning what can be inferred from a breach of the duty that correlates with the right. However, the right needs to exist in some shape or form – with the right-holder identifiable – before talk of any breach of (the correlative) duty is even tenable.

Following his critical comparison of will theory and interest theory, Sreenivasan proceeds to outline a hybrid 'third way' approach to rights-centred theoretical enquiry which, even if 'crude', is said to represent a 'new understanding' designed to meet the objections faced by will theory and interest theory.[71] The idea, in other words, is to overcome the 'objections' – shortcomings, failings – of the *two* theories. It is immediately apparent, however, that the opening position of this hybrid approach – what Sreenivasan refers to as his *Simple Hybrid* approach – is asymmetrical in that it mainly comprises a reconstruction, with modifications, of his previously attempted outline of the crux of *interest theory*.[72] Simple Hybrid does not engage, recognisably or credibly, with the most important elements of classical (Hartian) will theory that serve to make that theory distinctively tenable. Factored into the emerging hybrid is the right-holder's *power of waiver* which, Sreenivasan envisages, may or may not be available in a given case. It seems odd that the focus is on the power of waiver rather than on powers directly connected with the *exercise* of a right (such as the power to require performance of the correlative duty). Is the ability to give up a right more definingly characteristic of a right than the ability to exercise control over a correlative duty: which is the core characteristic of a right identified by Hart?[73] One would expect the focus to be on the thing given up, not on the giving up of the thing. In any event, the power of waiver is something that Neil MacCormick had regarded as *ancillary* to the possession of a right.[74] This is without doubt a valid position, though MacCormick also claimed that Hart had regarded such a power as indispensable to a right – that claim being questionable. What Hart in fact argued was that a right-holder need only have 'some measure' of control over a correlative obligation. And a *part* of that control is the ability or choice of the right-holder to waive the right.[75] The power of waiver thus does not exhaustively account for the control exercisable by the right-holder: it is only one element – and the power may be negated (or be absent) such as in the case of inalienable rights. It is all the more surprising that Sreenivasan gives such a central place to the power of waiver when, earlier in his analysis, he had taken the

[71] G Sreenivasan, 'A Hybrid Theory' (this chapter, n 56) 267.

[72] 'Suppose X has a duty to φ. Y has a claim-right against X that X φ just in case: *either* Y has the power to waive X's duty to φ *or* Y has no power to waive X's duty to φ, but (that is because) Y's disability advances Y's interests on balance.' (ibid 267) Sreenivasan appears to acknowledge that not having a power to waive a right somehow strengthens the right-holder's position. This might be so in a case where a right is inalienable. Simply put, in normal circumstances a right-holder might be prevailed upon to surrender a right (that is capable of waiver). But that cannot happen in the case of an inalienable right. Hence, the right-holder's interests are advanced – and the right-holder is in some sense the more empowered – by the inalienability of the right.

[73] See HLA Hart, *Essays on Bentham* (this chapter, n 27) 188.

[74] See DN MacCormick, *Legal Right and Social Democracy: Essays in Legal and Political Philosophy* (Clarendon Press 1982) 164.

[75] HLA Hart, *Essays on Bentham* (this chapter, n 27) 188.

view – shared by Simmonds – that it was intuitive to regard a person who is disabled from waiving a relevant duty as still holding the correlative claim-right.[76] (In other words, the power directly to control the correlative duty would remain central to the analysis regardless of the presence or absence of a power of waiver.)

Sreenivasan's first elaboration beyond his Simple Hybrid approach (Variant A) serves only to re-emphasise the elements of Simple Hybrid that already leave too much to the imagination.[77] The position outlined progresses little beyond the idea that Y has a claim-right if X is duty-bound to φ. This slightly states the (Hohfeldian) obvious; and indeed rather falls foul of the implacable 'charge of redundancy' levelled by Hart against *interest theory* (see discussion at section 3.2.1, Chapter 3, above) where rights (of one) could be considered exhaustively reducible to duties (of another), with the result that '… all that can be said in a terminology of such rights can be and indeed is best said in the indispensable terminology of duty'. By that account, rights were no more than 'an alternative formulation of duties'.[78] MacCormick, as we have seen, sought to address that criticism, demonstrating that use of the expression 'right' could extend beyond what is narrowly implied by a reduction of a right of one to a duty of another. For instance, use of a short, simple word such as 'right' could be seen as a convenient means of conveying a more complex idea without endlessly unpacking it into constituent parts – eg from any single instance of 'a right' we might infer the presence of a multiplicity of Hohfeldian atomic relationships.[79] But MacCormick never satisfactorily explained how his analysis served only to address Hart's 'charge of redundancy' while not at the same time operating as, potentially, an insightful elaboration of will theory. MacCormick's position (see discussion at section 2.3.3, Chapter 2, above) was not actually *incompatible* with will theory.

While Sreenivasan's Variant B factors in elements of Hartian will theory – in particular making reference to the idea of 'control' (of a duty) – it envisages (among other things) a situation where Y could have a claim-right against X *even if Y has no control over X's duty*. It is difficult to imagine in what meaningful sense Y (as right-holder) could exercise a right if Y has precisely *no ability* to control a duty correspondingly imposed upon X. That said, the presence of the Hartian idea of control in Variant B perhaps prefigures the element of control at the centre of Sreenivasan's Complex Hybrid (see below). So this is a step forward, arguably.

When examining Sreenivasan's two further variants – C and E (there being no D) – the explanatory thrust of those variants is not fully obvious. Sreenivasan returns to his familiar preoccupation with the right-holder's power of waiver, which emerged as a key feature of his Simple Hybrid approach, reinforcing the idea that Y's ability as right-holder to give up a right that X φ – in other words a

[76] G Sreenivasan, 'A Hybrid Theory' (this chapter, n 56) 260.

[77] ibid 269.

[78] HLA Hart, *Essays on Bentham* (this chapter, n 27) 181–182.

[79] DN MacCormick, 'Rights in Legislation' in PMS Hacker and J Raz (eds), *Law, Morality, and Society: Essays in Honour of HLA Hart* (Clarendon Press 1977) ch 11 (hereafter, in this chapter, 'Rights in Legislation') 206.

power of waiver – is somehow more critical to our understanding of a right than, for instance, Y's ability to exercise direct control over X's duty: such as by requiring performance of φ. This approach may, of course, enlighten our understanding of (eg) inalienable rights; but surely the point of a theory of rights is to enlighten our understanding of rights *in general*. Disproportionate attention appears to be focused on a category of rights that is plainly limited in its scope.

Sreenivasan's hybrid approach culminates in his *Complex Hybrid* model, which draws upon Simple Hybrid and its four variants. This is described as an 'omnibus formulation'.[80] While it is expected that this hybrid might exceed the sum of its parts, at first sight a few of the identified shortcomings of each of the (claimed) constituent parts of the hybrid return to 'haunt' it. At the same time it is difficult to discern precisely how the Complex Hybrid represents the end-point of a linear progression of ideas from Simple Hybrid through all of its succeeding variants: some elements of those variants are there; some are not. On the other hand, it is possible to look upon the Complex Hybrid not as the logical culmination of all of its five antecedents, but as an attempt to state a position that *independently* – on its own terms – synthesises aspects of will theory and interest theory. To that end, the Complex Hybrid model, while it must rely to some extent on its five antecedents, appears to transcend a few of their more problematic elements towards defining such an independent position.

As with the opening position of Simple Hybrid and other variants, the Complex Hybrid model invites us to 'suppose' that X is duty-bound to φ, and that Y has a corresponding claim-right to demand performance of φ from X. This is a situation that, as seen in Sreenivasan's other variants, simply *materialises*: essentially it is a pre-theoretical assumption. The existence of a duty to φ is the point of departure. Also, there is no reference to a 'sanctioned relation' which, in Sreenivasan's earlier characterisation of *interest theory* (not in any of his hybrids), had the merit of connecting an interest theory perspective on rights – certainly *legal* rights – with a background context of institutional structures having a (coercive) sanction-applying function. Such a reference might have enhanced the Complex Hybrid model. More positively, in the Complex Hybrid, there is less emphasis on the right-holder's power of waiver, though that power may be captured in the 'measure … of control' that Y is said to have over X's duty to φ: a power both to exercise and (presumably) to give up control. This probably represents a developed version of the element of control identified in Sreenivasan's Variant B: control, of course, being a key aspect of Hartian will theory.[81]

[80] G Sreenivasan, 'A Hybrid Theory' (this chapter, n 56) 271. 'Suppose X is duty-bound to φ. Y has a claim-right against X that X φ just in case: Y's measure (and, if Y has a surrogate Z, Z's measure) of control over a duty of X's to φ matches (by design) the measure of control that advances Y's interests on balance.'

[81] The idea of resting the *non*-existence of a right on the *absence* of a power of waiver is probably an error – this, of course, being the error misattributed by MacCormick to Hart. As previously noted, MacCormick holds Hart to a stricter position regarding powers of waiver than Hart himself concedes. This results in MacCormick's observation – sceptical of Hart's position – that if there be no power to waive or assert a claim upon some matter, upon that matter there is, by definition, no right either. See DN MacCormick, 'Rights in Legislation' (this chapter, n 79) 196. See also section 6.2.4 (Chapter 6, above).

Complex Hybrid implicitly recognises that if a more restricted measure of control – falling short of 'full' control, such as where a power of waiver is absent – nonetheless advances a right-holder's interests on balance, this neither counts against a finding that the right exists nor does it undermine the right-holder's possession of, and ability to enjoy, the right. Further – again in a positive vein – Complex Hybrid attempts to circumvent the (for some, intractable) problem centring on whether a right-holder has the cognitive and volitional capacity to exercise a right via an exertion of will. The claimed fragility of children's rights exemplifies this problem. Sreenivasan explicitly recognises that a 'surrogate' – a representative – might step in to act on behalf of the right-holder. This, as we have seen, was something that MacCormick gave no credit to Hart for recognising in the context of children's rights.[82] This element of Complex Hybrid does not feature as an element of Simple Hybrid nor of its four variants, adding to the perception that Complex Hybrid represents a straightforward *positing* of a hybrid position unconnected, or only tenuously connected, with its antecedents.

Be that as it may, when we take a step back not just from Sreenivasan's Complex Hybrid model, but from the full analytical span of 'A Hybrid Theory of Claim-Rights', we become aware of something quite striking. If we assume, not unreasonably, that the Complex Hybrid model represents the apex of Sreenivasan's synthesising project, it seems legitimate to hold Sreenivasan not only to the full implications, but also to the limitations, of the position adopted there. On doing that, what we find is that the main (or only) interest with which Complex Hybrid appears to concern itself is an *interest in control* – which doubtless extends, or translates, to an interest in *choices* – assignable to, and to the holding of, a right. (So Y's control over X's duty to φ, and attendant choices, advance Y's interests.) By implication, the same frame of reference accommodates *benefits* of control; and *benefits* derived from the availability of choices. Earlier in this chapter we saw that an interest in autonomous choice – touched upon by Sreenivasan[83] – might be viewed as a possible point of theoretical interpenetration of will theory and interest theory. This was hinted at early in Sreenivasan's critical appraisal *of interest theory*. Simply put, (Hartian) will theory centres around: (i) the control that a right-holder (Y) has over X's duty to φ; and (ii) choices associated with, and with the exercise of, that control. And while interest theory concerns itself generally with the interests and benefits assignable to, or arising from, the holding of a right, one of those interests – the interest in *autonomous choice* in exercising *control* of X's duty to φ – relies, at least in part, on will theory for a credible explanation of its characteristics, given will theory's focus on control and choice.

What is notable about the emergent image of a right, however, is not that Sreenivasan's attempt to outline a point of theoretical interpenetration of will theory and interest theory is necessarily untenable – on the contrary, Sreenivasan's analysis is

[82] See the discussion in section 3.2.3 (Chapter 3, above), especially at n 47.
[83] G Sreenivasan, 'A Hybrid Theory' (this chapter, n 56) 262.

credible in showing how theoretical interpenetration could be developed *beyond* his analysis. What is notable is Sreenivasan's narrow framing of the scope of the interest at the centre of his Complex Hybrid model. First and foremost there is an interest in *control*. And that interest parallels or complements the interest in autonomous choice mentioned in the context of Sreenivasan's earlier outline of interest theory: choices, centred around control, are exercised in relation to a correlative duty. So, the interest that Y has in controlling X's duty to φ – and in the choices around how to exercise that control – may be important but, at first sight, seems somehow secondary to the *wider* interests and benefits that attach to right-holding. The focus of classical interest theory is plainly on a wider range or constellation of interests. Take MacCormick's position, for instance. As we have seen, MacCormick holds to the view that a key tenet of interest theory is that 'the legal (or moral) *protection or promotion* of one person's interests as against some other person or the world at large' is 'essential to the constitution of a right'; and that this is realised by the imposition on a class of duty-bearers of 'duties, disabilities, or liabilities in respect of the party favoured'.[84] The orthodox position is thus framed in terms of protection or promotion of the right-holder's interests, conceived in the widest terms or, at any rate, not specifically reined in.

Does a right, however, protect or promote interests in the very mechanism – that of control (with its associated choices) – that serves to make the right operational at a practical level? A right-holder clearly has an interest in the (normative) mechanism of control, and institutional mechanisms of enforcement, which ensure the operational effectiveness of the right. The (normative) control provided to the right-holder is the basic ability to call upon the duty-bearer to perform a specified duty, making reference to the rule or norm or standard that defines the right. And this may ultimately be reinforced by the intervention of coercive agencies involved in enforcement. But a right does not *exist* to protect and promote *its own* mechanisms of control and attendant choices around control. This is what Complex Hybrid appears to suggest when referring to the right-holder's interest in control (and, by extension, related choices). A right exists, fundamentally, to protect those interests that are most closely associated with the substance of the right. So, for example, the interest that a property right protects ordinarily extends to the need or desire for exclusive enjoyment by the right-holder of an item of property: in the case of land, the right enables the landowner among other things to keep trespassers or intruders out and to prevent the neighbouring owner from encroaching (eg building) on the land. The right to an orchard, say, protects the interest that the owner has in harvesting apples to consume (personally) or to sell. Here, the *principle* remains intact that a range of interests can be protected or promoted by the control – by the exercises of (social) power, by the exertions of will, by the autonomous choices – that a right affords the right-holder. Those wider interests are primary interests, while the interest in control and associated choices (centred on the proper functioning of the right) is a secondary interest

[84] See DN MacCormick, 'Rights in Legislation' (this chapter, n 79) 192.

that emerges only after the right is already in place when the primary interests are already being protected or promoted by the right.

A reorientation of Sreenivasan's Complex Hybrid model to align more effectively with orthodox interest theory – where the interests identified for protection and promotion are in the nature of the wider (primary) interests, rather than the narrower (secondary) interests, mentioned above – would no doubt progress the model at least a step beyond the position which Sreenivasan outlines in the concluding section of his analysis – section 6. Such a reorientation would clearly part company with Sreenivasan's own analysis, offering a possible alternative framework within which a hybrid of will theory and interest theory might be realisable. The emerging framework would necessarily adopt as its point of departure some conception of the central tenets underpinning each theoretical approach. So, on one hand, Hartian will theory maintains that a right: (i) gives a right-holder, Y, a measure of control over X's duty to φ; and (ii) gives Y choices associated with, and with the exercise of, that control. On the other hand, classical interest theory maintains that the conferment of X's duty to φ – conceived as Y's right that X φ – expressed in terms of what the right delivers according to (i) and (ii) above (respectively control and (associated) choices characteristic of Hartian will theory) protects, promotes and advances the wider interests that Y's right, in substance, is designed or intended to secure. Against that background, we might assert that (A) what *interest theory* maintains regarding the interests protected and promoted by a right *complements* (B) what *will theory* maintains regarding the mechanism of control (and its associated choices) that the right provides to make such protection and promotion (of interests) possible and to make the right (involving control by Y of X's duty to φ) operational at a practical level.

This analysis hinges on complementarity; and it is only a sketch of a possible reorientation of Sreenivasan's Complex Hybrid model. Of course it does not go far enough in that, in merely demonstrating complementarity, it falls short of representing a more radical synthesis of the two theoretical approaches. However, it is beyond the scope of this chapter (and indeed of this book) to explore 'third way' rights theorising in any greater depth. Some further reflections on this are made in the concluding section of this chapter (below). It may be possible to attempt a proper exploration of 'third way' rights theorising elsewhere, as such theorising offers a prospect of combining the considerable insights of the two main theoretical approaches towards the construction of a unitary theory of possibly greater explanatory power than either theory is capable of in isolation.

9.4. Final Reflections

A final question for brief consideration in this concluding section is whether the image of a legal right presented in this book could be regarded as occupying a 'third way' beyond classical (Hartian) will theory and classical interest theory.

The approach outlined in this book attempts an elaboration of Hartian will theory, contextualised generally within social theory and drawing upon the idea (originating in Weberian sociology) of a legal right as an instrument of social power. The reliance upon a core aspect of interest theory – the idea that legal rights protect interests, which is not *of necessity* incompatible with Hartian will theory – serves to strengthen the overall theoretical position. The assumption is also made – traceable to Raz's version of interest theory – that the protection of interests by legal rights provides, in some measure, a reason for their existence. Moreover, the principle of protective empowerment – *that which protects also empowers* – reinforces the overarching theoretical position. A legal right empowers the right-holder normatively and institutionally: ultimately *coercively*. Protection (of interests) is overlaid upon the element of empowerment that resides in the ability of the right-holder (or a representative), by way of an exertion of will, to control the behaviour of an identifiable duty-bearer. This ability is *also*, in a sense, a 'protected' ability – one supported by institutional structures – ultimately coercive apparatuses – accessed by the right-holder and mobilised towards enforcement of the right. (This represents a further dimension of the right as an instrument of social power.)

The coercive apparatuses (in particular) are themselves controlled by courts and tribunals that make determinations as to (among other things) whether the right exists (at all); what its content and scope are; and what the consequences of that are in terms of orders made by the court to enforce the right. This underpins the adoption of a theoretical perspective from which legal rights are to be imagined: namely, that of an ultimate judge, *Iudex*, whose decisions are expressed in the hypothesis of the ultimate judgment. This is a (hypothetical) unappealable judgment of an ultimate (or even a lower) appellate court that *ex hypothesi* mobilises the coercive apparatuses of the legal system towards enforcement of the right.

Does this image of a legal right dovetail with the reorientation of 'third way' rights theorising – arising out of Gopal Sreenivasan's Complex Hybrid model – outlined at the end of section 9.3 (this chapter, above)? Briefly, the position outlined there envisages that further work might be needed towards developing a more radical synthesis of the two theoretical approaches. Nonetheless, it is clear that aspects of interest theory and will theory are mutually complementary not only in Sreenivasan's thinking but in the reorientation of Sreenivasan's Complex Hybrid model in section 9.3. In its particular manifestation, the reorientation of 'third way' rights theorising holds that a legal right is protective of, and promotes, interests, *as interest theory maintains*. At a more practical level this is accomplished, *as Hartian will theory maintains*, in that the right gives a right-holder, Y, a measure of control over the duty to φ assigned to a duty-bearer, X; giving Y choices associated with, and with the exercise of, that control. So, in the most straightforward terms, a legal right that gives a right-holder control over, and choices connected with, a duty assigned to a duty-bearer, is protective of, and promotes, interests of the right-holder. Not only is this perspective on 'third way' rights theorising compatible with the idea of a legal right as an instrument of social power, it also embraces the principle (outlined at various places in this book) of protective empowerment.

The possible reorientation of 'third way' rights theorising using Sreenivasan's variant does not, however, extend to anything that neatly corresponds to an institutional perspective such as *Iudex*: doubtless because, by and large, that idea lies some way beyond classical interest theory and classical (Hartian) will theory where, in both cases, the emphasis is on the respective (and narrow) standpoints of the right-holder and duty-bearer. What the analysis of *Iudex* contributes to the wider themes tackled in this book, perhaps, is a clearer sense of *perspective*. One key argument maintained throughout the book is that legal rights are thought to be inseparable from the institutional setting in which authoritative legal meaning is assigned – in other words the meaning of the legal standards in which the rights are grounded; and the content, scope, import and effect of those rights. The *Iudexian* perspective – that of an ultimate judicial actor – is an integral part of that institutional setting. There is a risk of distortion if legal rights are decontextualised from that setting (so the argument goes). At various points in the unfolding discussion, attempts have been made to capture an idea of legal meaning conceived within the *institutional imagination*. In the main this has been viewed as corresponding to the judicial consciousness – specifically that of *Iudex*. But it potentially extends to other institutional actors who wield significant social power and whose decision-making significantly replicates judicial reasoning or decision-making, often at the highest level, inevitably factoring in judicial precedents and other legal standards – for instance, institutions such as criminal prosecution authorities, tax authorities, governmental agencies and so on.

The *Iudexian* perspective is perhaps a good point on which to bring the discussion to a close. The main emphasis of this book has been on *legal* rights, not moral rights. In writings on will theory and interest theory, analyses of legal rights are often treated on a similar – if not, often, identical – basis to moral rights as if the structural similarities between the two types of rights were essentially a given, and differences were imperceptible. In analytical terms, what goes for legal rights (in traditional writing) largely goes for moral rights; and what goes for moral rights largely goes for legal rights. In these situations the institutional dimension of legal rights is taken for granted. Occasional reference will be made to 'real law', and judicial decision-making, in order to illustrate a point. (And often enough a very similar point could be made about moral rights, all things being equal.) Was there a rhinoceros in the room (or an elephant, or indeed a hippopotamus) when Wittgenstein famously debated this with Russell?[85] Russell was certain there was not; Wittgenstein was equally certain that we could not know for sure. In practical terms, the position is more straightforward when legal rights are under discussion in classical (Hartian) will theory and classical interest theory. There *is* an elephant

[85] See JF McDonald, 'Russell, Wittgenstein, and the Problem of the Rhinoceros' (1993) 31(4) *The Southern Journal of Philosophy* 409.

in the room, which is the institutionality of legal rights; yet it sometimes seems as if that is a matter of little importance, only worthy of discussion if coercion (and its justification) are on the agenda for exploration. Outside a doctrine such as that of papal infallibility,[86] mechanisms for the authoritative, final and conclusive determination of morals, and disputed questions of morality, are a rarity – probably as rare as an elephant in a room; yet corresponding mechanisms in the legal domain are everywhere to be found. The fact that institutionality – captured in the idea of the institutional imagination, itself contextualised within (mainly judicial) institutional decision-making structures – is *radically transformative* of the nature of legal rights often seems to escape the notice of will theorists and interest theorists alike.[87]

[86] See, for example, A Dulles, 'Newman on Infallibility' (1990) 51 *Theological Studies* 434.

[87] Neil MacCormick is the obvious exception; but, as mentioned in Chapter 3, he rejects the idea of the *Iudexian* perspective preferring, instead, a *professorial* perspective. He does not envisage his perspective – even if admirably eclectic – operating as a device (such as a Weberian ideal type) that replicates the position of an institutional insider such as a judge, validly appointed and recognised by the legal system as qualified (and empowered) to render a decision or judgment in a case before a court of law. Of course the professor in question may happen to be (simultaneously) a judge: even an ultimate one. And that would be undeniably a rarity.

BIBLIOGRAPHY

Adair-Toteff, C, 'Why Rickert? Regarding the Dogma about Heinrich Rickert's Influence on Max Weber' (2023) 53(2) *Journal for the Theory of Social Behaviour* 127

Anscombe, GEM, 'On Brute Facts' (1958) 18 *Analysis* 69

Auerbach, CA, 'On Professor HLA Hart's Definition and Theory in Jurisprudence' (1956) 9 *Journal of Legal Education* 39

Austin, J, *Lectures on Jurisprudence: The Philosophy of Positive Law* (abridged edn, R Campbell (ed), Henry Holt and Co 1875)

Bell, GJ, *Principles of the Law of Scotland* (1829)

Bentham, J, *Of Laws in General* (HLA Hart (ed), Athlone Press 1970)

Bergstraesser, A, 'Wilhelm Dilthey and Max Weber: An Empirical Approach to Historical Synthesis' (1947) 57(2) *Ethics* 92

Bohannan, P, 'Law and Legal Institutions' in WM Evan (ed), *The Sociology of Law* (Free Press 1980) ch 1, 3

Brownsword, R, and others, *The Law of Contract* (7th edn, LexisNexis Butterworths 2022)

Bruun, HH, *Science, Values and Politics in Max Weber's Methodology* (expanded edition, Routledge 2016)

Buckland, WW, *The Main Institutions of Roman Private Law* (Cambridge University Press 1931)

Cairns, JW, 'Institutional Writings in Scotland Reconsidered' (1983) 4 *Journal of Legal History* 76

Campbell, T, *Seven Theories of Human Society* (Clarendon Press 1981)

Campbell, TD, 'The Rights of the Minor: As Person, as Child, as Juvenile, as Future Adult' (1992) 6 *International Journal of Law and the Family* 1

Cobban, A, *Rousseau and the Modern State* (2nd edn, George Allen & Unwin Ltd 1964)

Coser, LA, *Masters of Sociological Thought: Ideas in Historical and Social Context* (2nd edn, Harcourt Brace Jovanovich Inc 1977)

Cotterrell, R, *The Politics of Jurisprudence: A Critical Introduction to Legal Philosophy* (Butterworths 1989)

Cross, R, *Precedent in English Law* (Clarendon Press 1961)

Cross, R, and Harris, JW, *Precedent in English Law* (4th edn, Clarendon Press 1991)

Cruft, R, 'Rights: Beyond Interest Theory and Will Theory?' (2004) 23 *Law and Philosophy* 347

Dahrendorf, R, *Homo Sociologicus* (Routledge & Kegan Paul 1973)

Dalrymple of Stair, Sir James, *The Institutions of the Law of Scotland* (1681)

Devlin, Baron (Lord), (PA Devlin), *The Judge* (Oxford University Press 1979)

Dulles, A, 'Newman on Infallibility' (1990) 51(3) *Theological Studies* 434

Dworkin, R, 'The Model of Rules' (1967) 35 *University of Chicago Law Review* 14

Dworkin, R, 'Hard Cases' (1975) 88 *Harvard Law Review* 1057

Dworkin, R, *Taking Rights Seriously* (Gerald Duckworth & Co Ltd 1977)

Dworkin, R, *Law's Empire* (Fontana Paperbacks 1986)

Dwyer, D, 'Beyond Kelsen and Hart? MacCormick's *Institutions of Law*' (2008) 71 *Modern Law Review* 823

Eliade, M, (ed), 'Syncretism' in *The Encyclopedia of Religion* vol 14 (Macmillan Publishing Company, 1987) 218–227

Erskine, J, *An Institute of the Law of Scotland* (1773)

Feinberg, J, *The Moral Limits of the Criminal Law. Vol 1, Harm to Others* (Oxford University Press 1984)

Feinberg, J, *The Moral Limits of the Criminal Law. Vol 2, Offense to Others* (Oxford University Press 1985)

Feinberg, J, *The Moral Limits of the Criminal Law. Vol 3, Harm to Self* (Oxford University Press 1986)

Feinberg, J, *The Moral Limits of the Criminal Law. Vol 4, Harmless Wrongdoing* (Oxford University Press 1988)

Finnis, J, *Natural Law and Natural Rights* (Clarendon Press 1980)
Flaubert, G, *Correspondance* (1852)
Forsyth, J, 'Lord Hope reflects on his life in law' *The Scotsman* (10 June 2013) www.scotsman.com/news/lord-hope-reflects-on-his-life-in-law-1571963 (accessed 28 July 2025)
Freund, J, 'German Sociology in the Time of Max Weber' in T Bottomore and R Nisbet (eds), *A History of Sociological Analysis* (Heinemann Educational Books Ltd 1978) ch 5, 149
Fuller, LL, *The Morality of Law* (rev edn, Yale University Press 1969)
Galloway, D, 'The Axiology of Analytical Jurisprudence: A Study of the Underlying Sociological Assumptions and Ideological Predilections' in TW Bechtler (ed), *Law in a Social Context: Liber Amicorum Honouring Professor Lon L Fuller* (Kluwer 1978) ch 5, 53
Giddens, A, 'Positivism and its Critics' in T Bottomore and R Nisbet (eds), *A History of Sociological Analysis* (Heinemann Educational Books Ltd 1978) ch 7, 237
Goble, GW, 'A Redefinition of Basic Legal Terms' (1935) 35(4) *Columbia Law Review* 535
Greenawalt, K, 'Policy, Rights, and Judicial Decision' in M Cohen (ed), *Ronald Dworkin and Contemporary Jurisprudence* (Gerald Duckworth & Co Ltd 1984) ch 5, 88
Gregory, A, '1,500 more patients of jailed breast surgeon Ian Paterson recalled' *The Guardian* (London: 1 February 2023): www.theguardian.com/society/2023/feb/01/1500-more-patients-of-jailed-breast-surgeon-ian-paterson-recalled (accessed 28 July 2025)
Gretton, GL, 'The Integrity of Property Law and of the Property Registers' (2001) 15 *Scots Law Times* 135
Griffith, JAG, *The Politics of the Judiciary* (5th edn, Fontana Press 1997)
Habermas, J, *Knowledge and Human Interests* [*Erkenntnis und Interesse*] (JJ Shapiro (tr), Heinemann Educational Books 1972)
Hacker, PMS, 'Definition in Jurisprudence' (1969) 19 *Philosophical Quarterly* 343
Hall, J, 'Nulla Poena Sine Lege' (1937) 47(2) *Yale Law Journal* 165
Harcourt, BE, 'The Collapse of the Harm Principle' (1999) 90 *Journal of Criminal Law and Criminology* 109
Hart, HLA, 'Definition and Theory in Jurisprudence' (1954) 70 *Law Quarterly Review* 37
Hart, HLA, 'Are There Any Natural Rights?' (1955) 64 *Philosophical Review* 175
Hart, HLA, 'Analytical Jurisprudence in Mid-Twentieth Century: A Reply to Professor Bodenheimer' (1957) 105 *University of Pennsylvania Law Review* 953
Hart, HLA, 'Bentham: Lecture on a Master Mind' (1962) 48 *Proceedings of the British Academy* 297
Hart, HLA, *Law, Liberty and Morality* (Oxford University Press 1963)
Hart, HLA, 'Bentham on Legal Rights' in AWB Simpson (ed), *Oxford Essays in Jurisprudence: Second Series* (Clarendon Press 1973)
Hart, HLA, *Essays on Bentham: Jurisprudence and Political Theory* (Clarendon Press 1982) ch VII, 162
Hart, HLA, *The Concept of Law* (2nd edn, Clarendon Press 1994)
Hobbes, T, *Leviathan* (E Curley (ed), Hackett Publishing Co Inc 1994)
Hodge, Lord, (PS Hodge), 'Property Law, Fiduciary Obligations and the Constructive Trust' in F McCarthy, J Chalmers and S Bogle (eds), *Essays in Conveyancing and Property Law in Honour of Professor Robert Rennie* (Open Book Publishers 2015) ch 6, 97
Hohfeld, WN, *Fundamental Legal Conceptions as Applied in Judicial Reasoning* (WW Cook (ed), Yale University Press 1919)
Honoré, AM, 'Real Laws' in PMS Hacker and J Raz (eds), *Law, Morality, and Society: Essays in Honour of HLA Hart* (Clarendon Press 1977) ch 5, 99
Honoré, AM, 'Rights of Exclusion and Immunities Against Divesting' (1959–1960) 34 *Tulane Law Review* 453
Hope of Craighead, Lord, (JAD Hope), *Lord Hope's Diaries: House of Lords 1996–2009* (Avizandum Publishing Limited 2018)
Hunt, A, *The Sociological Movement in Law* (The Macmillan Press Ltd 1978)
Jaffe, LL, *English and American Judges as Lawmakers* (Clarendon Press 1969)
Kant, I, *The Metaphysics of Morals* (M Gregor (tr), Cambridge University Press 1991)
Käsler, D, Max Weber: *An Introduction to his Life and Work* (P Hurd (tr), Polity Press 1988)

Kelman, HC, 'Further Thoughts on the Processes of Compliance, Identification, and Internalization', in JT Tedeschi (ed), *Perspectives on Social Power* (Aldine Publishing Company 1974) ch 5, 125
Kelsen, H, 'The Pure Theory of Law' (1934) 50 *Law Quarterly Review* 478
Kelsen, H, *General Theory of Law and State* (A Wedberg (tr), Harvard University Press 1945)
Kelsen, H, *Pure Theory of Law* (M Knight (tr), 2nd edn, University of California Press 1967)
Kelsen, H, *Pure Theory of Law* (published as Hans Kelsen, *Introduction to the Problems of Legal Theory* [*Reine Rechtslehre. Einleitung in die rechtswissenschaftliche Problematik*]) (BL Paulson and SL Paulson (trs and eds), Clarendon Press 1992)
Kirby, MD, 'Lord Denning: An Antipodean Appreciation' (1986) 1(1) *Denning Law Journal* 103
Kocourek, A, *Jural Relations* (2nd edn, The Bobbs-Merrill Company 1928)
Kramer, MH, 'Rights Without Trimmings' in MH Kramer, NE Simmonds and H Steiner, *A Debate Over Rights: Philosophical Enquiries* (Oxford University Press 1998) 7
Kramer, MH, 'Some Doubts about Alternatives to the Interest Theory of Rights' (2013) 123 *Ethics* 245
Kramer, MH, and Steiner, H, 'Theories of Rights: Is There a Third Way?' (2007) 27 *Oxford Journal of Legal Studies* 281
Kramer, MH, Simmonds, NE, and Steiner, H, *A Debate Over Rights: Philosophical Enquiries* (Oxford University Press 1998)
Lacey, N, *A Life of HLA Hart: The Nightmare and the Noble Dream* (Oxford University Press 2004)
Lacey, N, 'Analytical Jurisprudence versus Descriptive Sociology Revisited' (2006) 84 *Texas Law Review* 944
Locke, J, *An Essay Concerning Human Understanding* (26th edn, printed for T Tegg, R Griffin & Co and J Cumming 1828)
Locke, J, *Two Treatises of Government* (P Laslett (ed), Cambridge University Press 1988)
Lockwood, L, *Beethoven: The Music and the Life* (WW Norton & Company 2003)
Lukes, S, 'Methodological Individualism Reconsidered' (1968) 19(2) *British Journal of Sociology* 119
MacCormick, DN, 'Law as Institutional Fact' (1974) 90 *Law Quarterly Review* 102
MacCormick, DN, 'Children's Rights: a Test Case for Theories of Right' (1976) 62 *Archiv für Rechts- und Sozialphilosophie* 305
MacCormick, DN, 'Rights in Legislation' in PMS Hacker and J Raz (eds), *Law, Morality, and Society: Essays in Honour of HLA Hart* (Clarendon Press 1977) ch 11, 189
MacCormick, N, *HLA Hart* (Edward Arnold (Publishers) Ltd 1981)
MacCormick, DN, *Legal Right and Social Democracy: Essays in Legal and Political Philosophy* (Clarendon Press 1982)
MacCormick, N, *Institutions of Law: An Essay in Legal Theory* (Oxford University Press 2007)
McDonald, JF, 'Russell, Wittgenstein, and the Problem of the Rhinoceros' (1993) 31(4) *The Southern Journal of Philosophy* 409
McHugh, MH, The Hon Justice, 'The Judicial Method' (5 July 1998), accessible under the title 'The Australian Bar Association Conference, London, 5 July 1998, Democracy and the Law, "The Judicial Method"' here: https://www.hcourt.gov.au/resources-and-publications/speeches/michael-hudson-mchugh-ac-qc
McHugh, MH, The Hon Justice, 'The Judicial Method Revisited' (17 January 2007) www.hkcfa.hk/file-manager/speech/en/upload/75/20070117%20McHugh%20-%20The%20Judicial%20Method%20Revisited.pdf (accessed 28 July 2025)
Macmillan, Lord, (HP Macmillan),'The Writing of Judgments' (1948) 26(3) *The Canadian Bar Review* 491
Malinowski, B, *The Dynamics of Culture Change: an Inquiry into Race Relations in Africa* (Yale University Press 1945)
Mill, JS, 'On Liberty' in J Gray (ed), *On Liberty and Other Essays* (Oxford University Press 1998) 5
Mullock, A, 'Surgical Harm, Consent, and English Criminal Law: When Should "Bad Apple" Surgeons be Prosecuted?' (2021) 21(4) *Medical Law International* 343
Oakes, G, *Weber and Rickert: Concept Formation in the Cultural Sciences* (MIT Press 1988)
Parsons, T, 'Max Weber 1864–1964', (1965) 30(2) *American Sociological Review* 171
Parsons, T, 'Value-Freedom and Objectivity' in O Stammer (ed), *Max Weber and Sociology Today: Explorations in Interpretative Sociology* (Basil Blackwell 1971) 33

Paterson, A, *Final Judgment – The Last Law Lords and the Supreme Court* (Hart Publishing 2013)
Persky, J, 'Retrospectives: The Ethology of Homo Economicus' (1995) 9(2) *The Journal of Economic Perspectives* 221
Plato, *The Republic* (AD Lindsay (tr), JM Dent & Sons Ltd 1976) book V
Radin, M, 'A Restatement of Hohfeld' (1938) 51 *Harvard Law Review* 1141
Rawls, J, *A Theory of Justice* (Oxford University Press 1973)
Raz, J, *The Authority of Law: Essays on Law and Morality* (Clarendon Press 1979)
Raz, J, *The Concept of a Legal System: An Introduction to the Theory of Legal System* (2nd edn, Clarendon Press 1980)
Raz, J, 'Legal Rights' (1984) 4 *Oxford Journal of Legal Studies* 1
Raz, J, 'On the Nature of Rights' (1984) 93 *Mind* 194
Reed, Lord, of Allermuir (RJ Reed), 'The Supreme Court Ten Years On' (The Bentham Association Lecture 2019, University College London, 6 March 2019) https://supremecourt.uk/speeches/lord-reed-at-the-bentham-association-lecture-2019-university-college-london (accessed 28 July 2025)
Reid, KGC, 'Equity Triumphant: *Sharp v Thomson*' (1997) 1 *Edinburgh Law Review* 464
Rickman, HP (tr and ed), *W Dilthey Selected Writings* (Cambridge University Press 1976)
Ross, H, 'Hans Kelsen and the Utopia of Theoretical Purism' (2001) 12 *King's College Law Journal* 174
Ross, H, *Law as a Social Institution* (Hart Publishing 2001)
Ross, H, 'The *Pure Theory of Law* and Interpretive Sociology – a Basis for Interdisciplinarity?' in M Freeman (ed), *Law and Sociology* (Current Legal Issues 2005, vol 8) (Oxford University Press 2006) ch 5, 69
Ross, H, 'Children's Rights and Theories of Rights' (2013) 21 *International Journal of Children's Rights* 679
Ross, H, 'Children's Rights – a Defence of Hartian Will Theory' (2014) 22 *International Journal of Children's Rights* 43
Rousseau, Jean-Jacques, *Discourse on Political Economy and the Social Contract* (C Betts (tr and ed), Oxford University Press 1994)
Sartorius, R, 'Positivism and the Foundations of Legal Authority', in R Gavison (ed), *Issues in Contemporary Legal Philosophy: The Influence of HLA Hart* (Clarendon Press 1987) ch 2.1, 43
Scottish Law Commission, *Discussion Paper on* Sharp v Thomson (Discussion Paper No 114, The Stationery Office July 2001)
Scruton, R, *Kant* (Oxford University Press 1982)
Searle, JR, *Speech Acts: An Essay in the Philosophy of Language* (Cambridge University Press 1969)
Simmonds, NE, *Central Issues in Jurisprudence: Justice, Law and Rights* (Sweet & Maxwell 1986)
Simmonds, NE, 'Rights at the Cutting Edge' in MH Kramer, NE Simmonds and H Steiner, *A Debate Over Rights: Philosophical Enquiries* (Oxford University Press 1998) 113
Sreenivasan, G, 'A Hybrid Theory of Claim-Rights' (2005) 25 *Oxford Journal of Legal Studies* 257
Stair, James Dalrymple of, *The Institutions of the Law of Scotland* (1681)
Stampp, KM, *The Peculiar Institution: Slavery in the Ante-Bellum South* (Alfred A Knopf 1956)
Steiner, H, 'Working Rights' in MH Kramer, NE Simmonds and H Steiner, *A Debate Over Rights: Philosophical Enquiries* (Oxford University Press 1998) 233
Stephen, JF, *Liberty, Equality, Fraternity* (RJ White (ed), Cambridge University Press 1967)
Stewart, I, 'The Critical Legal Science of Hans Kelsen' (1990) 17(3) *Journal of Law and Society* 273
Tamanaha, BZ, *A General Jurisprudence of Law and Society* (Oxford University Press 2001)
Tamanaha, BZ, *On the Rule of Law: History, Politics, Theory* (Cambridge University Press 2004)
Tuck, R, *Natural Rights Theories: Their Origin and Development* (Cambridge University Press 1979)
Tur, R, 'The Kelsenian Enterprise' in R Tur and W Twining (eds), *Essays on Kelsen* (Clarendon Press 1986) 149
Unger, RM, *Law in Modern Society: Toward a Criticism of Social Theory* (The Free Press 1976)
van Mill, D, 'Freedom of Speech' in *The Stanford Encyclopedia of Philosophy* (Spring 2015 Edition), EN Zalta (ed) http://plato.stanford.edu/archives/spr2015/entries/freedom-speech/ (accessed 28 July 2025)
von Savigny, FC, *System of the Modern Roman Law* (W Holloway (tr), Higginbotham 1867) vol I, 2nd book, ch I, 6
Wagner, PA, 'The Idea of a Moral Person' (1983) 18(2) *Journal of Thought* 85
Wagner G, and Härpfer, C, 'Neo-Kantianism and the Social Sciences: from Rickert to Weber' in N de Warren and A Staiti (eds), *New Approaches to Neo-Kantianism* (Cambridge University Press 2015)

Wasserstrom, R, 'Rights, Human Rights and Racial Discrimination' (1964) 61 *The Journal of Philosophy* 628
Weber, M, 'Politics as a Vocation' ['*Politik als Beruf*'] in HH Gerth and CW Mills (trs and eds) *From Max Weber: Essays in Sociology* (Oxford University Press 1946) 77
Weber, M, *The Theory of Social and Economic Organization* (AM Henderson and T Parsons (trs and eds), The Free Press 1947)
Weber, M, '"Objectivity" in Social Science and Social Policy' ['*Die 'Objektivität' sozialwissenschaftlicher und sozialpolitischer Erkenntnis*'] in M Weber, *Max Weber On The Methodology of the Social Sciences* (EA Shils and HA Finch (trs and eds), The Free Press 1949) ch II, 49
Weber, M, *Max Weber on Law in Economy and Society* (M Rheinstein (ed), Harvard University Press 1954)
Weber, M, *Economy and Society: An Outline of Interpretive Sociology* [*Wirtschaft und Gesellschaft: Grundriss der Verstehenden Soziologie*] (G Roth, C Wittich and others (trs and eds), Bedminster Press Inc 1968)
Weber, M, 'The Concept of "Following a Rule"' in WG Runciman (ed), *Max Weber, Selections in Translation* (Cambridge University Press 1978) ch 5, 99
Weingarten, G, 'Pearls Before Breakfast: Can one of the nation's great musicians cut through the fog of a DC rush hour? Let's find out.' *The Washington Post* (8 April 2007) www.washingtonpost.com/lifestyle/magazine/pearls-before-breakfast-can-one-of-the-nations-great-musicians-cut-through-the-fog-of-a-dc-rush-hour-lets-find-out/2014/09/23/8a6d46da-4331-11e4-b47c-f5889e061e5f_story.html# (accessed 28 July 2025)
Wenar, L, 'The Nature of Claim-Rights' (2013) 123 *Ethics* 202
Wenar, L, 'Rights', *The Stanford Encyclopedia of Philosophy* (Fall edn, 2015) para [2.2] https://plato.stanford.edu/entries/rights/#2.2 (accessed 28 July 2025)
Wenar, L, 'The Nature of Rights' (2005) 33 *Philosophy and Public Affairs* 223
Williams, G, *Salmond on Jurisprudence* (11th edn, Sweet & Maxwell 1957)
Winch, P, *The Idea of a Social Science and its Relation to Philosophy* (2nd edn, Routledge 1990)
Wittgenstein, L, *Philosophical Investigations* (GEM Anscombe (tr) and GEM Anscombe and others (eds), Basil Blackwell Limited 1953)
Wolff, KH, 'Phenomenology and Sociology' in T Bottomore and R Nisbet (eds), *A History of Sociological Analysis* (Heinemann Educational Books Ltd 1978) ch 13, 499
Zijderveld, AC, *The Abstract Society: A Cultural Analysis of Our Time* (Penguin Books Limited 1974) 31

INDEX

www.ingramcontent.com/pod-product-compliance
Ingram Content Group UK Ltd.
Pitfield, Milton Keynes, MK11 3LW, UK
UKHW020801290926
15470UKWH00003B/883

9 781509 979004